INSIDE AGITATORS

Inside Agitators

White Southerners in the Civil Rights Movement

DAVID L. CHAPPELL

The Johns Hopkins University Press
Baltimore and London

The Johns Hopkins University Press
2715 North Charles Street
Baltimore, Maryland 21218-4319
The Johns Hopkins Press Ltd., London

ISBN 0-8018-4685-4

Library of Congress Cataloging-in-Publication Data will be found
at the end of this book.

A catalog record for this book is available from the British Library.

For Elizabeth Moore

The South is not "solid"; it is a land in the ferment of social change. . . . Discriminating and broad-minded criticism is what the South needs—needs it for the sake of her own white sons and daughters. . . . To-day even the attitude of the Southern whites toward the blacks is not, as so many assume, in all cases the same; the ignorant Southerner hates the Negro, the workingmen fear his competition, the money-makers wish to use him as a laborer, some of the educated see a menace in his upward development, while others—usually the sons of the masters— wish to help him to rise.

Through all the sorrow of the Sorrow Songs there breathes a hope—a faith in the ultimate justice of things. . . . Sometimes it is a faith in life, sometimes a faith in death, sometimes assurance of boundless justice in some fair world beyond. But whichever it is, the meaning is always clear: that sometime, somewhere, men will judge men by their souls and not by their skins.

—W.E.B. Du Bois, *The Souls of Black Folk*

CONTENTS

FOREWORD

One of the many virtues of David Chappell's fascinating study is that he does not romanticize white southerners who were sympathetic toward the civil rights movement. Rather than depicting them simply as courageous dissenters, he shows that their motives for supporting civil rights reform were varied and complex — a mixture of altruism, pragmatism, paternalism, guilt, and numerous other idiosyncratic sentiments.

Certainly there were courageous white southerners who not only responded to the civil rights movement but even became activists in it. Bob Zellner of the Student Nonviolent Coordinating Committee (SNCC) comes to mind as a white southerner who became one of the dedicated foot soldiers of the black freedom struggle. Similarly Sam Shirah and Sue Thrasher of the Southern Student Organizing Committee were among the dozens of southern white student activists who attempted to bring SNCC's radicalism into white communities. Anne and Carl Braden of the Southern Conference Educational Fund represented still another expression of southern white militancy on behalf of the civil rights movement.

But Chappell recognizes that the experiences of these exceptional southern white radicals were less crucial to the success of the black movement than were the far more commonplace actions of southern white moderates. The former had almost no influence in southern communities precisely because they were not in the mainstream of southern white opinion; the latter became an essential force for compromise between civil rights protesters and white segregationists.

By carefully examining the role of southern white moderates, Chappell also enables us to see the civil rights movement more realistically. Too often historians and journalists have seen the nonviolent strategy of black protesters merely as a morally and religiously based challenge to the southern system of racial domination. In this view, the black struggle succeeded because peaceful black demonstrators exposed the evil of segregation

through confrontations with intransigent southerners determined to preserve their racial privilege through brutal force. The iconography of the
civil rights movement is dominated by such confrontations of good versus
evil—Rosa Parks under arrest in Montgomery, Little Rock black students
enduring mob violence, Birmingham youths facing "Bull" Connor's dogs
and water hoses, or Selma marchers being clubbed by mounted state
troopers.

Such a depiction of the nonviolent strategy understates its impact,
however, by discounting its political as well as moral significance. The
strategy did succeed in arousing the consciences of many whites. But, more
importantly, it also convinced white leaders in the South and elsewhere to
give in to movement demands even when their consciences did not compel
them to do so. As Chappell points out, civil rights activists should not be
seen as utopians, more concerned with moral consistency than with political efficacy. They were accomplished strategists "using force against enemies to achieve political ends. The general philosophical question and the
general historical tradition they were involved in was that of the just war,
and the principles of just war provide the best summary of the relationship
they developed between ends and means."

As Chappell notes, Martin Luther King, Jr., was always careful to dis-
tinguish between the notion of nonviolence as a refusal to use violence and
as a determination to use nonviolent tactics militantly and even coercively
to overcome social evil. He saw nonviolence as more than a moral impera-
tive. It was also a well-tested, potentially powerful political strategy that
had "muzzled the guns of the British empire in India and freed more than
three hundred and fifty million people from colonialism." King insisted
that he was both a realist and an idealist. "If I am to merit the trust invested
in me by some of my race, I must be both of these things. This is why nonviolence is a powerful as well as a *just* weapon."

Others in the black freedom struggle were willing to go farther than
King in utilizing nonviolent tactics coercively to push hesitating southern
moderates—and national leaders—to speed the pace of racial change.
SNCC activists in particular were often prepared to intensify nonviolent
protests even at the risk of prompting civil disorder. For them, nonviolent
tactics were the most appropriate form of political action available to black
southerners. James Lawson and others often spoke of organizing a nonviolent army willing to sustain direct action until southern and national leaders agreed to accept change rather than face continued social disorder. In
the draft speech SNCC chairman John Lewis prepared for delivery at the

1963 March on Washington, he spoke for many activists when he referred to the civil rights movement as a nonviolent revolution: "We will not wait for the courts to act. . . . We will not wait for the President, the Justice Department, nor Congress, but we will take matters into our own hands and create a source of power, outside of any national structure, that could and would assure us victory."

Although some black militants of the last half of the 1960s turned away from the nonviolent strategy, understanding the reasons for its success in the early 1960s helps us to appreciate its contemporary relevance. Malcolm X once aroused black audiences with his sardonic criticisms of nonviolence, but neither he nor any of his Nation of Islam followers ever directly challenged white power with the same determination or effectiveness shown by the nonviolent activists of the early 1960s. After his break with Elijah Muhammad, Malcolm acknowledged what southern white leaders already knew — that black southerners had used nonviolent tactics militantly and deftly to overcome powerful and vicious opposition. In his autobiography, he expressed his disappointment in the failure of the Nation of Islam to become involved in the escalating black civil rights protests of the early 1960s: "It could be heard increasingly in the Negro communities: 'Those Muslims *talk* tough, but they never *do* anything, unless somebody bothers Muslims.'"

By the end of his life, Malcolm was also aware that the civil rights movement had given many black people confidence in their ability to confront and sometimes overcome white power structures. After his assassination, many black leaders adopted Malcolm's critique of nonviolence rather than his critique of the rhetorical black nationalist militancy. Black power advocates of the late 1960s power were too willing to abandon the nonviolent tactics that had enabled southern blacks to transform their discontent into effective political action. By rejecting nonviolence as unmanly and ineffective against monolithic white racist power structures, they deprived their followers of a set of tactics that had enabled discontented black people to achieve historic civil rights gains.

Because the southern black freedom struggle mobilized thousands of black people to overcome strong and powerful opposition, it remains a crucial episode in the history of freedom struggles throughout the world. During the past three decades, freedom movements through the world have benefited from the ideas of that struggle. As Marxian ideas have declined in their capacity to inspire oppressed people, the intellectual legacy of nonviolence has remained a source of hope.

Yet this intellectual legacy remains underappreciated among contemporary African Americans who trace their ideological roots to Malcolm and the black power movement. Rather than seeking inspiration in a mass struggle that gave millions of black people the confidence to demand social justice, many young black Americans have belittled the gains of the civil rights movement. Instead of developing a strategy that is effectively within the broader framework of American politics, many have replaced political engagement with posturing and escapist forms of racial separatism. Many African-American young people have adopted attitudes that express their anger and frustration, but they have been unable to transform their resentments into an effective political strategy capable of offering hope for the future. Without effective political outlets, black anger has become self-destructive.

The successful black community mobilizations and effective challenges to white authority that occurred during the period from 1955 to 1965 provide an antidote to the politics of racial resentment. To learn from this history, however, we must begin to understand the civil rights movement not as moralistic melodrama but as politics. Southern whites were not monolithic and intransigent but divided in ways that are similar to the divisions among those currently in positions of privilege and power. The ways in which southern blacks exploited those divisions for their own benefit offer profound lessons for the future. A revival of Gandhian/Kingian nonviolence offers the best alternative we have to an acceptance of racial divisions and racial injustice as inevitable. Against the claim that the present world order constitutes an end point of social progress, the tradition of nonviolent social struggle offers a trenchant social critique and a feasible political strategy for those at the bottom of the social order.

Clayborne Carson
Professor of history, Stanford University
Editor of the papers of Martin Luther King, Jr.

PREFACE

This study began with a simple, and to me at the time startling, observation: there were white southerners who supported the civil rights movement. There were white southerners, that is, whose actions belied the segregationist myth that all white people had an interest in keeping the black man down. Oddly, northern liberals shared a belief in this myth, insofar as they believed that all *southern* white people had an interest in keeping the black man down. Growing up during the 1960s in what must have been a typical northern white liberal family, I had an image of the white South as one big lynch mob waiting to happen. To me Bull Connor and Sheriff Clark represented the typical, not the exceptional, southerner. Through the mass media, northern liberals reassured themselves that vicious hatreds and prejudices were vestiges of the Old South, that Dixie remained underdeveloped in the twentieth century, clinging with recalcitrant desperation to outmoded notions. We could not see that Bull Connor represented only one end of a spectrum of southern white opinion, that there were quieter but equally representative voices at the other end. Nor could we see the vast middle, which was uncertain which way it was being led. Seeing these complexities would make the South, which was a synonym for racial trouble, too much like our own complex reality. Ignoring them was essential to the notion that racism was somebody else's problem.

The civil rights movement seems distant from us today because we think Martin Luther King, Jr., and his followers faced superhuman or subhuman monsters, not people like us. The Bull Connors and Sheriff Clarks were evil incarnate; they attacked innocent black people with electric cattle prods, with high-pressure hoses, with *animals*. Only supreme faith—the kind we label fundamentalist when it serves political ends we disapprove of —could have given the poor black minority the courage to stand up to them. The southern racial system, symbolized by the hooded Klansman, was so dark and demonic, so unmodern that we cannot identify with the people who lived within it. Instead we reduce them to abstract monoliths, literally black and white.

Yet black veterans of the southern movement—Coretta King, Charles Gomillion, Ralph Abernathy, Georgia Gilmore, Johnnie Carr, John Lewis, Hosea Williams, and others—have told me that in nearly every southern community there were white people on their side, back in the 1950s and early 1960s, when it was neither fashionable nor safe to be. Covert moral support from local white people was immensely encouraging to black protesters at a time when hopelessness was always a dangerous temptation. Covert material aid, legal advice, and inside information were useful in a direct, practical way. Andrew Young, the former program director of the Southern Christian Leadership Conference, one of King's closest advisers who lived to become the first black congressman from Georgia since Reconstruction and then the second black mayor of Atlanta, told me, "If it hadn't been for the kind of white southerners you are talking about, the South today would look like Beirut looks today."

Learning how that could have been so in a region and a period that I had misunderstood, like most Americans, in simplistic, black-and-white terms, took me across the South and through the records of the struggle over a period of four years. I could not have done it on my own.

To the white southerners I interviewed or otherwise got to know during my research, and to the civil rights leaders who first drew my attention to them, I am most indebted for whatever understanding may precipitate out of this book. Not all of their names appear in the narrative below, and those whose names do appear do not appear often or prominently enough to indicate how important they were in awakening and deepening my interest in their history. I was lucky enough to meet many of them and to read and hear enough about others to feel I knew them. There are surely many important, even heroic, ones I neglected to mention or never knew about. The ones who have most influenced my understanding are Porter Anderson, Sarah Patton Boyle, Anne and Carl Braden, Baxton Bryant, Will Campbell, Guy Carawan, Hodding Carter III, Connie Curry, Ken Dean, Patt Derian, Leslie Dunbar, Virginia and Clifford Durr, P. D. East, C. P. Ellis, W. W. Finlator, Harold Fleming, Sam H. Franklin, Paul Gaston, Robert Graetz, Winifred Green, Casey Hayden (Sandra Cason), Myles Horton, Frank Johnson, Mary King (southern by paternal ancestry), Floyd Mann, Florence Mars, Lucy Randolph Mason, Bill Minor, H. L. Mitchell, Charles Morgan, Walker Percy, Howell Raines, Roy Reed, Junius Scales,

Sam Shirah, Glenn Smiley, Lillian Smith, Jane Stembridge, Francis Stevens, Sue Thrasher, David Vann, J. Waites Waring, Robert Penn Warren, Pat Watters, C. Vann Woodward, Hogan Yancey, Bob Zellner, and Charles Zukowski. I owe these men and women much more than the book that follows.

There are many more immediate debts. The research for this book would not have been possible without the generous financial support of the history department and the graduate dean's office of the University of Rochester. I am deeply grateful to both. A predoctoral fellowship from the Frederick Douglass Institute for African and African-American Studies at Rochester gave me the freedom I needed to write most of the argument in a year and the criticism I often needed to focus and clarify it. I thank the institute and its staff.

I also benefited from two Moody grants from the Lyndon Baines Johnson Foundation for research at the Johnson Library in Austin, Texas, and a John F. Kennedy Foundation grant-in-aid for research at the Kennedy Library in Boston, Massachusetts.

I would like to thank my graduate school adviser, Christopher Lasch, for his patience and his faith. He did more than I ever thought possible to mitigate the cruelties of graduate study in the humanities in the 1980s. His criticism and suggestions made this book (which I submitted in modified form as a dissertation) far better than it would have been otherwise. He may be surprised to hear that he gave me hope. There is no greater and no more difficult gift.

I am also profoundly grateful for the inspiration and advice of Professors Karen Fields, Eugene Genovese, and Robert Westbrook. It was a tremendous privilege to know and work with them during the time I was working on this book.

My editor at the Johns Hopkins University Press, Robert J. Brugger, provided all the advice and encouragement I couldn't get from my professors, and they should be as thankful as I am that he did — for I would surely still be hounding them, with a reproachfully unfinished dissertation ever in hand, if he hadn't. Brugger, in turn, should be as thankful as I am to Grace Buonocore, who read the manuscript with care and insight, to the credit of both her and her employer. Michelle Davidson graciously shared her knowledge of Little Rock with me and improved my chapter on that city. Professor Dan Carter took time from his busy schedule to read the manuscript and offered several intelligent and helpful criticisms.

Professor Harold Stanley gave me rigorously well informed and humane advice about southern politics, often over the jealously guarded wall of an academic discipline that was foreign to him. His provocative comments, especially on the last draft of my dissertation, helped me see beyond my own conclusions, and if I live to develop what I have learned beyond the temporal and spatial boundaries of the present work, his words will guide and goad me profitably. C. Vann Woodward graciously agreed to read a substantial portion of the manuscript and then with a baffling and wholly unjustified humility made suggestions that improved it immeasurably. Even if he had not done that, however, I would owe him a great deal, as any one who studies the South must.

Other teachers had a less direct impact on what I argue below, but their criticism and encouragement, often years before this book popped into my head, put me deeply in their debt. They are Kip Macmillan, Madeleine Poster, Patricia Peterson, Phil Roden, Syd Lieberman, Ernie LePore, David Oskie, Richard Fox, Robin Winks, Bill Arkin, Barbara Ehrenreich, Seymour Hersh, Cheryl Shanks, Roger Wilkins, William Taylor, and Mary Young. Wherever you all are now, thank you.

Years ago, Leslie Dunbar inadvertently gave me the whole idea. For that and a great deal more I am forever indebted to him.

The process of research, often messy and frustrating, was eased and often made enjoyable by veteran journalists, local sages and oracles, and kind strangers who knew the local scene. These folks often gave me a bed or a meal, or just eased my mind with an engaging conversation, in some far-flung outpost where I sought, often in vain, an interview or a document: Hodding Carter III, Bob G. Corley, Patt Derian, Barbara Dozier, Jim Hall, Bette Lee Hanson, Jimmy Harper, Bill Minor, Alice Murray, Roy Reed, Verna Rivers, Chinda Roach, Jim Scott, Courtney and Elizabeth Siceloff, Steve Suitts, Randall Williams. If I have forgotten anyone I once thanked effusively for such help, I surely remembered you before you saw this and felt a greater pang at the indelible omission than you possibly could.

Librarians are the unsung heroes of any researcher's life. Their huge brains and tiny egos reliably ease and improve the work of those with reversed proportions, and of everyone in between. If there were any justice, they would inherit the earth. Among the many who helped me, the following stand out: at the Martin Luther King Center in Atlanta, Diane Ware and Danny Bellinger (a.k.a. Will'um Lee); at the Civil Rights Documentation Project at Howard University, Esmé Bahn; at the Southern Historical Center at the University of North Carolina, John White and Richard Shrader; at the JFK Library in Boston, Maura Porter, Ron Whelan, and

William Johnson; at the LBJ Library in Austin, Texas, Shelleyne Wucher, Claudia Anderson, Regina Greenwell, and Linda Hanson.

I had to live while I wrote, and those who helped me live well (including most of those already mentioned for other reasons) deserve perhaps a greater, if more diffuse, thanks. There is something faintly obscene about mentioning all the following at once. Each made a contribution whose uniqueness cannot be captured in the crude egalitarianism of a list. Still I thank each one, separately, as a beginning. The book could not have been written without their help:

Paulina do Amaral; Baxton Bryant; Carolyn Cartwright; Addison Chappell; Bogie Chappell; Jon Chappell; Mary Chappell; Misa Chappell; Sheryl Chappell; Mary Sue Chor; Patrick Cribben; Steve Downing; Barbara Dozier; Ben Ebenhack; Liz Forbes; Randi Greenspan; Mark Headley; Charlotte Henri; Larry Hudson; Walter Kitt; Chris Lehmann; Adrian McFarlane; Francesca Morgan; Jim Mott; Patti Neill; Doug Noble; Caroline Packard; Kai Pedersen; Martina Pils; Verna Rivers; Sharon Ryan; Ken Serbin; Cheryl Shanks; Robin Sherlock; Miriam Smalhout; Elyse Small; Julie Sorensen; Clay Templin; Jaime Templin; Cathy Jean Tumber; Elisabeth K. Valkenier; Lisa Valkenier; Robert Valkenier; Peter Wallace; Shelley Wallace; Karin Weaver; Suzanne Wolk; Quentin Young; Ruth Young; Corrine Zurbreugg.

My mother and father, mysteriously, made everything possible. They might have been satisfied with that. Yet they kept making more things possible and in doing so inadvertently filled me with more gratitude than I can express in a lifetime. A different mystery makes me even more grateful to the parents of Elizabeth Moore and leaves me powerless to dedicate this book to anyone but her.

As will be obvious to anyone who knows any of the above-mentioned persons, they bear a great deal of responsibility for worthwhile insights and conclusions that have crept into the work below, but none for any mistakes and omissions in it.

INTRODUCTION

This book is about the relationship between morality and politics. Its central question is, how did a poor, disfranchised minority win a political battle against a majority that outvoted, outspent, and outgunned it? The basic answer is that southern black leaders of the civil rights movement understood white southerners well enough to take advantage of covert white sympathy, and of fatal divisions among segregationists, in a wide variety of ways.

The reason behind the black leaders' advantage was that segregationist myths about the South were untrue, starting with the myth that black and white southerners lived in completely separate worlds under segregation. Martin Luther King and other black leaders had grown up in the midst of white southerners; they were not alienated from them, especially not as children. Southern black folks knew "their" white folks. They monitored their petty rivalries. They heard the little white lies they told themselves. They knew their institutions the way Shakespeare's gardeners, gatekeepers, and gravediggers knew those of their ruling class. Most of all, they knew their holy texts—their Bible and their Constitution—which they reverently shared with them. Thus they knew the white South's weak points. Starting with this knowledge, the leaders of the Southern Christian Leadership Conference were moral leaders in treating those weak points mercifully. They were political leaders in recognizing that merciful treatment opened up the widest possible opportunities for advancement of their own cause.

The material these leaders had to work with, the white South, had to contain keys to their victory. It was not a monolithic wall of resistance but a complex whole that had to be studied piece by piece. In the first stages of research for this book, I looked only at the tiny minority of white southerners who actively supported the civil rights movement. They were the ones who most directly contradicted the myth of the solid white South. They also made a fascinating human interest story. But I soon began to see that their story barely scratched the surface of historical explanation. I had assumed that each of these brave white southerners would serve as a prototype of the movement's interaction with the whole of white society. To join a movement against racism they first had to defeat it in their own minds, and their struggle to redefine their identity as white southerners without white supremacy would, I thought, provide a window into what the movement eventually did in the white South as a whole.

But it was only their relationship to the rest of the white South, it turned out, that made these unusually introspective and unconventional people useful to the civil rights movement. Attractive as they were in their own right as living contradictions to the ideology that defined their society, they mattered as much for their unexceptional as for their exceptional qualities. They rarely considered themselves radicals. They saw themselves as defending, not attacking, the best of southern tradition. Though opposed to southern racism, that is, they were still southern: they could exploit their familiarity with other white southerners for purposes of persuasion or espionage. Their being white southerners was perhaps more important than their being white liberals, and their effect on the outcome of the civil rights movement, especially in its early days, was far greater than that of the more numerous, more celebrated northern liberals.[1]

The more I studied the exceptional white southerners who out of a moral commitment actively aided the movement, the more my attention was drawn to a larger group who, without any moral commitment, found themselves compelled to break with the segregationists in order to restore social peace, a good business climate, or the good name of their city in the national headlines. These middle-road southerners sought a quiet role for themselves, and when exposed, they were accused of violating the southern way of life and betraying their race. Yet by their numbers and standing in the community, they undermined the credibility of their attackers.

I was discovering things about the white South that the civil rights movement had discovered long before. Black southerners who joined the movement knew that the dominant ideology of their society, racism, was wrong, but they knew it was wrong in more than a moral sense. They knew it was incorrect, in a factual sense. White people did not stick together in their endorsement (or even in their definition) of racial separation, let alone in their willingness to defend it. The black southern movement started by discerning the divisions in the white South and then set about widening them. The black leaders won largely because they understood the white South better than the segregationists who claimed to be defending it.

The first category of white southerners I examined—the small number of conscientious movement supporters—was vital to this process in two ways. In a practical way, they were often the only persons available with the legal training, social connections, inside information, and money that the local movement needed at crucial junctures. In a spiritual way, they gave the movement hope that white people in general might follow the lead of the ones who were facing up to the duty to grant justice to black people, even when doing so meant paying a price of ostracization or worse.

Practical help and grounds for hope were still not enough. The success of movement actions in the South can only be understood by looking at the precise ways in which civil rights organizations won the battles they did. In each of these battles, the central question was the ability of the segregationist leadership to hold the white community's allegiance throughout a long siege. Here the pragmatic or opportunistic white moderates became most important. They could compete with the die-hard segregationists for leadership. Unlike white movement supporters, they never stuck their necks out in the beginning of a local movement action. But precisely because of that, they could offer themselves as alternatives to extremism. Their need to show the public that they had a way to bring peace and restore order aided the movement during the middle and late stages of the struggle, when extreme segregationists became most desperate and most violent.

The movement depended on these white moderates for changing national policy as well as local practices. National Democrats, especially Lyndon Johnson, sought them out as the shortest and surest route to ending the disorder that threatened their party—which historically depended on the all-white system that kept the South Democratic, yet increasingly depended on the black men and women who escaped that system, and enfranchised themselves, by migrating northward. Johnson and other Democratic leaders needed large numbers of powerful white southerners to circumvent the political apparatus of southern states, controlled by racial demagogues, and show enough progress in civil rights to hold northern black votes without driving off too many southern white votes. As the southern white moderates became agents of federal authority, their usefulness to the civil rights leaders increased.

Since the appeal of the middle-road white leaders depended on their distance from their extremist rivals for control of southern cities, it became clear that it was also necessary to examine the role of a third group of white southerners, the rabid segregationists, whose tactics and social background may have done more to damage the respectability of segregation than any opponent of segregation could have done. A complete explanation required analysis of the relationship of all three groups to the movement. There was a source for this explanation, as things turned out, in the movement's own strategy, the heart of which was best expressed in two points made by Martin Luther King, the first a sociological one, the second a philosophical one.

King's sociological point was that there were three kinds of white people in the South: extreme segregationists who were willing to fight; middle-roaders who favored segregation but would sooner see it destroyed than take personal risks to defend it; and the tiny minority who would, with varying degrees of caution, support action to undermine segregation. Those are the categories on which the civil rights movement based its relationship to the white South. They are the basis of this book.

King's philosophical point was that moral thought must focus on tactics and not simply on goals. King's preoccupation as a social theorist, and his central disagreement with Marx, was his belief that the end does not justify the means. On the contrary, he argued that means and ends must cohere, that a moral end cannot be achieved by immoral means. Arguments over what constitutes human happiness or social justice at some hypothetical time in the future were usually beside the point, since they did not spell out how, exactly, human beings in the here and now could achieve such ultimate goals. After all, it was on the road to such goals that the worst crimes against humanity were committed. How to take the first steps needed the most attention. A moral victory would not be possible if black southerners attacked white southerners or dehumanized them with the stereotypes that attack required. Not only would attack be immoral, it would be impractical. It would impel white southerners, who outnumbered and outgunned black ones, to close ranks and defend themselves, to live up to the stereotype. On the other hand, as long as white southerners were not under attack, the assumption that they all had something in common to fight for—the central assumption of segregationist doctrine—was fatally unrealistic. The political task was to attack the institutions of the white South in such a way as to divide rather than unify its people—or in the movement's moral language, to hate the sin but love the sinner. That was a delicate task and required resourcefulness and self-restraint. The southern civil rights movement, while it lasted, imposed on its ranks the collective mental discipline necessary to achieve that task.

The black movement pressured white southerners in two interlocking ways. Moral appeals inspired a few white persons to follow their best instincts and traditions. Political manipulation impelled others to follow their worst instincts and traditions in mostly self-destructive ways. At the same time as the movement appealed to the goodness in all white southern-ers, it sought to get them to do something against their will. It aimed both to redeem and to coerce them.[2] The synergistic effect of both kinds of pres-sure made the black minority far stronger than its numbers, its money, and its political power would have indicated.

The civil rights movement never faced a simple choice between force and moral suasion because there was never a simple division between black and white. A few white southerners were sickened by segregation. Usually they were unable or unwilling to do anything to change it. Many more white southerners endorsed segregation enthusiastically in principle yet found it terribly inconvenient in practice. They too did nothing to change it. Yet the knowledge that both groups of white southerners existed was the greatest moral and political resource the civil rights movement had: each group wanted in one way or another to be pushed. That knowledge gave millions of black southerners, despite a dispiriting history of crushed hopes and broken promises, confidence in their ability to win — not simply confi-dence in the righteousness of their cause but in the usually unrelated prospects of that cause for victory in the real world.

In the minds of black southern protesters, racist institutions were not just evil, they were weak; their administration was diluted by human com-passion and human cupidity. Southern white resistance, if determined and vicious, was surmountable because its very determination and viciousness imposed too high a cost on southern society. Two frequently repeated expe-riences reinforced these basic intuitions: the movement found local white allies it could rely upon, and perhaps more important, it found that it could usually rely on the stupidity and disorganization of its opponents to alien-ate the white population they claimed to represent[3] (except in Albany, Georgia, the exception that proved the rule). The mixture of the move-ment's moral appeal to potential allies and political manipulation of the extreme segregationists and middle-roaders produced a far-reaching social result and revealed a basic historical truth: there was no white solidarity in the racist South.

The key to the civil rights movement's success lies in the attitude of its members toward their circumstance, especially toward their allies and ene-mies. The black protesters said, and believed, that what they were doing was good for the white South: they were freeing the white man from the guilt and superstition that inhibited him as much as them. Black southerners had listened for centuries to patronizing white statements about what was good for the Negro, but from their own powerless position, they could not afford to have illusions about what was good for white people. They had to look for real signs of willingness for change and vulnerability to pressure. The movement's attitude toward the white South, forged by a very exacting history, was one of unyielding yet rational hope. Keeping the hope alive required gaining some measure of fulfillment in the real world from time to time. That, in turn, required careful analysis of southern white society.

Hope guided the strategy that enabled an oppressed minority to change the institutions that had given the majority its power. It is by looking at the strategy that I think we can best understand the relationship of the objective to the subjective, the social to the psychological causes of social change. We can examine not "ideas" as opposed to "realities" but ideas about reality which happened to work out as plans to change reality. In strategy, the ultimate goals of a movement must be tied to the means. Plans to achieve the goals must meet the test of reality: those that succeed, even in a limited way, cut the path of social change which we must retrace to explain history. In the case of the civil rights movement, the strategy to redeem the South and coerce it to abandon its defining institutions was not moral or political but inextricably moral *and* political.

The civil rights movement's combination of moral and political strength is the hardest thing to understand about it. Americans today tend to put morality and politics into separate, watertight compartments in their minds. The meaning of each term, it seems, depends on the absence of concerns about the other. Politics, like high finance and show business, respects only ambition; those held back by moral ideals are considered too good, or too soft, for anything but private life. There are public figures we can point to as exceptions, but they only seem to prove the rule that morality is an impractical basis for public life. Those whom we call moral leaders — Gandhi in the movies, Mother Teresa and possibly Lech Wałęsa and Nelson Mandela on the news — make inspiring speeches and become the subjects of inspiring biographies, especially for young readers. When it comes to actual administration, however, they never appear able to make ends meet. They seem in our culture to play a role that is closer to entertainers on stage than to responsible authorities in our day-to-day lives. They are not considered part of what we blithely refer to as "the real world."

Political leaders appear as photographic negatives of the moral leaders. The outlines are similar: both depend on popular support and both make lots of speeches. Both occasionally win the Nobel Peace Prize. Yet where Gandhi sacrificed himself for his people and his dream, as the story goes, political leaders are expected to do the opposite: to sacrifice the public weal, to manipulate public hopes and aspirations, for their own fame and power. Deep down, most people who are not politicians themselves would agree with the cynical cliché: all that distinguished Richard Nixon from other successful politicians is that he got caught. (And an alarming number who are politicians would no doubt agree with this too.) To be political in our world means to be power hungry to the point of ruthlessness. To be moral means to be selfless to the point of ineffectuality.

To be sure, some distinction between the two is warranted. The idea of complete compatibility of moral and political demands is utopian. But complete polarization is unrealistic, too, as the civil rights movement ought to make clear. Black Christians in the South saw their social reality stand condemned by their moral law. Yet they insisted that their moral law was not unrealistic. The moral and the political are in constant tension, and can probably coincide only temporarily, but their temporary coincidence is what makes the civil rights movement momentous and interesting.

That formative event of our recent history, for all its idealism, was grounded in the organizational drudgery and strategic calculation of day-to-day politics. It politicized masses by making their fervent moral beliefs seem realistic. Only then could they overcome the powerful inclination to find the drudgery and calculation alienating. They remained unalienated for years of excruciating risk and in doing so brought moral concerns to bear upon political institutions. Without morality, politics became frightening, or just plain dull, to all but the ambitious and lucky few. Without politics, morality became a series of disappointments and delusions. The movement's success in maintaining a relationship between the two demands close attention, the more so because it was incomplete.

PART ONE

The Strange Career of Racial Dissent in the South

Liberalism that is sincere must will the condition of achieving its ends.

—John Dewey, *Liberalism and Social Action*

Everything seems stupid when it fails.

—Dostoyevsky, *Crime and Punishment*

The "Silent South"

The Founding Fathers of
Southern White Dissent

T he white southerners who dissented from the racial status quo in the
1950s did not just pop up out of nowhere. They had a long history.
The main question in that history is why it failed so utterly for so long to
produce any effective aid to the struggle for black rights before the 1950s.

Before proceeding, some definitions are in order. It is necessary to dis-
tinguish between a liberal and what I will call a racial dissenter (or simply a
dissenter). The "liberal" seeks a formalized legal structure, believes in
progress, and sees education as a way to achieve material progress and
overcome moral "problems." There is in liberalism as such nothing that
precludes racial prejudice. Most liberals in the South (and, it seems, the
North) were racists in the late nineteenth and early twentieth centuries, in
the sense that when they thought about it at all, they accepted the "scientific" finding that Negroes were biologically or culturally inferior to the
more developed "race" of white people. Negroes might deserve help or
someday achieve "uplift," but if so, that was not a central question to liberals, who generally supported segregation and disfranchisement.

The dissenters, on the other hand, were the small number of white
persons who expressed opposition to specific racist laws and policies. Dissenters did not necessarily reject the doctrine of racial inequality (indeed,
they usually endorsed it). Their opposition to specific policies may have
been based on self-interest, opportunism, or even a more thoroughgoing
racism than their contemporaries (as when some argued that racial distinc-
tiveness, a strong, natural force, would withstand integrated schooling,
which was desirable because it was cheaper than separate schooling). Their
motives are not examined here: those are a psychological matter. What will

be examined is a political and historical matter: the tendency of their dissent, whether individual or organized, to fail.

The historical significance of southern white dissent should not be exaggerated. There was a "silent South," to use the phrase that George Washington Cable (one of the most prominent dissenters) coined as he tried to awaken it in the late nineteenth century. Before and after Cable, many southern white dissenters shared his bold vision of racial justice. But Cable's "silent South" was, as he and his followers mournfully acknowledged, above all silent—until the black movement finally gave it an effective voice in the 1950s and 1960s. What is important about this dissent before the 1950s and 1960s is that, though it never infected a significant portion of white opinion, it nonetheless conveyed, by its very persistence in the face of failure, a message to the southern black community: that the white community contained figures who were repulsed by the system of segregation and disfranchisement and, more important, that white allegiance to the system was divided and full of weak spots.

The Founding Father of Southern White Dissent: Atticus Greene Haygood

The first significant example of white racial dissent after Reconstruction is Atticus Greene Haygood. Haygood used his authority as president of Emory College in Oxford, Georgia (which later became Emory University in Atlanta), and as a leading Methodist minister (he later became bishop of the Southern Methodist Episcopal Church), to exhort the white South to treat black folks more charitably.

In his 1881 book, *Our Brother in Black, His Freedom and His Future*, Haygood argued that true Christianity demanded changes in the existing pattern of black-white relations in the South, and denounced perpetrators of racial violence as un-Christian. He also insisted that it was impractical for white people to exclude black people from their communities—he dismissed the widely discussed alternatives to integration, deportation and reenslavement, as unfeasible. Most important was his prediction that efforts to keep black people poor and illiterate would in the long run drag their white neighbors down. It would be kinder, and more prudent, to provide former slaves with a day's work than a day's rations, and there was no way out of providing one or the other. If society "will not build schoolhouses and churches, it must build jails. Thus reason and justice get their grim revenge."[1]

Though Haygood put his own money where his mouth was—he served from 1884 to 1891 as the first head of the Slater Fund, a northern-based philanthropic organization that helped build black schools in the South—he did not make great demands on his southern white brethren. White employers had to allow only so much education for black people as could fit into their working schedules. Nor would white society have to assume a long-term burden of financing black education. To make education a completely "free-gift," he argued, would reinforce black character traits of dependence. He believed that it would be best for black fathers to shoulder the burden of educating their children after white people, who at the time "ha[d] the money," primed the pump for a generation or so.[2]

As things turned out, however, the passing of a generation weakened Haygood's case for black education. Writing before systematic legal disfranchisement, Haygood based his case on the premise that black men could vote: "This new citizen is a voter, and unhappily for all, he is not ready for his responsibilities. . . . Woe to the land where those who hold the balance of power are in ignorance. This tremendous engine of political power, the ballot, must be in hands that know what they are doing." There was no need to pretend to be happy about black suffrage, but from its establishment Haygood concluded as a charitable pragmatist that there must be black education.

Haygood's audience concluded from the same premise that the most pragmatic solution was simply to deprive black people of the ballot. Education was hard enough for white people in a poor and war-torn region to establish for their own children, and Haygood's professed pragmatism failed him when it came to specifying means to his ends: "I claim no mastery of this question [how to finance a new public school system] for it is very large and complicated." He averred that it might be a good idea to try applying federal appropriations to black education, but he was "not sure of this." If the South would only develop a willing mind, he assured, "ways and means" would be found to solve the admittedly difficult problems of educating all its children.

Haygood's views, which were not unusual for prominent white southerners in Reconstruction years, were becoming increasingly unacceptable. The Democratic party was hardening in its campaign against black rights, and its growing hegemony in the South made Haygood a regional heretic. But he was not a complete heretic: he shared the growing white belief in segregation, as most progressive thinkers of the New South did. Though he was not sure how to provide black education, he was sure that "there

should be separate schools for Negro children." It was "best for all parties."[3] Today this may appear to be a hypocritical endorsement of unequal
facilities. But the establishment of separate schools was tied up with several
other issues, not least the establishment of public schools per se. The alternative to establishing separate schools for black children was often no
schools at all, rather than mixed schools. At the time Haygood wrote, it was
not at all clear that separate schooling would underwrite subordination and
exclusion of black people from society in general, for in 1881 segregation
had not yet triumphed. One of the reasons it did triumph was that white
liberals like Haygood—whether they personally sought to discriminate
against black people or not—believed separation would prevent the emergence of harsher systems of race relations, such as all-out race war.[4] Haygood's position was significant in its insistence on black education, but also
in the example it provides of how narrow and tentative were southern
white pleas for racial justice after Reconstruction.

As it was, Haygood did not end up winning many sympathizers for the
ideas he proposed. At the end of the last words he ever wrote on race relations, in 1895, he prophesied that by 1965 his white southern descendants
would look back and "build monuments to the heroic men and women
whom their grandparents ostracized." There were but "half a dozen" of
his people and time who, he said, shared his vision. "Would God there
were more!"[5]

More than the limitations of Haygood's own position, its inconsistency
with other southern white dissent shows how it was doomed to fail. While
others opposed segregation and supported disfranchisement, Haygood
accepted segregation and opposed disfranchisement. His strongest point
was a plea for black education. But he also took a strong position against
mob violence, and while that was the one point on which all southern dissenters (and many supporters of the emerging system) agreed, even in that
area Haygood's arguments undermined their own conclusions. Though he
said violence was un-Christian and denounced "the deviltry of Ku Klux-
ism," he voiced an opinion that later researchers would establish as almost
always mistaken: that lynchings were responses to actual sexual assaults on
white women.[6] This was the standard apology for lynching among the
respectable class of white southerners. It did not do much good to condemn lynching without questioning the basic justification for it. That the
justification was genuinely believed does not absolve the believers of the
charge of wishful thinking.

Within the framework of such assumptions, which southern dissenters began to question publicly only in the 1920s and 1930s, scholars have held Haygood up as "one of the South's most eloquent and consistent defenders of black aspirations."[7] Certainly the moral fervor of his sermons was sincere. At his best, however, Haygood's was a lonely voice. Those who try to afflict the conscience are never popular, even when, as Haygood did, they embrace the fundamental assumptions and wishful thoughts of their audience. He faced the limitation moral reformers always face: faith in the good will of one's audience may be necessary to hold its attention, yet it shades into flattery. It can come across as praise even though not meant that way. Exhortations to live by one's best instincts, because they emphasize the existence of the instincts, convert easily into excuses for putting off living by them. Assured and confident appeals to a conscience can become its balm.

A Hard-nosed Approach: Lewis Harvie Blair

The very different rhetorical tactic of the next great white southern dissenter suggests that Haygood's limitations did not derive fully from his reliance on moral suasion. Lewis Harvie Blair, a Richmond businessman and free-trade advocate, turned his argument for increased black rights and equality on the material self-interests of white people. Blair's was, in his words, an "appeal to the pocket." He relied on "facts" and repudiated "sentiment." All experience proved "that human nature must be interested on its material side before its intellectual and moral instincts can be permanently stimulated. In order to move men to practice justice and right they must first be convinced that it will be profitable for them to do so."[8]

Blair's economic determinism (common among liberal reformers of the Gilded Age, North and South) led him to many of the same conclusions Haygood had reached through religion. Blair too told white people that attempting to impede black progress only wasted energy. "We must trample or we must elevate," he wrote, and when trampling upon the Negro, the white South found (whenever it was rational enough to notice) that the downtrodden Negro just dragged it down with him. White people could conserve energy by elevating the Negro. The Negro in his present state, Blair wrote, was an "extremely defective tool" in the campaign for prosperity. But if the Negro was to become "an intelligent voter," a "citizen capable of taking a sensible part in the affairs of his community," and a "valuable co-worker in adding to the wealth of the State," then white southerners had "a vast deal to do in order to elevate him." The rational motive for educating the Negro, Blair argued, was "to make him *our* assistant in the production of wealth." Considering that reenslavement was impractical, his only alternative was to induce the Negro to hard labor "by ambition," or "the hope of enjoying in full the fruits of his labors." He was retooling Horatio Alger for application to black southerners.

Unlike Haygood, Blair advocated integration in the schools. The best way to inculcate ambition and industriousness in black people, Blair maintained, was to put them in schools with white people, who already possessed such traits and would provide both an inspiring example and bracing competition. Mixed schools were a social necessity in any case, as the number of white children in so many districts in the South was too small to allow a separate school, what with shortages of funds and teachers.[9]

C. Vann Woodward finds underneath this flint-nosed practicality a genuine "moral indignation over injustice and strong impulses of ethical idealism"; there is "a good deal of the iron glove on the velvet hand" in Blair's rhetoric.[10] Other readers may have trouble detecting those qualities, but whether they are present between the lines or not has little to do with the political effect of Blair's lines. Blair's premises, like Haygood's, could be taken to simpler conclusions than those he proposed. If his assumption of progress and perpetual abundance turned out to be unfounded, then Blair's premises (which lack Haygood's leaven of moral sentiment) could lead to the disastrous racial war he hoped to prevent. Blair's rhetorical game had high stakes. He was aware of the logical trap he had set to convince his audience: "If the elevation of the Negro would not make us wealthy and prosperous, instead of advocating his cause it would be the part of wisdom to promote any and all measures that would tend speedily to wipe him off the face of the earth."[11] In this light, it is not so strange that Blair methodically and completely (though privately) recanted his racial egalitarianism, adopting in its place a belief in repeal of the Fourteenth and Fifteenth amendments, complete disfranchisement, and total segregation. It is not such an "enigma," to use Woodward's description, that "the prophet" Blair was "swept up in the storm of reaction" of the late 1890s.[12]

Blair, in other words, followed the pattern of the white South in general: entertaining proposals for equal justice and opportunity for black men toward the end of the nineteenth century, when a repetition of past economic, military, and political disaster was a constant threat and the future was open to social experiment and political competition, and then reversing itself around the turn of the century, when powerful white southerners discovered that their resources were scarcer than ever, that northern industrialization was leaving their region behind, that the alleged ravages of Negro rule made for great crowd-pleasing speeches (punctuated with lurid hints about Negro sexuality), and above all that they could get away with progressive and systematic denial of equal justice and opportunity as far as northern opinion and federal power were now concerned. The mild-mannered and practical Blair followed, in other words, the course of that more incendiary and famous egalitarian-turned-bigot, Tom Watson.[13]

Even in the early Blair there are healthy seeds of the later growth of Negrophobia. "[The] Negro is not a competent voter," he wrote in 1889, "and he should never have been entrusted with the ballot." True, Blair immediately qualified this statement with the assurance that the average white man was not competent either, and since white men already had the ballot, nothing special had been lost by turning it over to black men. Still, Blair's assumption that the franchise could not be taken away from uneducated, illiterate voters, black or white, was conspicuously weak and, events would prove, quite wrong. It was also the only thing that kept his mind open on race.

Blair's final point in urging the white South to let black men continue voting had been that the North would not tolerate another massive infringement on black freedom. In a nation whose sectional divisions continued in "full vigor," Blair believed in 1889, the alternative to conceding black rights was a northern campaign for black rights, which, if repulsed by the white South, would lead to political penalties that might be as crippling as the war and Reconstruction—in Blair's words, "complete disfranchisement of every Southern state."[14] That assumption, as bolder bigots soon discovered, was completely wrong too.

Thus there was very little in Blair's argument to keep the majority of white southerners from concluding that black southerners should be driven utterly to the margin of southern society, and ultimately nothing to keep Blair himself from coming to this conclusion. Just as the line between moral suasion and flattery was thin, so was the line between practicality and resignation to the status quo.

On the other hand, Woodward is surely right to point out that Blair exemplified a moment in southern history when possibilities for social change were open, "when public commitment and decision were still in suspense," and the best minds of the South could think freely about other systems of racial order than the rigid and degrading one they later adopted. Blair pointed a way that the South could have gone, a way of openness and flexibility in race relations, before the "great freeze" of the 1890s. More important for present purposes, Blair was also part of a heritage on which white and black southerners could later draw as evidence that the racial system was not an unchanging monolith. Blair's bigotry did not make him useless to those who sought to end bigotry—any more than Haygood's good intentions made him useful. If Blair's original assumptions about reality could be revalidated—if the North could be made somehow to care about justice in the South, or if white southerners could find someday that the sacrifices required for racial justice were not as great as in the days when black men demanded land as well as votes—then southerners might begin to read their "interests" differently.

Culmination and Synthesis: George Washington Cable

Historians have singled out George Washington Cable as the most thoroughgoing of southern white dissenters in the late nineteenth century. His failure was the most complete.

Like Blair, Cable appealed to material interests. Making his pitch for the New South program of industrialization and urbanization, Cable told of his visit to Birmingham, where he had seen the future and concluded that it worked. He rhapsodized about seeing "the crude ore of the earth, so long trampled underfoot, . . . being turned by great burnings and meltings into one of the prime factors of the world's wealth." The most important lesson of Birmingham was the spectacle of the black men, with "the wild glare of molten cinders and liquid metal falling upon their black faces and reeking forms," proving that they were "no longer simple husbandmen" or mere "companions of unfettered nature." To Cable, who viewed racial oppression as the "stump" of slavery, the "felled institution" of the Old South, black men not only *could* but *had to* rise under industrialization, in order to lift the South out of its past. Southern poverty made it urgent to elevate the black man: "For our own interests, one and all of them, we ought to lose no time."[15]

Like Haygood, Cable also appealed to a moral sense. Petty and short-sighted "politics," he claimed, were blocking the "moral and intellectual intelligence" of the South, which would normally seek "that plane of universal justice and equity which it is every people's duty before God to seek." Party politics had rendered racial justice a secondary question, but the "best people" of the South, left to their instincts, would have made it their top priority. Cable called these people back to their instincts. The responsibility of the "best people" increased in the midst of all the unscrupulous types—carpetbaggers, scalawags, and their successors—

who stood ready to take advantage of the social discord that results from injustice: "[T]hey spring and flourish wherever, under representative government, gentility makes a mistake, however sincere, against the rights of the poor and ignorant."[16]

Cable shared with Haygood and Blair a faith that helping the black South would help the white South, that morality and self-interest, wherever one put the emphasis, did not conflict, even in a time of economic scarcity and intense social conflict. There was, despite the rather breathtaking optimism of this assumption, a tone of desperation in it. The dissenters *had* to believe that their morality was not naive and outdated; they *had* to believe that their self-interests were not rapacious and evil. This was only the first sign of their faith outrunning their circumstances.

Haygood, Blair, and Cable, among the most sensitive and supple-minded thinkers of the New South, were troubled by the legacies of the Old South, whose destruction left a vacuum in their moral as well as their economic and political worlds. Slavery was gone, but so was any sense of obligation to the slaves. The dissenters still felt a strong tug of paternalistic duty. Now that war had destroyed the customary ways of satisfying that duty, what was left of morality? Either there was no moral basis for society, or the dissenters had to do some fast footwork to replace paternalism with something new. That something new was progress.

To most of the New South movement, the ideal of progress—as yet nothing but an ideal—promised that even the lowliest members of society would survive and flourish as a part of a natural, accidental process. Prosperous members of society no longer had to do anything to help the poor folks, except get out of the way of that process. Though the racial dissenters were never as fully convinced as other members of the New South movement that progress would work moral miracles, they strained to accept the general faith that moral obligations would wither away with economic growth.

To make the idea of progress come true, Haygood, Blair, and Cable—unlike most New South men—believed they had to convince the South that black people had rights and deserved schools. This was the issue on which all their other social and economic dreams depended, and they were not above a little intellectual terrorism in pursuing the goal. Their audiences feared a renewed northern occupation. Always aware that their logic and facts might fail to persuade, Haygood, Blair, and Cable sooner or later pulled their rhetorical trump card: if you do not do what we good southerners say you should do, Sherman's army will march again. The North will impose an even sterner, more sudden version of Reconstruction. Efforts to hold the Negro down will always backfire, not only because they will impede southern progress, but because the Yankees will sooner or later spring to the Negro's defense. In this way, racial dissenters sought to excite sectional fears and southern nationalism even as they (with the rest of the New South men) repudiated all "sectionalism" and irrationality.

This threatening manipulation of white southern fears was the strongest tactic the dissenters used. It is easy to see why it failed. After thirty years of ever-bolder taunting and testing by southern vigilantes and legislatures, the threat of renewed federal intervention proved to be a paper tiger. By the end of the century, southern white audiences quite rationally concluded that they could do as they pleased with the black population, at least as far as northern lawgivers and judges were concerned. They now had to face only their own consciences, and their black population.

Out of the failures of these three southern white dissenters in the late nineteenth century, a pattern emerges. The tone of their writings is always plaintive. They sound not only defeatist but defensive, especially on two points: their affirmation of their southern identity and their disavowal of "social equality." In these two themes southern white dissenters reveal how hard it was, and how hard they tried, to change the course of southern history. In them, one can see the deepening imprint of the forces arrayed against dissent—forces that any future dissent would have to understand and overcome.

Defending Their Southern Identity

Establishing one's *bona fides* as a southerner required showing that the "race problem" was neither the South's fault nor the North's business. The whole nation, Cable wrote, brought the Negro to our shores, for the whole nation's profit. "The African slave was brought here by cruel force, and with everybody's consent except his own. Everywhere the practice was favored as a measure of common aggrandizement . . . with the full knowledge and consent of the nation."[17] On the other hand, the South had for some time assumed full responsibility for the burdensome Negro question and was best left alone to work that question out. Whatever desire the North had to help black people would come to naught without the South's cooperation. Northern benevolence tended to go awry. Southern dissenters, with the rest of the South's leadership, asked northern patience in return for assuming the racial burden of the whole nation.[18] "Southern

whites understand the negroes better," Haygood asserted, "[and] they have
done unspeakably more than they have had credit for." Although there
were "a few desperate and lawless men" in the South who persecuted black
people, Haygood assured northern audiences that they did so "to the dis-
may and horror of the mass of the Southern people."[19] This was also meant
to assure southern audiences of Haygood's loyalty.

The defensiveness grew even stronger when dissenters addressed their
own neighbors directly. White southerners were the audience they had to
convert to a strenuous belief in fairness for the Negro. The first order of
business was to convince them that such fairness was not an alien idea.
Blair avowed that southerners might see his book as presumptuous and
hostile; he nonetheless believed that his "Southern ancestry, birth, rearing,
residence and interest" preserved him from the charge of invidiousness."[20]
Cable, too, declared with peremptory pride that he was "prosouthern" and
had lived in the South "all through Reconstruction." He had argued from
the first that the solution to the race issue had to come from the South.
And who better to recommend the solution than one who could announce,
"I am the son and grandson of slaveholders," moreover a "citizen of an
extreme Southern state, a native of Louisiana, an ex-Confederate soldier,
and a lover of my home, my city, and my state, as well as of my country"?
Cable's enemies insinuated that he was tainted with New England blood,
seeking for Cable's deviance on the race question — as they did for so many
other difficulties — a genetic explanation. Cable's fierce assertions of his
own purity demonstrate the insecurity as well as the importance of southern identity in this debate.[21]

In a period of radical transformation of southern society, any effort to
stake out one's southern identity had ambiguous implications. Not only
were the dissenters torn between asserting national loyalty and southern
loyalty, but southern loyalty itself seemed to pull in two directions. Defeat
in war, with all the resentment and nostalgia it entailed, meant that the
South had no single, unified character but an uncertain duality. The southerner was a ghost of the past and an unborn child of the future. This led
the dissenters to make two conflicting appeals to "the South."

First, they appealed to the Old South, often by simply hanging the
verdant decay of past southern glory as decoration on whatever argument
they happened to be making.[22] That was the literary fashion of the day. But
there is in the dissenters' writings a profound and insistent sense of obligation inherited from the past, too. Dissenters sought to revive the defiant
strength of the Old South and keep it free from the taint of Yankeedom.

They saw kindness and gentility in that Old South, which they genuinely believed would work longer and more effectively in favor of the poor Negro than the available alternative, the meddlesome schoolmarmism of carpetbaggers. Second, they appealed to a healthier, livelier South: Henry Grady's New South of industrialization and urbanization. This New South existed as yet only in their imaginations. To convert it into reality they strove to repudiate the image of the past, which was a disastrous series of temptations to self-destruction, and replace it with the image of the future, which was a promising series of exhortations to prosperity. Southern dissenters, like southerners in general, were caught in a tug of war between the failed but glorious past and the promising but unproven future. The past pulled hard but threatened to lead them into repeating the catastrophes of the past. The future pulled hard but, because of its associations with the North, could never be fully trusted.

Disavowing "Social Equality"

Between section and nation, between past and future, between the bonds of paternal obligation and the fluidity of industrial progress, southern dissenters found only narrow and shifting ground on which to stake their claims for racial justice. The cramped and unstable quality of their dissent shows through most strongly on the second front of their defensiveness, their reaction to charges of "social equality." So hard did they strive to avoid any hint of support for this dread (but ill-defined) shibboleth that they contradicted one another in their disavowals of it.

Haygood lumped his disavowal of social equality together with his opposition to integration. Those who perceived a danger of social equality in black suffrage, which he supported, failed to understand the "facts": southern white children "won't sit at the same desks with Negro children" and southern black children "don't want to sit at the same desks with white children." Only "a small class of fanatics" could be troubled by these facts. The vast majority wishes to let man's social instincts dictate their own wisdom rather than impose fanciful schemes, such as integration. Haygood gave an example of a "wild and rattle-brained Federal judge" who declared in 1867 that the South must accept not only emancipation and Negro suffrage, but "social equality, amalgamation, and all." In dismissing the judge's "exquisite absurdities," Haygood sidled up to the prejudices of his society and enlisted them in the cause of black voting rights. Haygood assured that the races would always separate, like oil and water, no matter how much they were shaken together by misguided reformers. He apparently believed that such assurances would quiet his society's fears about continued black exercise of basic rights.[23]

Blair and Cable, on the other hand, favored integration, and they lumped their disavowal of "social equality" with assurances that integration would never produce intermixing. Black and white children might attend the same schools for years, but they would always follow their instinct to keep separate in social relations. Schools were not strong enough to break that instinct. To Blair, the educated were especially disinclined to mix. Blair dismissed the fears of those who sometimes saw "degraded white men mix with Negroes" and imagined that the mixing caused the demoralization: "The fact is, they did not mingle with the blacks until they had become demoralized." Thus it was "thoroughly illogical" to believe "that the simple mingling of the two colors in the same school, however well guarded and however well regulated the public schools were, would also cause demoralization." As both races became more educated in common schools, they would increasingly shun each other outside school.

After arguing that social mixing was unlikely in integrated schools, Blair took another tack and argued that much interracial mingling already occurred in society and no degradation of the white people had resulted: black "mammies" had been nursing the finest of white children for generations. Even with this most intimate form of mingling, both races still followed a general (and, to Blair, salutary) pattern of separation. "Even in separate schools, both private and public, children do not form many intimate acquaintances and in mixed schools there is little likelihood of white children forming any intimacies with black children."[24]

Cable conceded a vast amount of "common ground" to those who opposed him on civil rights and integration, including the assumption that the black race was "inferior." But Cable turned that assumption into an assurance that integration did not threaten to bring about "social equality." Restraint of racial oppression would not undermine the social order, Cable maintained, because class differences would persist. Social equality, he insisted, could never arise "where a community is actuated, as every civilized community is, by an intellectual and moral ambition." That was clear from all history. Social equality was "a fool's dream," and therefore the fear that one change or another in society's laws would create it was "a fool's fear."

Taking a less confrontational approach later, Cable reassured white southerners that they had too long held an "absurd fear" that the "common herd of clowns and ragamuffins" would usurp the civil rewards of decent dress and behavior. Past attempts to bring about reconciliation of social classes had proven this point. Some northern churches, for example, had recently tried to mix the races in a social setting—to do, in other words, "what none of the Protestant churches in America, faithfully as they have striven for it, has ever been able extensively to accomplish. That is, *to get high and low life* to worship together." The northern churches' experiment failed because the white people involved were "cultured" people, trying to mix with "an ignorant, superstitious race of boisterous worshipers just emerged from slavery; one side craving spiritual meat, the other needing spiritual milk." Classes would always tend to separate willingly and spontaneously. The log (the church or, implicitly, any other institution) could not split the wedge (the social impulse to mix only with one's own class).[25]

Effects of Early Southern White Dissent

To say these assurances fell on deaf ears would be to miss the point. They fell on confused ears, barraged by far more numerous appeals to support the emerging pattern of segregation. Such ears ferreted out the self-assured clarity and simplicity of the segregationists and, understandably, turned away from the defensive and inconsistent subtlety of the defenders of black rights.

Apart from confusion, different kinds of white southern audiences were predisposed to mistrust Cable's assurances. Poor white southerners could not have been gratified by Cable's assurances that class barriers would remain as a bulwark against social equality. That implied that the barriers would remain between themselves and upper-class whites, even as some black folk found opportunities to rise and lord their success over the poor whites. Well-heeled white leaders could not have welcomed Cable's acknowledgment of class barriers among white folks, when they were straining to deny the existence of those barriers and flatter the poor white voters with assurances that, although poor, they were on the winning side —as long as they did not make common cause with poor black voters.

Even if Cable, Blair, and Haygood had had sympathetic audiences, their basic premise that political equality did not entail social equality was very hard to sustain. For what, in the final analysis, had guaranteed the social distinctions of racial slavery if not the legal sanction and codification of those distinctions? Could slavery have persisted if escaped slaves were not legally returned to their masters? What hope was there of maintaining a distinction between black and white when some black persons, freed from the restraints of slavery, had already shown their ability to learn and work and save?

The mass of southern white people, who remained desperately poor and uneducated, tended to be jealous of those who rose in status. The small number of black people who jumped, as it were, from below them on the social ladder to a rung above them took on a symbolic importance, with the aid of racial propaganda, which magnified poor white jealousies. Poor whites feared that black self-uplift, aided by northern philanthropy, would create a vacuum at the bottom level of society into which they themselves would be sucked. By 1900 one of the leading New South spokesmen remarked that what the South needed was a "white Booker T. Washington" who would "do for the poor white boys of his section the effective work which has already been accomplished at Tuskegee."[26] But as no one was willing to provide funds or leadership for such a program, how could poor whites hope to hold on to the few advantages they had left? If their land and their livelihood were being taken away, and previously landless freedmen were fighting for land and competing for the jobs that were sometimes available to disinherited white farmers, how could the poor whites pass up the opportunity to create barriers to black mobility—especially when the alternative, political efforts to band together with blacks to defeat rich whites, failed again and again?

New South leaders, wanting sectional peace and social peace within the section, tried to flatter the poor white man of the South into believing that he was the equal of the white planter, banker, and lawyer. As if to lend credence to that implausible notion, they added that he was *better* than the former slave. At the same time, they (and they here includes Booker T. Washington) assured the former slave that he could rise, in a separate sphere, to the same level if he would take his energy out of politics and put it into vocational education and hard work. They also sought to flatter northern and southern defenders of the Constitution (no longer the "proslavery compact" that abolitionist and slaveholder had agreed it was, but a program for unprecedented equality in national and state laws) with assurances that they had done all they could for black equality. They need not feel guilty about doing no more.

The Road Not Taken:
John Marshall Harlan and the Last Battle against Segregation

In competing for the allegiance, or at least the acquiescence, of these disparate groups, the New South men hit upon a formula that relieved the guilt and sense of failure each of these groups felt. The formula was popularized by the leading ideologue of the New South movement. Henry Grady, welcoming the Supreme Court's 1883 decisions to undercut the Civil Rights Act of 1875 and allow discrimination by "private" entities, as opposed to the state governments, had written that nothing untoward would result from the growth of private discrimination: the races could remain "equal, but separate."

The success of this formula in law courts and in public opinion was not a foregone conclusion. The need to divert and suppress conflict intensified in the 1890s as the Populist revolt and depression shook the foundations of southern politics. Legislators, hoping to maintain their power, had to act to restore stability, and since the promise of industrial progress had failed to placate the poor farmers, the separation of races by legislative fiat appeared as a way to provide a sense of privilege to those on the white side. Segregation would compensate them for their loss of economic status. Poor white folk might be induced to defend their new status and at the same time would face increased difficulties whenever they tried to communicate with potential allies among the black folk. It was not at all clear that this tactic would work, but by fits and starts, the legislatures experimented with it.

Cable had begged his countrymen to see that separate could never be equal. But if he had ever had a chance of influencing southern white opinion, that chance evaporated the very year he began to plead his case. After hearing the universally negative response to his pleas in the public opinion organs, he went into what C. Vann Woodward referred to as "exile" in Northampton, Massachusetts; the South lost "a fearless critic and a point of view that could thenceforth be dismissed as foreign."[27] The southern legislatures gambled on Grady's formula, constructing a Jim Crow system bit by bit, each state waiting for reinforcement by the other states, which copied and exceeded each other's initiatives. They gained reinforcement from the organs of northern liberal opinion, especially Horace Greeley's *Tribune* and E. L. Godkin's *Nation*.

The decisive contest, though, was in the Supreme Court. The battle there brought out the last cries of southern white opposition to segregation and redefined southern white dissent for the next half-century.

Shortly after Louisiana passed an "equal but separate" railroad law in 1890 (over the protests not only of organized black groups in New Orleans but also of the railroads), a young black attorney named Louis A. Martinet began developing a strategy for a test case to overturn the law. Martinet, son of a creole father and a slave mother, and editor of the militant black paper the *Crusader*, had lobbied unsuccessfully against passage of the law as a form of "class legislation" that was "unjust" and "unchristian." He was in touch with his fellow Louisianan, George Washington Cable, who was now a member of the National Citizens' Rights Association, a northern-based organization formed in 1891 by former carpetbagger Albion Winegar Tourgee to oppose new forms of racial oppression.[28]

Martinet chose Tourgee to be his main lawyer but for various reasons decided to put some white southerners on the case, too. The plaintiff was to be Homer Adolph Plessy, a man who, though legally a "Negro," appeared to be so white that Martinet had to enlist the cooperation of the East Louisiana Railroad even to detect his presence in the "white" car and have him arrested. Plessy's white appearance, Martinet and his associates believed, would strengthen their case for overturning the law. After losing in the Louisiana courts and waiting nearly four years before the U.S. Supreme Court put *Plessy* on the docket, Tourgee found himself too enmeshed in other difficulties to appear before the Court.[29] The task of arguing the case fell to the white southern lawyer Samuel Field Phillips.

Phillips had been a Whig legislator in North Carolina before the war, supported the South's war effort, and helped draft the state's new Black Code and exclusionary political laws in 1865 and 1866 under Presidential Reconstruction. Then, following a four-year retirement, Phillips returned to public life as a Republican supporter of Congressional Reconstruction and, in time, espoused Radical views on the race question. Out of line with most fellow white southerners, Phillips did find favor with the federal government. He served as U.S. solicitor general under Ulysses S. Grant. He had argued several civil rights cases before the Supreme Court before appearing on behalf of Plessy in 1896.

In trying to persuade the Court to overthrow the Jim Crow law of Louisiana, Phillips did not challenge the distinction between social and political equality. His brief emphasized that the Jim Crow statute attempted "to enforce by law an inequality betwixt White and Colored citizens that otherwise [was] *at most* only a social matter, if one at all." He said it was not proper for "a statute to give *force of law* to mere social inequalities turning upon color." Everybody agreed that the white man was "socially" at "the head of the table," he said, and nobody was complaining about that situation. "It is only when social usage is confirmed by statute that exception ought or legally can be taken thereto."

Phillips conceded that the state governments had an interest in some social matters, in particular "the institution of *Marriage*, including the *Family* and rearing of the young." As such, Phillips said he could raise no constitutional objection to laws prohibiting racial intermarriage, an "interesting and delicate subject."[30] The subject was so delicate that Phillips took pains to make it clear that nothing in his brief against segregation in railroads would challenge segregation in public schools. The overriding point in Phillips' challenge to railroad segregation, in other words, was that segregation was necessary and that the state had the right in some instances to ensure it in law. The case at hand, however, was not one of those cases. Phillips argued that "*separate schools*" came under "different orders of consideration" from *separate cars*, because "[i]n educating the young, government steps '*in loco parentis*' and therefore may . . . conform to the will of the natural parents." Educating the young, he went on, was "all part of *Marriage and the Family*," and was to be "treated conformably therewith." His brief aimed narrowly at segregation in railroads. That put the argument into a muddle.

Cable and Blair, in contrast to Phillips, had lumped schools and transportation together as equally unjustifiable arenas for segregation.[31] Proponents of segregation, too, had always lumped schools and transportation together, as equally "social" spheres whose segregation would not infringe upon black "political" rights.[32] If the color line were justifiable, as Phillips said, in the schools, the Court could not be blamed for thinking Phillips a bit perverse to claim that it was unjustifiable in transportation. Justice Henry Billings Brown, writing for the seven-to-one majority, decreed that the framers of the Fourteenth Amendment "could not have intended to abolish distinctions based upon color, or to enforce social, as distinguished from political, equality."[33] So the Court ignored Phillips' hairsplitting. Yet at bottom Phillips' plea was in the strongest spirit of southern white dissent — which is to say, not very strong. His concession of school, as distinguished from railroad, segregation was not qualitatively different from Cable and Blair's disavowal of "social equality." If the southern white dissenters accepted a color line anywhere, they were hard-pressed to prevent it from being drawn everywhere.

The greatest southern white dissenter of them all was therefore not Cable or Blair but Supreme Court justice John Marshall Harlan, the lone dissenter from the *Plessy* decision. A Kentucky gentleman and former slaveholder, Harlan opposed abolitionism and Republicanism before the war but became a strong unionist and served in the Union Army in the war. He converted to Republicanism and the cause of black rights after the war and dissented strongly from the Court's curtailment of black rights in the *Civil Rights Cases* of 1883.

When *Plessy* came up, Harlan dismissed the suggestion that "social equality" might result from repeal of the law. "That argument, if it can properly be regarded as one, is scarcely worthy of consideration." If the Court were really worried about social equality, then it would have to strike down not only its recent opinions rejecting segregation of jury boxes and political assemblies but the Fifteenth Amendment itself, which put black and white voters into the same room whenever they register or approach the ballot box. By accepting railroad segregation on the premise of preserving social inequality, the Court was paving the way for more absurdities based on the same premise: "[A]stute men of the dominant race, who affect to be disturbed at the possibility that the integrity of the white race may be corrupted, or that its supremacy will be imperiled, by contact on public highways with black people, will endeavor to procure statutes requiring white and black jurors to be separated in the jury box by a 'partition.'"[34]

Harlan's main contribution was to put the focus where it belonged: repeal of the recently enacted railroad segregation law could hardly "enforce" social equality, as Justice Brown's opinion for the majority suggested. The legislation in question was designed to *create* social inequality. It was segregation that required the positive act of law. "The arbitrary separation of citizens, on the basis of race, while they are on a public highway, is a badge of servitude wholly inconsistent with the civil freedom and the equality before the law established by the constitution." He charged his brethren with rendering an opinion that would, "in time, prove to be quite as pernicious as the decision made by this tribunal in the *Dred Scott Case*." He predicted that the *Plessy* decision would "not only stimulate aggressions, more or less brutal and irritating, upon the admitted rights of colored citizens, but [would] encourage the belief that it [was] possible, by means of state enactment, to defeat the beneficent purposes . . . of . . . the recent amendments of the Constitution."[35]

But the greatest dissenter was the greatest failure. His words failed to convince his northern brethren (six of the seven who voted with the majority were upper-class New Englanders; Justice Edward White, a Louisiana planter-lawyer and Confederate Army veteran, was the only southerner who voted to uphold Jim Crow) and gained no sympathetic hearing among southern white jurists and legislators. The battle was over.[36] From that point on, segregation movements were emboldened by the very clear message of nationwide endorsement. The segregation system hardened into law. The restrictions grew tighter and tighter. From that point forward, there was scarcely any white dissent from the segregation formula. Harlan spoke, as Woodward noted, "the convictions of a bygone era."[37]

Southern White Dissent after *Plessy*

After this point, southern white dissent became even narrower and more defensive. It fragmented and turned in different directions, including northward. William English Walling, born in 1877, was heir to a rich Kentucky slaveholding family, became a socialist and settlement house worker in his early twenties, and then married a Russian Jew, writer Anna Strunsky, who had been jailed for revolutionary activity. After visits to czarist Russia, Walling and his wife became alarmed by racial discrimination and conflict in the States, believing the treatment of the American Negro to be more severe than that of the Russian Jew.[38]

Walling repeated a theme often sounded by southern intellectuals (including Haygood, Cable, and Blair) since the Civil War when speaking to the North about racial issues: set thine own house in order. When tempers were short on either side, this could be abbreviated: so's your old man. Reporting on the Springfield, Illinois, riot of 1908 in the *Independent*, Walling complained that "a large part of the white population of Lincoln's home, supported largely by the farmers and miners of the neighboring towns," had ignited a "permanent warfare with the Negro race." Yet Walling did not absolve the South of responsibility. He attributed the outburst in Springfield in part to "the existence of a Southern element in the town." Most important, he noted that racial warfare was occurring even where the excuse that white southerners made for it—the possibility of being overwhelmed by a black majority—did not apply. "The Negroes, constituting scarcely more than a tenth of the population, in this case could not possibly endanger the 'supremacy' of the whites." As in the South, the respectable class of white folk condoned the mob's action. The local press exonerated the white rioters, Walling complained, saying their outburst was "inevitable" and that "citizens could find no other remedy than that applied by the mob." The press blamed the violence on the Negro's misconduct and "general inferiority or unfitness for free institutions" rather than "the fact of the whites' hatred toward the negroes." One "leading white minister recommended the Southern disfranchisement scheme as a remedy for *negro* (!) lawlessness." White Springfield, Walling concluded, "had no shame."

The 1908 riot proved that sectional peace, which was premised on northern acquiescence in southern disfranchisement and segregation, had not eliminated racial conflict. The only way to eliminate it, Walling insisted, was "to treat the negro on a plane of absolute political and social equality." If not, southern racial demagogues such as James Vardaman and "Pitchfork Ben" Tillman would soon transfer "the race war" to the North. Perhaps the transfer was underway. "Already Vardaman boasts that 'such sad experiences as Springfield is undergoing will doubtless cause the people of the North to look with more toleration upon the methods employed by the Southern people.'" Walling countered that if Vardaman's dream came true, "every hope of political democracy [would] be dead, other weaker races and classes [would] be persecuted in the North as in the South, public education [would] undergo an eclipse, and American civilization [would] await either a rapid degeneration or another . . . civil war."[39]

The northern white reformer Mary White Ovington, one of the founding mothers of the National Association for the Advancement of Colored People, put Walling on a par with W.E.B. Du Bois for helping to inspire, with these words, the founding of that organization in 1911.[40] But that affiliation, along with Walling's use of the phrase "absolute political and social equality," marked him as an outsider. He was southern born and bred but had cast his lot with a northern organization. The growing militancy of the northern NAACP frightened southern white dissenters into an even more timid position.

The utter hopelessness of moving the race question *in* the South reinforced the dissenters' sad, demoralized sense of fighting for another lost cause and impelled them to oscillate between two tactics. The first tactic was to try to awaken what Cable had referred to as the "silent South" — the "better sort" out there who deplored racial oppression and violence. The second was to try to attach themselves to an independent force, a force that would play the role "northern capital" had played in the New South dreams of industrialization. Attracted to the South for its own self-interested reasons, such a force would serendipitously spread wealth, opportunity, and intelligence and thus cause social "problems" to wither away. Eventually, these tactics enabled southern white dissenters to gain a wide enough hearing to help make the system of segregation and disfranchisement vulnerable to attack. Until then, however, they produced a long record of failure that proved southern white dissent insufficient, by itself, to change the system.

From Silence to Futility

Southern White Dissent
Gets Organized

The two tactics that southern white dissenters adopted in their efforts to influence southern opinion after *Plessy* took different forms. The first tactic — trying to awaken the "better sort" of southerner, who was repulsed by racial oppression and violence — ranged from individual appeals to conscience and practicality, to forming, by fits and starts, region-wide reform organizations. The second tactic — attachment of proposals for racial reform to external sources of power — also moved by fits and starts. It did not develop great potential until the New Deal appeared as a new independent force that, unlike northern capital during the New South era, had reason to dissociate itself from the political structure of the white supremacist Democracy. Most significant, the second tactic led southern white dissenters in the 1930s to overcome a fatal weakness of southern reform: the repudiation of "politics" that had been central to programs for progress since the New South era.

Raising the Stakes and Narrowing the Limits of Dissent:
Andrew Sledd and John Spencer Bassett

Despite native white dissenters' narrowing and muting their pleas for racial justice after *Plessy*, they faced the threat of losing their jobs. That further demoralized them and undermined their faith in the "silent South." The careers of two university professors who tried to awaken the silent South in the first years of the twentieth century illustrate this trend.

Andrew Sledd, a native Virginian and professor of Latin at Emory College in Oxford, Georgia, began his attack on southern racial policies in the July 1902 *Atlantic Monthly* by charging that previous attacks on those policies had had a "largely sectional" motive behind them. Careful to set himself off from those attacks and identify himself with the South, Sledd put the first blame on the Yankees. "Northern writers, with practically no knowledge or experience of actual conditions, have theorized to meet a condition that they did not understand." They championed the Negro cause "with a bitter and undiscriminating zeal as earnest as it [was] misguided." Yet Sledd looked to his own house and found much out of order there. "The South, in answer to what is unjust in the charge of the North, recalls former days, persuades herself of the righteousness of her cause, and continually recommits herself to an antiquated and unsound policy." Southerners' "surly invitation to 'mind your own business'" failed to deter northern critics and diverted the South from the reforms it needed.

Though Sledd was (as it turned out) taking great risks to utter such criticism, he did not depart from the New South orthodoxy. In rethinking the Negro question, he did not call on southerners to rethink the basic framework that had foreclosed searching discussion of that question so far. He located the source of the South's trouble in the distant past, for example, conceding that racial inequality was a vestige of the world of slavery and secessionism—the responsibility of dead and discredited men rather than a creation of positive law, being made and remade by living men.[1] Thus Sledd did not go beyond Cable, or the *Plessy* verdict, in arguing for black equality.

Sledd was even more careful than Haygood, Blair, and Cable to disavow any suggestion of social equality. "The Negro is lower in the scale of development than the white man," Sledd proclaimed. "His inferiority is radical and inherent, a physiological and racial inequality that may, indeed, be modified by environment, but cannot be erased [without the passage of] indefinite time." This was now becoming widely accepted, despite "ill-advised cant" about Negro equality. He endorsed legal equality but rejected "all those schemes that used to find favor in the North . . . for the establishment of social equality and the amalgamation of the races."

It was not enough anymore to reject "social equality," however. Eighteen years after Cable wrote the "Freedman's Case," Sledd had to reckon with a great deal of political change in the South. He could not write about the Negro question with "candor" (one of his favorite words) without writing about disfranchisement, which he saw as an acceptable alternative to social equality.

It is not necessary, nor desired, that the Negro should be the social equal of the white man. His political privileges may be curtailed, and without injustice or offense, provided the curtailment work impartially among blacks and whites alike. If fifty percent of the Negroes are deprived of the right of suffrage by reason of illiteracy, and the same legislation is fairly permitted to work the disfranchisement of all whites (fifteen to twenty percent of our voting population) of the same class, no injustice is done.[2]

His candor forced him to see the link that Blair and Cable denied between "political" and "social" equality. To him denial of one entailed denial of the other, and he therefore had to support disfranchisement.

Yet this man was a racial heretic. Accepting all the latest institutions of inequality, he still excoriated his fellow white southerners for carrying "the idea of the Negro's inferiority almost, if not quite, to the point of dehumanizing him." Worse than that, "blatant demagogues, political shysters, courting favor with the mob," ignored the facts and asserted "with frothing vehemence" that the Negro was "fairly and kindly treated in the South." If one paid attention to the "facts," one would soon see evidence of "our brutal estimate of the Negro."

Sledd concentrated on the most brutal aspect of southern race relations, the aspect that was the safest to criticize, for everyone agreed in finding it—or at least in professing to find it—distasteful: lynching. This was the one form of outrage, Sledd pointed out, which could justifiably be blamed on the South, for 70 to 80 percent of all lynchings in the United States at that time occurred in the South. Moreover, lynching was clearly racial. About three-quarters of the victims of lynching were black.[3]

Sledd's most fateful step was to attack the assumption that white southerners used to rationalize lynching. In contrast to Haygood, Sledd argued what northern investigators had begun to document with extremely convincing testimony: that the vast majority (in some years 90 percent) of lynchings were not a response to a rape, or even a suspected rape, and that even in cases of genuinely suspected rape the lynching party did not include a relative of the rape victim.[4] The true motive for the lynching, Sledd argued, was to provide a reminder to black people in general to know and keep their "place," to teach "the niggers a lesson." The mob, he wrote, would "teach the Negro the lesson of abject and eternal servility, would burn into his quivering flesh the consciousness that he ha[d] not, and [could] not have, the rights of a free citizen or even of a fellow human creature."[5]

Sledd did not refute all of the South's evasions and justifications. Lynchings were the work of "the lower and lowest classes" of white folk. This locating of the blame among rednecks, hillbillies, and white trash was a way of saying, especially to the North, that the racial oppression was a vestige of the benighted southern past.[6] Those who had not yet risen into the New South, the uneducated, did not represent the South to come. Indeed, Sledd compared the lower classes of his day—"the classes that supply our lynchers"—to the slaveholding class of the Old South; they were marked by their "self-conceit," "marble-hearted insensibility," "violence in cruelty," and total lack of "correct views of equity." The implication was that more progress, under the kind of leadership Sledd represented, would eradicate lynching.

Still, he had gone too far in criticizing the present South. In response to this article, the only thing Sledd had ever written on the subject, the *Atlanta Constitution* denounced his "northern foolosophy" and published a letter from racist crusader Rebecca Latimer Felton, who recommended deporting him, after a tar and feathering, to the North: "It is bad enough to be taxed to death to educate negroes and defend one's home from criminal assault . . . but it is simply atrocious to fatten or feed a creature who stoops to the defamation of the southern people only to find access to liberal checks in a partisan magazine." The *Atlanta Journal* agreed with Felton's recommendation and called upon Emory to fire Sledd. The *Atlanta News* equated Sledd's position with "treason."

So rigid had southern ideology become that the Emory faculty did not come to Sledd's defense, even though he was the son-in-law of a former president of the college. The most favored members of a private, cloistered institution could not be protected from the consequences of stepping out of line. The episode was a disaster for Sledd's career. After pressure on Emory increased, he had to resign. He ended up doing graduate work at Yale University. Though he returned to the South a year later, and returned quietly to Emory itself in 1914, he ceased to write social criticism.[7]

The year after the Sledd affair, in 1903, history professor John Spencer Bassett of Trinity College (which later became Duke University) found more to condemn than lynching, but his condemnation assumed a milder tone than Sledd's. Bassett's concern was that racial antipathy in the South had increased greatly since the war, mainly because politicians had discovered that racial agitation could work wonders for candidates otherwise lacking in talent. Racial antipathy seemed to defy the laws of economics in that it grew in value as more and more of it was produced.

Racial demagoguery was a consequence of the fracture of the Democratic party in the 1890s, Bassett wrote. "Ten years ago the South was in the embrace of the Populist movement." Had that movement succeeded, it "would have broken up the Democratic party. . . . To fight it down, the leaders of the old party were led to seek a strong issue." The Negro issue "lent itself to the exigency because the Populists, wherever they triumphed, had been in alliance with the Republicans and had brought a few Negroes into office." Since these Negroes were "frequently unfit for office," and "sometimes unduly elated over their success, being merely ignorant Negroes," aspiring demagogues saw "an opportunity to cry 'Negro domination.'" Though he came close to blaming the victim here, what is more significant is that, unlike Sledd, he saw racial trouble as a deliberate, recent creation rather than a hangover from antebellum excesses. He did not blame benighted, ignorant classes, at least not directly, but the leaders of the New South's primary institution of political authority: "It is now good party tactics to keep the Negro question before the people." Yet political success for the Democrats spelled disaster for the South. Demagogues had created a deplorable politics and a social climate of growing hatred in which each race seemed to be "caught in a torrent of passion" that Bassett feared would lead the country to an end he dared not name.

There was only one way to avoid cataclysm: "the adoption of these children of Africa into our American life. In spite of our race feeling, of which the writer has his share, they will win equality at some time. We cannot remove them, we cannot kill them, we cannot prevent them from advancing in civilization. They are now very weak; some day they will be stronger." Economic need was already leading white employers, in spite of themselves, to uplift black workers, who were already showing that they could uplift themselves. It was pointless to resist the inevitable. "Someday the white man will beat the Negro out of his cowardice. . . . Someday the Negro will be a great industrial factor in the community; someday he will be united under strong leaders of his own. In that time his struggle will not be so unequal as now. In that time, let us hope, he will have brave and Christian leaders."

Having raised more challenging questions than Sledd, Bassett admitted he did not have answers. He called upon his fellow white southerners for forbearance and courage. Rare among liberals of his time, Bassett did not foresee progress just around the corner. "The conflict will be fiercer in the future than in the present. Lynchings and 'outrages' will, perhaps,

become more frequent than they are now. As long as one race contends for
the absolute inferiority of the other the struggle will go on."

Yet, no doubt unwittingly, Bassett himself joined the struggle for the
absolute inferiority of the black race. Like Sledd, he included a stern
injunction against social equality in his plea for mercy on black people.
Separation of the races was established by nature and enforced by tradition, starting with marriage laws in the colonial period. "The commingling
which we then set our hearts against in regard to things sexual we have also
opposed in regard to most other matters of life. There must be no social
equality, no eating together, no joining in amusements, and finally no mingling in religious worship."[8] Given the immutability of social differences,
the point that needed stress was the obligation of the superior race to act
decently toward the inferior: "[If] the spirit of conciliation shall come into
the hearts of the superior race the struggle will become less strenuous."
Brave and wise men had a duty "to infuse the spirit of conciliation" into the
politicians who led white men. "Shall they also be beasts, like the dull-
faced black men who stand over against them?" If the white man was superior, was he not "superior in obligation to do acts of charity?"[9]

For all his racism, Bassett did not push segregationism hard enough to
satisfy his critics. The reason was probably that he did not feel a need to
worry about social equality. Like Cable, he felt sure that class differences
would prevail to keep the worst sorts from commingling with the best.
Although Cable had extended that point and argued that therefore integration (which Cable favored because it would bring economic efficiency and
intellectual competition) was acceptable, Bassett endorsed segregation.
Criticism of racial agitation and propaganda was as far as he went. Perhaps
segregation seemed to Bassett, as it had not seemed to Cable nineteen years
earlier, an ineradicable *fait accompli;* over that nineteen years the limits of
permissible social ideas had narrowed greatly. For suggesting considerably
milder reforms in race relations than Cable, Haygood, or Blair, Bassett and
Sledd suffered much more vituperative and threatening attacks.

Bassett's essay, "Stirring Up the Fires of Racial Antipathy," published
in the *South Atlantic Quarterly* (which Bassett founded in 1902 and edited
until 1905), drew fire from the same types who had driven Sledd out of
town. Leading the pack this time was Josephus Daniels, editor of the
Raleigh News and Observer, which began to run headlines about Professor
"bASSett." In one editorial Daniels asked whether Bassett prayed "with
his face turned toward Tuskegee." That Daniels was a liberal on virtually
every major issue—indeed, a rather bold and innovative one—illustrates

how anachronistic is the habit of associating liberalism with support for black rights. Daniels was the newspapering trendsetter in North Carolina (and one of the leaders for the whole South). The other papers of the state followed his lead by labeling Bassett "disloyal" and a "nigger lover."[10]

This publicity put considerable pressure on the Trinity trustees. One of them, Furnifold M. Simmons, a state Democratic party leader who had played a key role in the disfranchisement campaign of 1898–99, came to the December 1903 meeting of the trustees in Durham ready to fight what he referred to as "the last fight for white supremacy." Bassett offered to resign. But in contrast to Sledd's colleagues at Emory, the Trinity professors and administration took their stand for academic freedom, and Bassett managed to hold on to his job, and his journal, for a few years.[11]

Instrumental in Bassett's defense was the Trinity president, James Kilgo, who himself had gained some notoriety in 1902 by writing a *South Atlantic Quarterly* article that denounced lynching in somewhat stronger terms than Sledd's. (He argued that even rape did not justify lynching — after all, the South had laws, and police, judges, and jurors who could be counted on to deal with that crime stringently enough — and that southern editors and politicians, who whipped up racial hysteria, were the real cause of lynching.)[12] Kilgo and twelve of the thirteen faculty members all vowed to submit their own resignations if Bassett's were accepted. North Carolina businessmen, following the lead of tobacco tycoon and Trinity trustee Benjamin Duke, were prominent among Bassett's defenders on the board of trustees. They had received much correspondence supporting Bassett from their business colleagues around the state.[13]

The grounds on which all these men defended Bassett were revealingly narrow. President Kilgo was careful to point out that Bassett's speech deserved protection, not because it might help persuade the South to act in a more humane and decent fashion, or even because it might spark healthy debate, but because there should be a place in the South, namely his college, where one could speak without fear of abuse. The twelve faculty members, in a signed statement, went further in specifying the cause for which they were standing up: "It is the cause of academic freedom, and we, the professors of Trinity College, by reason of the very circumstance that we do not assent to the views of our colleague which are being criticized, feel that we are left exceptionally free to devote ourselves to the great and general principle involved." That principle was that "it is far better to tolerate opinions which seem to be wrong rather than to punish the expression of opinions because they are contrary to those generally accepted."

They stood up to protect their institution, not their colleague, and stood apart from him and his principles to protect themselves.

But it was not enough to dissociate oneself from Bassett's views. It was also necessary, apparently, to assure that Bassett's views were not all that radical in the first place. After the trustees voted not to accept Bassett's resignation, they ended their statement with a reminder: "Professor Bassett does not believe in, nor does he teach, social equality."

Though Bassett kept his job, it was a Pyrrhic victory. Historian Bruce Clayton concluded that after one more article defending his views, "public opinion" silenced Bassett, who felt plagued with guilt that he had caused so much trouble for the college. He gave an interview, at the urging of his colleagues, and used it as an opportunity to make clear that he was not preaching "social equality." Within a few years of his eponymous "affair" (now a legend in the official folklore of Duke University), Bassett left the South. There is today a statue of Bassett in the main quadrangle at Duke, but his influence on southern opinion seems to have been quite transitory, if detectable at all.[14]

Sledd and Bassett are emblematic. They illustrate the weakness and narrowness of dissent, or to look at it the other way around, the growing strength and breadth of racist ideology. Yet at the same time, they increased the feeling that there was a "silent South," which would speak up if only something were different. If only there were more education, if only there were less poverty, if only we had better leaders: then freedom of discussion would allow a sensible search for solutions to this Negro question. But above all, the time for southern white dissent was hostile, and dissent reflected the hostility by being as muted and defensive as it could be.

Early Attempts to Organize the "Silent South"

It was just at the time of its greatest defensiveness that southern white dissent began to get organized. For those who remained in the South, Sledd and Bassett were prototypes, both in the narrowness of their dissent and in their failure. But something new was added in the years just before World War I: collective effort. No longer were white southern dissenters loners. No longer did they suffer the loneliness, or enjoy the luxury, of isolation.

At first there were short-lived and mostly ineffectual efforts to improve conditions for black southerners within the new system of segregation and disfranchisement. These included Alabama's all-white Southern Society for the Promotion of the Study of Race Conditions and

Problems in the South, known as the Montgomery Conference, organized by Edgar Gardner Murphy in 1900; the Race Relations Committee of the interracial Southern Sociological Congress, founded in 1912; the University Commission on Southern Race Questions, founded in 1912; and the Southern Publicity Committee, founded in 1919.

The Montgomery Conference often hosted speakers who were openly hostile to black rights. Its chief organizer, Edgar Gardner Murphy, favored disfranchisement on the paternalistic grounds that the poor, uneducated Negro was a ward of the state even when he did vote. Thus, wrote Murphy, "the vote of every Southern representative is a vote of stewardship, a vote in representation of the claims of a dependent people. . . . If you think the Negro, with his weakness and his ignorance, could secure better representation . . . if permitted in every case the individual exercise of the suffrage, I can only say you have forgotten the history of the reconstruction period." Murphy carried on the New South Creed, supporting not just white supremacy but the supremacy of "the forces of intelligence and property," of "men of the highest type." Murphy believed that explicit, legal suffrage restrictions were superior to the fraud and subterfuge that had previously restricted voting. The old, informal techniques created racist restrictions. Murphy wanted to replace those racist restrictions with legitimate discrimination against the illiterate and irresponsible class of voters in *both* races. A formal, legal system based on regular principles was better than an informal one that bred illegality.[15]

The Montgomery Conference echoed Cable's and Sledd's opposition to lynching: lynch mobs did not represent "the best of the South" but an unsavory minority. Though the conference had an undoubtedly genuine dislike of violence, it also wanted to keep violence from giving the South a bad name. That was the key to why Murphy's critique, unlike those of Sledd and Bassett, caught on and gained adherents. It was a tactic to get the North to leave the South alone.

To succeed fully in restoring national confidence in southern autonomy, and in assuaging the respectable white southerner's conscience, this tactic would have to produce at least a modicum of actual changes in society. But the halfheartedness and opportunism behind it are suggested by the fact that the Montgomery Conference members found it unnecessary to continue meeting after the 1901 Alabama Constitution succeeded in disfranchising nearly all black men, and a good many poor white ones, thus removing the "Negro question" from politics and public view. It is probable that in representing the "best men" of the South, and evincing a genuine if paternalistic concern for black people, the Montgomery Conference actually helped to legitimize disfranchisement.

The Southern Sociological Congress, the University Commission on Southern Race Questions, and the Southern Publicity Committee, like the Montgomery Conference, all tried to encourage the "best people" of the South to support better treatment of black people. At best, these organizations pricked the southern white conscience. The SSC, the UCSRQ, and the SPC undermined the legitimacy of lynching by printing evidence that lynching victims had rarely even been accused of criminal assault, that they were far more frequently suspected of petty crimes, or of nothing at all. They also argued that the respectable, silent majority of white southerners could not escape responsibility for the lawlessness and mob rule represented by lynching statistics. The UCSRQ and SPC especially appealed to the sense of responsibility that privileged whites should feel for violence in their region, the UCSRQ concentrating on college students, the SPC on a broader educated class of newspaper readers.

At worst, these organizations further legitimized the new racial order of the South by drawing more attention to themselves as decent liberals in positions of authority than their actual power and accomplishments would justify. These groups all supported black education, but all within a theory of separate development. Most of them agitated for industrial, as opposed to academic, education, though it should be noted that they tended to favor industrial education for the majority of white people, as well as for black people. They all rejected "social equality" in principle and endorsed segregation in practice.

Other than raising the level of awareness and discomfort among respectable white southerners—an achievement almost impossible to measure—these organizations could point to little in the way of accomplishments. Above all, they were short-lived—all of them were defunct by the early 1920s—and fragmented. They focused on different social bases within the southern white middle class and adopted different strategies to raise consciousness; they centered around the personalities of strong leaders rather than bringing together a regionwide "silent South" under common principles.

The Commission on Interracial Cooperation

The effort to organize racial dissent did not really come together until 1919, when Will Alexander organized the Commission on Interracial

Cooperation. In that year, marked by the spreading disillusionment that followed America's participation in World War I, the formation of the Pan-African Congress, and a series of racial riots all over the United States, it became apparent that progress and modernity did not eliminate social conflict but rather intensified it. Many southern liberals, their optimism thus undermined, asserted their optimism with an ever-greater fervor.

Alexander, a Vanderbilt-trained Methodist minister born and raised on a Missouri farm, had been greatly influenced by YMCA organizer W. D. Weatherford, the moving force behind the race relations section of the SSC and author of two books, *Negro Life in the South* (1910) and *Present Forces for Negro Progress* (1912). Oswald Garrison Villard, one of the founders of the NAACP, pointed to Weatherford as a hopeful sign of changing attitudes in the South. The War Department found Weatherford a hopeful sign too, mainly on the basis of his work in the YMCA movement, and enlisted his and the YMCA's cooperation in setting up racial harmony programs on military bases. Weatherford recruited Alexander to supervise these programs in the South.[16] Alexander found cause for great hope in the war. Since black southerners enthusiastically supported the war effort, Alexander believed their example of patriotic sacrifice would inaugurate a new era of racial cooperation. Alexander was "deeply stirred" by President Wilson's ideal of spreading democracy and came to believe that "any effort to make democracy function in the South would go to the heart of the racial problem."[17]

Alexander was deeply shocked when the riots broke out after the war. Still working under War Department auspices, he tried to bring leading white and black citizens together to form ad hoc committees in areas where racial disturbances had broken out, hoping their cooperation and leadership would influence the masses and avert further violence. To keep these committees going on a permanent basis, Alexander got the YMCA and northern philanthropists to fund a federation of the local committees. That federation became the Commission on Interracial Cooperation.

Though the commission owed its origins to the War Department, an external, nonsouthern force, Alexander devoted his energy to pulling together the leading white men of the South, in the name of the South. "I kept reminding them how well we had behaved during the war." There had been "a new kind of contact between the Negroes and whites," with the result that white leaders discovered worthy black leaders. "Up to that time the contacts between the Negroes and the whites were closest at the bottom of the social and economic level, and as you moved up culturally and economically, the distance between the groups increased." No longer. Besides echoing Blair's analysis of lower-class racial mixing, Alexander voiced once again the basic assumptions of New South ideology: that economic progress was the paramount aim, and that economic progress would elevate black people more or less automatically. From the vantage point of 1919, ignoring the riots, Alexander could say it already had lifted them somewhat.

Alexander found many white people of like mind all over the South. Typical of them was John Eagan, a Birmingham industrialist who employed large numbers of black workers. During the war Eagan got a good impression of black soldiers, with whom he had had much contact. Alexander described Eagan as "a sensitive, high-minded man with a great distrust of force," who joined the "search for some means besides force to meet the problems of the South." With men like Eagan, Alexander carried on the New South quest for ways to avert both racial warfare and northern intervention. By the mid-1920s, Alexander had about seven thousand members.

The CIC was the largest effort to date to organize white racial dissent, yet it was terribly limited. Alexander set up local committees in thirteen southern states, but there was significant action in only three of these states and little coordination between the states. Moreover, the program of "cooperation" was vague. The members all believed in improving race relations and in aiding black uplift but did not put forward much in the way of specifics. Historian Morton Sosna concluded that the CIC remained "more or less an expression of sentiment rather than an official group with carefully defined policies."[18]

The sentiment itself was timid. Thomas Woofter, CIC research director, laid down the organization line in CIC pamphlets and in his 1925 book, *The Basis for Racial Adjustment*. Woofter stressed that white people, most of whom were ignorant, needed to learn about the conditions of Negro life, but he warned that agitation for change would only impede progress. Black-white cooperation was growing slowly in groups like the CIC, Woofter argued, but pushing these efforts too fast would jeopardize them. In light of the progress of cooperation, Woofter even argued that the press should ignore the occasional outbursts of racial violence and stress the good side of southern race relations. Although it tried to decrease bad publicity for the South, the CIC feared reaction to its own limited efforts so much that it never publicized its meetings.[19] The strongest effort yet to awaken the silent South did not dare to disturb the quiet. CIC members were closet dissenters.

Even privately, the CIC did not take issue with the system of segregation. Most of the members endorsed segregation wholeheartedly. When Alexander cautiously hedged his own support for segregation, he quickly ran into the limits of southern tolerance. Alexander told a Birmingham audience in 1936 that he could not justify the segregation laws, but whether to repeal them was a different matter on which, he said, one man's opinion was as good as another's. This was not a sufficiently solid apology for the system. The statement provoked several CIC members to restate their commitment to segregation publicly, and the Birmingham ministers who had hosted Alexander's speech drafted a statement declaring that the speaker was unfit to represent their group. The incident served as a warning. The silent South would not wait for reaction against any deviation from orthodoxy to materialize but would head it off at the pass.[20] The art of self-censorship that individual social critics cultivated—a legacy of the Sledd and Bassett affairs—became institutionalized.

The only thing the CIC did challenge was lynching. Differences over how to challenge lynching soon divided the organization against itself and revealed the fundamental weakness that underlay the whole outlook of southern white dissenters in this period.

Lynching was the least controversial part of the southern system of race relations because all agreed that it was a distasteful, unfortunate practice. Even those who said lynching was a necessary evil to keep black men in their place recognized that too much of it might arouse the carpetbagging tendencies that the New South had worked so hard to sedate. Woofter's book, which was used as a textbook in CIC-sponsored college courses all over the South, urged white readers to see lynching as a threat to civilization—as great a threat as "the raids of the red savage against the early pioneer settlements"—and in the same breath questioned the constitutionality of the Dyer antilynching bills, introduced into Congress in 1922 and 1924, and discredited their supporters as "partisan" and "sectional" and therefore counterproductive.[21]

The CIC, of course, was not the only organization that crusaded against lynching. The NAACP, now under the leadership of Walter White, had also been investigating lynchings in the South and stole the CIC's thunder by publishing its findings in 1929 in White's *Rope and Faggot*, a book explicitly pitched at Congress, to demonstrate the need for federal intervention.[22] Southern liberals as a whole greeted this book as an outside intrusion.

The most dynamic leader to emerge from the southern antilynching crusade, former Texas suffragist Jesse Daniel Ames, director of the CIC's Women's Division since 1924, was the most adamant in her opposition to federal legislation. She believed, like most in the CIC, that the only way to reduce lynching was for "respectable" white southerners to speak out against it and in doing so educate away the quiet tolerance and blind-eyed apologies most white southerners indulged in. Federal laws would sabotage these efforts by pushing white southerners into a sectional belligerence that would encourage rather than discourage mob violence.

The CIC strategy, according to Morton Sosna, was to convince fellow white southerners "that lynching hurt them more than blacks" and to offend white sensibilities as little as possible in the process.[23] Ames believed that upper-class women stood in a particularly good position to convince the southern white community that lynching was bad for civilization. As the symbols of racial purity and gentility, women had special authority to testify that, far from deterring sexual crimes, lynching was an anarchic menace to social order, especially to women and children, who frequently had to witness orgies of violence and were corrupted by the experience. If enough of the women renounced their desire for this kind of protection, the men could no longer justify it. If southern ladies could cast off "the crown of chivalry" that had been "thrust like a crown of thorns" on their heads, as Ames put it, mob violence would cease. With that in mind, Ames formed a separate organization of twenty-six prominent white women, the Association of Southern Women for the Prevention of Lynching, in November 1930.

The ASWPL, which eventually grew to 40,000 members, worked energetically whenever a lynching seemed to be in the offing. Ames kept a card file of 1,074 women upon whom she and the CIC could call whenever there was an arrest for rape, or a mob formed. Ames herself would get in her car and drive to the jail where the intended victim was being held, and with her local recruits she would shame the incipient mob from action.[24] Although this unquestionably showed tremendous courage on the part of Ames and her followers, the ASWPL as an organization, like the CIC, operated behind the scenes, calling as little attention as possible to itself. Many of the demonstrations against lynching thus appeared to be spontaneous and local, which added legitimacy to them, but also revealed once more the cautious, defensive tendencies of southern white dissent.

There were signs of success. Counterorganizations, such as the Women's National Association for the Preservation of the White Race, founded in 1932, were fairly ineffectual, especially in their appeals (full of grammatical and orthographic errors) to the educated classes. That signified some provisional acceptance of the ASWPL. Still, however heroically ASWPL members intervened in gathering mobs, they only opposed what was already against the law. They left alone the broader system of institutionalized discrimination, of which lynching was but one of many techniques of enforcement. This is not to say that the ASWPL was insignificant: Ames's group of "ladies in their white gloves and heavy silks and flowered cottons," leading clubwomen and church pillars all, probably succeeded in undermining the respectability of lynching.[25] As James Weldon Johnson said, the antilynching crusade of the 1930s "dented the American conscience,"[26] and the CIC and ASWPL were important parts of that crusade. But the deepest, most visible part of the dent bore the imprint of the harder-hitting NAACP and barely extended into the southern quarter-panel of the national conscience.

Regional Allegiance Strengthens the Legitimacy but Limits the Power of Dissent

The effect of the southern white crusade against lynching was ambiguous: its effect (as distinct from that of the northern-based crusade) became clearest in an ironic way in the behavior of southern congressmen who filibustered against antilynching laws. As Ames said, few southern politicians were willing to "lay themselves open to ridicule" by defending lynching on the grounds of gallantry. Instead, they pointed to the activities of the respectable southern white folk who were dealing with the problem in their own way. Federal intervention was therefore unnecessary. Ames's organization wholeheartedly endorsed this line.[27]

Part of the southern white crusade against lynching did begin to favor federal antilynching laws, however. Arthur Raper, who replaced Woofter as CIC research director in 1926, led the CIC-spawned Southern Commission for the Study of Lynching, which undertook years of investigations and published its findings in Raper's *Tragedy of Lynching* in 1933. Raper took respectable white southerners to task for their habit of justifying lynchings and was surprised to find the response to his book among southern white readers rather favorable. On the strength of this response, Raper converted to support of antilynching laws. The southern readers who welcomed his book, he reasoned, were just so many witnesses who would be able to testify in investigations and indictments, if only they could get the protection—and the hope of a fair hearing—which federal courts alone could provide.[28] But the emergence of support for federal intervention divided an already weak movement. Ames continued her determined opposition to federal law, even aiding her fellow Texan, Senator John Connally, in his fight against the Gavagan antilynching bill in 1939.[29]

Some historians have credited the CIC and ASWPL efforts for much of the decline in lynching in the 1930s. These historians admit that direct connections are hard to demonstrate and fail to acknowledge a general secular decline in lynching before and after, as well as during, the years of the antilynching crusade in the 1920s and 1930s.[30] Even assuming that the CIC and ASWPL caused illegal mob violence to decrease, the decline in lynching, against the background of a rising tide of "massive resistance" to federal authority on civil rights issues (a reaction that Numan Bartley dates from the New Deal years),[31] suggests a more fundamental weakness of southern white dissent in these years. Even without the internal division over federal law, the southern antilynching movement would have run very quickly into the limitations of its own assumptions. By focusing on illegal activity as the most offensive manifestation of southern racial oppression, as Morton Sosna notes, the CIC and ASWPL failed to make more than glancing blows at the system, the heart of which was a strong body of segregation and disfranchisement laws. This became clear in the 1931 trial of "the Scottsboro Boys."[32]

Nine young black men who were arrested on charges of raping two white women on a freight train were given a speedy trial in the local Alabama courts and sentenced to death. The irregularities in the trial were striking to the most casual observers, and journalists from all over the country churned up considerable testimony undermining the credibility of witnesses for the prosecution, including especially the two plaintiffs. The case became one of the celebrated political trials of the decade, not least because of its sectional character: respectable white southerners defended the southern white women against all accusations and refused to countenance any "outside" interference in the administration of justice, especially when motivated by "radical" forces—a label that included the NAACP as well as the Communist-aligned International Labor Defense, which competed with each other to represent the Scottsboro Boys on appeal. Southern antilynching crusaders, whose movement depended on the extralegal character of mob action, had nothing at all to say about justice as usual. The trial was an example of what William English Walling had referred to as "lynching by law," or "legal lynching," and the decline in the "lynching" figures fails to account for the vast numbers of black men executed by kangaroo courts—which were often shamed into giving death sentences just to prevent a mob from embarrassing their community with an illegal lynching.[33]

Though CIC investigators discovered beyond doubt that the Scottsboro plaintiffs were disreputable characters who lacked credibility even among their bigoted friends and neighbors, the CIC kept its findings silent during the trial. Southern dissenters' opposition to the NAACP, the federal government, and "outside" forces in general would probably have been enough to keep the CIC off the case—even if supporters of the racial system had not succeeded in discrediting the ILD as "red." Though all the Scottsboro defendants were finally released alive by 1950, the number of legal lynchings obscured by their famous rescue makes a mockery of the success of the antilynching crusade.[34]

Red-baiting increasingly threw southern white dissenters into attacks on other racial dissenters and diverted them from attacks on racist policies and practices. Supporters of the system used red-baiting as a tactic to put its critics on the defensive. But the critics' tradition of defensiveness made the tactic enormously easy to employ.[35]

The CIC and the rest of the antilynching crusade broke down not only because of their conflict over strategy and the peripherality of their target but also because the silent South they sought to awaken lacked legitimacy and unity. The CIC leaders were still fatally defensive about their "southern" identity. They either censored themselves or divided their ranks to avoid scalawag-baiting. Most of all, they were wary of using (perhaps realistically aware of their inability to use) force. Efforts to rouse the silent South failed again and again because of the fundamental assumption that ideals and benevolence were sufficient, that power was not the primary issue.

The Rediscovery of Politics and the Wages of Demagoguery

The next significant and durable organization of southern dissenters did not completely abandon the effort to awaken a silent South, but it defined itself from the beginning by its effort to enlist an independent force, the New Deal. In doing so, the Southern Conference for Human Welfare made changing the political structure of the South its primary goal.

The founding of the Southern Conference for Human Welfare in 1938 was the first time since disfranchisement that southern white dissenters deviated from the New South Creed's taboo on politics. Henry Grady and his fellow prophets of southern progress had insisted (along with the "best men" of northern mugwumpery) that politics was irretrievably corrupt. Rather than try to change politics, they sought to circumvent politics, partly by putting the functions of government into what they hoped would be nonpartisan, disinterested, "professional" organizations, and partly by investing their hopes in the gradual moral uplift that they assumed would be a by-product of economic growth. Believing they could overcome the need for politics, they failed to develop a sense of politics, let alone a power base from which to fight politics with politics. The New South men proved even more credulous than northern mugwumps in their faith that politics would wither away. Their strategy amounted to an abandonment of politics, an effort to wash their hands of the inevitable corruptions of power rather than assume responsibility for those corruptions and struggle against them. That they ended up, as they saw things, with a band of slobbering demagogues as their representatives in Congress seems only fitting. Demagoguery, in time, became their main enemy, and to some degree their scapegoat.

Demagogues, according to southern racial dissenters, won elections by fanning the flames of racial antagonism, blaming black people for all the poverty and desperation the voters suffered. In doing so, demagogues encouraged voters to vent their frustrations on black people and thereby made enforcement of segregation more brutal and insulting than it would have been otherwise. The larger effect of racial demagoguery was to reduce southern politics almost to a single issue, white supremacy, at the expense of economic development and reform, at precisely those times when economic development and reform were most needed. Virginius Dabney, a liberal member of the *Richmond Times-Dispatch* editorial board (he became editor in 1939 and remained in that post until 1969), expressed the disappointments of southern liberals who once hoped to keep the race issue from sabotaging southern progress. In a book that did not center on the race question, *Liberalism in the South,* published in 1932, Dabney summed up the unfulfilled promises that had led southern liberals to endorse disfranchisement and segregation a generation earlier. "It was hoped that the wholesale disfranchisement of the Negroes . . . would remove the blacks from the political picture, but this expectation was not realized."[36] Dabney followed the liberal tradition of seeing racism as a product of the "lower class whites." As a political force, they were "in the saddle virtually throughout the Southern states" and "were too keenly aware of the Negro's potentialities as an economic rival to permit any soft-pedaling of the race issue." For that reason, the South developed "a class of demagogues" who appealed "to the 'poor whites' . . . by means of blatant agitation of the race question." According to Dabney, the "most brutal Negrophobe in the South," former senator James Vardaman of Mississippi, was the "spokesman for the 'hill billies' and 'red necks.'"[37]

The dissenters' inability to influence southern politics, and their habit of blaming racial tension on the uneducated, backward masses, both contributed to and grew out of their abiding sense of failure. This sense of failure is detectable in Dabney's *Liberalism in the South*, though it is probably the most optimistic, and unquestionably the longest, book imaginable on the subject.[38] But the dissenters who formed the SCHW sensed a new opportunity in the stifling political landscape of the South: racial demagogues had a hammerlock on national politics as well as southern politics. At one point in the 1930s, 75 percent of Senate committee chairs were occupied by southerners. By virtue of the two-thirds rule in the Senate, the South could filibuster to death whatever legislation its chairmen could not keep off the floor. A similar rule in Democratic national conventions gave southern delegates a veto on presidential nominees. Southern political power, based on racial oppression, was an impediment to the personal ambitions and political programs of northern politicians, even if (as was generally the case) they had no ethical or ideological qualms about racial oppression itself. There lay the great opening for southern white dissent.

In the late 1930s, no one felt more constrained by the South's grip on national politics than Franklin Roosevelt. Southern white dissenters could not help identifying with his frustration. By chance, someone who championed something quite different from either FDR's or the southern dissenters' causes brought them together. Joe Gelders' cause was civil liberties. A physics professor at the University of Alabama who had been fired for privately holding the view that "capitalism" was the cause of the Great Depression, Gelders went to New York to join the National Committee for the Defense of Political Prisoners and returned to Birmingham in 1936 as its southern representative. Gelders and Lucy Randolph Mason, the Virginia aristocrat and CIO organizer, contacted Mason's friend Eleanor Roosevelt to enlist her aid in setting up a conference to defend civil liberties, which were particularly valuable to the CIO in its southern organizing campaigns and, they believed, therefore essential to the New Deal coalition. Mrs. Roosevelt met with Gelders and persuaded him to expand his idea into a conference to discuss all southern problems.[39] Gelders then set about pulling together representatives of labor, socialist, religious, and philanthropic organizations, plus liberal politicians and academics, for a meeting to be held in December 1938. It might have amounted to just another aimless, inconsequential meeting had it not been for high-level disasters in the Democratic party's power base which came at the same time.

President Roosevelt had his own ideas about how to break the hold of southern politicians on Congress. After increasing southern opposition built up to New Deal legislation, which opposition rallied to defeat his "court-packing" bill in 1937, FDR went south in a breach of party protocol to campaign against incumbent Democratic senators Millard Tydings of Maryland and especially Cotton Ed Smith of South Carolina and Walter George of Georgia. He labeled these senators "feudal," even "fascist," and endorsed inexperienced candidates against them in the primaries. Senator George referred to FDR's campaign visit to his state as "Sherman's second march." Part of the president's strategy to defeat these men was the National Emergency Council's report, released the same month as FDR's trip to Georgia, which detailed the effects of years of conservative Democratic rule in the region: the South was the nation's "Number One Economic Problem," and in order to overcome that problem the South and the nation needed to clear out the politicians who, if they did not create it, opposed solutions to it.

This strategy failed miserably. Tydings, George, and Smith all won reelection in campaigns of intense southern sectionalism and Negrophobia. Henceforth, FDR's domestic policy would teeter over a sectional rift.

When Gelders' conference convened in December 1938, its stated purpose was to respond to the NEC report. Though the variety of groups gathered came up with a variety of solutions, the one concrete idea the Southern Conference for Human Welfare, as the organization formed in the conference came to be called, came up with was to fight against the poll tax. The organization suffered immediately from bad publicity. Dabney refused to join because some members were suspected reds. Word leaked out that some attendees of the conference favored "social equality" and the "sectional" Wagner antilynching bill. Prominent politicians who had attended the first meeting hastened to dissociate themselves from it. Representative Luther Patrick and Senators Lister Hill and John Bankhead II, all of Alabama, withdrew from the organization, and Representative Brooks Hays of Arkansas continued to have only secret contacts. Representative Maury Maverick of Texas, chairman of the SCHW's Civil Rights Committee as of 1939, was the only southern politician who served in any official capacity, and Senator Claude Pepper of Florida was the only other one who remained open in his support of the organization. These last two were men of the peripheral South, not the Deep South, and their involvement was neither as risky nor as potentially effective in striking at the heart of Jim Crow as a Deep South politician's would have been.

The central idea of the SCHW's campaign against the poll tax was that repeal would enfranchise the New Deal's natural constituents, the poor of both races, and thereby drive out the reactionary opposition. This was an unsure strategy. One of the New Deal's earliest and strongest opponents, Senator Josiah Bailey of North Carolina, came from the first state to repeal (in 1920) its poll tax. Huey Long's forces succeeded in making Louisiana the second state to repeal its poll tax, in 1934, but that led to a decrease in Roosevelt's control of that state rather than an increase. Florida, on the other hand, the third state to repeal (and the last before the SCHW formed), repealed under the influence of Claude Pepper, who was a strong supporter of the New Deal; he and it thus probably did benefit from repeal there. Still, the political logic of poll tax repeal was shaky. There was no guarantee that black voters in the South would abandon the party of Lincoln the way that northern black voters had only begun to do in 1934 and 1936. Though FDR sent private letters of encouragement to the SCHW, he never publicly associated himself with the organization.

In any case, the SCHW's offer of aid to the New Deal came too late. As southern opposition pushed New Deal reforms from the top to the bottom of FDR's agenda, foreign policy pulled southern politicians from the bottom to the top of FDR's list of supporters. As war spread in Asia and threatened to erupt in Europe, FDR no longer needed to shake anti–New Deal senators and representatives out of office. Warmongering was as useful as race-baiting to the careers of such men.

Timing was not the only weakness of the SCHW. It failed to become a mass organization. It failed, in other words, to organize the potential voters it aimed to enfranchise. Without these constituents as supporters, the SCHW could not develop the independent power base it needed to move its agenda.[40] It remained an organization of prominent middle-class liberals who, having had the vote, as well as control over universities, leading newspapers, and professional organizations for decades, had already proven their inability to overthrow the southern political system—despite the new power they gained through New Deal patronage. FDR probably could not have done anything more to help them, even if he had been committed to poll tax repeal for ideological or tactical reasons, which he was not.

The SCHW, though it recognized the need to seize political power to

alter the racist system, and even had the right idea in seeking to comman-
deer the national state as part of the effort, failed to achieve power. In
appealing to the tactical interests of New Deal Democrats, the SCHW
could not even draw upon the moral revulsion that northerners and southerners tended to feel when confronted with lynching. The task was to unify
an ability to channel moral outrage with a political sense of force and timing. Until a new power rose in the South, rivaling the southern demagogues
in their ability to hit the emotional jugular with one hand while offering
votes with the other, Democratic presidents had to reckon with those who
already had power in the South.

The Eleventh Hour of Southern White Dissent

War, and a rising tide of black power in the North, raised the stakes of dissent and shifted its paths of least resistance in the South and the nation.
The organization that rose up at the end of World War II, in the ashes of
the CIC, was born in controversy over the inconsistencies and shortcomings of its predecessor. The Southern Regional Council, founded in 1944,
aimed to fight racist propaganda and prepare southern opinion for gradual
amelioration of black social conditions. It made a point of not questioning
the institution of segregation, however, and therefore alienated a small
fringe of southern liberals, most notably novelist Lillian Smith, who were
beginning to make defiant public statements against segregation. It also
alienated some black leaders, who believed that the SRC would not have
any greater effect on southern institutions than the CIC, whose structure
and membership it absorbed.[41] It probably would not have, had it not
become an instrument first of the black southern movement that rose up in
the mid-1950s and then of the federal agencies that began to turn against
segregation in the mid-1960s.

There was also a new successor to the SCHW, called the Southern
Conference Educational Fund, which began as a tax-exempt branch of the
SCHW and survived the financial and organizational crises that did in its
parent organization. Although its members explicitly opposed segregation
and it became a rallying ground for the fringe who opposed the SRC on
that issue, its agenda was narrower than the SCHW's had been, partly
because tax exemption required it to restrict its activities to "education." It
returned to the tactic of trying to awaken a "silent South" by mere repetition of dissenting ideas. (The SRC, without a tax motive, restricted itself to
the same kinds of activities.) Not driven to harness the power of the

national state, it lacked the strategic program of the SCHW and appeared more tentative and less ambitious than its predecessor.[42] At any rate, the SCEF, like the SRC, took whatever shape it had increasingly from black civil rights organizations. The story of white southern dissent from the mid-1950s on is a story of response to the new black movement.

There were other forms of southern white dissent before the 1940s and 1950s, which were less prominent and less organized than the CIC and the SCHW and their successors. Most important was what could be called a neo-Populist tradition that centered in collective farm and labor organizations, including the Brotherhood of Timber Workers, the Southern Tenant Farmers' Union, and the CIO's early southern efforts in the 1930s. These dissenters overlapped with Christian socialists and Christian radicals, influenced especially by Reinhold Niebuhr, who formed prolabor and pro-farmer organizations such as the Fellowship of Southern Churchmen. The Christians were especially prominent in the work of the Highlander Folk School, an important training center in rural Tennessee for national labor and civil rights protest, and in communal farming experiments such as the Koinonia cooperative in rural Georgia. These programs were desegregated from the start.[43]

Some of the exponents of this neo-Populism joined the SCHW and the SCEF and later worked with black movement organizations. The historical record probably underrepresents the extent of this kind of radicalism, since it did not have the intellectual audience in the North that intellectual dissent had, and since its organized opposition to racial institutions was part of a broader social program that was dismissed as a fringe movement, even within the labor movement. These neo-Populists often opposed the liberalism of CIC and SCHW members and were far more inclined to oppose segregation, even to the extent of integrating their meetings.

The neo-Populists might thus strike present readers as more authentic dissenters than the Blairs, Cables, Alexanders, and Ameses. They may be. But that does not make them more historically significant. However interesting or admirable for their courage or purity of thought—or more precisely, their more complete foreshadowing of views that are fashionable, and cost-free, today—they would be of central importance only if we substituted good ideas for actual political change. In other words, the history of neo-Populist dissent is a history of failure, just as much as the history of middle-class liberal dissent is, and for many of the same reasons. Though of different social background, and often opposed to the class interests associated with the CIC and the SRC, the neo-Populists fell victim to the same disorganization and disunity and, especially in the late 1940s and 1950s, the red-baiting (much of it self-inflicted) that crippled the liberal dissenters.[44]

The civil rights movement of the 1950s and 1960s alone is responsible for changing southern race relations from top to bottom, but the previous history of southern white dissent left its mark on the consciousness of those who followed, black and white. That history was above all a history of failure, which is not to say it was a useless history. Given the weakness and disunity of southern white dissent, it is hard to say exactly what it consisted of. Whenever it had ideals, it appealed to a sense of paternalistic obligation, which it schizophrenically altered with contradictory hopes for industrial progress. Dissenters tried to awaken the silent South by appealing to its conscience and at the same time wished that progress would render conscience unnecessary. In holding those contradictory hopes, southern white dissenters (before the SCHW) ignored the question of political power; they tried to wish, rather than strove to will, their ends into existence. Perhaps they understood that they had no power and did all they could without power. But they fell into habits of believing that mere assertion of ideals, or accidental changes of history, would somehow exempt them from answering the moral and political questions left unanswered in the birth of their social order.

Conversely, when the dissenters did try to develop a power base, through the SCHW, they hoped too much that that power base would share their interests or their ideals. The ideals of the New Deal were at bottom no stronger than those of northern capital in the New South era. (The SRC revived the northern capital strategy after World War II but ended up hitching itself to an altogether different force, the civil rights movement, and the related federal agencies. But that was unintentional—a result of the black movement's strategy and planning, not of the SRC's own.) The power brokers in both cases sought out alliances with those who had something to offer. The southern white dissenters had little more than a wish list.

The most sensitive of the dissenters were acutely aware of their failures. Jonathan Daniels, the influential liberal editor of the *Raleigh News and Observer* (successor and son of Josephus Daniels, who had hounded John Spencer Bassett), campaigned for improved treatment and expanded rights of black people, yet like most dissenters he opposed integration. Daniels found himself caught in between the growing militancy of black leaders (especially in the North) and the equal and opposite growth of segregation-ist resistance. He foresaw a showdown, in which liberal gradualism, and all the progress it could achieve, would be foreclosed. "We seem to be almost back to the extreme abolitionists and the extreme slaveholders in the lines of discussion," he wrote to his fellow liberal gradualist, sociologist Howard Odum, during World War II. "Between them, people like ourselves seem to be left in a sort of awareness and futility together."[45]

Black leaders in the South, who watched these developments very care-fully, learned not to repeat the mistakes of the white dissenters, avoiding both their wishful thinking about the power of white people with good intentions and, at least until the mid-1960s, their assumption that eco-nomic progress entailed moral progress. More important, southern black leaders gained from the white dissenters' history the complex and supple strategic insight that some white southerners had an interest in abandoning the system that claimed to help *all* white southerners. Those white south-erners needed to be pushed, but they were there and could make valuable allies. The lesson of greatest consequence for black leaders, however, was that they could not rely on white dissenters. It had become obvious that white dissenters failed, regardless of the character of their motives, their organization, and their strategies. Black leaders therefore had to seize the initiative with organizations of their own. They learned, in short, that a civil rights movement was necessary.

A new generation of white southern dissenters inherited from their predecessors a conscience inflated to fantastic proportions by the belief that they were somehow responsible for the system, and further burdened by a sense of their failure over the last half-century to improve it. The greatest proof of that failure, the emergence of a mass movement of black southern-ers taking history into their own hands, excited their consciences to an even higher pitch of obligation and gave them a new school for learning political realism.

PART TWO

The Strategy of Nonviolence and the Role of White Southerners in the Movement

It cannot be called prowess to kill fellow citizens, to betray friends, to be treacherous, pitiless, irreligious. These ways can win a prince power, but not glory.

—Machiavelli, *The Prince*

Every man who has not wit to rule his inner self will be most apt to rule his neighbor's will.

—Goethe, *Faust, Part Two*

The Montgomery Bus
Boycott, 1955-1956

In the middle of the 1950s, a handful of black preachers found an opportunity to lead the white South away from the demagogues who had
dominated racial politics since the end of the Populist revolt in 1896. These
preachers knew that those who dominated politics never represented the
whole white South, yet they also knew that the dissenters only complained
ineffectually against the demagogues or, more often, kept a glum silence.
They observed the white dissenters, unable to lead, spending a good deal of
their time blaming the South's ills on the absence of proper leadership.[1]
Though white dissenters undoubtedly expected proper leadership to
emerge from the ranks of the educated white elite, it emerged instead from
an educated black elite, among the preachers, in the mid-1950s. A central
question in the history of southern white dissenters was how they
responded to this surprising development.

Two representatives of the dissenting tradition, Clifford and Virginia
Durr of Montgomery, Alabama, were called upon quite directly to respond
to the new black leadership. The character of the call did not seem new at
first, however, for black leaders had been calling on the Durrs for many
years. Clifford, who had been assistant counsel to the Reconstruction
Finance Corporation in Washington, was a white lawyer who had a reputation for helping black clients. He was a close friend of Aubrey Williams, the
white southerner who headed the National Youth Administration, one of
the few New Deal agencies that defied state laws by operating without
racial discrimination in the South. Virginia was perhaps even better known
as a Democratic National Committeewoman, who had been active in the
campaign to abolish the poll tax.[2]

Clifford Durr's early resistance to the Red Scare led Mississippi senator Jim Eastland to subpoena him and his wife to appear in March 1954 before his Senate Investigating Committee's special hearings in New Orleans. These were Eastland's effort to improve upon Senator Joe McCarthy's anticommunist investigation, which had left the South virtually untouched up to that point. Eastland, anticipating the Supreme Court's ruling in favor of the NAACP in the *Brown* decision (which was to come in May 1954), had vowed to fight the Court, which he characterized as a central part of the Communist Conspiracy. He seemed to be using the Durrs for target practice.[3]

Though Virginia Durr took advantage of her political connections, not least with then–majority leader Lyndon Johnson, to reduce Eastland's "committee" hearing to a one-man campaign stunt, the red taint stuck to the Durrs and cost them a great many business connections and social entrées back in Alabama. None of their old friends sent a message of support during their ordeal with Eastland, which produced among other difficulties a heart attack for Clifford.[4] The only message from Montgomery was one telegram, signed by Jo Ann Robinson, Irene West, and several others whom the Durrs had never met. "So when I came back to Montgomery," Virginia Durr said, "I was determined to find out who these women were. . . . I didn't know if they were black or white."[5]

E. D. Nixon, head of the Montgomery NAACP and one of Clifford's clients, told Virginia that the signers were all members of the Women's Political Council—educated black women, that is, who were struggling to improve their lot. "So I looked each one of them up and thanked them," Virginia recalled, asking each of them how it was that they were willing to take her "on faith" and to send such a potentially dangerous telegram. "We knew if Senator Eastland was after you," the black women replied, "you had to be all right."[6]

Encouragement from Conscientious White Supporters

Through E. D. Nixon, Virginia Durr also met Rosa Parks, secretary of the local NAACP. Durr hired Parks as a seamstress, and the two became friends. There was nothing unusual about this friendship in Durr's mind. Herself an upper-class lady from a long line of Alabama gentry, she found Rosa Parks to be "one of the gentlest" women she had ever met — "the epitome of what you'd call the southern lady."[7]

Through the poll tax crusade, Virginia Durr had become well connected to other dissenters from racial orthodoxy across the South, particularly those with socialist leanings and ties to organized labor.[8] One of her favorites was Myles Horton, a poor white sharecropper turned theologian, who studied under Reinhold Niebuhr at Union Theological Seminary and then, in 1932, established the Highlander Folk School at Monteagle, Tennessee. Patterned on a Danish model that was influenced by the settlement house work of Jane Addams and the educational ideas of John Dewey, Highlander was an interracial training center for labor, socialist, and religiously oriented community organizers in the South.[9] Through his support of unionization and his fights against racism, Horton had also become friends with E. D. Nixon, who had been an organizer for the Sleeping Car Porters. Clifford Durr and Aubrey Williams were among the financial sponsors of the Highlander School.[10]

Virginia Durr thought her seamstress could use a vacation from the Deep South and that she was a perfect candidate for Horton's program at Highlander — and perhaps that Highlander could benefit from her. So she arranged for Parks' pilgrimage to Monteagle in the summer of 1955.[11] There, as Parks traded ideas about political action with other organizers, she experienced life without segregation for the first time.

Parks returned to Montgomery a changed woman, saying, in July 1955, that she hoped to attend another workshop at Monteagle soon, eager as she was "to make a contribution to the fulfillment of complete freedom for all people."[12] She got her opportunity at home, though, on the first of December. When she refused a driver's order to give up her seat for a white man, the driver summoned the police, having no idea what his action would lead to. As Irene West mused, "If the man who had called the cop had known it would come to this, he would have been willing to let her sit in his lap."[13]

Bertha Butler, another member of the Women's Political Council who happened to be on the bus, got off and went immediately to tell E. D. Nixon what had happened. Nixon first called Fred Gray, one of two black lawyers in Montgomery, but Gray was out of town. Nixon then called the police station and asked what charges Parks was being held on. The desk sergeant told him that was none of his business. Needing a lawyer, he called Clifford Durr. Durr made a few inquiries and called Nixon back to tell him that Parks was charged with violating the state segregation laws. He volunteered to accompany Nixon to the station and post Parks' bond. Nixon came right over to pick him up and took Virginia Durr along, too.

The three of them got Parks released and took her home to discuss

using her as the plaintiff for the test case for which they had all been waiting. Her husband was against it, telling her, "The white folks will kill you,
Rosa. . . . Don't do anything to make trouble, Rosa." Her mother did not
like the idea either. But Rosa Parks elected to go ahead with it, encouraged
by Nixon and the Durrs.[14]

Soon the local NAACP representatives, Nixon and Parks, joined forces
with the Women's Political Council; both groups had been toying with the
idea of direct action to supplement the attack on segregation through the
courts. The WPC contacted nearly all of Montgomery's ninety-two black
clergymen, urging them to inspire their congregants to stay off the buses
the following Monday. The preachers and their flocks came together to
form the Montgomery Improvement Association, with a new young
preacher in town, Martin Luther King, Jr., at its head. Both of the Durrs
continued to give legal, financial, and moral support to the MIA throughout the boycott and after.[15]

Other white southerners heard the call of the new black leadership of the
South less directly than the Durrs. There was one major black church in
Montgomery that Nixon and the WPC did not notify: the Reverend Robert
Graetz's Trinity Lutheran Church. Graetz heard about the boycott only as
a rumor, not too differently from the way the police heard about it. He was
in the odd position of being a white pastor to an all-black church. His congregation would not tell him about the boycott when he asked them.
Though white folks in Montgomery shunned him, he was not fully welcomed into the confidence of his black congregants, some of whom openly
stated that they did not want a white man leading them, especially on risky
matters like a boycott. By coincidence, though, he knew Rosa Parks. She
was not a member of his congregation, but he had participated in her
NAACP activity. He called her to see if she could substantiate the rumor
that someone had been arrested and that a boycott was planned in protest.
Parks told him the rumor was true and that she was the one who had been
arrested.[16]

Graetz wanted to support Rosa Parks all he could. The day after speaking with her, he preached a sermon giving the boycott, scheduled to begin
the following day, his blessing. He knew where *he* would be tomorrow, he
told his flock. He would be ferrying boycotters all over the city in his car.
He warned them sternly of the hazards of disunity: "Let's try to make this
boycott as effective as possible," he said, "because it won't be any boycott if

half of us ride the buses and half of us don't ride. If we're going to do it, let's make a good job of it."[17]

The one preacher left out of the boycott alert soon found himself playing a key role in it. Eyes always on the conscience of the nation, Martin Luther King recognized that emphasis on Graetz's role could be particularly valuable in appeals to white liberals. Visiting journalists found their attention steered, perhaps disproportionately, to episodes involving the lone white minister leading hordes of black protesters. The first national attention Graetz got came from the black press: *Jet* featured him as early as December 22, 1955.[18] In the first month of the boycott, Graetz brought in an impressive seven thousand dollars in donations by mail from northern Lutherans.

Graetz had less success with the local clergy. He later claimed, "If we forced all the white ministers in the area to take a stand one way or another, about half of the white ministers in our area would be on our side." But although he stated that "many" of the local white clergy were "already getting more active" in the protest campaign, most were silent. Not a single white church contributed financially to the boycott, though many individual white Christians did. Graetz sent letters to every white minister in the Montgomery area asking their support for the boycott. The answers were evasive or negative, with a handful of exceptions. Graetz told King that the majority "dared not get involved in such a controversial issue." King said this "was a deep disappointment" to him and that the white ministers as a whole remained "appallingly silent throughout the protest."

J. E. Pierce, a black professor at Alabama State and close associate of Nixon's on the MIA, spoke apologetically about the white ministers: "We have to take into consideration that the white minister is between the bite. If he comes out to the Negroes, he is going to be squeezed by the Citizens' Council. And by his church, see." He told the story of one white minister (the Reverend Ray Wadley of St. Mark's Methodist), president of the local Council on Human Relations, who was run out of town for being too soft on the race question. Graetz always kept Wadley's experience in mind, as well as a White Citizens' Council bonfire he had witnessed, in which two effigies, one black, one white, were burned. The black one was labeled "NAACP," the white one, "I talked integration."[19]

Graetz soon became a member of the executive board of the MIA, and a year after the boycott ended, he became the organization's secretary. Coretta King said that Graetz "paid dearly" for all his activity in support of the movement. Apart from almost nightly telephone threats and broken windows, the police jailed and threatened him for helping the carpool. In August 1956, while he was at Highlander teaching boycott strategy to future protesters, his house was bombed.[20]

Within two months of its founding, another white southerner, the Reverend Glenn Smiley, had become a prime mover in the Montgomery Improvement Association. Smiley was then a staff member of the Fellowship of Reconciliation, A. J. Muste's pacifist organization, which Aldon Morris classifies, along with Horton's Highlander School, as one of the "movement halfway houses" — an institution that provided vital organizational support to the movement but, unlike the main movement organizations such as the MIA, did not grow out of the southern black communities.

Like both of the Durrs, Smiley was raised as a southern segregationist. His father owned a cotton plantation in west Texas which employed seasonal labor, mostly braceros from Mexico and black migrants from Arkansas. His mother, from east Tennessee, occasionally retained "colored help" around the house, when the family could afford it, and treated them with warmth and condescension in public; the warmth grew and the condescension diminished in private, but the two never seemed inconsistent with each other. Smiley was aware of racial barriers very early and was taught not to cross or question them. He studied religion in college and became a minister in the Southern Methodist Conference.

His entry into civil rights work was indirect. Just about the time he was ordained, fascism was on the rise in Europe. He came into contact with two organizations that opposed it, the Communist party and the pacifist FOR. His religious principles pointed to the pacifist response — even if this meant opposition to class warfare, to which he was otherwise attracted. By the time the United States joined the war, Smiley had become an FOR staff member and had withdrawn his draft registration. In 1943, the army assigned him to a conscientious objectors' camp. He refused this offer as hypocrisy, choosing imprisonment at McNeil Island Penitentiary in Puget Sound instead.

In prison he witnessed a firmly institutionalized segregation that lacked the leaven of human indulgence he had known back in his father's fields and his mother's kitchen. "It seemed incumbent upon me to attempt to change this. . . . So we began to refuse to practice segregation." By the time he was released in October 1945, he and roughly forty other conscientious objectors had disrupted prison life sufficiently to make some minor inroads toward desegregation. But he understood that the culture surrounding the federal penitentiary in Atlanta, Georgia, or Segoville, Texas, would have resisted the kind of changes they achieved in Washington State. Though his father's family had practiced what seemed a more humane segregation than the northern institutions, Smiley recognized that it was also more ingrained and harder to break down.[21]

While he was in prison, the organization he was part of had followed a similar route from antiwar activity to antiracist action. When Gandhi's disciple Krishnalal Shridharani (whose manual *War without Violence* [1939] had become popular among nonviolent activists in the United States) visited the United States in the early 1940s, the FOR leader, A. J. Muste, met with him and with A. Philip Randolph, head of the Sleeping Car Porters' union and the March on Washington Movement, to discuss whether the book's principles could be applied to the American racial scene. Other FOR members, especially James Farmer, Bayard Rustin, and George Hauser, put the idea into action; they formed the Congress of Racial Equality. CORE, a spinoff from the FOR, focused exclusively on racial issues and demanded less piety of its members in adherence to nonviolent principles. Smiley, on the FOR staff in Los Angeles after his release in 1945, helped establish the CORE chapter there.

When the Montgomery bus boycott broke out in December 1955, Bayard Rustin, then on the CORE and FOR staffs, decided he had to go there to indoctrinate the ranks in the principles of nonviolent warfare. But Rustin had to leave town shortly after he arrived. King told Rustin he needed someone to fill in, and Rustin told King to send for Smiley: "Why I don't know," Smiley said, "except I [had] some experience and I was a southerner, which they felt might have helped." On February 14, 1956, Smiley showed up at King's house and attended a press conference there that day. He said King was already imbued with the ideas of nonviolent direct action; all he lacked was experience, and it was Smiley's job to bring the experience of CORE and the FOR to bear on the day-to-day crises of the Montgomery boycott.[22]

"I had two assignments with Dr. King," Smiley said. "One was every mass meeting in which I was in town, I was given a spot on the program to discuss tactical nonviolence. Then, I was supposed to go around to the different churches and meet with small groups and try to whip the clergy and laity into line about nonviolence. My other assignment was to make every contact possible in the white community and attempt to do the same thing, to get them to understand and try to meet with Negroes."[23] In the latter capacity, Smiley says he acted as "a sort of intelligence service as to what people, including the White Citizens' Council and others, were saying. The fact that I was white and could speak and act like a southerner gave me access to public meetings of the WCC and even the Klan."[24]

Smiley supervised the training program in nonviolence which built up the discipline of the mass protesters in Montgomery (and subsequently in other southern cities). The last effort he led in Montgomery was a "workshop" in Ralph Abernathy's church of some five thousand black protesters on the eve of the victory celebration—the boarding of buses on a nonsegregated basis on December 21, 1956, after more than a year of siege. Smiley directed this dress rehearsal. The purpose was to anticipate acts of violence on the newly desegregated buses. Black people had to play all the white parts, as Smiley was the only white person there, and they played the most hostile, intransigent hoods they could imagine; others rehearsed nonviolent appeals to their consciences (with less success than was to be the case in real life the following day).[25]

Smiley's role culminated, symbolically, just before going to bed that night. Sitting alone with King at King's dinner table, Smiley said, "Dr. King, tomorrow I want to be paid for the fact that I have worked 381 days with you here on the bus protest, and it has not cost you a penny, because my salary and my expenses have been paid by my organization the FOR." King looked at him quizzically and said, "What do you mean?" Smiley said, "Well, I just want to be paid." King then saw that he was joking and said, "Name me a price." Smiley replied, "Dr. King, it's a high price, but tomorrow when we board the bus I want to be the first white man to ride with you in the integrated buses of Montgomery." Smiley said that King "laughed with his very deep laughter for which he was famous" and stood up and hugged him and said, "'Glenn, you shall be paid to the last farthing.'" The payoff came the next morning:

> At 5:30 when we boarded the first bus—I've never seen so many TV cameras and radio reporters and lights and so on in my life—[there were] four of us, Dr. King and myself, the Rev. Ralph Abernathy, and a Mrs. Bascomb, and in fact there was a fifth, the fifth was a young man who ran errands for the committee when they were in session. And when Dr. King, being the first to get on, spoke to the bus driver, the bus driver smiled and said, "You're Dr. King, aren't you?" and he said yes, and [the driver] said "Well, I'm glad to have you aboard"—and well he might have been, because he

had not been working for over a year. [King and I] sat in the second vertical seats back, the two seats, Ralph Abernathy and Mrs. Bascomb sat in the front of the two vertical seats, and then the gopher sat behind Dr. King and me. And so the bus driver went on down to the main part of town.

Smiley's picture, in King's account of the boycott, *Stride toward Freedom*, is featured on the last page of photos, headed "The End," with King's caption, "The first non-segregated bus rides down the streets of Montgomery with Glenn Smiley, a white Southerner, sharing a seat with M. L. King."[26] The bus driver made an unscheduled stop in front of Graetz's home and honked the horn to summon Graetz to board the bus on its way to meet the crowd of thousands who had assembled downtown to meet the dawn of the new day in person.[27]

The support of these conscientious white southerners for the boycott was not, on the whole, very public. Sometimes, when they wanted to come out in public, they did not get the chance. At the grand mass meeting after the first day of the boycott, other than newsmen, Graetz was the only white person there. Smiley had not yet come to town. Clifford and Virginia Durr were not able to get near the door: the cars and crowds thronged outside the doors were too thick for them to penetrate.[28] It did not matter that he was a legal adviser to Rosa Parks and she a friend and confidant. This was not their movement. They found themselves, so to speak, on the back of the historical bus. It was no longer a matter of doing things for the Negroes, as they had been accustomed to doing. The day they thought they were waiting for — the day when they would simply do things with the Negroes — had been passed over. It seemed as though Negroes were now doing things for themselves, and even, in a sense, for the whites.[29] Now the only position the white dissenters could find themselves in, sometimes sheepishly, was to react to initiatives that rose more or less fully formed out of the black community.

The Response of the Middle: Mixed Signals

Sometimes the new black leadership of the South called on followers to do no more than be honest and stick to their principles. Sticking to one's principles, in the years before mass protest, had been virtually risk free for nonracist white people in Montgomery: individual acts of kindness and private gestures of fairness did not threaten the system. (Indeed, they may have made it more palatable, to both black and white people, and thus put off the day when the black community banded together to challenge the system.) When the boycott came, white people who were in the habit of making such acts and gestures did not have to change their feelings and opinions, but staying the same became a strain. The solidarity of the black masses in a public confrontation with the system changed the definition of what could be taken as kindness and fairness.

The white people of Montgomery were not initially united against the boycott. Much had happened already to prepare them for the incremental change being demanded by the boycotters. Black leaders had pressed demands and won concessions, with little calamity resulting. In September 1955, for example, black Montgomerians had packed a local church to pay tribute to the outgoing fire and police commissioner, Dave Birmingham, who had, in what the local paper called a "precedent-shattering action," hired four black policemen in the spring of 1954. Birmingham rose to speak at the September meeting and told the (mostly black) crowd, "It was a privilege to have had a place in helping you people take a place in the sun of this city, a place you richly deserve." He did not say, and the papers did not report, that he had made a deal with E. D. Nixon during his January 1954 campaign for the office. Nixon promised to deliver the black vote for Birmingham in what was sure to be a close election; in return, Birmingham promised to hire four black officers. Though small in number, the black voters (about 1,800 in a total population of about 125,000) did provide Birmingham's margin of victory.[30] It was thus apt that the tribute to Birmingham, also attended by prominent white business, labor, and religious leaders, evolved into a rally to kick off a new registration campaign, the goal of which was to sign up 5,000 new black voters. Birmingham, according to one witness, "got lost in the shuffle" as the topic of discussion turned to registration.[31] Another example of black demands leading to some concessions came the same year when the local minor league baseball team added a black player to its roster for the first time in history, George W. ("the Infield Star") Handy. The team was named the Montgomery Rebels.[32]

These usually quiet, behind-the-scenes changes were so incremental and so few as to seem mere tokenism. But other signals from local whites suggested the time was ripe for a frontal assault on white supremacy. Rosa Parks had defied bus drivers before.[33] If she had never gone so far as to refuse a direct order to give up her seat, she and others had refused to follow the unusually insulting rule that required black passengers to pay their fare at the front of the bus, get off, and reenter at the rear. She was not arrested for that. One of the reasons segregation could not command wholehearted moral support was that, however rational and right most whites believed it to be in principle, obeying its rules on a day-to-day basis involved so many such contortions that southerners, never a punctiliously law-abiding people, got in the habit of winking at a humane bending of the rules now and then. Another reason it could not command wholehearted support was that those who did rigorously uphold the rules were typically tiresome, if not cruel and unusual, types.

Rosa Parks said it was up to the whim of the driver whether to enforce segregation on his bus. Most drivers tried to avoid confrontations over it, out of a natural laziness and inertia as well as a southern politesse and aversion to controversy. When they did go so far as to evict a black woman to enforce the rules, according to Parks, white passengers were typically too ashamed or too proud to take the seat vacated for their benefit: "If a driver would ask, say, four women to stand up for a white man to sit—it would usually be that—the person wouldn't take the seat. He would just remain standing."[34] Even Claudette Colvin, who had been arrested for refusing to give up a seat months before Parks, and who in contrast to the ever-composed Parks was indignant and cursed the driver, had a white woman come to her defense.[35]

Though segregation commanded widespread southern white support in the abstract, its actual enforcement in so many instances was so clearly a gratuitous insult to black people (and sometimes to white people) that it was vulnerable to political attack. The critics could attack the specifics of enforcement rather than the principle, the means rather than the end, and tap into a huge reservoir of inarticulate sympathy.

Thus it was not against ironclad resistance that the leading black churches of Montgomery rose up in December 1955. In the first mass meeting of the boycott, Martin Luther King electrified the crowd with righteous impatience. The phrase "there comes a time" punctuated his speech, and the time was unmistakably now. Black people as a whole would never again appear meek and cowering to the white people in Montgomery.

But King's demands in retrospect appear quite mild. The main "demand" was simply to let black people sit from back to front, white people from front to back, with no one ever having to vacate a seat unless (if the passenger was black) an empty seat existed farther back or (if white) farther forward; in no circumstances should whites and blacks sit in the same seat. Two ancillary demands, the hiring of black drivers to serve on predominantly black routes, and "courtesy" from all drivers, did not threaten "the southern way of life." Nor, in substance, did the seating demand, as the MIA took pains to point out in negotiations and public statements: state law required only separate seating. It did not require evicting seated passengers or forcing black passengers to stand when empty seats to the front of seated whites were available. Leaders of the NAACP, so often viewed today as meliorists who were outpaced by the new direct action of the 1950s and 1960s, initially wrote the Montgomery boycott off as a flash in the pan, whose ill-considered demands stopped short of total integration.[36] In retrospect, it seems that the MIA put its thinnest edge forward, but at the time it was not apparent how wide the wedge would be, or how loudly and violently the rail of southern society would split. In 1955 and 1956, the movement could portray itself as the moderate force in town. Though asking enormous sacrifices and risks on the part of blacks, it was not asking much of the whites.[37]

Not all white liberals went as far as the Durrs, Graetz, or Smiley in their support for this kind of change, yet their acts had significance when added together. The governor of Alabama, "Big Jim" Folsom, had been elected to his second term the year of the *Brown* decision. In that election he received the majority of the black votes, as he had in his previous election.[38] The meaning of his Delphic campaign statements — that he would settle the segregation issue "within the framework of the law"; that the Supreme Court decision had the effect of law, which must prevail; and most characteristically, that he was not going to force the state's "fine colored children to go to school with white folks" — became clear as the year developed. In November he voted against the segregation resolution passed at the Southern Governors' Conference of 1954 — the only Deep South governor to do so. He publicly referred to the "interposition" resolution that his state legislature passed in 1954 (one of many neo-Calhounian measures by which southern states intended to nullify *Brown*) as "hogwash."[39]

In February 1956 Folsom proposed — through the good offices of his chauffeur, Winston Craig, who was a member of Martin Luther King's church — a compromise for the bus boycott in the capital city. He appointed a biracial commission to resolve differences between the races in Montgomery. He proposed that these "moderate leaders of both races" get together and just talk things through. Alabama's newspaper editors responded favorably to this leadership, but this and Folsom's subsequent attempts to get Montgomery mayor W. A. "Tacky" Gayle to settle with the MIA went unrewarded. Within a month of its appointment, Folsom's commission was dead.[40]

The black-owned *Atlanta Daily World,* in an editorial entitled "Alabama Might Take the Lead," eulogized, "While Governor Folsom did not do all that he might have done for our particular racial group, he made an excellent beginning towards the ends of impartial administration in the affairs of state. In the dispute between the colored citizens of Montgomery and the transit authorities, the governor has not impugned the motives of the leaders of the cause nor has he suggested violence."[41]

Grover Hall, Jr., the editor of Montgomery's morning paper, the *Advertiser,* initially took the position that white Montgomery should accept the movement's demands—despite his negative opinion of the new black leadership.[42] When Smiley, on a good will mission to the *Advertiser,* asked Hall what he thought of King, Hall replied, "Dr. King is a dangerous communist son of a bitch."[43] King was less harsh toward Hall. King said that Hall, like the vast majority of white southerners, liked segregation but could not stomach segregationists, whose tactics extended to bombing the houses of preachers.[44]

Hall and his paper did not support the boycott,[45] but having the editor of the leading newspaper in town against the movement's enemies, if not in favor of the movement, was a form of lukewarm support as valuable as the more wholehearted support of the Durrs and Graetz. Lukewarm moderates and liberals like Hall, in Montgomery and in later struggles, were to get more credit in the press for the ultimate settlement of the issue than the wholehearted opponents of racism like the Durrs and Graetz. Though their motives may have been less idealistic, their influence on white opinion was greater than wholehearted idealism could be.

If Folsom's popularity and Hall's *Advertiser* were any indication of the climate of opinion, many white Alabamians were ready for change. None of them was willing to take the initiative for change. But once the MIA took matters into its own hands, if direct support from whites was rare, surely the lesser signs of sympathy helped the morale of the movement.

Several white people, especially women, wrote letters to the editor in defense of the boycott. Frances P. McLeod confessed on December 9, 1955, "The treatment of Negroes on our city buses has caused us to bow our heads in shame." She did not see any reason why Montgomery could not meet the black demands, which would give Montgomery's bus system the same kind of seating arrangements that prevailed by law in such eminently southern centers as Nashville, Richmond, and Mobile.

Mrs. I. B. Rutledge wrote the same day, recalling with shame and embarrassment being "the only white person occupying one of 10 vacant seats at the front of the bus" while the back was packed to overflow with black passengers returning tired from a day's work. She asked the driver, she said, to "let these people sit down." The driver had not objected to her suggestion in principle but declined to follow it because, he said, he was "afraid" lest someone criticize him. Rutledge went on to say that in canvassing her friends and neighbors, she had "yet to find one white person" who felt that it was right "that a Negro be made to stand so that a white person [could] sit." Like McLeod, she waved the southern flag over her peroration. We southerners, she wrote, "like to think of ourselves as a courageous people with the courage not only to face danger in war, but the moral courage to face issues and adverse public opinion." Clearly, therefore, it was time for those who really believed in "Christian and democratic principles of consideration of others and fair play" to start speaking out, to "help create a public opinion" that would encourage a resolution "satisfactory to all."[46]

A Mrs. E. R. J. told *Advertiser* readers on Christmas day, 1955, "I was born and reared in the Black Belt of Alabama, but I, like a lot of others, have been forced to do a lot of thinking on the race question lately. I am afraid the Negro is not now, nor has ever been, as happy and content with his place as we southern white people have believed. There has been peace, true, but some of it has been peace imposed by fear. Such peace always brings its dangers." She did not want to forsake southern virtues. She evinced the South's bruised allegiance to the home territory, which always balanced a prideful complacency with a goading sense of inferiority. "We southern white people may not have as much money as the Yankees, but we could go them one better and give the Negro our cooperation and good will." This was to be no mere Christmas homily, she made clear as she got to the point. "Take the Negro bus strike. They are asking for so little. 'First come first served' is certainly not much of an innovation. Very few white people could object to it. But we are slow in granting even this little change." She compared the crisis to the disruption of Western civilization by the rise of liberal democracy and industrial capitalism: "We have two choices, we can, like the British, bend with the wind, and rise stronger after the storm, or we can be stiff and brittle like the French and be broken and wounded in the conflict."[47]

Grover Hall duly printed such letters, along with what seem to have been, at least initially, less frequent letters denouncing the boycott or calling for more "time."[48] The mail received by the *Newsletter* of the Alabama Council on Human Relations (an organization that worked quietly for better understanding between black and white leaders), while hardly representative of white opinion in general, is significant: it ran five to one in favor of the MIA position on bus seating. The ACHR even suggested that white bus patronage had "slackened somewhat" and noted that white people occasionally appeared as carpool drivers.[49] The local white newspapers also reported sightings of white drivers in carpools.[50]

The motive behind much of the white help to carpooling — which white drivers did not always refer to, or even recognize, as such — was simple self-interest: white women needed their maids and there was no other way to get them. Such motivation did not, of course, bother the boycott leaders, who understood with Eliot that people can be counted on to do the right things for the wrong reasons. But there is evidence that at least some of the white aid to the boycott was a deliberate and purposeful expression of support, if always given on the sly. This evidence consists of the letters that many local white people sent to King and the accounts and rosters of the mass meetings which show local white carpool drivers in attendance from time to time.[51]

Many local white people also gave money to the MIA. Though financial contributions were probably more helpful to the cause, they were less risky than driving (of which the police and vigilantes began to take note as the boycott wore on) because they could be covert. The fundraising apparatus was designed to make the contributors' identities impossible to trace, not to protect white dissidents' reputations but to protect the black contributors who were far more vulnerable to reprisals, and whose contributions were, in the minds of the initial planners of the boycott, far more crucial. That white contributors benefited from the diffusion and secrecy of fundraisers, and that the boycott benefited from their contributions, were unexpected side effects.

The contributions suggest how widespread white support for the boycott in Montgomery really was. They tell more than opinion polls, which suggest no more than superficial sentiments, and more than carpooling, which may suggest only selfish need. Giving money was a deliberate, concrete action, which usually required the white contributor to take the initiative to track down a fundraiser and then keep the whole thing secret, for the fundraiser's sake if not the contributor's. Unfortunately, under such circumstances, thorough recordkeeping would have been too great a risk, so the historian has to rely on the testimony of the participants.

Everyone told some version of the story, perhaps apocryphal, of the mistress who snuck up one day and pressed a ten-dollar bill into her maid's hand, professing in a hushed frenzy her belief in the cause and begging for secrecy about it: if news of the transaction leaked out, it would just kill her husband (or, in some versions, he her). Later the same day, the husband appeared in some out-of-the-way corner, motioned the same maid aside, handed her another ten, and winkingly enjoined her from saying anything about it to the Missus, who was so old-fashioned, you know, and just wouldn't understand.[52]

There is more credible testimony to financial support from local whites. The MIA treasurer, Irene West, stated that "a number of white people contributed" to the boycott, indeed, that she "turned in a lot of money but mostly [from] white people."[53] Jo Ann Robinson told of a great two-way loyalty between maids and the families that employed them. "White wives were grateful for the services their house workers rendered. The 'good' white employers increased the so-called twenty-cents bus fare to taxi fare. Some also increased wages. A number of domestic workers," Robinson said, "informed me that their employers often put extra money in the pay envelopes to put in the MIA collections at the Monday night meetings."[54]

These contributions were almost all secret. West said she collected a hundred dollars from a white man (an unusually large contribution) but she couldn't tell his name. She just had to say " 'a friend.' "[55] Rosa Parks said that white people typically sent their contributions "with a preference to remain anonymous."[56] Georgia Gilmore, a black cook, midwife, and mother of six, was one of the mainstays of the movement. In addition to providing food for the ranks, at the only eatery in town where blacks and whites could be served (illegally) at the same table,[57] she headed the famous "Club from Nowhere." Next to the plate passings at church, this was the greatest source of MIA funds: tiny contributions—typically fifty cents or a dollar—given anonymously by often terrified black people and, she said, a substantial number of white people.[58] Aubrey Williams, the former head of the National Youth Administration who was in semiretirement and publishing a faltering magazine, *The Southern Farmer* (which had lost subscriptions and advertising in response to integrationist editorials), made it known to the MIA that he would put his property up for bond for any black protester who needed it.[59]

Apart from practical assistance, such contributions gave concrete evidence that there were many white people in Montgomery who were willing to see the system change. A segregated society was not some abstract, alien thing to the black participants in the movement but a form of degradation and insult maintained by a particular group of white people in the name of all white people. The white community was not some abstract category but a number of flesh and blood persons the black protesters had known, between them, all their lives. The protesters knew that if pressed, many of those persons would gladly give the system up, with all its pretenses and inconveniences.

Just as important, white acts of support affected the white community. They opened up a wide space in which support of the boycott, rather than being outlandish or daring, became so commonplace that everyone in town was talking about someone he knew who had given material aid to it. Supporters were not easy to isolate and ostracize. The black leadership came, to all appearances, from the most respectable quarters of the black community —the choice of Rosa Parks over Claudette Colvin indicates that that was no accident—and that surely contributed to the legitimacy of the protest. But the added effect of white people, who almost always seem to have been upper-class, aiding the movement suggested that desegregation was acceptable to white citizens of stature and influence and that the transition to a new order might be much smoother than anticipated. The peaceful desegregation of transportation (and, shortly, even schools) in many a southern city before the Montgomery boycott was on the minds of the protesters in Montgomery and elsewhere. Those episodes suggested to the protesters that their city might follow the lead of the sympathetic white people of the South rather than the militant segregationists.[60]

Die-hard Segregationism Drives Away the Middle

In Montgomery, however, sympathetic white people did not prevail. The resistance of such white leaders as bus company lawyer Jack Crenshaw and the new police and fire commissioner Clyde Sellers, who (with a 43 percent plurality) had defeated Dave Birmingham in a race-baiting campaign in March 1955, kept such sentiments from influencing the local government and bus company.[61]

To the mildest of the MIA demands, a plea for courtesy from the drivers, Crenshaw replied that discourtesy was a natural reaction to the rudeness or misbehavior of passengers and furthermore that there had been no cases of driver rudeness reported to the management.[62] As to the substantive demands, Crenshaw replied that changes in seating rules would lead to a situation in which black men were "practically rubbing knees" with white women on buses.[63] King came to regard Crenshaw as the "most stubborn opponent" of black rights in town.[64]

Sellers, for his part, did not drop the race-baiting campaign after he had won election as police commissioner. In early January 1956, he attended a White Citizens' Council rally in Montgomery, jumped up out of the crowd, garnered a standing ovation by boasting that he was as rigid a bigot as anyone there, and rode the wave of mob approval to the podium, where he declared he would never trade his "southern birthright for a hundred Negro votes." Commenting on the rally, which had been held to honor two guest speakers from Arkansas, the *Advertiser* said that Sellers "stole the show." Later that night, Sellers completed the ritual by joining the WCC.[65] Within a couple of weeks, Mayor Gayle and the other member of the three-man city commission, Frank Parks (who had shown signs of moderation and had won his election on a margin of black votes), followed Sellers' lead and joined the WCC too.[66]

Thus the elected leaders of Montgomery took every possible precaution not to appear soft on integration. They pitched rumors about Martin Luther King at black audiences. (He was an uppity troublemaker who rode in fancy cars, paid for by their contributions, while they got blisters on their feet walking to work.) They denounced King, who was from Georgia, as an outsider. Then all three commissioners hosted a rally for Mississippi senator Jim Eastland, on February 10, 1956. Eastland taunted his hosts with such lines as "I am sure you are not going to permit the NAACP to control your state." He warned all white citizens of the need to "organize and be militant."[67]

The negotiating position of the bus company, led by Crenshaw, and of the city commission, led by Sellers, was that they had to uphold the law. There was something to this, since segregation was, after all, the law. However, given the moderation and strict legality of the boycotters' original demands — which is to say their acceptance of segregation in principle — that position was hard to sustain. (The original three demands were never dropped by the MIA during the boycott but were in a sense superseded by Fred Gray's federal case, filed February 1, 1956, which challenged the constitutionality of segregation per se and which the MIA leaders, for that reason, had delayed filing.[68]) It was all the more difficult to sustain, considering, as the ACHR and other white moderates pointed out, that

Mobile, Alabama (among other southern cities), was covered by the same laws as Montgomery and had already done as much as the boycotters were asking Montgomery to do. Not only was Mobile's system legally sound, but adoption of it had resulted in no calamity; social peace, indeed white supremacy, seemed to remain intact.

What seems more compelling as an explanation for the intransigence of the bus company and the commission is their fear that any bending in the particulars of white rule, at least by force, at that moment in history, would open the floodgates to other changes to which the South seemed vulnerable. Crenshaw, though he stuck to his legal argument tenaciously, if not recalcitrantly, at one heated moment blurted out, "If we granted the negroes these demands, they would go about boasting of a victory they had won over the white people, and this we will not stand for."[69]

Subsequent events would show that the floodgates *had* been opened at Montgomery, despite the resistance of the city commission. The beginning of mass direct action by black southerners in Montgomery was only the beginning of much more fundamental and disruptive challenges to the status quo than the MIA's proposed change in bus seating. The militant segregationists, if their tactics were unsuccessful, at least perceived this more readily than the mild-mannered segregationists, like editor Grover Hall, who argued in favor of accepting the boycott's mild demands in the hope of getting it over with.

The White Citizens' Council put an ad in the *Advertiser* a year later which summed up its position and its frustration: "There are only two sides in the Southern fight—those who want to maintain the Southern way of life or those who want to mix the races. . . . Whites must stand by whites just as Negroes are standing by Negroes. . . . There is no middle ground for moderation . . . that middle ground has been washed away by the actions of the NAACP in seeking to destroy the freedoms of the Southern white man."[70] This was typical of segregationist appeals. The WCC and other such organizations called for unity among the white people, in increasingly exasperated tones, because no such unity existed. The efforts of Crenshaw and Sellers were aimed at achieving unity through the political agency and authority of the local state. The conversion of all three city commissioners to WCC membership suggested that they were well on the way to achieving their goal.

Chaos and Conflict Bring the Middle to Compromise

Against such resistance, the good will and sympathy of the Durrs, Graetz, and Smiley, the occasional white carpool drivers, and even the financial contributions of perhaps hundreds of local white donors were not enough. The MIA needed access to the corridors of power, and a distinctly different type of white southerner was needed for that.

The Durrs, Graetz, and Smiley had put themselves outside the "power structure," which defined itself, in those instances in which the civil rights movement faced resistance, as the guardian of segregation. White southerners who turned against it were "traitors" and could not be expected to provide inroads that might lead to compromise, or even reliable information about what the leaders of the power structure were planning to do. Nor were white sympathizers who attended MIA meetings on the sly, or gave cash under the table, able to lend further help to the strategic aims of the movement, except perhaps as occasional sources of information, which they leaked deliberately or inadvertently to the movement planners. But such white sympathizers did not exhaust the white resources available to black protesters.

A different kind of white person who aided the movement's larger aims was typified by the Montgomery chapter of the Alabama Council on Human Relations. The ACHR, one of many state Human Relations Councils that operated in all the southern states, counseled its members (and all others who would listen) to engage in dialogue with the educated, well-dressed, and well-spoken black leaders who were eyed with suspicion by radical bigots as "uppity." The council asked the educated white leaders of the community to face racial "problems" and to urge upon their political representatives an open-minded course of negotiation and compromise with black representatives. The Human Relations Council did not ask its members to support the boycott; many members opposed it. The group was well positioned, however, to supply negotiators who could interpose themselves between the boycott leaders and the city officials who had locked horns with them.

It so happened that the rector of Mayor Gayle's church, Thomas Thrasher, a white Episcopal priest, was a member of the Montgomery chapter of the ACHR. Thrasher had racially liberal leanings, but he kept a low profile and never became publicly identified with the movement. All available evidence suggests he did not support the movement privately, either. He was, however, instrumental as a middleman between the city commissioners and the movement. The commissioners would not meet with the movement leaders on their own initiative; they had their reputation to maintain, after all, and they had their pride. But if a white minister —one well connected with the established clergy and civic groups and not identified with the black community or civil rights organizations in such a way as to cause his business and political connections to write him off (as Clifford Durr's had written him off)—set up negotiations aimed at ending the disruption of order and downtown business, they might forgive themselves for meeting with him.

That is what happened.[71] Of far greater significance here than the direct outcome of these negotiations—evidence of bad faith on the part of the city commissioners seems to explain adequately the failure to arrive at a negotiated settlement in Montgomery[72]—is the effect of the negotiations on public opinion. More important to the life of the movement than winning a concession per se was just getting its foot in the door with the city government, achieving an opening in the power structure.

That the city would, by whatever circuitous route, grant that the MIA was the legitimate representative of the black community, and would sit down to negotiate the economic future of downtown and the fate of the public transportation system with it, was the kind of coup that was vital to the legitimacy of the movement. And not just its legitimacy in white eyes. Maintaining mass support in the black community, and morale in the hardcore movement cadres, was a constant difficulty. To get people in the neighborhoods talking—these leaders are negotiating with *the mayor*— suddenly made the movement seem much more serious, and its ultimate victory much more plausible, to a generally and justifiably demoralized group of people who had no idea, in 1955 and 1956, how things were going to turn out. They had seen more than a hundred years of steps backward, of promises broken, of guaranteed rights ignored and abused with impunity, and a few years of opportunistic tokenism that seemed to reinforce rather than challenge the established pattern. They had seen upstart leaders and agitators challenge the system and fail.

Outflanking the ACHR was a group of white citizens who were even less committed to racial change. The white businessmen of Montgomery were vulnerable to the bad publicity that the movement and the segregationist response to it were generating, as well as to the direct economic effects of the boycott. Because they needed black dollars as much as they needed white ones, the businessmen needed a settlement, even at the risk of injuring their reputations as segregationists. They suspected that if businesses and buses began to desegregate, militant segregationists would not be able to muster the numbers or the party discipline to mobilize a counterboycott of the desegregated facilities; therefore they leaned toward appeasing their much more organized black customers. Thus businessmen tended to be unusually flexible, which is why boycott leaders made them a priority target.

Still, individual initiative (that is to say leadership) was hazardous; to become the *first* businessman to desegregate, whatever the predicted long-term economic logic of desegregation, was too risky a move for the typically risk-averse businessman. The boycott leaders could not depend on the white businesses to solve this problem on their own. They had to solve it for them, and force rather than suasion seemed the way. The task for a numerically inferior and resource-poor movement was to find a weak point in segregationist armor and pound away at it.

Although small businesses felt the economic effects of the boycott most directly, their fear of losing white customers led them to resist desegregation most rigidly. The larger industries felt the effects of national publicity more than the small ones. They needed northern capital, which was extremely gun-shy in the face of social upheaval. If bombs were going off night after night, transportation systems were on the verge of collapse, and local politicians were incapable of reaching a settlement, then outside investors would pick less newsworthy spots to spend their dollars. Big industries also depended on handouts from local and federal government, especially in the South, where industry was born late (relative to the North) and had the disadvantage of an underdeveloped infrastructure and an undereducated population (white as well as black). Booster clubs sprang up all over the South, to help the South catch up; they gave institutionalized expression to southern capital's collective inferiority complex. Booster clubs tended to make the business communities even more sensitive to bad publicity than the investors they were trying to attract.

In Montgomery, a booster club organized in October 1955, just over two months before the boycott, calling itself, modestly enough, the Men of Montgomery. The MOM, in the words of one contemporary observer, was a group that was "trying to bring industry to the city." The boycott was attracting precisely the wrong kind of attention. "They think this is giving Montgomery a bad name."[73] The MOM could be seen as the pragmatic, economic side of the religion- and psychology-oriented Human Relations Council. In fact, according to Graetz, the membership of the Human Relations Council was "mostly wives of white businessmen."[74]

King had no illusions about the motives of the Men of Montgomery. Though he granted that they were "men of good will who abhorred the increasing tension they saw around them," he made clear where he thought their efforts originated: "They had already begun to see the effects of the protest on trade, and realized that a prolonged conflict could be disastrous." They were not integrationists: "far from it. Some of them believed firmly in segregation, and even those who did not would probably have agreed with [the Reverend Henry] Parker [head of the mayor's negotiating committee] that the Negroes were 'pushing things too fast.'" Members of the Men of Montgomery met with members of the MIA in what King called "an earnest effort" to settle the conflict. King had no doubt that they would have come to a solution "had it not been for the recalcitrance of the city commission."[75]

More Help from the Die-hard Segregationists

But the encouragement the movement got from these middling whites still did not exhaust the white community's contribution to the black community's victory over segregation. The militant segregationists, ironically, helped embolden and solidify the movement's appeals to southern whites in general. The commissioners demonstrated their desire to polarize opinion by adopting a "get tough" policy shortly after they joined the WCC.

The first step toward getting tough was an attempt to put one over on the public: the commissioners announced on January 21 that they had reached a negotiated settlement with "representatives of the Negro community." This "settlement" amounted to the black "representatives'" endorsement of the terms the commission had been offering all along: in other words, no concessions to the boycotters. The commissioners had found three obscure black preachers from the backcountry who were willing, with some prompting, to sign on to such an "agreement," and got the *Advertiser* to report the news. The fabrication failed to convince the black masses. It should not be overlooked that, in their effort to try to convince those masses, the commissioners, despite a militant commitment to segregationism, demonstrated that they wanted the public to *believe* that they were willing to negotiate and settle. The fabrication of a settlement must thus be understood, at least in part, as a profession of moderation. That the effort backfired spectacularly should not draw attention from that intention.

The movement cleared up the misunderstanding with impressive efficiency. Taking the spurious settlement seriously, the MIA hierarchy got to the bottom of it through its contacts with the black clergy of the area. Even before the story appeared, the MIA chiefs located the three preachers, whose names the commissioners had not divulged to the press (reporter Carl Rowan had seen the story come over the wire in Minneapolis and immediately called King to check it out), and called them in for a meeting.

It turned out that three country preachers had been coaxed, under somewhat false pretenses, into agreeing to the commissioners' statement. They were just as easily uncoaxed by the movement leaders. That same night the MIA spread word of what had happened to all the black preachers and Graetz, who were thus prepared to discredit the story from their pulpits on the morning that it appeared in the *Advertiser*, a Sunday. That the buses remained completely empty the following Monday morning indicated a unanimous repudiation by the black masses; this was followed by formal retraction from the three black signatories of the city's statement at a press conference that afternoon. They had been "hood-winked," they told reporters.[76]

The whole episode came off as an insult to the black community and only hardened its resolve behind the boycott. In the process, it undermined white confidence in the segregationist leadership. The commission's demonstration of bad faith in the negotiations signified a general failure of intelligence on the part of the segregationists. They underestimated the organizational ability, solidarity, and popular appeal of the movement among local black people and in doing so undermined the strength of their own cause among local white people.

It is hard to say whether the failure to take the boycotters seriously was a simple product of racism or an independent mental shortcoming. What can be determined and what has great historical significance is that the most intelligent political strategists in southern society were not lined up in defense of segregation. There certainly were intelligent thinkers and political operators among the militant segregationists, but they were not the norm, and they seem to have been absent altogether in places like Montgomery.

The segregationist authorities in general assumed either that the blacks were contented with their lot or that they were too stupid, too weak, or too disorganized to do anything about it. These assumptions kept segregationists from making serious efforts to mobilize white opinion in defense of segregation, until the truth of black power caught up with them and it was too late. For example, the *Montgomery Advertiser* sent an investigative reporter to find out who was behind the MIA. He came back with a story on the one man who, being white, *must* be the mastermind. Thus Robert Graetz, a mild-mannered, soft-spoken pastor, whose flock seemed to be leading him more than he them, and whose public statements evinced a naiveté bordering on giddiness, appeared as a dynamic and tenacious strategist who had thrown the whole city into disorder. It was the kind of assumption that was necessary to maintain the myth that underlay white support for the status quo: our Negroes, for whom we have always presumed to speak, and whose true interests we understand better than Yankees and at times better than the Negroes themselves, are so contented that they would never protest on their own. Some evil genius, not of their own kind, must have led them astray.[77]

Similar assumptions lay behind the reports, printed in the papers, that black people were staying off the buses because "goon squads" were intimidating them. These reports, like those that focused on a white evil genius, drew attention away from the mass support that the protest actually had. These were variations on the theme of infiltration by "outside agitators"; something abnormal had only to be removed and everything would return to normal. These assumptions gave the MIA a tactical advantage: they kept the segregationists looking in all the wrong places while protesters organized themselves and kept a step ahead.

The assumption that 90 percent of the black passengers would return to the buses if not intimidated by goons gave the boycotters a more direct advantage: it led many white employers to drive their maids to carpool pickups, in the belief that they were protecting them from harm.[78] Black supporters of the boycott were not above allowing this assumption to flourish.

The commissioners' "get tough" policy brought police harassment of boycotters and supporters. As could be expected from any crackdown against such a large and diffuse form of defiance, enforcement was so haphazard that many innocents, including some white people, were detained. This further hardened the black resistance and thinned the ranks of segregationist support. On February 21, 1956, a Montgomery grand jury, empaneled as part of a secret investigation that had begun on January 11, indicted eighty-nine of Montgomery's most respected black leaders for violating an antiboycott law (an old antiunion measure passed in 1921 to fight Birmingham steelworkers). The eighty-nine indicted included twenty-four clergymen, one of whom was Martin Luther King.[79] The Human Relations Council expressed moderate whites' exasperation by commenting that King's arrest only sealed his "martyrdom."[80] This recognition must have eroded the white community's confidence in the ability of its leaders to handle themselves in a crisis; their efforts to restore order persistently had the opposite effect.

The "get tough" policy did not produce the closing of white ranks that the commissioners expected and needed but rather an open split. At this point the Men of Montgomery took their boldest initiative. They began almost daily meetings with the MIA leaders, and with the commissioners. The MOM said, in effect, let us tough-minded leaders who are capable of seeing the city's true long-term interests, unclouded by emotion and stubbornness, work things out in a practical way. The failure of these negotiations to produce a settlement (as with previous efforts arranged by the Human Relations Council) was less important than the immediate effect they had in legitimizing the MIA and discrediting the official posture of the city commission, which had announced on January 23 its refusal to meet anymore with the MIA.

The city commission, meanwhile, began to exhort the white masses to take a much more militant stance than they were willing to take. Mayor Gayle tried to goad the employers of domestics (a large proportion of bus passengers) by announcing that the disruption could end in one day if the white women would refuse to drive their maids back and forth to work. According to Virginia Durr, the reaction of the white women in Montgomery was, "If Tacky Gayle wants to nurse my children, if Tacky Gayle wants to wash my clothes, if Tacky Gayle wants to wash my dishes, if Tacky Gayle wants to clean my house, let him do it. In other words, they absolutely refused to give up their maids and they wouldn't listen to him." The movement leaders had no illusions about the innate goodness of people, white southerners or any others. They could make do turning the self-interests of others to their advantage. Durr did not think any of the white mistresses drove their maids "from any desire to help the boycott. They did it from the fact that they didn't want . . . to have to do their own work." So the mayor's injunctions "fell completely flat."[81] Perhaps at this point the movement no longer needed white people like Virginia Durr, who did have a desire to help the boycott. Between the trigger-happy city commission and the peace-seeking business boosters, the segregationist majority wore itself down to a beatable size. With enemies like that, who needed friends?

When the police started systematically arresting white women for transporting their maids, a few days later, they only added injury to insult. Next, Mayor Gayle appealed to white businessmen, trying to "get them to fire anybody that drove" or had anything to do with the boycott. "That also fell flat, because nobody wanted to give up their labor." Of course this de facto white opposition to the segregationists' policy required an elaborate justification, which the ranks of the black movement were only too happy to provide. The black and white women of Montgomery "carried on a kind of a game," Virginia Durr said. "The maids would tell their white mistresses that they didn't ride the bus because they were scared that the hoodlums would beat them up. . . . The white women said, 'well now of course *my* maid is not a part of the boycott.' And the maid, you know, would lie to her. And it was, you know, just this terrific game that went on." Underneath the game was the inescapable reality. The mutual dependence that gave southern black folks an intimate, strategic knowledge of their white folks also gave them a measure of direct power. The white people of Montgomery could not "give up the labor of the Negro community," Durr said. Segregationist solidarity "splintered on that rock. . . . If everybody fired everybody that was connected with the boycott, maybe they would have broken it, but they weren't willing."[82]

The few who were willing to make sacrifices for segregation inadvertently divided their ranks by increasing resort to guerrilla tactics. On January 30, 1956, someone threw a stick of dynamite on King's porch.[83] When King arrived at his house that night, Mayor Gayle and Commissioner Sellers were on the scene and getting increasingly nervous about the black crowd that had gathered in front of it. Both men expressed their regret to King that such an incident had taken place in their city. One of King's deacons, expressing a view widespread among the crowd, replied to the mayor, "You may express your regrets, but you must face the fact that your public statements created the atmosphere for this bombing. This is the end result of your 'get tough' policy." According to King, "Neither Mayor Gayle nor Commissioner Sellers could reply."[84] Two days later, someone threw a dynamite cap into E. D. Nixon's yard. If the city leaders were sincere in their condemnation of violence, they had lost control of their movement.

The bombings at once revealed the desperation and futility of the segregationist cause. The commissioners offered a reward for the names of the offenders. There was a certain duplicity here: in later public statements, the commissioners countenanced a segregationist rumor that the MIA itself had planted the bombs as media stunts to elicit financial aid from northern liberals. But such rumors remained at the level of hint and innuendo: Gayle and Sellers never could identify themselves publicly with bombing and other extralegal tactics.

The organization Gayle and Sellers had joined with such fanfare the month before, on the other hand, if it did not officially urge violence, did base its appeal on beliefs like those expressed in a pamphlet circulated among participants in a White Citizens' Council rally in February 1956: "When in the course of human events it becomes necessary to abolish the Negro race, proper methods should be used. Among these are guns, bow and arrows, slingshots and knives. We hold these truths to be self-evident: that all whites are created equal with certain rights; among these are life, liberty and the pursuit of dead niggers."[85] It was impossible for segregationist leaders to maintain their respectability except by dissociating themselves from such sentiments; that meant stern public denunciations of the perpetrators of violence and some convincing gestures at catching them as well. On the other hand, the leaders had to keep up some gestures of solidarity with the militant segregationists, which only added to the impression among voters that these leaders had no sense of direction, and probably to the impression among the respectable classes (white as well as black) that they were really winking at violence and lawlessness. No conspiracy cooked up in secret councils of the MIA could have been better calculated to divide the segregationist camp.

The segregationists' resort to desperate measures increased the commitment of the black community to the continuation of protest. One MIA board member said, "Our protest showed signs of weakening, but the bombings and the indictments came just in time to bring us back together."[86] Since all this took place, increasingly, before the eyes of the world, black protesters had an added incentive to maintain their resolve — out of responsibility to a larger cause, and concerns about their reputation.

At the same time, the "get tough" Montgomery police fatally began to alienate a national press, whose allegiance in the conflict was yet to be determined, by prohibiting a *Life* photographer from photographing a street scene of the boycott, telling him the scene was "not public property."[87] There began a whole train of abuses — mob attacks on cameramen and reporters, while police looked the other way, and in a few instances even helped out — which seemed all but deliberately designed to turn the national press against segregationism. Meanwhile, Montgomery police reported a marked drop in crimes and drunkenness among Negroes, and black pastors recorded an all-time high in church attendance. The press, eyes of the nation, could not help noticing.[88]

On the other side was a thin, but potentially growing, sympathy, which could be seen in parts of the white church. A *Time* magazine profile of Martin Luther King in early 1957 noted:

"Baptist King's impact has been felt by the influential white clergy, which could—if it would—help lead the South through a peaceful and orderly transitional period toward the integration that is inevitable. Explains [white] Baptist Minister Will Campbell, one-time chaplain at the University of Mississippi, now a Southern official of the National Council of Churches: "I know of very few white Southern ministers who aren't troubled and don't have admiration for King. They've become tortured souls." Says [white] Baptist Minister William Finlator of Raleigh, North Carolina: "King has been working on the guilty conscience of the South. If he can bring us to contrition, that is our hope."[89]

Important as such pangs of white conscience may have been, baser considerations were probably more important. When King told his followers, "We are not struggling merely for the rights of Negroes but for all the people of Montgomery, black and white," he did not envision a happy utopia of cooperative souls. His Christianity and his politics were grounded in the real world; the sins he fought were social sins, and the weapons he used were economic pressure and mass protest, held together by what could be called party discipline. He believed that white southerners held back their region by holding down their black neighbors. He believed that the violence, dishonesty, and miseducation of white people which were necessary to maintain white supremacy, hurt white people in material as well as spiritual ways.[90]

King and other leaders found reinforcement for that conviction in their relationships with white southerners throughout the boycott. The MOM and the *Advertiser*'s Grover Hall saw the indictments of virtually every prominent black leader in Montgomery in late January as above and beyond the call of sanity.[91] Bombings further alienated moderate white opinion, which held social peace in higher regard than segregation itself.[92] The bombs damaged more than the investment climate. They exploded in the homes of the upstanding, well-dressed black leaders who were well known to influential white leaders; one did not have to be a pacifist or a civil rights supporter to find this selection of targets counterproductive. The bomb that went off in the home of a white man, Graetz, broadcast the message that no white person who had given support to the boycott was safe. The "get tough" policy condemned even passive, innocent, or self-interested support.

A Pattern for Future Actions

The black movement's self-disciplined and dignified appeals to biblical and constitutional principles provided a stark contrast to the crassness and clumsiness of the segregationists. The White Citizens' Council forced a polarization by taking an extreme and often wildly impulsive position. That was a recipe for defeat. The movement leaders, recognizing the inbred conservatism of white southerners, knew their only hope was to appear on the opposite side of disorder. As the struggle continued and both sides became more determined, the movement became more disciplined and the segregationists became sloppier. That dynamic made it easier and easier for white southerners in the middle camp to slip over into sympathy for the protesters. Even those who did not slip over into sympathy had less and less confidence in the segregationist leaders, at a time when the segregationists demanded more and more polarization and closing of ranks.

That was the pattern Montgomery established. The black leaders and disciplined ranks would strike at a vulnerable point in the segregation system. A handful of white sympathizers would support them, usually in private, but in crucial instances in public also. Caught off guard, the militant segregationists would cast about for different tactics of response and usually find them insufficient. Frustration would drive them to intransigence and scattershot attacks that would scare away more allies than opponents. Competition for alternative leadership among white people would grow and exacerbate divisions in the segregationist ranks. "Compromise" leaders would emerge from "moderate" quarters of the white elite, and if these failed to settle the dispute, they certainly helped build the movement's hopes as they stole legitimacy from the segregationist leadership.

All these developments contributed to the feeling of futility that segregationism increasingly took on. The civil rights movement's action made it clear to enough white southerners that segregation — which their ancestors had adopted as a moderate measure to stave off social conflict — was not living up to its promise. That was not quite enough to kill the institution of segregation, but it was enough to hobble it — and the entire society built around it — to the point that the federal government, which alone had the power to kill the institution, could no longer avoid moving in. Most important, this process determined which side the federal government took when it did move in.

The future of the movement depended on adherence to that pattern. In Tallahassee and Little Rock, the pattern would hold. After that, it would face a severe test in Albany, Georgia, which showed that the pattern — which depended on black leaders' careful analysis, timing, and target selection — was not inevitable.

━━━━ 4

Tallahassee,
1956-1957

Before 1956, the black community of Tallahassee, Florida, had been quiescent. The local NAACP chapter was "small and weak," according to a study of the community done by two local sociologists, Charles Smith and Lewis Killian. In the wake of the *Brown* decision in 1954, some local black leaders joined white moderates in forming a Florida Council on Human Relations, which soon established an interracial unit in Tallahassee. But this group did little more than talk.[1]

The white community also appeared unconcerned about desegregation. Tallahassee, in the northern Florida black belt, was culturally part of the Deep South, in contrast to the southern part of the state, which had a very high concentration of nonsouthern migrants. But the segregationists, who like the moderates had organized in the wake of *Brown*, were no more active than the FCHR or NAACP chapters. The White Citizens' Council in Tallahassee was also "small and weak," and a Klan revival that had centered in Tallahassee for a few years after World War II had died out completely by 1952.[2]

Beneath the surface of organized activity, the same three-tiered pattern in white opinion that Martin Luther King had detected in Montgomery and elsewhere in the South seemed to exist in Tallahassee, as a series of opinion polls taken before the boycott illustrates. Of the white people polled, 11 percent said that *Brown* was a good decision and that Tallahassee should let black students into white schools immediately; another 11 percent said that *Brown* was a bad decision but that "we should start trying to let them in" anyway. Though a total of 84 percent of white Tallahasseeans said that *Brown* was a bad decision, only 17 percent recommended keeping black children out of schools even if doing so meant breaking the law. A total of 56 percent recommended that the city do all it could, within the law, to keep the schools segregated. (Five percent replied "other" or "don't know.")

The extreme segregationist element was probably not as large as this opinion survey would suggest. Those who recommended breaking the law probably aired more bluster than commitment to action: it was one thing to endorse breaking the law, another to follow handcuffed hooligans into the paddy wagon. Another survey, which asked respondents what they would do if they were on a bus in the North and a Negro sat down next to them, found that only 4 percent would order him to move to another seat. Even that tiny minority, according to the pollsters, seemed unwilling to break the law without at least the tacit support or acquiescence of public officials;[3] the ranks of lawbreakers among the segregationists would have been greatly thinned, it seems, had not law enforcement officials made it clear that the normal consequences of lawbreaking were suspended.

Conversely, the group at the other extreme, those supporting compliance with desegregation, seemed to be emboldened by initiatives of white political figures. The question "What would you do if a Negro sat next to you [on a bus in the North]?" asked the respondents to imagine themselves in a different world, where desegregation was already legal and an established fact. In that world, the legal authorities would be on the side of desegregation rather than segregation. Resistance to their authority would be futile and probably embarrassing. Twenty-six percent of white Tallahasseeans said they would not like a Negro sitting next to them but admitted they would not do anything about it. Again, the large middle (44 percent) took the perhaps unattractive but altogether harmless view that they would move to another seat themselves. Twenty-one percent said a black person sitting next to them would be "perfectly alright" with them. This last group corresponded roughly to the earlier survey's extreme left: the 11 percent that approved of *Brown* plus the 11 percent that disapproved but advocated letting black students into the schools anyway. More than a fifth of Tallahassee's white people were ripe for the appeals of the desegregation movement, and all but a smaller fraction were ready to acquiesce in its actions.

The civil rights movement in Tallahassee began by taking advantage of the legal legitimacy desegregation now had in the wake of the *Brown* decision, and before long, the more directly applicable decision on bus desegregation won by Montgomery protesters. White southerners who lived by law either had to abandon segregation laws or had to change the wording of the laws enough to conceal their purpose, a tactic that would inevitably attenuate the practice of segregation. The leadership of the state of Florida seemed at first to cooperate with desegregation, and adherence to the law was not its only reason. Political arithmetic made Florida different from most southern states. The absence of a literacy test, the abolition of the poll tax in 1937, and the highest level of urbanization of any southern state allowed registration of 48,157 black voters by 1946. In 1952 Florida had the highest percentage of its black voting-age population registered of the southern states. Blacks constituted about 15 percent of the voting-age population and 10 percent of the registered voters.[4] The presence of some competition from the Republican party magnified the presence of black voters.[5] Florida also had a large population of migrants from the North, in its modern cities and retirement centers, who presumably felt no deep commitment to legal segregation. Thus it seemed that political leadership could accommodate racial change at little political cost. Leaders in the state capital had called for a "calm moderate approach" to desegregation; "local leaders, both white and Negro, seemed to wait to take their cues from the leaders of the state," according to Smith and Killian.[6]

Unfortunately, fulfillment of the Court's mandate was not automatic. It required creative initiatives from local officials, and neither the Florida delegation in Congress, which included such old liberal mainstays as Claude Pepper (already a supporter of civil rights), nor the state leadership, headed by Governor LeRoy Collins, took any action to follow the Supreme Court's lead. The business community, the ministerial association, and the local intellectuals (professors at Florida State University, editors at the *Tallahassee Democrat*) provided no direction either; they remained largely silent on the desegregation issue.[7] This silence practically guaranteed the emergence of the kind of militant black leadership that had emerged in Montgomery.

On May 26, 1956, two students from the local black university, Florida Agricultural and Mechanical, refused a bus driver's order to give up their seats near the front of the bus. They had apparently been invited to take those seats by a white lady.[8] Yet they were arrested, and their protest immediately provoked an extreme segregationist reaction. The evening after their arrest, which got front-page coverage, one of the two students, Wilhelmina Jakes, opened her door to find a cross burning on her lawn. The following day, the president of the Florida A&M student government, citing the inspiration of the Montgomery boycott, called on his fellow students to "refrain from riding the city buses" for the rest of the semester. His listeners proceeded to block the next bus that drove through the campus and asked all black passengers to get off.[9]

The Reverend C. K. Steele, president of the local NAACP, called on black religious leaders to support the students' initiative. Those leaders met to form the Inter-Civic Council, an all-black, church-based organization. The ICC, supplanting the NAACP, provided the militant leadership and extensive organizational relationships necessary to finance and sustain a long boycott.[10]

Active White Southern Support

Soon after its formation, the ICC asked Glenn Smiley to give nonviolent training to the rank and file. Smiley, "answering the fire alarm," rushed into Tallahassee to repeat the training he had given King and others in Montgomery. The chairman of the ICC's transportation committee, the Reverend Daniel Speed, later recalled that the masses remained nonviolent because "some experts in nonviolent training" were there at all times. "One person in particular was Dr. Glenn Smiley. Glenn was the active chairman for the committee of the nonviolent group that talked to all of the various assemblies. When he didn't do it himself, somebody out of his committee would be there." Though Smiley believed that his being southern and white had little to do with his being chosen (by Rustin and King) to serve in this capacity, he said "it turned out to be helpful," since he knew the ways of the white folks from the inside.[11]

There were very few local white residents who sympathized with the protesters. With some exceptions, those who did, notably a small number of students and faculty at Florida State, were marginal to the life of the city. According to Glenda Rabby, author of the most thorough study of the Tallahassee boycott, "A few local white families outside of the University lent their monetary and vocal support to the civil rights struggle, usually at the price of social ostracization and, occasionally, of economic retaliation."[12] Once the boycott erupted, some of these whites contributed material aid. Dan Speed recalled that he had "about fourteen" white drivers helping him in the carpool. "I was very proud to have had some whites who were very nice. They would bring their hired help sometimes as far as certain streets and tell me where they were going to be and I'[d] have a car there or go myself. . . . I don't think I should forget that either."[13]

One local white family gave more direct aid. George Lewis, president of the Lewis State Bank, and his wife Clifton van Brundt Lewis, who both came from distinguished old families (Clifton's mother was one of the Byrds of Virginia), had grown up among Tallahassee's white elite. They kept their heads low. Before the bank opened in the morning, Lewis sneaked black leaders in to borrow money to finance the ICC's operations. Glenda Rabby comments, "Although both Clifton and George Lewis remain modest concerning their role in the Civil Rights Movement in Tallahassee, many blacks consider the monetary and moral support they provided an important contribution to the movement." The Lewises' stance cost them some business at the bank; without their family history and social connections, "they would have been literally run out of town," according to one local observer.[14] With the fourteen-odd white people who helped the carpool, the Lewises constituted the extreme group that aided the boycott directly and consistently.

The Middle's Weakness for Legality

Sympathizers like Smiley and the Lewises obviously did not represent the white community as a whole. The middle group, those who wanted to keep segregation but were unwilling to put up much of a fight, contained most of the leaders of the local power structure. From the beginning city officials revealed the weakness of their commitment to segregation. The police arrested the two students who touched off the boycott, not for breaking the segregation law, but for "putting themselves in a position to cause a riot." The evasiveness of this charge betrayed a reluctance to engage in legal battles over a supposedly sacred institution. The *Tallahassee Democrat* voiced the reluctance with greater clarity. The two arrested coeds "may have been impelled by a misunderstanding of what the United States Supreme Court ruled was their right in intra-state bus seating." They could hardly be blamed for what they did, considering that the Supreme Court was so "vague."[15] The unwillingness of legitimate authority to take a stand explicitly for segregation became clearer still when the city authorities dropped the charges against the two offenders and remanded them to the custody of their college president.

The city commission had been unprepared for a challenge to segregation; it now tried to meet the challenge by passing new laws. On July 25, 1956, it introduced an ordinance to outlaw carpools—an attempt to save segregation without mentioning it by name. When the Florida attorney general advised the commissioners that carpools were already illegal, they withdrew the ordinance. On August 25, ICC leaders C. K. Steele, Daniel Speed, K. S. DuPont, and eight others were arrested under a law requiring "for hire" tags on vehicles used for public transport. A month later, however, the city dropped those charges and arrested the executive committee of the ICC on the new charge of operating a transportation system without a franchise. If there was a clear pattern of harassment here, there was also a pattern of vacillation growing out of the attempt to find a plausible grounds for a legal defense of segregation.

Meanwhile, the boycott was costing the city a great deal. The city gave the faltering bus company a tax reduction and allowed it to raise fares on June 12, two weeks after the boycott began. Those measures failed. The bus company president publicly acknowledged that the boycott had led to the loss of 60 percent of the company's revenues. The bus company manager, Charles L. Carter, later testified that the boycott had caused profits to shrink from fifteen thousand dollars a month to nine thousand dollars a month.[16] At the end of the first month of the boycott, June 30, the company went out of business.[17]

To revive it, the Chamber of Commerce initiated a "Ride the Buses" campaign and declared the campaign a success when it had collected eight hundred dollars in voluntary contributions (this compared with twenty thousand dollars the ICC claimed to have in its legal defense fund). On August 2, the bus company started up service again with great fanfare. It assured police protection for black riders who would break the boycott. It passed out lapel buttons that read "I'm riding the bus, are you?" and offered not only free rides but free orange juice, coffee, and newspapers.[18]

It was a losing battle. These tawdry temptations to ride again, insulting enough to boycotters who had risked jail to stand on principle, also heightened their feeling that disciplined protest could force concessions from the other side. From the start, black passengers had been 60 to 70 percent of the bus company's clientele; at least 90 percent of black Tallahasseeans observed the boycott rigorously. The ICC saw the city's Ride the Bus campaign as nothing but a demonstration of the financial weakness of the bus company.[19] The bus company's counteroffensive, together with its concession in hiring two black drivers, only strengthened the boycotters' sense of power.[20]

Tallahassee officials, like their counterparts in Montgomery, underestimated the boycott's strength by attributing it to the work of outside agitators. An investigating committee of the state legislature, headed by the race- and red-baiting Charley Johns, investigated the ICC at the behest of city officials. The Johns committee spent its time trying to establish the NAACP connections of the boycott. The assumption that a northern organization, rather than local masses, was at work diverted the segregationist authorities from the true nature of the boycott. Even the moderate and often astute governor of Florida, LeRoy Collins, denounced the boycott leaders as "outsiders."[21] Such statements falsely reassured the defenders of segregation and left them unprepared for the determination and tenacity of protest.

The Divisive Tactics of the Extremists

A vacillating defense of segregation left the defenders vulnerable to attack, not only from the movement but also from extreme segregationists. When the Ku Klux Klan met outside Tallahassee on September 2, after making threatening gestures at the black leadership, its speakers denounced the *Tallahassee Democrat* and Governor Collins for their "moderation."[22] Such attempts to enforce white solidarity only made the illusion of white solidarity more difficult to maintain.

The boycotters, for their part, showed little readiness to quit. In response to the October 20 conviction and sentencing of the entire ICC executive committee, the ICC officially discontinued the carpool, but a covert, unofficial carpool straggled along, while the visible boycott continued on foot and bicycle.[23] When the U.S. Supreme Court ruled (on November 13, 1956) that intrastate bus segregation in Montgomery was unconstitutional, the ICC decided to declare a victory. After taking a vote at an ICC mass meeting, Steele announced on December 22 that the boycott was over and that black people would return to riding the buses, unsegregated, the day before Christmas. He urged black riders to turn the other cheek if attacked, and he handed them detailed instructions (modeled on those used in Montgomery) on how, exactly, to do that. He called on the city to assist in maintaining order.[24]

The next day, however, Mayor John Humphress asked both races to cooperate with the city in maintaining segregation. He indicated a lack of confidence in the loyalty of his principal ally by calling on the bus company for help: the bus company had shown no inclination to abandon segregation before, but its willingness to flout the Supreme Court could not be assumed. It was time to close ranks. Two days later, the city commission held an emergency session at which it ordered the company to enforce segregation—on just what legal basis was not clear. On December 26, the city commissioners suspended the company's operating franchise because, they said, Negroes were making efforts to integrate its operations. The bus company announced that it would not respect the suspension. On December 27 the City reacted by arresting not black passengers but the bus company manager, who had previously been one of the principal spokesmen for segregation, and nine bus drivers.

That night federal judge Dozier DeVane, as if called to duty by the confusion of local authority, issued from his home a restraining order forbidding interference with integration on the buses. He also made known his personal opinion that "every segregation act of every state or city [was] dead as a doornail."[25] Judge DeVane was a native Floridian who, after serving as solicitor for the Federal Power Commission, was nominated to the Federal Court for the Northern District of Florida by FDR in 1943. Like most Democrats, he was a staunch believer in states' rights. Nearing retirement in late 1957, he said that all his years on the bench had not changed to any extent his views "as to the rights of the states under the United States Constitution." In later years as a circuit court of appeals judge, DeVane was to be the lone dissenter from the majority opinion ordering James Meredith's admission to the University of Mississippi in 1962. In Meredith's case, DeVane went beyond upholding states' rights, offering gratuitous agreement with the Ole Miss registrar's assessment of the plaintiff's character: Meredith, DeVane said, "bore all the characteristics of becoming a troublemaker."[26]

Throughout his career, DeVane ruled many times that state segregation laws were legitimate, despite federal orders against segregation. Still, he understood that in the Tallahassee case in 1956, the legitimacy of the segregation laws was too thin to allow him to uphold them. Florida's supreme court had elaborated a strong segregationist doctrine — stating, for instance, that "when God created man, he allotted each race to his own continent according to color, Europe to the white man, Asia to the yellow man, Africa to the black man, and America to the red man" — and had already refused three direct orders from the U.S. Supreme Court to stop delaying desegregation in Florida. But it had always justified its delaying actions on the narrow grounds of a state's right to maintain order, implicitly conceding the substantive issue that there was no state right to maintain segregation itself.[27] DeVane therefore had no basis for upholding a state right to segregation.

A Reluctant Moderate Governor Loses His Reluctance

On December 31, Governor LeRoy Collins intervened, intimating that local authority had abdicated. Using emergency powers recently granted to him by the Florida legislature, he suspended bus service. It did not improve the city commission's image that Collins justified the suspension by referring to threats of violence and vandalism. Collins left the impression that imminent lawlessness had brought a reluctant governor to interfere in local affairs, that local authorities were not competent to maintain order.

The aimlessness of Tallahassee's white leadership, as much as its evident inability to preserve segregation, seemed to encourage vigilantism, which further alienated middle-road sentiment in the city. A wave of brick and rock throwing, shotgun blasts, and car smashing began on New Year's Eve. Just after New Year's, a cross was burned on the lawn of Steele's church.[28] The city commission, still searching for a way to preserve segregation without using the word *segregation,* passed a new "seat assignment" law while the buses were still under suspension. The new law gave bus drivers the authority to tell passengers where to sit; it explicitly forbade consideration of race but allowed such considerations as public health, maintenance of order, and proper distribution of weight on the bus.[29] Such loophole spinning could not have been very reassuring to those who held segregation to be a fundamental principle.

The conflict between the bus company and the city continued, with all the fierceness and futility of a family feud, in the courts. Early in January, the bus company sued the city for $100,000 in damages and sought a permanent injunction against interference in its operation. The city countersued, hoping to gain clarification of the segregation act, which — even before the legal challenges to it — the city had shrunk from invoking in its arrests of the boycotters. Both suits were then dropped, as were the city's charges against the nine bus drivers and their manager.

With violence in the streets and bickering and dickering in the city government, the ICC could plausibly portray itself as the only force for law and order. It called on Collins to restore bus service under "effective and forthright law enforcement." These words must have struck a chord in those white citizens who wanted to see an end to violence and disorder and recognized that segregation, whatever its merits, was a lost cause.

Not least among such white citizens, as the ICC knew, was Governor Collins himself, an opponent of desegregation who had nevertheless gained a reputation as a racial moderate among southern politicians.[30] In March

1956, Collins had faced a militant segregationist in a single-issue campaign. He became more vocal in his support of segregation: "We are just as determined as any other southern state to maintain segregation," Collins said. "But," he added significantly, "we will do so by lawful and peaceful means." He denounced his opponent, Sumter Lowry, as a "one-track candidate" given to "buffoonery and demagoguery." Collins refused to have his state "torn asunder by rioting and disorder and violence and the sort of thing that [Lowry] is seeking to invite."[31] The Florida Council on Human Relations gave an "unprecedented endorsement" to Collins in 1956, because of "Governor Collins' continued emphasis upon not circumventing the law, and his refusal to become part of the emotional atmosphere."[32] According to Earl Black, Collins created "abstract respect for the *Brown* decision as the law of the land," even though he did not at any time encourage actual desegregation. Collins won, with strong majorities in the urban areas associated with racial liberalism (and, in Florida, with high concentrations of northern migrants) and a plurality of the rural areas that had low black populations, though he lost the traditionally segregationist black-belt counties.[33]

When the boycott began two months later, in May 1956, Collins, who had grown up in Tallahassee, shied away from involvement in what he called a "local" dispute—despite the importance of local transportation and commerce to state administration (Tallahassee is the state capital). In July 1956, he told reporters that the boycott leaders, sponsored by "outsiders" and the NAACP, were pushing too hard too fast. He said the protest was a "miscarriage of ambition" on the part of "short-sighted and unreasonable" Negroes.[34] Though these statements encouraged the bus company to resist the boycott, they also angered the protesters and strengthened their resolve.[35] Collins avoided involvement until the disorder and demagoguery he had campaigned against in 1956 grew too powerful to ignore.

The Inter-Civic Council and the White Citizens' Council pushed Collins into a corner. The ICC, having abandoned its boycott, called on the governor to restore order. Then, on the day Collins suspended bus service, the WCC asked him to seize the buses to protect segregation. This was a crafty move: by asking the governor to suspend service, the WCC made Collins' suspension—which he and the *Tallahassee Democrat* saw as a move to restore order[36]—appear to be a victory for segregation. As the *Democrat* had complained since July, the protesters "wiped out the middle ground. They . . . left no room for the moderate."[37]

Collins began moving toward the position he would later take as a leading southern moderate — "Liberal Leroy," the only governor to endorse, though in a qualified way, the sit-ins in his state in 1960.[38] On January 8, 1957, he made his inauguration speech. White people, he said, had to recognize that black people did not enjoy the equal opportunity supposedly guaranteed them by the laws. He was convinced that the average white citizen did not object to non-segregated seating on a bus any more than he objected to "riding in the elevators or patronizing the same stores." The same average white citizen, quite understandably, did resent "some of the methods used to achieve certain ends." But Collins asked Floridians to start "being honest" with themselves and recognize realities. "Man's greatest failures have come when he has refused to admit the reality of a changed situation. We should admit that our attitude toward the black populace generally in the past has been obstructive all along the line." It was the first time Collins himself had admitted it.[39]

Collins made good on his statement about equal opportunities for black citizens when on January 11 he lifted the bus company's suspension order to allow for a "good will" test. The ICC urged black people to ride, provided that they be allowed to do so on a "democratic" (i.e., integrated) basis. The buses returned to service on January 12 without incident. Elsewhere in Tallahassee, the violence that had broken out after the new year continued, but more sporadically than at first.

After Collins indicated the direction leadership would henceforth have to take, there were other signs of a reassertion of local authority. On January 15, police chief Frank Stoutamire announced that he was going to "put a stop" to the stoning and shooting of Negroes and their property. "I don't stand for that sort of thing," he told the press. "That's not my kind of law enforcement." On January 18, Governor Collins announced that he would step in to restore order if local law enforcement officials did not take positive action to halt the violence. Shortly after that, Chief Stoutamire brought in eleven white youths rumored to know something about the acts of violence. He made no arrests. He merely warned and lectured the youths, but the violence came to a halt soon after.[40]

The Position of the Moderate Politician

The tide was turning in favor of the ICC. The new official support for law and order, a partial victory for the boycott, emboldened white people who sympathized with the movement. By this time some thirty white supporters were regularly attending ICC meetings.[41] There was still a price for defiance, however. On January 20 two white students and one white employee of the State Road Department joined three black students for a "sightseeing ride" to test the desegregation order. Two of the black students and one of the white ones were arrested under the seat assignment ordinance (which had passed on January 7). They were given the maximum sentence of sixty days in jail and five-hundred-dollar fines and subpoenaed to appear before the anticommunist special investigating committee of the Florida legislature, headed by arch-segregationist Charley Johns.[42] Judge DeVane called the seat assignment law a "subterfuge" and called upon the federal courts to declare it unconstitutional. But he declined to intervene in the case.[43]

Because of the political strength of black voters in Florida, nearly all of whom told opinion pollers that they supported desegregation, Collins was in a more precarious position than Governors Ross Barnett of Mississippi and George Wallace of Alabama, who interposed themselves to prevent the integration of their respective state universities in 1962 and 1963. Governor Collins had to adopt a more flexible stance on segregation. In Mississippi and Alabama in those days, disfranchisement of black people was nearly complete and two-party competition did not exist. In Florida, by contrast, the GOP's division of the "white" vote made the small percentage of black voters decisive — potentially as decisive as in the liberal northern states — and therefore gave Collins' Democrats a strong incentive to make statements in support of black demands.

Not just any Florida Democrat would follow that incentive. It took a politician with national ambitions to buck the local Democracy, and segregationists rarely had national ambitions (George Wallace being the outstanding exception). The Republican threat in Florida was still confined almost exclusively to "presidential Republicanism": state and local politicians rarely faced Republican competition at the polls, and thus they did not see the black vote as a serious threat. Yet segregationists alienated the national party (including the southerners within it who desired national positions) by failing to deliver their state consistently in the Electoral College. For the local candidates, segregationism was still a safe position, yet for candidates who needed to maintain good relations with the national party, it was becoming more and more dangerous.[44] Collins was in the latter category. He may have been driven by a growing sense of racial justice too, but only by associating himself with the national rather than the local Democrats could he hope to keep that sense from driving him to political ruin.

Though Collins, in Smith and Killian's words, "recognized the inevitability" of change in Tallahassee, or in C. K. Steele's, "went through a normal process of growth and change," he never condoned direct action. Such methods as "boycotts, ultimatums," and the like were ineffective as well as counterproductive, he argued, and could not do what "persuasion, peaceful petitions, and normal judicial procedures" could do for the Negro.[45] Though few segregationists in Tallahassee could have recognized it, Collins was taking precisely the line that the NAACP—which the Johns committee had been trying, against Collins' vetoes, to ban—was taking in opposition to direct-action organizations like the ICC. Collins called upon his fellow white Floridians to recognize "realities" and admit that their attitude generally in the past had been "obstructive all along the line."[46] By May 1958, after two years of attrition warfare, all the legal and illegal resistance to desegregation of the Tallahassee buses had ended, and the system was fully desegregated.[47]

In Tallahassee, as nowhere else, the governor's leadership aided the settlement of the protest in favor of desegregation. But Collins was just another would-be white moderate who waited until the power of the civil rights movement made moderation possible. Others like him existed all over the South, and the movement used them elsewhere to achieve its ends. It had to use them very skillfully, for the position they were in was always a precarious one.

Little Rock,
1957-1959

T he biggest difference between the capital cities of Little Rock and Tallahassee was the governor who sat in each city's statehouse. For a
while it looked as though Governor Orval E. Faubus of Arkansas would
follow the moderate route of Governor Collins of Florida. Like Collins,
Faubus said he supported segregation but pledged to maintain it only "in a
calm, orderly, thoughtful and completely legal manner."[1] Faubus also had
shown signs of mild integrationism. One of his first acts after being elected
governor in 1954 was to expand the state Democratic Committee to
include six black members. Subsequently, he met with the presidents of
colleges in the state to advise them to desegregate. By 1957, most of them
had done so, without any fanfare or violence. Following the precedent of
his mentor Sid McMath (governor, 1948–52), under whom Faubus served
as administrative assistant and then as state highway director, Faubus
appointed black men to state boards and commissions; Faubus appointed
more black officials than any previous governor.[2]

The black lawyer who was to lead the legal battle against Faubus,
Wiley Branton, and the white liberal editor who gained a reputation (and a
Pulitzer Prize) as a leading southern integrationist in the years of the Little
Rock crisis, Harry Ashmore of the *Arkansas Gazette*, supported Faubus for
reelection in 1956.[3] The challenger was Jim Johnson, a militant racist who
accused Faubus of being "soft" on integration, and who said his first act as
governor would be to replace the six black members Faubus had appointed
to the state Democratic Committee. Faubus denounced Johnson as "a
meringue-headed demagogue," a professional "purveyor of hate," and a

"willing mouthpiece" for a "handful of vicious men . . . for whom the stirring up of strife and racial hatreds and tension [was] a cheerful past-time."[4] At the time of the desegregation crisis that made Faubus famous, his son was attending an integrated college.[5]

Moderate Leaders Initiate Desegregation

In leaning toward integrationism, Faubus was leaning away from the established habits of Arkansas politics. Faubus's victory over Johnson aside, the statewide contests were still generally dominated by segregationists, typified by Senator John McClellan, who referred to the Supreme Court of the *Brown* case as "nine men lacking in judicial capacity."[6] Leaders of the capital city, however, leaned even further toward integrationism than the upcountry governor. With the support of the local newspaper and the mayor, Little Rock's elected superintendent of schools, Virgil Blossom, attached his name to the plan to desegregate the Little Rock schools voluntarily and gradually, starting at the top with one of Little Rock's three high schools.

The Blossom Plan aimed to put as little strain as possible on Little Rock's school system. Blossom wanted to start with a high school because he believed that the parents who fought desegregation were invariably those who had little children in school, and because the high school system contained the smallest number of schools and the smallest number of students. In making his plan purely voluntary, he assumed that only a small number of black high school students would go to all the trouble of moving away from their friends. Those who did volunteer would go on a trial basis only, for the first stage of the plan, which was to last at least two years. If the first stage went well, Blossom's plan would extend small-scale, voluntary desegregation to junior high schools, and two or three years later, elementary schools. At all times, pupils who did not want to stay in the integrated schools would be permitted to transfer to other schools: at no time did the plan contemplate the disappearance of all-white schools within a desegregated district.[7]

This plan fit the general trend of reform led by business and professional people who wanted to attract new businesses and investment dollars to their city in competition with other cities. In 1952 the Chamber of Commerce created an industrial district on the outskirts of Little Rock, designed to attract northern capital with land grants, tax breaks, and other subsidies. Winthrop Rockefeller told the Little Rock Women's Republican Club in 1956, "Big industry is shying away from Southern states," because they were defying the federal government on segregation.[8] The federal government was directly involved in Little Rock's economic growth: the successful effort to attract a major air force base to the area was a boon to industrial development. The base provided free job training as well as payrolls and local construction and supply contracts. As an outpost of the recently desegregated air force, the base made a dent in the institution of segregation. Businessmen might have debated whether that institution theoretically impeded economic growth by inhibiting the free play of the market, but none could deny the direct association of integration with the receipt of federal military funds. The enthusiastic welcome the base received from the business leadership of Little Rock signaled that these men had no special attachment to segregation, as long as some advantage could be gained in giving it up.

That did not mean, of course, any positive enthusiasm for desegregation. In fact, the business elite of Little Rock has been faulted for imposing desegregation on the children of the working class and avoiding it themselves by creating desegregation plans that focused on the inner city while the elite kept its own children in suburban or private schools.[9] In a March 1957 school board election that amounted to a referendum on the Blossom Plan, opposition came from a minority (about one-third of all voters) concentrated in the working-class wards of the city, which opposed the business elite on many grounds and might have seen the Blossom Plan as a form of class legislation.[10] From the start, the struggle over segregation in Little Rock was not merely black against white but one kind of white person against another.

While Governor Faubus did not identify strictly with either kind of white person in Little Rock, he was clearly alienated from the business-reform leadership. He was from the hill country. Like his former boss Sid McMath, and not unlike Huey Long, he devoted himself to opposing the Arkansas Light and Power Company, which dominated Arkansas politics the way Standard Oil dominated Louisiana.[11] McMath's main campaign issue had been rich against poor; he championed the small farmer and the worker against the plantation landlord and the banker. Faubus followed this example. He had been raised to be as suspicious of the Little Rock business elite as he was of segregationist demagogues.

To one who was sympathetic to the business-reform leadership in

Little Rock, *Gazette* editor Harry Ashmore, who became one of Faubus's strongest critics, the important thing was that

> Orval could never stand to be looked down upon. As an unexpected tenant of the Governor's Mansion he had ample reason to feel that the Little Rock establishment resented his populist assault on [previous governor] Francis Cherry, and tended to write him off as a rude demagogue. He suspected that liberal Democrats, who should have been his political allies, didn't take him seriously. He saw, correctly, that when the Blossom Plan worked through to its conclusion the affluent whites in the suburbs would be largely exempt from integrated schools while the working class whites in the downtown section would have to send their children to class with blacks.[12]

If Faubus had shown stronger signs of favoring desegregation than any of the other politicians in the state, he might still have been tempted here by the opportunity to get back at the rich elite and to tap into the voting strength of the urban working class of Little Rock, who had as much reason to resent the elite of Pulaski Heights as his own upcountry folk did.

Thus it was anybody's guess where Faubus would come down on the desegregation question in Little Rock. Despite his appointment of black men to state office and his opposition to racist campaign tactics, Faubus had stated in March 1956 that the people of his state were "overwhelmingly" opposed to "sudden and complete" integration and that time was "absolutely necessary to allow the citizens to cope."[13] If there was any sign here of his later challenge to the federal courts, he was throwing down the gauntlet in a most gingerly manner. Coupled with his earlier statement that he would uphold segregation only legally and calmly, this kind of hedging about "time" sounded like the face-saving device that many a southern politician had set up for himself: he had desegregation forced upon him by higher powers, against his will and better judgment, and it was all he could do to minimize the shock of the inevitable. Although this line expresses segregationist sentiment, it is, as we have seen, substantially the position of those forces in town who had formulated and were identified with the integration plan.

A White Population Prepared for Desegregation

Despite his later reputation as a champion of last-ditch, fire-eating segregationism, Faubus was never demagogic or incendiary in his rhetoric. He was tentative, even wishy-washy, in the days leading up to the confrontation at Central High. He was, after all, a pioneer in massive resistance, the first southern leader to face federal troops since Reconstruction, and he was a reluctant candidate for that role. He had no idea which way the South, or even his own voters, would go. He evinced the schizophrenic quality of massive resistance: he had to present himself as a calm, rational defender of constitutional tradition against carpetbagging intrusions from Washington and the black ghettoes. He also had to grandstand, to provide an emotional outlet for the frustrations of white southerners, especially the economically insecure ones who needed reassurances and scapegoats.

As if unaffected by the governor's March 1956 statement of opposition to rapid desegregation, Faubus's state witnessed desegregation in several places that year and the following year. In April 1956, for example, Little Rock's bus system desegregated, as did that of North Little Rock, the city on the capital's northern border. The mayors of the two cities simply stated that henceforth the police would "pay no attention" to mixed seating, and none of the protest that brought Montgomery and Tallahassee to a standstill occurred.[14] Most of the Little Rock eating establishments quietly desegregated as well. Even the public schools, which tended to occasion more resistance than transportation or commerce, began to desegregate in the state. Before the clash at Central High, Arkansas had more public school districts desegregated than nine other southern states combined; the only former Confederate state that had more desegregated schools than Arkansas was Texas.[15]

There were indications that white opinion would not be hostile to continuation of this trend. Not only the *Gazette* but the much more conservative *Arkansas Democrat* had endorsed the Blossom Plan by August 1957.[16] Private groups gave indications of the depth and breadth of white acceptance of desegregation. The State Disciples of Christ resolved in April 1956 to "exert efforts toward orderly compliance" with court orders and called upon political candidates to refrain from centering the upcoming campaign on issues that divided one race from the other and tended to "fan the flames of fear and hatred." Earlier that year, the Methodist Women's Society of Little Rock formed a committee of "Christian citizens of integrity of both races" to recommend ways to guide the people of their state in "lessening racial tensions" in many areas of their common life. On April 23, Little Rock's white Ministerial Alliance approved a proposal to merge with its black counterpart, the Interdenominational Ministerial Alliance, which had approved the same proposal on April 9. The merger involved sixty white and thirty black ministers. The local Council on

Human Relations formed ten biracial teams of preachers, which in January 1957 began to travel around the state to speak to any church group that would listen about race relations and presumably smooth the way toward compliance with desegregation.[17] White businessmen and civic groups underwrote Blossom's plan as the quiet, gradual way to avoid conflict and bad publicity. Especially prominent in this regard was the Committee of 100, a group like the Men of Montgomery which formed to promote economic development.[18]

White opinion from other positions of authority carried more weight. In August 1956, Judge John E. Miller of the Federal District Court for East Arkansas rejected a challenge from NAACP lawyers to implement the desegregation plan more speedily. But his opinion probably strengthened the Blossom Plan by reinforcing its image as a white, moderate program that "radicals" in the NAACP did not find sufficiently strong. Wiley Branton (the third black graduate of the University of Arkansas Law School and chief NAACP lawyer in the case) stated in April 1957, when the federal appeals court at St. Louis upheld Judge Miller's verdict, that although the courts had ruled against him, their opinions still gave integrationists "a cloak of protection against some of the hard, anti-integration groups who might still try to delay integration."[19] Most tellingly, when the Citizens' Council asked Faubus in July 1957 directly to "interpose" himself against the impending desegregation of Central High, the governor rebuffed it, saying, "Everyone knows no state's laws supersede a federal law."[20]

Of course there were strong signs of segregationist resistance. In April 1956, one Methodist church in Little Rock publicly dissociated itself from other southern Methodist groups that had gone on record against segregation. The white Baptists who spoke out were almost unanimous in their opposition to desegregation. The American Baptist Association (some three thousand churches in twenty-four states, most of them in the South, not to be confused with the Southern Baptist Convention, some thirty thousand churches) was particularly adamant. On June 27, 1956, the ABA adopted a resolution, drafted by the pastor of Little Rock's Antioch Baptist Church, condemning integration as not only ungodly but unlawful, and something that most southern Negroes opposed. In November 1956, Arkansas voters, though they rejected the extreme segregationist gubernatorial candidate, approved three segregationist resolutions.[21]

Even in approving these resolutions, however, the voters revealed how divided they were. Those who endorsed strictly legal efforts to save segregation outnumbered desegregationists by two to one, but the majority endorsing defiance of the law was much smaller, only outnumbering those who rejected defiance by 13 percent Some of the defiant segregationists organized to increase their strength. The Capital Citizens' Council, emboldened by the growing controversy, began to attract more than the accustomed handful to its meetings. In the late summer of 1957, under the name Mothers' League of Central High, a women's auxiliary to the CCC formed and tried to steer opinion against desegregation. One Citizens' Council leader vowed in June 1957 that there would be "hell on the border" if integration occurred in Little Rock that fall.[22] That was precisely what the school board and business leaders wanted to avoid.

Governor Faubus Takes His Stand

The school board bent over backward to try to lure as many segregationists as possible away from defiance. A little more than a month before the first day of school, in response to baiting from segregationist leaders who asked whether black students would be admitted to school dances as well as classrooms, the school board gave out a written statement saying, "Social functions which involve race mixing will not be held" and "Teachers can and will avoid situations such as love scenes in class plays featuring students of different races."[23]

Segregationists, seeking a local white scapegoat, turned on Faubus.[24] As elsewhere, the segregationists preferred to ignore the real prointegration forces in Little Rock, the local NAACP president Daisy Bates and her husband, editor of the local black newspaper: to focus on them would be to concede that local black folks, rather than outsiders, were the force behind change. Faubus was a doubly tempting target because segregationist baiting might convert him to the cause, which lacked direction and desperately needed legitimacy. In late August two of the Citizens' Council's leading heroes flew into Arkansas (again revealing the hypocrisy of its opposition to "outside agitators"): Governor Marvin Griffin of Georgia and WCC leader Roy Harris. Faubus telephoned them and, after securing their assurance that they would refrain from inflammatory speeches, invited them to spend the night at the Governor's Mansion. This invitation was a surprise because the segregationists had been attacking Faubus, but it did not change Faubus's reputation as soft on integration. Roy Harris said,

> We had to accept Faubus' invitation to stay at the Mansion, but we had to apologize to the [Citizens'] Council folks for staying there. When we got to

the airport there at Little Rock, Marv went over and greeted the Governor's delegation—the state troopers and all—and that gave me time to get to one side with *our* people. I apologized and told 'em that Marv figured it was just courtesy to accept another governor's invitation, and that being discourteous wouldn't do any good. And then I told 'em, "Why, having us two there at the Mansion's the worst thing could happen to Faubus. It'll ruin him with the integrationists and liberals." And they said, "We never thought of it that way. That's fine."[25]

The segregationists made it clear that they needed Faubus, and for a time it seemed that they needed him more than he needed them.

Faubus had one more force to contend with: the federal government. His earlier stance against the Citizens' Council consisted of a scolding and peremptory observation, "Everyone knows no state's laws supersede a federal law."[26] He knew that any defiance in Arkansas, whether he was directly implicated in it or not, would test the federal government's resolve. State forces were surely outgunned. Avoiding a showdown was therefore paramount: Faubus knew that much of the defiance mouthed by Griffin and the others was bluff. On the other hand, he also knew that the federal government in the 1950s (indeed, since Redemption) was not inclined to call the bluff, and that gave him a certain amount of room to maneuver. However unequivocal and revolutionary the federal courts' orders were, testing and taunting those who were supposed to enforce the orders seemed to be a safe political game.

When Faubus shifted toward defiance of federal authority, he did not do so in the name of segregation. He insisted that his aim was to preserve local peace.[27] If this justification seems disingenuous, a more candid segregationism was hard to find in Arkansas in 1957. After the Griffin-Harris visit on August 22, Faubus encouraged the Mothers' League of Central High to sue for an injunction against desegregation in the chancery court, which they did on August 29. Volunteering to testify in favor of that injunction, Faubus did not make any statements about the purity of the white race or the sanctity of states' rights. Rather, he spoke of increased sales of knives and revolvers to students. He said he had personal knowledge that some students, black and white, had recently had revolvers confiscated from them; "violence and bloodshed and riots" would result if the schools were desegregated that fall.

Faubus's statements in court were the first concrete indications of the stance he would take. The *Gazette* editor the next day wrote that Faubus had "abjectly surrendered" to the White Citizens' Council's pressure. The WCC strategy had paid off, Ashmore wrote. Now that "it was no longer possible to continue straddling the fence," Faubus had fallen on the wrong side.[28] Faubus explicitly credited outside pressure for his move toward the die-hard camp: "In my judgment the sentiment within the past three weeks has changed." He said "one thing that triggered" the change was Georgia governor Marvin Griffin's August 22 speech to the Capital Citizens' Council: "People are coming to me and saying if Georgia doesn't have integration, why does Arkansas have it?" Chancery court judge Murray O. Reed ruled in favor of Faubus and ordered an injunction against immediate desegregation.[29]

Other white leaders, at the highest levels of local government, dissociated themselves from Faubus as soon as he took the plunge against the Blossom Plan. The school board immediately appealed Judge Reed's injunction in federal court. Police chief Marvin Potts, when asked about the governor's testimony on knives and revolvers, stated that his men had found no evidence of any planned violence. Potts said, "Let's say I haven't heard what Governor Faubus says he has heard." School superintendent Blossom said the same was true of other police intelligence, including that of the FBI (whose agents were present in such numbers in Little Rock as to put a strain on hotel accommodations).[30]

Just who in Little Rock had confiscated the students' revolvers, if not the police or school authorities, Faubus never made clear. That did not stop chancery judge Reed from issuing his injunction, but federal judge Ronald Davies threw out Judge Reed's injunction the next day.[31] The way was now clear for desegregation. All legal avenues of opposition had been closed off. Faubus's effort appeared feeble and unsuccessful—too little, too late.

On the eve of the opening of school, the *Gazette* drew back from its attack on Faubus. Aiming at the unconverted middle, it made a more oblique attack on prophets of violence. In a front-page editorial calling for acceptance of the now-inevitable entry of a small number of black students on September 4, the *Gazette* separated itself from those who predicted violence. "They have, we believe, too little faith in the respect of our people for law and order." The editor allowed, "Few of us are entirely happy over the necessary developments in the wake of changes in the law," but he went on to add, "We must recognize that the school board is simply carrying out its clear duty—and is doing so in the ultimate best interests of all the school children of Little Rock, white and colored alike."[32] The *Gazette* played on respect for tradition and concern about the city's "image." Its parting shot expressed confidence that the citizens of Little Rock would demonstrate on the opening day of school "for the world to see" that they were "a law abiding people." The paper also tried to soft-pedal the impending "integration" as a "limited, gradual" integration of only fifteen black students (this number was soon reduced to nine) at only one school in town, and as a resolution of a painful conflict between state and federal laws, which could now at last be put behind them forever. But the main point was that it was not necessary to *like* integration in order to lean away from Faubus.

Winthrop Rockefeller, whom Faubus had appointed chairman of the Arkansas Industrial Development Commission, visited Faubus after Faubus's testimony in chancery court to plead with him not to interfere with admission of the black children to Central High. Faubus reportedly told him, "I'm sorry, but I'm already committed. I'm going to run for a third term, and if I don't do this Jim Johnson and Bruce Bennet [state attorney general and segregationist] will tear me to shreds."[33] The segregationists, however, were still uncertain about his stance. His testimony in the chancery court, and the earlier hospitality to Harris and Griffin, were weak and ambiguous signals of support. At best Faubus was a Johnny-come-lately to segregationism; a generally paranoid movement demanded much more unequivocal signs of support than the governor of Arkansas felt free to give.

When Faubus suddenly called in his National Guard on the morning school opened, eight of the nine students scheduled to enter Central High were nowhere to be seen. The local NAACP, seeking to avoid violence, called them on the phone to delay their arrival at school. One of them, however, did not have a phone and went to school alone. Elizabeth Eckford thought the troops had come to protect her, and she tried to enter several doors before realizing the troops were there, like the mob whose presence she understood from the start, to keep her out. The segregationists were as confused as she was about whose side the troops were on. The mob hesitated and remained passive until she tried the last possible door and was turned away.[34] When Roy Harris, back home in Georgia, heard that Faubus had sent troops to Central High, he said, "I sat there . . . just scratching my head and wondering if he called 'em out *for* us or *agin'* us."[35]

Opponents and Proponents of Desegregation Both Claim the Mantle of Law and Order

Eight out of Little Rock's ten aldermen issued a statement in support of Faubus's use of troops. The local American Legion post adopted a resolution supporting Faubus with similar language.[36] But even now, the segregationists' public face had to be a moderate one. If they were animated by hidden motives of racial exclusion and defiance of federal authority, those motives were no longer fully legitimate in the mid-twentieth-century middle class of southern cities and had to hide behind rhetoric about maintaining peace and order. The segregationists had to say they were trying to prevent violence. And what they had to say is the significant thing here. Segregationism, whatever motives lay underneath it, was a public movement. To be sure, racism drew on dark psychological yearnings and phobias, and it ensured the power of a well-heeled minority against possible majority insurgencies, but southerners tried to keep such things private. People with varying, unexpressed, and probably ill-understood motives came together and acted on those motives only after translating them into commonly acceptable forms. The aldermen defended Faubus's use of troops "in this crisis to protect the lives and property of all [the city's] people." Protecting lives and property was still an honorable function of local government. Protecting the purity of the white race and state sovereignty was not.

These statements reflected not only the unwillingness of leading segregationists to take a stand explicitly for segregation but also the effort to confuse the uncommitted middle as to what Faubus's troops were actually doing. Rather than keeping black students out and allowing the mob to intimidate Elizabeth Eckford in defiance of a court order, the aldermen and other supporters gave the uninformed public the impression that the troops were preventing violence that was otherwise sure to occur, at the hands of freelance extremists — not merely black integrationists, as racists were free to infer, but white bitter-enders, as moderates were free to infer.[37]

It was against this background that the nine black students at Central High gained support from a small cohort of white southerners. The visible expression of this support came in the first days of school when two white southern clergymen, and the son of one of these, accompanied the children to school. The first was the Reverend Will Campbell, who had grown up poor in Mississippi during the Depression but managed to get a ministry in the southern Baptist church and some educational credentials, including a degree from Yale Divinity School. Rare among white Baptists, he insisted on socializing with and defending the rights of fellow Christians who happened to be black. These habits got him into trouble in his second preaching job, as chaplain of Ole Miss. He started there in August 1954. Within the first year he became the main target of campus segregationists, whose intimidation culminated in an ugly incident at a YMCA party he was hosting. Someone spiked the punch with what looked like human feces sprinkled with powdered sugar. He left Ole Miss, seeking a pulpit where he would be free to interpret the gospel as he saw fit, but word was out that he attracted controversy and trouble, and that could be deadly to a southern Baptist's career. At just that time, however, the National Council of Churches was looking for a white southern preacher of a kind the organized church in the South did not want. It was opening up a social mission in the South and asked Campbell to direct its southern office of the Department of Racial and Cultural Relations. To Campbell's brother, who advised him not to take the job, it was "like saying [one was] going to work for the Communist Party." Campbell felt called to go to Little Rock (and other major and minor desegregation battles) to help the young students there get through an ordeal.[38]

The other white preacher, Dunbar Ogden, had been preaching at the Central Presbyterian Church in Little Rock since 1954. Active in many civic organizations, he was elected president of the recently integrated Interdenominational Ministerial Alliance, in June 1957. In that capacity, he received a call from Daisy Bates asking him to escort the Nine. Though Ogden became a committed integrationist after this experience, which led him to see segregationists as vicious people, he first felt a simple duty to offer whatever protection his presence among them might afford the children. Ogden's twenty-one-year-old son David came along, telling his father that he needed a bodyguard.[39]

These and quieter expressions of support from white people in Little Rock gave Bates and the Little Rock Nine a degree of solace and hope, which may have strengthened their determination. But in Little Rock as elsewhere, the effect of such direct expressions was most significant at the beginning; soon after the struggle was joined, the split between mild and hard-core segregationists— "mouth segs" and "real segs," in the local parlance[40]— was what gave the movement the opportunity it needed to achieve victory. That split was not visible before the local activists applied pressure.

The schism in white leadership broke through the surface only after the National Guard troops made Faubus's purpose clear. The troops turned Elizabeth Eckford away and let the mob have its way on September 4. That made it clear that they were preventing something other than mob violence. Faubus had become the first politician to make good on the "interposition" movement among many southern state legislatures and "state sovereignty commissions," which invoked John C. Calhoun's constitutional philosophy and harkened back to antifederalism. The idea was to "interpose" the state government between the people of a particular state and an extension of national power beyond the limits set by the Constitution. Before the federal government swung into action to restore the supremacy of federal over state law, and the rule of law in general, the mayor of Little Rock, Woodrow Wilson Mann, quipped that he was "tempted to issue an executive order interposing the city of Little Rock between Governor Faubus and the Little Rock school board." Even Mayor Mann's reason for not yielding to that temptation was a dig at Faubus: all that kept him from this "interposition," he said, was his "own respect for due process of law."[41] Mayor Mann had put Faubus in the position of a scofflaw and an outside agitator meddling in local affairs.

Reporters had no trouble finding other white leaders who, if they did not exactly endorse desegregation in their hearts and minds, urged compliance with the law and pinned the blame for the violence on Governor Faubus. Most significant of these, perhaps, was the student body president of Central High, Ralph Brodie. Asked how long he thought the tension at his school would last, he told CBS's Mike Wallace that that was "up to Governor Faubus." Asked whether he personally thought Negroes should be admitted immediately, he replied, "Sir, it's the law. We are going to have to face it some time. . . . If it's a court order we have to follow it and abide by the law." He said he would not object to sitting next to a Negro in school, though he had no Negro friends at present, but that he would object to interracial dating. Pressed on the latter point, he said he did not know why. "I was just brought up that way." On the general question of equality of intellect among black and white he was first noncommittal and when pressed said, "If they have had the same benefits and advantages, I think they're equally as smart." He was clearest and wavered least on the question of respecting the law and obeying court orders.[42]

Breakdown of Local Authority Invites Federal Intervention

Faubus had been drawn out into a precarious position, opposing many of the respectable white leaders in Little Rock, including his former allies. His one-time boss and mentor, former governor Sid McMath, said, "The last man I would have expected to have called out the National Guard in defiance of federal court orders was Orval Faubus." He said that even if Faubus's pretext about guns and knives among students had been accurate (he did not believe that it was), the governor "should have used the National Guard to protect the children, instead of blocking their entry; his actions gave encouragement to the racist rabble-rousers, and slowed down industrial development in the state."[43] The greatest of the rabble-rousers, Faubus's race-baiting rival Jim Johnson, reinforced McMath's point from the other side. Looking sullenly at the overnight sensation who had upstaged him and every other veteran in the segregationist movement, Johnson remarked, "He used my nickel and hit the jackpot."[44] McMath, who had gained a reputation for developing state highways (largely through the office of his highway commissioner, Orval Faubus), said during the crisis at Central High that his only mistake as governor had been "to build that one paved road in Madison County that let Faubus out."[45]

The governor's own father wrote several letters to the editor of the *Gazette* which sharply criticized Faubus's administration of the desegregation crisis. Old Sam Faubus was a populist and socialist from the upcountry who believed that all working people, black and white, had to stand together to achieve social justice. His letters appeared over the pseudonymous signature "Jimmy Higgins" in the *Gazette*'s "From the People" column.[46] It is not clear whether Sam Faubus kept the identity of Jimmy Higgins secret from his son or only from his son's constituents; but more and more prominent white folks in the state began to make public statements against Faubus, using their real names. It still took time before, in historian Elizabeth Jacoway's phrase, "the respectability of opposing Governor Faubus had been established,"[47] but the process was well underway soon after school opened in September 1957.

So when Elizabeth Eckford and eight other black students braved the mob at Central High for the rest of that year, they faced a divided and confused opposition. There were those who claimed to support desegregation in general and only objected to the suddenness of the change. They did not, for whatever reason, say they wanted to keep black students out, but only that they wanted to prevent the white rabble from attacking black students and disrupting the education of black and white alike. Spurious as those claims might have been (any real change would have to be sudden), they put a large part of the white community into an anti-

Faubus position, now that he had abandoned his previous position of accepting a lawful and gradual plan for desegregation and gave material support to the mob.

Historians have tended to suggest that after Faubus put the military power of Arkansas in direct opposition to the orders of the federal court, a firm reply from the national state was inevitable. It was certainly not immediate. President Eisenhower's federal troops did not come to Little Rock for three full weeks after Faubus's National Guard blocked Elizabeth Eckford's entry on September 4. Eisenhower, not given to decisive and controversial actions in any case, had made it clear that he did not agree with the Supreme Court's decision in *Brown*. Prior to that, campaigning for the presidency on September 3, 1952, Eisenhower told an audience in Little Rock that he deplored the meddling of the government in affairs where it did not belong.[48] As of September 1957, Eisenhower had never put the executive branch to the task of enforcing the Supreme Court's interpretation of the Constitution and laws on school desegregation.[49]

Besides Faubus, two other white southerners were instrumental in pulling the president off the fence: *Washington Post* publisher Phil Graham and Little Rock's liberal congressman Brooks Hays. Having built his empire of opinion and influence in the nation's capital, Phil Graham's continued drive for power required imaginative and decisive political leadership to change the status quo (as had happened in the 1930s and 1940s). This in turn required a Democratic president with a personality powerful enough and political connections wide enough to unify the party. To Graham, only Lyndon Johnson could fulfill that historic mission, and Graham saw himself as something of a kingmaker. Like many leading Democrats in the late 1950s, Graham was convinced that LBJ, as a southerner, could never make it as a national politician unless he committed southern heresy on civil rights; also, Johnson was the only southerner who had enough muscle to get away with such heresy. So Graham helped Johnson push the first Civil Rights Act since Reconstruction through Congress in 1957. Graham led the fight for that bill as much as Johnson; Graham took on the liberals, while Johnson worked the conservatives. Graham had to convince his contacts, the big idea men in the party, the liberal lobbyists, bankrollers, and interest group heads, that the bill, watered down to please enough of Johnson's conservative senators to squeak through passage, was not a defeat for civil rights; Johnson had to convince enough conservatives that the bill would be an ineffectual sop to civil rights groups and thus delay really harmful court action. During the long fight to pass the bill, according to David Halberstam, the two "were virtually living together." As soon as it passed, Graham collapsed, exhausted.[50]

At almost precisely that moment, Faubus sent in his troops, and Graham felt personally responsible. Johnson's image was tarnished by racial tension and lawlessness in the South. His liberal contacts felt that after gambling for a half step forward, they were suddenly being dragged three backward. Faubus was a two-bit hick who threatened the whole plan Graham had painstakingly put together.

Though exhausted, Graham picked up the phone and began arranging deals and negotiations to get the errant Faubus to cease and desist. One of the first people he contacted was Arkansas congressman Brooks Hays. Hays' first task was to call former president Harry Truman. The connection, in Graham's scheming mind, was that Faubus admired Truman and might listen to him. Truman was a Baptist, and Hays, as well as being a liberal who had an interest in cleaning up the national image of his home city, had considerable authority with his coreligionists; the congressman was moonlighting at that time as head of the Southern Baptist Convention. Whatever Truman did is not known, but the former president—one of the earliest Democratic converts to civil rights—did not bring Faubus to heel. The fallback plan was to use the current president. Hays' White House contact was Sherman Adams, Eisenhower's chief domestic adviser, whom Hays had befriended in Congress some ten years earlier. Through Adams, Hays set up a meeting between Eisenhower and Faubus, at Newport, Rhode Island. In the course of setting this up, Hays convinced Adams that Faubus was not "a stubborn, last-ditch segregationist." Hays told Adams his one great concern was to handle Faubus carefully, lest he be "driven into the arms of the few extremists in the Southern governors' group." Hays reported that Adams was sympathetic on that score, and after considerable haggling between Hays and Adams, the meeting was arranged.[51]

But before Eisenhower's staff would agree to Faubus's conference with the president, Faubus had to make a formal, public assurance that he would appear before the federal district court to answer a summons to testify on a petition challenging his use of troops to block desegregation. He also had to agree to affirm publicly that the federal courts were already clear in their opinions on desegregation at Central High, that "all good citizens must of course obey all proper orders" of the courts, and that it was his "desire to comply with the order" that had been issued by the District Court in this case. He gave this statement to the press on September 11. At Newport,

Rhode Island, on September 14, 1957, the president and the governor met. Faubus, who brought Hays along with him, was agreeable and diplomatic. He agreed to abide by court orders and to withdraw his National Guard troops soon.[52]

Faubus had wavered at first but then swung impulsively over to defiance and then to capitulation in his face-off with Eisenhower. Next he seemed to abdicate altogether. Following his pledge, he pulled his National Guard troops out on September 20, and he left town the next day to attend the Southern Governors' Conference in Sea Island, Georgia, leaving his lieutenant governor, Nathan Gordon, in charge with "no suggestions for dealing with the integration issue."[53] Despite his agreement with Eisenhower, and despite Mayor Mann's stern announcement that local police would prevent any interference with desegregation, Faubus told the Associated Press on his arrival in Atlanta that in his opinion there would be violence in Little Rock if black students tried to enter Central High.[54]

Many on both sides interpreted that statement as encouragement for the mob and discouragement for the police. On September 23, 1957, known as Black Monday to the segregationists, assistant police chief Eugene Smith said he walked a hundred miles keeping his own troops in line. He told his men "that if any sonofabitch even thought about falling out [he'd] shoot him in the back of the head" and said he "had to be in a position to deliver."[55] Eventually Smith, fatigued and under pressure, concluded that his forces could not protect the black students and arranged to have them escorted out the back door of the school and spirited away in police cars before the mob caught on. One of the students recalled a suggestion from one of the authorities present that if the police allowed the mob to hang one student as a diversion, the rest could be gotten out safely:

> The police chief said, "Unh-uh, how are you going to choose? You're going to let them draw straws?" He said, "I'll get them out." [The police took them to the basement and put them into two cars, and Smith told the drivers,] "Once you start driving, do not stop." And he told us to put our heads down. [As the driver came up,] I could just see hands reaching across the car, I could hear the yelling, I could see guns, and he was told not to stop. "If you hit somebody, you keep rolling, 'cause the kids are dead." And he did just that, and he didn't hit anybody, but he certainly was forceful and aggressive in the way he exited this driveway, because people tried to stop him and he didn't stop. He dropped me off at home. And I remember

saying, "Thank you for the ride," and I should have said, "Thank you for my life."[56]

Mayor Mann then telegraphed the White House that the situation had passed beyond the control of local authorities.[57] Only then did Eisenhower, who up to that point had respected Faubus's turf, call in the army. Segregation had broken down completely at the local level before the national state stepped in to fill the power vacuum. Law and order, so long a staple of segregationist ideology, could not be maintained by segregationists. Faubus's vacillations, followed by his absence from the scene at the moment of confrontation, weakened the legitimacy of his newly adopted cause. Those inclined to dissent from segregation gained confidence with the assurance that the power of the U.S. Army was now arrayed against it.

Segregationists Drive Away White Supporters

The aesthetics of mob action undermined segregationism still further. In the morning paper and on national television, photos of a white child in the grip of an abusive tantrum, taunting and spitting at a lone black child, usually pictured with head held high in calm dignity, could embarrass if they could not shame. Mob attacks on several reporters and photographers, including the beating of the entire staff that *Life* magazine deployed to the scene, ensured that the press's sympathies would gravitate toward the brave black students and their articulate, if few, white supporters. Asked if northern reporters were sympathetic with her cause, Bates responded that "most of the reporters, period, north and south" were "sympathetic," including the local reporters.[58] Mobs ranging about the city, randomly attacking black men and women and beating them, left the distinct impression that the police had lost control. Incidents involving lit cigarettes down the black children's collars suggested the mob's lack of restraint and put all on notice that anyone, child or adult, white or black, might fall in the aimlessness of the frenzy.

One student, sickened by the mob, felt himself cross over to sympathy for the black students. Craig Rains, a white senior and student council member, recalled that the mob seemed to have traveled to his town from somewhere else, just to stir up trouble.

> There were license plates from out of state. Very few people from Little Rock were there causing these problems, that I could see. But it was an ugly attitude. Especially when Elizabeth Eckford came to try to get into school.

And the crowd began to heckle her, and cheer and shout, as she walked along. I was just dumbfounded. I had my camera at the time; I ran up and took a picture of it. And then as she went on I thought, Well, I can't believe people would actually be this way to other people. I began to change from being somebody who was a moderate, who, if I had my way, would have said, "Let's don't integrate, because it's the state's right to decide," to someone who felt a real sense of compassion for these students. I also developed a real dislike for the people that were out there that were causing problems. It was very unsettling to me.[59]

The white students at Central who showed sympathy with the nine black students suffered reprisals and got little protection from the troops posted on guard duty in the halls, whose attention was strained keeping track of the black students.[60] Some local white sympathizers, including a woman who had come to Elizabeth Eckford's aid her first day of school, Grace Lorch, and her husband, Lee Lorch, were harassed by state red-baiting committees.[61] The *Arkansas Gazette* reportedly lost over two million dollars in subscriptions and advertising revenue as a result of its endorsement of desegregation. Daisy Bates named six local white citizens who kept in contact with her throughout the crisis, although all of her friends stopped coming to visit, "because they were afraid."[62]

In its effort to intimidate the entire black population, the mob inevitably created a climate of fear among white people. Very few white people probably changed their opinion of segregation as an issue. But the issue itself changed from segregation to mob rule. That in turn changed the political arithmetic in a population whose majority favored racial separation but, as they soon discovered, favored law and order more.

After Black Monday, the mob, frustrated in its attempts to keep black students from entering Central, contented itself with trying to coax white students out. There were some walkouts. But according to Superintendent Blossom, few were willing, even if they privately disagreed with desegregation, to make even so mild a protest as leaving class—a form of protest which school authorities, voluntarists to the end, did nothing to discourage.[63] One white girl told reporters that there was "very little trouble at all" inside the school and that the majority of her classmates were "disgusted" with the students who walked out. Superintendent Blossom said "the great majority of students acted with dignity and tact."[64] Many white students even "spoke words of encouragement to the Negro children and urged them to 'stay and fight it out.'"[65]

In February 1958, however, a majority of the school board filed suit in federal court to suspend implementation of the Blossom Plan until things calmed down. (The minority who opposed this move, including Superintendent Blossom, resigned.) Though this move pleased segregationists—the suit was an admission of the failure of integration—it put the blame for violence on the leading segregationist. The school board complained that Governor Faubus's illegal interference with desegregation had created the disorder that made suspension necessary.[66] In June 1958 federal district judge Harry J. Lemley, an avowed segregationist, granted the suspension on the grounds that although the black students had a right to attend an all-white school, the testimony concerning chaos and tension indicated that the time had not quite arrived when they could enjoy that right. The suit and the verdict, like other moves to forestall integration elsewhere, conceded the main point of law and based the argument for an exception to it somewhat perversely on disapproval of segregationist tactics. The overturning of Lemley's verdict was only a short logical step beyond the verdict itself: if the threat of violence could delay the enforcement of the law, then all who opposed the law could evade it indefinitely by threatening violence. So the federal appeals court argued, granting the NAACP's request for repeal of Lemley's ruling, on August 18. Inescapable as this ruling was for any court interested in upholding the rule of law, the larger historical point should not be obscured, namely that both sides were agreeing, in their public appeals, to fight for order and social peace against disorder and mob violence—not for or against segregation. The civil rights movement had succeeded in shifting the terms of battle from ends to means.

The Costs of Moderation—and the Greater Costs of Immoderation

Faubus did not admit defeat. He called a special session of the legislature to prepare for the Supreme Court's decision to uphold the appeals court ruling, which came on September 12, 1958. Soon after, the special session passed a bill that empowered Faubus to close the high schools in Little Rock, and he ordered the schools closed. They remained closed the following academic year.

School closing was another example of self-defeating segregationist desperation. From that point on, the issue was not segregated or integrated education but segregation or education. The main vehicle of racial moderation became the Women's Emergency Committee to Open Our Schools, founded by Adolphine Fletcher Terry, a white aristocrat. Originally, the women who began this group had conceived of an organization to work for racial justice in general, but they had reined in their ambitions because of the lack of support for change. The closing of the schools was their opportunity to mobilize moderate white opinion behind a conservative, sensible-sounding cause. Being women of the upper class and upper middle class in the 1950s, moreover, they had a degree of freedom from economic reprisals, which their husbands, who tended to share their political views, did not.[67]

Their husbands did begin to follow suit, however, probably pulled along by increasing awareness of the harm that all the publicity was doing to the city's investment climate. Chamber of Commerce committees that traveled to other states to entice expanding companies to open branches in Little Rock were reporting that no one was interested. The loss of a bid for a $10 million shopping center in late 1958 was attributed to the desegregation crisis too. In the beginning of 1959, the new president of the Chamber of Commerce, E. Grainger Williams, used his inaugural address to call for an end to the crisis. It was the first time someone with authority in Little Rock took a strong public stand against the segregationists. The board of the Chamber of Commerce soon polled the membership and found that 819 of them favored, while only 245 opposed, "reopening the Little Rock public high schools on a controlled minimum plan of integration acceptable to the federal courts" (83 did not vote). In March the Chamber of Commerce issued a statement:

> The decision of the Supreme Court of the United States, however much we dislike it, is the declared law and is binding on us. We think that the decision was erroneous and that it was a reversal of established law upon an unprecedented base of psychology and sociology. But we must in honesty recognize that, because the Supreme Court is the court of last resort in this country, what it has said must stand until there is a correcting constitutional amendment or until the Court corrects its own error. We must live and act now under the decision of the Court.[68]

Once the issue became law and order, even the most risk-averse, publicity-shy authorities — that is to say, the average business and civic leaders — joined the battle against segregation.

The school board became the main vehicle for resistance to integration. It tried to fire forty-four teachers and administrators who supported compliance with desegregation. If the closing of the schools had not been enough, this was. The same quarters of the city that organized the Emergency Committee to Open Our Schools spawned an even more militantly moderate group, Stop This Outrageous Purge (STOP). The Chamber of Commerce and the PTA joined forces with STOP, putting together a voting coalition of black and affluent white voters strong enough to knock the three segregationists off the school board in a recall election in May 1959 and replace them with three who campaigned as moderates.[69]

At the head of the new school board was Everett Tucker, Jr., grandson of a Confederate veteran and landlord of a Delta cotton plantation, who described himself as "typical of the conservative enlightened southern viewpoint." To him this meant that one rebelled against doing away with what one had "grown up knowing." And he had grown up knowing that, "without any personal vindictiveness or any ill feeling toward the colored race," children had just always gone to separate schools and that "this was the way it was supposed to [be]." According to Tucker, "This is what you learned at your mother's knee, and you don't learn anything bad at your mother's knee." Still a conservative had to face reality. Once he "got over the shock of the realization that this was coming to an end, this way of doing things," he regarded Virgil Blossom's plan as "a very practical, intelligent, token approach to easing into the thing." By then, he said, he had begun to think that it was really "for the good of both races to adopt sensible programs for letting white and Negro children go to school together."[70]

That put an end to defiance of the court orders. The moderates had rallied around an apple-pie issue, keeping the children in school, and, predictably, carried the day. The segregationists, in an equal and opposite reaction, lost all scruples. At the moment when segregationism's defeat was closest, ironically, dissent from it became most costly.

When the schools reopened in August 1959, Eugene Smith, now chief of police, found himself escorting black children into Central High and facing the mob again. (The federal troops had gone home after the first year.) He ordered his men to use force against any who tried to interfere, and they followed his orders, using billy clubs and other weapons while arresting twenty-four segregationist protesters. For that, according to Daisy Bates, Smith became "a villain, an object of hatred, a turncoat to the white supremacists." Since the force Smith's men used included fire hoses, the Little Rock fire chief had his car bombed. The mayor and the school superintendent had their offices bombed. Smith investigated several segregationist leaders for the bombings and eventually convicted some of them.

Though he was a former football hero (at the high school that later
changed its name to Central) and navy veteran, Smith became terribly
unpopular, and in a state that elected its sheriffs that was more than an
emotional burden. Bates saw Smith's fate as perhaps the greatest tragedy of
Little Rock. She described him as "a man trained to withstand much more
than the ordinary pressures of life. But who can possibly term as 'ordinary
pressure' the grinding horror that had settled on Little Rock?" Seven
months after the sentencing of the bombers, news came that his own son
had brought a real dishonor by pleading guilty to a series of thefts in a
nearby town. The next day Smith was found dead at his breakfast table.
The county coroner established that he had fired three fatal shots into his
wife before shooting himself.[71]

Bill Hadley, a friend of Smith's who ran a public relations agency,
appeared on television to help urge the acceptance of desegregation. He
lost several accounts from controversy-shy businesses and ended up,
according to his financial adviser, "in serious financial condition." Bates
reflected on how lonely the white man became in the South when he took
"certain 'unorthodox' steps." Hadley lost all confidence in his abilities, he
told her: "Suddenly it was as if I had no talent, no intelligence. I thought
only in spasms, in jerks. . . . I couldn't go to the store and come back with
what I was sent for. . . . I couldn't sleep." At length, he contemplated suicide. "I came close, very close." Instead, he left town. But before he did, he
gave Smith his gun. "So you can imagine my shock when I heard about
Gene. That's the gun I almost used on myself." Reflecting on this story,
Bates wondered what it would be like "to be white and see for the first time
how sadistic white people [could] be, and how craven even the more 'progressive' intellectuals and 'liberal' businessmen [could] be." Her husband
told her, "Maybe, hon, it's better to be black or brown and not be under any
illusions. At least when we have a surprise it's a pleasant one."[72]

No less severe was the fate of Dunbar Ogden. After accompanying the
nine students to school their first day, he organized a statewide meeting of
ministers that released a manifesto supporting the desegregation movement. While his parishioners were willing to forget about his escorting the
children, the manifesto openly courted controversy, which he met by making further public statements. Members stopped attending his church, and
contributions declined sharply, finally forcing him to resign and leave town.
Though he took most of his family with him to his new church in West Virginia, his bodyguard stayed behind and began absorbing all the anger his

father had provoked. David Ogden was mobbed and heckled on the street; he lost two jobs and more than a few friends. In June 1960, he shot himself through the chest with a shotgun and died.[73]

But by this time, the Little Rock Nine had gotten through safely. One had graduated after the first year, one had transferred to a school in New York, and one had moved to California; the last of the remaining six graduated from Central in 1960, with increasingly desegregated classes coming up behind them ever after. The violence withered away.

It was far from the end of Jim Crow in particular or discrimination in general. But it was the end of widespread, organized, and potentially legitimate defense of either in Little Rock. The moderate, gradualist tactics of the NAACP's initial assault on school segregation determined the marginalization, and thus the defeat, of massive resistance in Little Rock, even though massive resistance there went as high as the governor and had military force behind it. A wavering president, who had grave doubts about desegregation, might have allied with (or acquiesced to) a governor who could guarantee order and stability. But because the governor was identified with the mob and because he was in open conflict with local officials who had legitimate claims to authority over Little Rock's schools, he could not maintain the respect and allegiance of local opinion. Without that he could not maintain order. His rival leaders in Little Rock claimed that their efforts to maintain order were compromised by Faubus's failure to respect their jurisdiction and by his encouragement of the mob. Unable to maintain such a position, the governor abdicated, and his rivals asked the president of the United States to enforce their version of a federal court order.

The civil rights movement's victory in Little Rock derived from its taking careful advantage of the peculiar circumstances and tendencies of the segregationists in that community. Little Rock was different in some of these particulars from previous battle sites. The governor there was vulnerable to segregationist baiting and took a stand that Folsom and Collins before him did not take. Though Faubus made a greater show of strength than any previous or subsequent segregationist could muster, he was impulsive in his choice of methods to court segregationist favor and inconsistent in his simultaneous assurances to Little Rock moderates and the like-minded President Eisenhower. He was unprepared to organize a defense of the southern way of life on the scale of the Nullifiers or the Secessionists of the previous century. But he was bold enough to provoke the federal government and inept enough to make intervention worth the political risk to an extremely reluctant president.

The result of the civil rights movement's victory in Little Rock (which came before the local victory of school desegregation there) was to put the federal executive power on the side of desegregation. The movement achieved this result by defining the side of desegregation as inescapably the side of order — the side that had the least political risks associated with it — where the federal executive would naturally want to be. Despite the unusual federal intervention, the general outlines of the struggle were the same as elsewhere. The segregationists in Little Rock, as in Montgomery and Tallahassee, were well known to the black community; their vulnerabilities and self-delusions were well understood. Above all, the segregationists had a tendency to indulge in unorganized violence and to suspect, offend, and confuse their natural allies — the vast majority of white citizens who shared their belief in segregation. These tendencies alone were inconsequential. The segregationists' weaknesses were perfectly suited to living with segregation (or any social system) as long as the system faced no serious challenge; if no one had forced them to represent and defend segregation before the world, they would have lived and died as most people do, unheroically as disparate individuals without historical significance. But when integrationists organized and maintained solidarity and discipline, they forced a confrontation that brought the segregationists' weaknesses to the fore. Integrationists gained allies of convenience from local (and, increasingly, federal) forces who had an interest in order and peace. This wore the segregationists — and eventually segregation — down.

These general trends were not absolute, however. There was one place where the segregationists surprised the movement — and probably themselves — by returning the movement's fire, by remaining, that is, as unified, as disciplined, as respectful of law and order, and as well led as the movement. It was the only place where the segregationists did this — other places where they may have been capable of doing so the movement began to avoid — and in doing so they mounted the most serious, and most damaging, resistance the movement ever faced. To that instructive episode we now turn.

Albany, Georgia, 1961-1962

A lbany was the hardest battle for the nonviolent army. The outcome there derived directly from the unique strategy of the white people who supported the status quo and from the movement's defensive efforts to compete with those white people for the mainstream of white (and black) opinion. To Charles Sherrod and Cordell Reagon, two leaders of the Student Nonviolent Coordinating Committee who arrived there in October 1961 and set up an office to encourage black voter registration, Albany appeared to be a typical southern town. A few years later, it turned out to be unique, and uniquely destructive to civil rights organizing.

The most striking difference between Albany and other battle sites was that in Albany there was no open conflict among white residents over how to respond to the protests. Though private opinion among the white people may have been as divided as it was elsewhere, there were no visible white dissenters, like the Durrs and Graetz in Montgomery, or even moderates bold enough to stand up in favor of compliance with court orders, like certain FCHR members in Tallahassee or Harry Ashmore and assistant police chief Eugene Smith in Little Rock.[1]

There were efforts to find white dissenters and moderates. Two white women, for example, tried to enlist the white clergy in support of civil rights, but their effort came too late and had little effect.[2] The white executive director of the Georgia Council on Human Relations, Mrs. Frances Pauley of Atlanta, sent letters to virtually every white family in Albany (approximately 10,000 letters in all), pointing out that other Georgia communities had gotten over their racial "problems" by reasoned negotiation with black leaders. She tried to persuade Albanians to urge the same course upon their city officials. Of the 250 replies she received, all but 2 were negative, and many denounced and cursed her obscenely.[3] Though a few white southerners came into Albany with the SNCC leaders to help organize the voter registration campaign and test the desegregation rulings at public accommodations there, their presence in the city neither allied with significant white support within the community nor generated it.[4]

Principals of the two movement organizations that attempted to organize Albany, SNCC and the Southern Christian Leadership Conference, stated categorically that there was no white support, covert or overt, for the movement in Albany.[5] Instead, as the most thorough historian of the movement in Albany observed, there was "an amazing cohesiveness in the white community."[6] The cohesiveness did amaze those who witnessed it, but neither this historian nor any other has ventured to state the reason why it amazed: such cohesiveness had never before been witnessed, and was never again to be witnessed, in any southern white community during the years of the civil rights movement.

Albany's white folk had not always shown such solidarity. In fact, in the voting booth and in opinion polls they showed signs of moderation that were as strong as in any city in the South—and these signs were particularly noteworthy, given Albany's Deep South, rural, black-belt location. Though in the heart of white-supremacy country, Dougherty County, of which Albany is the seat, was the only county in that part of Georgia to vote in favor of moderate gubernatorial candidate Carl Sanders in his 1962 victory over archracist Marvin Griffin (the former governor, who had flown into Little Rock with Roy Harris to agitate the white people there in 1957). Sanders' total in Dougherty County was two times the number of registered black voters there.[7] Albany's white residents in the late 1950s seemed as divided as those of Little Rock, Tallahassee, or Montgomery.

When black activists tried to desegregate Albany's churches in August 1962, though they were denied entry at one Baptist and one Methodist church, they were admitted into the Catholic church and the Episcopal church. At least one white Baptist minister, the Reverend Brooks Ramsey of First Baptist, preached in favor of letting black worshipers into his church. "This is Christ's church," he said, "and I can't build any walls around it that Christ did not build. And Christ did not build any racial walls." His board of deacons voted unanimously to retain him and upheld his right to speak his mind.

Moreover, as one observer with strong sympathies toward SNCC reported, several white businessmen in Albany had "shown a willingness to negotiate differences" with black leaders. Although a majority of the seven-member city commission censured such businessmen for their efforts, it is worth noting that the mayor, Asa Kelley, opposed the majority's intransigent racist stance on this and other matters and turned a moderate ear in general toward black demands.[8]

The Importance of White Leadership and Planning

Despite such apparent signs of white flexibility on racial separation in general, white people in Albany showed no flexibility toward the civil rights movement's particular challenge. There was no open dissent from the city government's official policy of staunch opposition to the movement. On that the white residents were unified.

At the apex of this amazingly cohesive white community was police chief Laurie Pritchett. With his swaggering manner and unschooled speech, Pritchett seemed to fit the cliché of a rural southern sheriff. But he had a touch of the gentleman, too. As a politician he tended to follow the model of Odysseus rather than Achilles, outwitting his opponents rather than challenging them belligerently and bludgeoning them into submission. In this respect as in others, Pritchett resembled Martin Luther King more than his fellow southern lawmen.

The resemblance was no accident. Pritchett studied King. He prepared for King's arrival in his city, which he had anticipated for some time. Long before the movement began in Albany in earnest, in December 1961, black leaders had been attempting to negotiate with the city commission and getting nowhere. Pritchett had developed good contacts with these leaders and heard from them ahead of time that Sherrod and SNCC were coming to town, aiming to make Albany a focal point of the national movement. The response of his police department was to prepare: "We'd been training for it and getting ready for whatever."[9] For Pritchett, this first involved studying the theories and experiences of Martin Luther King. Subsequently, Pritchett received information that Dr. King himself was coming to town too. "And you know his philosophy was nonviolence," Pritchett explained. King's philosophy was based on Gandhi—"the march to the sea where they just filled the jails to capacity" and forced a surrender. Pritchett was not going to let that happen in his city. He contacted the sheriffs in surrounding counties, requesting arrangements to guarantee the use of their spare jail space. Preparing for King's arrival, Pritchett claimed that he had set up the capacity to confine ten thousand prisoners, and yet "never put a one in our city jail." He had confidence in his scheme because he had studied the movement. "I'd read a lot about King and . . . on Gandhi, on overpower them by mass arrests." Since King knew the city jail facilities were limited, Pritchett arranged to overcome that weakness. He would wear his enemies down by sheer capacity to absorb their capacity to absorb suffering.

In his annual report to the city commissioner, Pritchett stated that on the basis of his study of the movement's experience in other cities, his police force conducted "for the first time in any civil rights struggle a nonviolent operation. For a period of four to five months, members of the Albany Police Department were indoctrinated to this plan of non-violence by the staff officers. . . . At each roll call the members of the Albany Police Department were lectured and shown films on how to conduct themselves in this non-violent operation." Albany had a supply of police dogs, but "they were deactivated." Pritchett says he instructed his men "that if they were spit upon, cussed, abused in any way . . . they were not to take their billy clubs out. . . . And this is what they did; . . . there was no bloodshed." During the time Albany was under movement siege, Pritchett claimed, "there was never any violence on the part of the police."[10]

Unlike other segregationists, Pritchett respected his opponents. In fact, he admired King and other movement leaders. He described Dr. King as "a close personal friend." The Albany Movement president, Dr. William Anderson, too, was "a real close personal friend." Wyatt Walker, Andrew Young, and Ralph Abernathy, were all "real close personal friends."[11] Pritchett claimed that the admiration went two ways. During one of the trials, Pritchett referred to movement lawyer C. B. King as "C. B.," and King referred to him as Laurie. "Well," Pritchett recalled, "the Judge didn't say anything when I referred to him as C. B., but when he referred to me as Laurie he [gaveled] and said, 'You will refer to him as Chief Pritchett.' And I said, 'Look, your honor, we're friends. My friends can call me Laurie.'" Dr. King apparently admired Pritchett at least enough to give him an autographed copy of his book *Strength to Love,* inscribed, "with best wishes and deep hopes that the system of segregation will soon pass away so that we can be brothers indeed."[12]

Pritchett kept his office open to the movement leadership throughout the crisis, and Martin Luther King and others negotiated with him formally and informally on many occasions.

[One night] Dr. King came to my office and my secretary come in with a telegram. I opened it up, and it was from my wife. . . . Dr. King says, "Did something disturb you, Chief Pritchett?" I said, "Well, yes, in a way. This telegram's from my wife. It's our anniversary, and I haven't been home in weeks." Dr. King looked at me and he says, "All right. You go home tonight, enjoy your anniversary, do anything you want to. There'll be nothing happening in this town tonight." And he said, "In the morning we'll take up where we left off." So I said, "Do you mean this?" He said, "You have my word." So I got in my truck and went home. We went out to dinner. . . . And then the next morning we took up where we left off.[13]

Even after King left Albany, they "corresponded with each other for a long time." As of 1976, Pritchett was still getting Christmas cards from Coretta Scott King.[14]

The two leaders got along like Erich von Stroheim and Pierre Fresnay in *Grand Illusion*, except that these two enemies were not in prison taking respite from the war but actively engaged in day-to-day combat against each other. They were in battle, and the good manners on both sides were weapons which, for once, King's adversary used as skillfully as King himself. Pritchett knew that King's success depended on his ability to get the segregationists to attack nonviolent demonstrators. "We never did what they intended [for us] to do."[15]

Pritchett's study of and admiration for King were only the beginning. Once he had carefully laid his plans to foil the movement, he had a huge logistical operation to conduct—one that rivaled in complexity the movement's own operation of the Montgomery bus boycott. He had to keep his overstaffed department working overtime without breaks, to arrest "every man, woman and child," in one of his critics' words, "who dared protest in any way the infringement of rights guaranteed them by the Constitution."[16] This often meant arresting seven hundred to eight hundred demonstrators in a single day, always shipping them out to outlying county jails.[17]

Historians often leave the impression that the arrests and other workings of the southern machinery of repression were automatic, as though it were a foregone conclusion that any black person who stepped out of line would quickly feel the grip of southern justice. On the contrary, civil rights leaders planned their actions in the knowledge that mass arrests were enormously difficult and time-consuming, as well as deeply embarrassing to southern authorities. The civil rights leaders' aim, especially in Albany, was not merely to inflame the conscience of the American public but to put direct and severe strains on the resources of the state. In so doing, they hoped to force politicians to divert resources from other priorities, and force a practical or financial crisis that would impel white citizens to reconsider their priorities: was segregation worth fighting for, especially if fighting meant a costly war of attrition against telegenic protesters? In contrast to white people in other cities, the white people in Albany, under Pritchett's leadership, consistently and almost unanimously answered yes to this question. Understanding why they did and why others answered no requires understanding what Pritchett was up against.

The forces of massive resistance tried to make an even stronger showing in Albany than they had in Little Rock. This meant that, in addition to the black protesters, whose arrests have been the focus of nearly all historical treatments of the movement, Pritchett's men also had to arrest hostile white counterprotesters. The numbers here were of course much smaller than those of the black protesters, but the white lawbreakers were often more difficult to handle, both as prisoners and as political liabilities. It was not enough for Pritchett to protect the demonstrators from police violence. He had to protect them against freelance vigilantes as well. After all, as police chief he was responsible for the safety of all citizens, not merely for the good behavior of his own men. The Imperial Wizard of the United Klans of America, Robert Shelton of Alabama, marshaled his forces for a confrontation in Albany, and it must be said that Pritchett treated Shelton's forces with less consideration than he treated his other visitors from Alabama. If segregationists in other cities hid a racist exclusionism behind the legitimate idea of defending local autonomy, Pritchett insisted on consistent application of the respectable components of segregationism. Outside lawbreakers were outside lawbreakers. "Shelton and all them came in from Alabama," Pritchett recalled. "We would not let them come into Albany, Georgia. . . . The American Nazis out of Washington came in; we wouldn't let them parade. We packed them up in their car and they went back. Shelton and all of the Ku Klux Klan, they met on the outside of the city limits; we wouldn't let them come in. They never did come in for parading or anything."[18] Although Chief Pritchett arrested black demonstrators, he never barred them or their supporters from the city.

Not only did he prevent white groups from demonstrating, he also tried to keep them away from black demonstrators. "We arrested a great number of whites that were trying to intimidate or interfere with some of these peaceful demonstrations," Pritchett said. Whenever the movement planned a demonstration, he recalled, "we'd go down and cordon off three or four blocks where whites couldn't come through. You know, we wouldn't let anybody through there." After one movement leader was assaulted by a local county sheriff, Pritchett feared the incident would embolden other angry white people to violence:

> All the whites (and we had them in there with their lunches, you know, with shotguns in the back of their cars and baseball bats; and they'd bring the kids with lunches and just sit waiting for something so they could come out), they figured that when the sheriff did this this would give them the right. And we had to go out on public address systems and state that there would be no violence. We would not tolerate it. And we cleared the whole town. I closed the bars; I closed everything in that town. There wasn't anything open. And we cordoned it off where nobody could come in.

It is an unexplored irony that restricting the liberties — and possibly the constitutional rights — of segregationists may have been easier for a sheriff under the scrutiny of the national press in the 1960s than doing the same to civil rights workers.

Pritchett, though he seems to have approved of the segregation system it was his job to defend, had strong practical reasons for keeping such a tight rein on segregationists. While many southern lawmen tacitly declared open season on civil rights workers, Pritchett saw to it that he would not have a martyr in his town, especially not a nationally prominent figure like Dr. King. Pritchett said to himself, "Wherever this man is killed, hell's going to break loose." For this reason Pritchett kept in constant contact with King and provided him an escort to, from, and within Albany: "As soon as he'd leave Atlanta he'd tell me approximately what time he'd be coming into Americus, which was forty miles north of Albany. We'd meet him. One of my men would get in the car, he'd get in our car, and then they'd come in by two cars. And we took him everywhere. There was a plot down there to kidnap him, and we found out about this and got it stopped."[19] Pritchett did not live by shrewdness alone; his shrewdness was tended by vigilance. "We had a bodyguard with him at all times. . . . We'd take him everywhere he wanted to go. Where he spent the night, we had people there all the time. . . . This caused some criticism that we were payin' taxpayers' money to protect this man, and . . . I told them, if this man was killed in Albany, Georgia, the fires would never cease."[20] Obviously the protection had a certain surveillance value as well, but that the Albany police dealt with their frustrations about civil rights in a patient, organized manner at all distinguished their city from all the other major sites of civil rights protest.

This activity consumed enormous resources. Pritchett's police set up operations for his overtime-working staff outside the police station in two commandeered hotels downtown. "All my police officers were living in the hotels. We lived in the hotels for months at a time."[21]

Logistics were only half of Pritchett's battle. He had entered a war on the propaganda front, too, which required him to appear purer than Caesar's wife. The press by this time was expecting just the kind of martyrdom Pritchett feared. One national editor instructed his reporter on the civil rights beat, "Go where the Mahatma goes; he might get killed."[22] While media attention was focused on the nonviolent movement in Albany, Pritchett never wavered from his posture of watchful restraint, and unlike many a southern sheriff, he never made the mistake of underestimating the intelligence and the power that the black community had to influence the press. Though he first followed the segregationist line blaming all disturbances on "outside agitators," by the summer of 1962 he was trying to persuade Albany's white leaders not to lull themselves with such delusions: he told a businessmen's club meeting, "It must be recognized that the movement has the support of most of the city's Negroes."[23] That Pritchett, unlike Clyde Sellers and Orval Faubus, and the more notorious Bull Connor and Sheriff Clark of subsequent years, did not assume black people to be incompetent and complacent suggests, as the Albany story does in general, that segregation could be effectively defended only by those who were not racists: only they could make adequate provision for the battle ahead. That could be the central contradiction that explains the breakdown of the system in the South as a whole.

The Press and the Nation's Conscience

Pritchett knew he had to study the protesters with care to keep one step ahead of them in public relations, which were extremely delicate, as the movement was being covered by a national (that is to say, northern) press. The sympathies of the press came to lie with the protesters, who as articulate and principled victims of wild outrages usually made better copy, and who at any rate never smashed cameras. Those circumstances more than any others affected the movement's ability to stir the national conscience in other battles; Albany was to be the one exception to the pattern of press sympathy.

The best example of the press's susceptibility to Pritchett's tactics came on Labor Day, 1962, when seventy-five northern clergy and laity drove to Albany to express their support for the city's black protesters. They aimed to bring national attention to racial injustice, but Pritchett parried by pointing out that his city's response to civil rights activity was benign compared with that of Little Rock or Montgomery—or with what could be expected, for that matter, from northern cities should protest erupt there. For the benefit of the press listening nearby, he said to the Yankee faithful, "Clear your own cities of sin and lawlessness."[24] No doubt he converted few of the northern liberal pilgrims with this line, but he clearly impressed the members of the press, who repeated it in their dispatches. The great pilgrimage to Albany, an event conceivable only in an era that depended on media coverage to define events, flopped in the press. The city commission artfully decided to resume negotiations just before the northerners arrived.[25] Pritchett's rhetoric, broadcast beyond the sealed ears of civil rights sympathizers who had traveled far into what they considered the belly of the beast, must have given less committed northern Christians pause to think about setting their own houses in order.

Asked by an interviewer if he had been "conscious of press relations" and "very careful about [his] language," Pritchett answered in the affirmative. "You know," he explained, "the press had been to other places and been intimidated (cameras broken, they were not able to walk the streets), and so we had set up that every day, twice a day we'd have news conferences. They'd come to my room at the hotel. . . . They'd come to my room at night and we'd sit down and talk. But they could go anywhere they wanted to. We kept them alerted as to what was going to happen, because we had sources of information. We knew when they were going to march, where they were going to march, what they were going to do." The press was often in a position to return the favor and thereby improved Pritchett's intelligence force: "We had a mutual understanding," he said.[26] While he had to pay his police informants, the information he received from the media was free.[27] Pritchett's victory in the court of public relations was not a foregone conclusion; that he (unlike other defenders of the southern way of life) understood that ironically ensured his victory.

Pritchett understood, in other words, the need to make ends and means cohere in a political strategy to win the hearts and minds of the public. He realized that there are limits to what the public—now with ringside seats, owing to recent changes in the technology and organization of news reporting—will accept as reasonable, fair, proportional, necessary. Even if the public agrees with the reasons for which its political leaders are fighting, it may be so repulsed by the way they fight that it ceases to feel a com-

mitment to the fighting. To hold the public's allegiance, which is more necessary than ever in an age of mass communications and total war, the
politico-military commanders had to be very careful about how as well as
why they fought.

Not that the public is fundamentally nonviolent. Far from it. Movement leaders were never so naive or so zealous in their nonviolent faith as to
think any such thing about the southern white public. Movement leaders
knew that white southerners had nothing against the use of physical force
to maintain the social order. But they also knew that enough white southerners had enough of a sense of fair play that repeated exposure to flagrant,
gratuitous, and unprovoked brutality would sicken even the segregationists
among them. So the movement contrived to expose them to precisely that.
Pritchett's main task was to deny movement leaders that objective, and he
took great care in carrying it out. He disciplined his ranks so well that they
never exposed the public to segregationist brutality. If other segregationist
leaders had matched his skill, the victory of the nonviolent movement —
which historians so often treat as though it were an inevitable product of
some natural (or American) force of "progress" — might have been prevented everywhere. It was prevented in Albany.

Pritchett's careful study of his adversary was a sincere form of flattery: it
was not surprising that it often carried over to direct imitation. After
reaching an unwritten truce agreement (which was later broken by the city)
to get King to leave jail before Christmas, 1961, and to cease demonstrations in return for a city promise to desegregate the bus and train facilities,
release all demonstrators from jail, and hear black demands at an unspeci-
fied future meeting of the city commission, Pritchett said, "We met 'nonviolence' with 'nonviolence,' and we are indeed proud of the outcome."[28] He
was trying, with some success, to steal the nonviolent movement's thunder
in the national arena and beat it at its own game in the local arena.

Not only did Pritchett keep his side from publicly engaging in violence, he was able to capitalize on the lack of discipline and cohesion in the
movement ranks when many in the black community yielded to the temptation to engage in violence. On July 11, 1962, a crowd outside the Albany
Movement's mass meeting at Shiloh Baptist Church turned unruly and
began throwing bottles and bricks at police standing watch across the
street. Pritchett shocked everyone, including a deputy he took at his side,
by walking right through the crowd, in which some officers thought they
had seen guns being wielded, and into the church. "If you get hit," Pritchett

told his deputy, "don't stop." One eyewitness, reporter Pat Watters, said it was "one of the strangest, most deeply significant happenings of all the southern movement." Inside, while Slater King was trying to restore order and calling upon the crowd to remember the "dignity" befitting the occasion, he suddenly caught sight of the white men at the back of the church. "I notice we have in our presence Chief Pritchett," he called out. "No fear. Nothing here is secret. Would you like to say a few words?"

Someone in the crowd cried out, "Let's give him a big hand." And they applauded the chief of police. Pritchett took the pulpit. "I appreciate the opportunity to be here," he said. "I have often been told I would be welcome. I didn't know whether I would be or not."

Over nervous chatter and laughter, an old man cried out, "Let's hear. . . . Let's hear de chief."

Pritchett continued, "I never have interrupted your peaceful assemblies before. All through this there has been no incident of violence. Many people misunderstand your philosophy of non-violence, but we respect your policy. I ask your cooperation in keeping Albany peaceful. This business of throwing rocks is not good."

A voice called out, "Sho' ain't."

"Throwing bottles," Pritchett went on, working the crowd like a southern Baptist preacher, "is no good." A voice in the crowd sounded agreement. "We want to continue to see that nothing happens. We ask your cooperation. I know that you as citizens will respect and abide by our wishes that there be no disturbance. Go about your business the way we've had it." Amens rang out, and applause. Then Pritchett and his deputy went back out to the bricks and bottles.

Back at the station, when Watters interviewed Pritchett, he said the chief's ears were still scarlet. He knew he had the respect of the movement, but he was scared of the mob. "I don't care how much they dislike you in principle. They respect you. . . . That's as close as I want it to get. Something — a spark — could have set things off, and it would still be rolling down yonder. But [the protesters] proved to me tonight that they don't want . . . mob violence. I argue with them not about what they are trying to do, but the way they go about it."

The officer who had accompanied Pritchett into the church said, "Don't take me back in there, Chief. Nobody but the laundry man will know how scared I was."

Pritchett himself came out looking bold and unbeatable, to the press and to much of the rank and file of the movement as well. Movement leader

Slater King found this frustrating. The unwillingness of the crowd to challenge Pritchett's authority openly was the psychological root of segregation, he believed; to him their show of respect for the chief was a step backward at a crucial moment. "We want to give him respect," Slater King said, "but not like he's some kind of God. Maybe I am guilty of this myself. It's the system we've been conditioned by—like we've been brainwashed."[29] This seems harsh to the point of unrealism. There was nothing inconsistent between fighting courageously for freedom and showing what King called "adulation" for a speaker: the same audience showed powerful enthusiasm for the authority of black preachers who were courageous and principled enough to command their respect. Pritchett, because he had the same qualities, earned the same respect.

On July 24, when another demonstration gave way to rioting, Pritchett loudly called out to reporters, "Did you see them nonviolent rocks?" Again, by printing his words, the press gave Pritchett the power to shape public perceptions of events in a way that served his cause rather than that of his enemies. The day after this outburst, King and Albany Movement president William G. Anderson declared a "day of penance" for the black community, asking all to pray for their Negro brothers who had "not yet learned the nonviolent way."[30]

The rioting was evidence of a breakdown in movement solidarity—the kind of thing segregationists needed and rarely achieved—and King and Anderson's attempt to reimpose discipline was a further test of that solidarity. Some rivals for leadership, in particular SNCC's new executive secretary, James Forman, who claimed to have opposed King's presence in Albany from the start and later styled himself a "black revolutionary," were angered by King's seeming to blame the violence on the black community. But other SNCC members resolved not to break ranks. One of them, Charles Jones of Charlotte, North Carolina, who was among the first SNCC workers to arrive in Albany, toured the pool halls and juke joints of Albany's Harlem with King, pleading with the young toughs to maintain the nonviolent discipline (and the issue was discipline as much as it was nonviolence) of protest. King took a cue and had a few shots himself, to show that he was not putting himself above the men who hustled and drank and brawled, and told them that the power of souls could outlast that of guns and ammunition. Jones tried a different approach, claiming that the brick throwers were traitors who had been bribed by white officials to provoke police attacks upon innocent black protesters who were on the verge of winning through patience and determination.[31] Apparently these tactics worked, for there was no more violence from the poor black men in Albany as long as the press kept the national focus on the city.[32]

But the damage to the movement's image had, however unjustly, been done. The rioting of black people in Albany, though they were not members of the Albany Movement, was news. Elsewhere the minority of protesters had come to stand for the whole of the black community in the South while, in the necessarily simplistic perceptions of the press, vigilantes and undisciplined police represented the whole of the white. For once, the positions were reversed. Violence was always news, and the movement's ability to put itself on the innocent and dignified side of every news story up to this point had given it a positive image in the news.[33] Albany on July 24, 1962, was a case of man bites dog. In one night of rioting, the moral images of segregationist and desegregationist were equalized, in the literally black-and-white terms of press reporting, and it would take the desegregationists a long time to regain the high ground.

A Contest of Nonviolent Discipline

Pritchett's tactics were paying off. Discipline had broken down in an unusually frustrated and disunified black community that, facing an unusually well-disciplined and united white community, had trouble repressing hopelessness and desperation. Such feelings were held in check elsewhere by the hope of victory, which in turn fed on the enemy's ineptitude. Just after the rioting, James Bevel, an SCLC field secretary in Albany, explained to a reporter what was unique about Pritchett's forces in Albany. "In the movement you generally just set up a situation and wait for your adversary to make a mistake. But these are very shrewd people."[34] The incident suggests what a delicate task the movement's image building was, and what a feat of skill (and perhaps luck) that it did not break down elsewhere.

Pritchett's nonviolent discipline was not perfect either, however. Three incidents threatened to pull Albany back into the pattern of Montgomery and Little Rock. The earliest of these was the abuse of SNCC leader Charles Sherrod in the Terrell County Jail in December 1961. Rumors got back to the Albany Movement that Sheriff Zeke Matthews, who presided over "Terrible Terrell," had severely beaten Sherrod. Pritchett, with the same combination of conscience and opportunism that characterized King's strategy, intervened. A violation of Sherrod's rights in the next county did not directly implicate Pritchett, but a delegation of the Albany Movement went to Pritchett to protest. He surprised them with an offer to get movement associates admitted to Matthews' jail to see about Sherrod. (Even that seemingly minor first step was impossible elsewhere in the South; in later incidents Matthews himself steadfastly refused to show reporters arrest warrants and other documentation for detaining protesters. Asked why he was holding civil rights workers in July 1962, Matthews responded peremptorily, "Investigation, vagrancy, and all that crap.") But the next day, Pritchett delivered far more than what he had offered the day before. He showed up at a mass meeting at Shiloh, with Sherrod in tow.

It was a coup for Pritchett. The crowd was awed. They began to question Sherrod about his experience: "Did they beat you?"

"No. They slapped me a couple of times. . . . A man named Zeke with a sling on his arm . . . wanted me to say 'yes, sir' and 'no, sir.' I was not badly beaten. I was struck twice in the face while under arrest." The crowd was reassured that its worst fears were in this case unfounded.[35]

Sherrod, whose release had been secured through a "gentleman's agreement" that Pritchett was able to make with Sheriff Matthews, was a somewhat lesser hero that day than the man who had delivered him.[36] In most movement battles, a distinguishing feature — which made clearer than anything else what a watershed the new direct-action protests by the southern black masses were — was that beatings by white sheriffs began to backfire regularly. In previous times, when southern lawmen and vigilantes sought to show blacks (and to reassure themselves) what their "place" was, beatings had worked well because there was no hope of appeal to a larger system of justice. Under the special conditions created by the movement, which put southern justice under a national microscope, the beatings had begun instead to steel the movement's flagging resolve and restore its often crumbling solidarity. Any such outburst showed the world the true colors of its enemy and thus weakened the enemy's position. But in this case, Pritchett managed to twist the abuse of Sherrod back around to his own advantage. He could play himself as the good cop against Matthews' bad cop — just as Martin Luther King could play himself against Malcolm X and later black "militants."

More serious than Sherrod's incident with Sheriff Matthews was an assault on Slater King. Unlike Sherrod, an interloper who had to cultivate delicate new friendships and alliances in the Albany black community, Slater King (no relation to Martin Luther King), a successful real estate broker, was a longstanding Albany native and a member of the most distinguished family in town. Moreover, he was assaulted in Albany, not in the outlying redneck badlands of Terrell County. That such an assault could occur on Pritchett's turf undermined Pritchett's credibility with the black community, and the rest of the public, in a way that incidents in Terrell County, especially those involving a stranger (and, as some saw it, a troublemaker) like Sherrod, could not.[37]

Still, as they had done when Sherrod was abused, the local black leaders went to Pritchett to see about Slater King. King was being held in the Albany City Jail in December 1961 for a five-day contempt of court sentence after he had led a demonstration and had refused orders to disperse. When rumors of his beating reached the Albany Movement and the press, Pritchett responded with alacrity. He found out that King's refusal of food had angered a jailer, who responded by shoving him roughly backward into his cell. Pritchett shared this information readily with the movement and the press. In doing so, he immediately dissociated himself from the perpetrator, recommending that the jailer be fired even though King's injury was not serious: "I don't want a man like that in my jail," he told reporters.[38] This was an isolated incident, Pritchett implied, an internal discipline problem rather than a systematic pattern of repression and degradation.

Finally, in the third such incident, another leader from Slater King's family, movement lawyer C. B. King, was attacked in Albany. On July 28, 1962, C. B. King had gone into the Dougherty County Courthouse, across the street from Chief Pritchett's office, to see county sheriff Cull Campbell about the rumored beating of SNCC worker William Hansen, a white student from Cincinnati who had been jailed for participation in a march the day before. Fellow inmates had reportedly broken Hansen's jaw. The 76-year-old Sheriff Campbell ordered Albany's only black attorney out of his office, promptly decided he was not moving fast enough, and began to chase him. At the door, Campbell grabbed a wooden cane and hit King on the head with all his might. Then, as King turned to flee, Campbell hit him a second time from behind.

Pritchett pointed out that it was highly significant—of his own good behavior and of his relationship with the local black community—where King fled. He ran across the street, blood streaming from his head wounds, into Chief Pritchett's office. Pritchett shouted, "C. B., who did this?" and King told him. Pritchett ordered a squad car to transport King to the hospital and then went out to meet his public.

Word was out that Campbell had not denied beating C. B. King in his office. Campbell later told the FBI agent on the scene (who had to make an official report), "Yeah, I hit him in the head. I told the son of a bitch to get out of my office, and he didn't get out." When reporters asked him about it, Campbell denied nothing, acting as though the beating were necessary and proper.

When Pritchett got to the same reporters, he presented a different face of southern law enforcement. "This is exactly what we've been trying to prevent," he told them. Later, Pritchett talked Campbell into letting his officers check up on Hansen, who was then allowed to go to the hospital for a broken jaw, several broken ribs, and facial lacerations and was finally transferred to the city jail—Pritchett's jail, out of range of Campbell's men (who, according to some in the movement, had paid or made deals with inmates to abuse Hansen).[39] Even the archsegregationist *Albany Herald* criticized Campbell's behavior in this instance.

Pritchett's speedy response to the incident might have had something to do with why only five protesters showed up the next day at city hall for a public prayer against the outrage. Though angry segregationists urged Pritchett to follow his accustomed pattern of locking up every demonstrator who stepped outside the black section of town, Pritchett declined, telling the demonstrators that this time they could pray there all night if they wished. Pritchett later referred to Campbell as "a fine old man," who was, however, very old, and "probably senile" at that time. More important, Pritchett reflected, "He didn't believe in my philosophy."

Pritchett was criticized for not arresting Campbell. After all, he had arrested hundreds of demonstrators for far lesser crimes. In his own defense, Pritchett argued, "The chief of police's powers [do] not supersede the powers of the sheriff. He is the chief law enforcement officer of the county." Pritchett had other evidence of his own clean record: he noted that several nationally prominent lawyers had gone after him for civil rights violations in federal court and five federal judges had found him innocent. C. B. King himself "never uttered a word" against him, Pritchett said, and insisted on what was to him the central point of the episode: "Where did he come to for help? He came to me. . . . C. B. ran to my office, and he knew there he'd be protected. He was taken by my people to the local hospital." Though criticism of Pritchett would abound in civil rights organizations and in the literature on the movement, Pritchett was unperturbed: "There's an old saying that goes, 'Where did he run to?' "[40]

On these occasions when his own side had been responsible for an act of violence, Pritchett was most brilliant in mimicking the movement's non-violent posture. As Dr. King and Dr. Anderson had done, Pritchett reprimanded the perpetrator of violence, dissociated himself from the act, offered some symbolic penance, lectured his followers on the dangers of such indulgences, and reclaimed the moral high ground. The Albany Movement's "day of penance" following the rioting that had broken out in Albany's Harlem on July 24 was the model to hand of good press relations, of what today's public relations managers would call damage control, and Pritchett followed it.

Means Determine the End

With all these forces in his favor, as the *New York Herald Tribune* put it, Pritchett handed King "one of the most stunning defeats in his career." In virtually every southern city where King or like-minded activists had struck, they had gone away with at least some kind of token victory. Here they had lost a big one to the segregationists. They did not lose because white people in Albany were any more intransigent in their segregationism than those in other cities; as we have seen, inwardly they were as divided on their commitment to segregationism as the white people of Montgomery, Tallahassee, or Little Rock. The difference was that the white people in Albany—including especially those who in other cities would have lost confidence in their political leaders and found a quicker route to restoration of order through compromise with civil rights leaders—had confidence that their chief of police had the situation and the public relations under control.

An Associated Press reporter noted that white residents of Albany showed "little close-range interest in the incidents" (the numerous arrests and jailings for sit-ins, picketing, praying, applying for library cards, and so on). The Georgia Council on Human Relations reported that "the City Commission of Albany ha[d] officially given to the Chief of Police the power to be its spokesman in dealing with Negroes."[41]

As movement leader Marion Page put it, "The people of Albany did nothing but turn their backs and let him do whatever he saw fit to do."[42] That tacit unity behind their chief was as unique as it was essential. Those who fell into line behind Pritchett in Albany were exactly the kind who fell away from segregationist leadership in Montgomery, Tallahassee, Little Rock, and other southern cities—and Albany's white residents kept ranks for precisely for the same reasons that other white southerners broke ranks. Pritchett had a successful formula for maintaining order at home and the good name of the city nationwide. Elsewhere, the only road to the same ends appeared to require breaking with extreme segregationist leaders and making a compromise with the civil rights leaders. Moreover, Pritchett's ability to keep the white residents united worked to strengthen the position of the city commission, the commission's militant segregationism notwithstanding, and thereby discouraged the protesters and hastened their dissolution—for the protesters' hopes for success depended on dividing the white residents.

Pritchett was apparently not boasting idly when he declared, "I had more power than the mayor." And in the eyes of the nation, as well as the South, Pritchett had done a remarkable job. The *New York Herald Tribune*'s Fred Miller concluded that Pritchett "brought up to Albany a standard of professional achievement that would be difficult to emulate in a situation so made-to-order for violence."[43] Pritchett attributed the city's success in handling racial disturbances to the operation of "the non-violent movement by the Albany Police Department": "The credit goes to each individual member of the Albany Police Department who so successfully carried out [the non-violent] plan."[44] The executive director of the Georgia Municipal Association commended Pritchett for his handling of the Albany protests, which he referred to as "the number one job of law enforcement in recent Georgia history."[45]

Not all southern white observers approved of Pritchett's tactics. A few hours from Albany, in Atlanta, the head of the Southern Regional Council, a sort of central committee of white liberals in the South, complained that there were "legitimate grounds" for saying that in Albany "sophisticated police work" had done "the traditional—almost legendary—job of the mob."[46] The police, that is, led the fight against integration. But therein lay Pritchett's achievement. Pritchett's police did what the mob always wanted to do—defeat the civil rights leaders—but never could do precisely because it used mob methods. There is little reason to doubt that Pritchett's police were as contemptuous of federal court decisions, which they saw as radical and dangerous, as the Klan and the Citizens' Councils were. But just as the history of civil rights before the 1950s had shown that revolutionary methods—alliance with Populists, Socialists, or Communists, all of whom had at one point or another earnestly taken up the Negro's cause in the South—could not achieve revolutionary ends in their own day, so the history of massive resistance up to the Albany struggle showed that mob methods—which are inherently anarchic, if not radical—could not achieve conservative ends. Pritchett's police understood, exactly as King's protesters did, the importance of the relationship of means to ends.

Winning a cultural war for the hearts and minds of Christians and patriots depended on the segregationists' ability to maintain that they were defending established principles against an unjustified attack: that the segregation laws under attack were moral, that is to say, Christian and constitutional. That a small fraction of Christian authorities and a slightly larger fraction of judicial authorities had recently tendered their opinion that the laws were in fact un-Christian and unconstitutional clearly did not sway most white southerners, who, even when they accepted desegregation (especially token desegregation) as a practical expedient, had ample and well-established arguments to counter the recent deviation of the fringe clergy and Yankee-dominated Supreme Court from their traditional paths. There was little doubt in the southern white mind, that is, that segregation was a just cause—a worthy plan for social order and, potentially at least, social justice, order and justice that they could not, in fairness, discern in the urban ghettoes over which their Yankee critics presided. But the justness of the segregationist cause was still contingent: it could not, in the eyes of the white South or the rest of the nation, be merely a matter of the *jus ad bellum*. Prolonged moral support depended on scrupulous attention to the *jus in bello* as well. Such a war could not be waged by unseemly and unscrupulous means. Mob rule and slaughter of innocents could taint apple pie.

Despite the criticism of Pritchett expressed by the head of the Southern Regional Council, there is no evidence in the council's records of local white opposition to Pritchett's methods. If there was any feeling among local white residents of dissent from Albany's peculiar brand of orderly segregationism, as those who sought such dissent in vain testified, they kept it to themselves.[47] Elsewhere, white southerners who loved order may have held the card of potential dissent close to their chests and only played it when an irresistible opportunity arose—after the bluff of segregationist defenders of law and order had been called. In Montgomery, Tallahassee, and Little Rock, and cumulatively in the South as a whole, the civil rights leaders, aided by a small local fringe of white dissenters, called that bluff shrewdly time and again. In Albany they never could.

Pritchett was able to do much more than maintain the respect of potentially dissident whites. He maintained that of much of the black leadership as well. The latter gave him additional advantage. Pritchett gained reliable intelligence from the Albany Movement's meetings. Some of this came from paid informants and some from the press, but much of what was most valuable came voluntarily and freely from the Albany Movement hierarchy. Pritchett thought that Albany's traditional black leaders, in contrast to newcomers associated with SNCC and the SCLC, needed to maintain their accustomed *entrée* into the white power structure.[48] Movement secretary Marion Page, Pritchett said, "was talking both sides of the street. He'd talk to them and then he'd come to me."[49] Some of the major leaders of the Albany Movement, as well as the NAACP local president, were in almost nightly contact with Pritchett. Pritchett boasted that no meeting of the movement, public or private, occurred without his getting complete information, including often a full tape recording, ten to twelve hours afterward.[50]

Chief Pritchett's explanation for his most decisive *coup de main*—getting King and Abernathy, as they put it, "kicked out of jail" in July 1962—had a plausible ring to it, though the full truth behind the incident will probably never be known. On July 12, 1962, an unidentified, well-dressed black man, Pritchett said, showed up to pay the fines for King and Abernathy, who, sentenced the day before to $178 or forty-five days, had chosen jail in the time-honored movement tactic to draw media attention and thereby provoke federal intervention on behalf of constitutional rights. Years later Pritchett claimed that the decision to spring the civil rights leaders was reached at a meeting of white segregationists and black conservatives.[51] Whether his version of the plot was true or not, the incident showed that Pritchett could not only forge unusual cohesiveness in the white community but could also take inordinate advantage—at least rhetorically—of the inevitable divisions and dissension in the black.

Apart from the handful of lapses into violence in jails outside his jurisdiction, Pritchett helped Albany segregationists avoid the foot shooting in which segregationists elsewhere engaged. Many in the movement retained an abiding respect and even admiration for him. Much of this can be explained by contrasts: compared to other southern sheriffs, Pritchett did not have to do very much to demonstrate sufficient decency to make the protesters somewhat grateful for the difference. But much of it was surely heartfelt, too. Pritchett was able to kill them with kindness.[52]

For all his professed affection for them, Pritchett did not let his adversaries win; he never so much as yielded the initiative to them. By the end of July, two weeks after King and Abernathy were "kicked out of jail," the *New York Times* reported that the Albany Movement was "losing momentum." By August 4, city officials claimed that by "firm but fair law enforcement they had 'broken the back' of the Albany Movement." After tremendous press attention and outpouring of capital—Wyatt Walker said that nowhere in the South had the SCLC ever had such a "concentration of resources"; the SCLC spent ten thousand dollars in Albany, the Albany Movement twenty thousand—the movement there petered out.[53]

When Albany Movement president William Anderson, himself emotionally unstable from repeated jailings and threats, was pressed for an assessment of his organization's achievements and prospects, he could only reply that the campaign was "settling down for the long haul." Ruby Hurley, head of the Atlanta NAACP office, perhaps gleeful for the opportunity to bash a limelight-stealing and popular rival, said "Albany was successful only if the goal was to go to jail." King himself admitted that the movement "got nothing and the people were left very depressed and in despair."[54] Pritchett, with as much a note of melancholy as triumph, said of the man he had emulated and defeated, "Dr. King, when he left Albany, in his own words and in the words of the *New York Herald Tribune,* was a defeated man."[55]

The story of Albany, with Pritchett's story at the center of it, throws the relationship between ends and means into its highest relief. Before Albany, the movement had demonstrated that it could sway a southern white majority, and eventually an apathetic national population, a reluctant Congress, and a temporizing federal executive, to acceptance of its own radical position. It did this by taking the focus of battle off its own disagreeable (to the majority) ends and forcing a decision on its opponents' disagreeable means; the movement leaders achieved their end by scrupulous attention to means. Pritchett, disavowing the means of massive resistance, achieved its only victory. In doing so he explicitly gave credit to the movement by imitating it and implicitly criticized segregationism by disavowing virtually all of its assumptions—indeed, all but the central one, that segregation was worth saving. This was an amazing feat, one whose repetition the movement leaders averted by targeting cities led by men very different from Pritchett.

To preserve the system, Pritchett had to repudiate the basic illusion on which it relied, that black people were inferior and inherently suited to a system of racial hierarchy. In that assumption were grounded the basic tactics of segregationist mobs, who did their best to deny the humanity of their black opponents but in doing so fatally underestimated them as well as their audience, southern and national. Pritchett showed that an effective defense of segregation, ironically, required abandonment of the racist ideology on which segregation was based.

Pritchett's exceptional performance, like any abnormality, tells us, by its contrast, a great deal about the normal. That contrast was implicitly, and often explicitly, understood by the members of the civil rights movement, and it was a key to their general success in the South and the nation as it was to their particular failure in Albany. From this point on, civil rights leaders never faced another Albany. Their losses, or the limitations of their victories, henceforth derived from contradictions and patterns they did not fully understand and could manipulate only partially to their advantage: those of the North and the national state.

PART THREE

The Art of the Possible: The White Southerner in the National State

The Republican Party is the ship. All else is the sea.

—Frederick Douglass

Law is like sausage. Those who love it should not see how it is made.

—Winston Churchill

The Late 1950s

Saving the Party from Civil Rights

I n the late 1950s, the civil rights movement discovered that white southern moderates were vital to the way every battle turned out. There was
another group that had an interest in the way battles turned out, the
national Democratic party, and it found its attention drawn increasingly to
the same moderates, with whom it shared a fundamental interest in southern order and stability. The party's interest in order and stability was
diluted only by its deference to the de facto leaders of the South, all of
them Democrats, virtually none of them moderates. With far higher than
average seniority in Congress, southern Democrats wielded power far
greater than their numbers. An increasingly liberal New Deal coalition in
the North thus depended on an increasingly reactionary southern political
leadership for its national majorities at the polls.

The Democratic party now faced unprecedented pressure from millions of new black voters (who had enfranchised themselves by migrating
northward) to dissociate itself from southern demagogues. Southern moderates, if they became strong enough to supplant the demagogues, could
provide a way for the Democratic party to relieve itself of the demanding
presence of the demagogues without losing the southern vote — something
the northern liberal-labor coalition had been trying to do since the southerners formed a conservative coalition with Republicans against labor and
the New Deal in the late 1930s. The Democratic leadership, which hoped
to expand its appeal in the North, where liberals in many states still voted
Republican — partly because Republicans (with no southern responsibilities) supported civil rights with impunity — had the means and the motive
to make the southern moderates more viable, by supporting them.

Supporting southern moderates was a delicate task for Democratic leaders. Demagogues could turn instability to their advantage, as Governor Faubus proved by getting reelected after his showdown with the president. Local politics, moreover, was dangerous for southern moderates, who naturally preferred to remain insulated from the voters, in business and the professions. Supporting moderates was dangerous for the party because popular demagogues who now contributed to the Democratic majority might form a third party, as they did briefly in 1948. And there was no guarantee that the moderates, if they gained power, would feel any loyalty to the Democratic party that had stifled their efforts in the South for so long.

The civil rights movement, in its early years, had no competition in its efforts to obtain politically useful knowledge of white southerners. But by the late 1950s, the Democratic party was becoming an effective competitor for that knowledge and its use. The party's effort to break the civil rights movement's monopoly on strategic knowledge of white southerners, the key to its policy from roughly 1956 through the passage of the Civil Rights Act of 1964, grew out of Senate majority leader Lyndon Johnson's efforts to lead the party in the mid-1950s. Johnson, his eyes on the White House, needed this knowledge to fight rivals for the party leadership. Specifically, he needed to make himself indispensable to the faction of the Democratic party most dangerous to him, northern liberals. He could do this by delivering progress toward resolution of civil rights crises, which, as the nation's most powerful white southerner, he discovered he was uniquely positioned to do. He began, then, to deliver, and in doing so he succeeded in forcing the Democratic party to rely on him. To keep the game going, he found himself driven increasingly to find and organize men like himself—southern white men who sought power and control and were willing to disown ideological commitments that had once been essential to their power and control. He made powerful northerners rely on those men as well.

The High Stakes of Ensuring Domestic Tranquility in the 1950s

Johnson's efforts, and his success, must be understood against the backdrop of the crisis his party was in during the late 1950s. The crisis was a result of the civil rights movement and, preceding it, of the cityward migration of black southerners. We have seen how the Eisenhower administration's frustration increased as the disorder over civil rights forced it to act, at Little Rock. Democrats in Congress and in the Democratic National Committee felt an even greater frustration, for the disturbances were all occurring in areas of Democratic monopoly. Worse, they were dividing Democratic constituencies: the South was now finding it impossible to compromise, as it had managed to do since 1932, with the northern urban-liberal strongholds, whose power had grown in the 1930s and 1940s with their absorption of millions of recent black exiles from the South.

The bewilderment of the press and the electorate over civil rights–related violence demanded relief, and that gave Democrats an opportunity. If they could blame the showdown at Little Rock, say, on the Republican president — whose fecklessness and hesitation up to the eleventh hour offended northern liberals, and whose seemingly rash deployment of troops at the last minute offended southern believers in states' rights — they could divert attention from their own complicity in the chaos (which had occurred under the Democratic government of Arkansas). The Democratic task was to make the Little Rock disaster appear to originate in the last-minute decision to send the federal troops rather than in the age-old politics-as-usual that had sent segregationists like William Fulbright to the head of the Senate Foreign Relations Committee and Wilbur Mills to the head of the House Ways and Means Committee.

Northern Democrats were torn. Party tradition dictated giving southern Democrats free rein on racial policies within their states. Yet the growing body of new black voters threatened to hold the balance of power in many state and local contests in the North. To play up to them, however, might very well alienate the Democratic establishment in the South. The party had to choose which way its future lay: giving up on large numbers of northern black voters or giving up on the South. Neither way went anywhere near the White House.

The Democratic National Committee's Attempt to Advise Party Division Away

In November 1956, the crisis of party unity gave birth to a new institution, the Democratic Advisory Council. In the course of a postmortem on the second Stevenson disaster, the Executive Committee of the Democratic National Committee resolved to form an advisory committee of "outstanding Democratic leaders in Congress and elsewhere, including Democratic Governors, Mayors, and leaders at large." The committee (which soon changed its name to Advisory Council) would find ways to help "all elected Democrats in Congress and throughout the nation to implement the platform adopted by the Democratic National Convention at Chicago, August

15, 1956." In private deliberations and public statements, DAC members stated that their aim was to promote unity and harmony in the party.[1]

Innocuous as these aims sounded, the DAC backfired loudly. It seemed that an unelected central committee of the party was about to dictate policy to elected leaders in Congress. That had no precedent in the history of American parties,[2] and congressional leaders took unprecedented offense. Speaker of the House Sam Rayburn and Senate majority leader Lyndon Johnson saw the DAC as a usurpation of their authority. They not only refused invitations to join but advised their colleagues not to join, and since the advice of those two Texans carried more weight than most politicians' threats, hardly any of them did. A few who had joined hastily withdrew. The DAC became a symbol (and in the minds of congressional leaders a cause) of the party split it had been created to mend.

Congressional Democrats tended to go along with Eisenhower's drift in policy. Cooperation with the GOP made their business easier, and so they ignored or muted partisan differences in ideology. Those in the DNC *apparat*, by contrast, needed to emphasize how much their words differed from those of their presidential opponents, the Republicans; they tended to amplify differences of ideology, even where none existed. During Eisenhower's second term, the DAC functioned as a shadow cabinet for the so-called "presidential," or Stevensonian, wing of the party, battling against the more conservative and southern-dominated congressional wing.[3] It criticized the administration more than the comparatively nonpartisan Democrats in Congress were willing to do. Each of its pronouncements was thus an implicit dig at the Democrat-controlled Congress, and sometimes even an explicit one.

The digs had considerable force. The DAC and its staff included New York governor Averell Harriman, former president Harry Truman, former secretary of state Dean Acheson, former U.S. senator from New York Herbert Lehman, former director of the State Department's Policy Planning Staff Paul Nitze, popular economist John Kenneth Galbraith, and former air force secretary Tom Finletter. The two prominent members of Congress who did serve actively on the DAC, Hubert Humphrey and Estes Kefauver, in a way confirmed the suspicion that the DAC was anticongressional. Humphrey, who had introduced the 1948 civil rights plank that led the Dixiecrats to bolt from the ticket, had become a disgruntled crusader for legislation that Congress would not pass. Kefauver, Stevenson's running mate in 1956 and one of only three southern senators who had refused to sign the Southern Manifesto of opposition to the *Brown* decision, was known as a renegade.

The more heated division that lurked beneath, and to a great extent created, the split between congressional and "presidential" wings was between southerners and northerners. In the DNC Executive Committee meeting that created the DAC, no one dared go out on a limb to advocate civil rights in strong terms. To do so would alienate southern Democrats. In private, however, Executive Committee members agreed on the undeniable need for "the Negro vote" and groused about LBJ's defense of southern power in the party. The only point they took to the public was that they were determined to fulfill the platform of 1956. A southerner on the Executive Committee pointed out that the only thing on the platform about which there was any dispute was its civil rights plank, but the public statement announcing the DAC's creation left that point implicit.

The DAC became an object of hope, and something of a refuge, for civil rights advocates and northern liberals in general. Such types were the main authors of the DAC policy papers and the ones associated in the press with DAC thinking. The five southern politicians on the DAC had an effective veto over the council's resolutions and thus kept the DAC from saying anything too strongly in favor of civil rights. But compared to Congress, with its southern committee chairmen, its antimajoritarian rules, and its disinclination to rock its own boat, the DAC looked like the best vehicle for the northern activists who wanted their party to do something about civil rights.

The Trials of Getting Along With Southern Democrats

Northerners in the DAC clearly wanted to start a real fight for civil rights. But the way they chose to fight through the DAC showed a desire not to alienate southern Democrats. Like the Executive Committee that created the council, they framed their advocacy of civil rights obliquely and euphemistically, citing the binding effect of the 1956 platform's mild civil rights plank. All southerners had approved the platform: it had passed nearly unanimously. (A strengthening amendment to the plank, offered by extreme liberals, had been defeated.) Both pro– and anti–civil rights forces had made compromises to achieve that unanimity, and the pro-civil rights forces felt they deserved a reward for their sacrifices, in the form of continued adherence to the contract. They chose to forget that the candidate who ran on the platform lost, thereby nullifying it in the minds of many Democrats.[4]

After making oblique references to civil rights at first, northern liberals met strong resistance in their efforts to become the tiniest bit bolder. In 1957, they proposed a declaration of specific acceptance of the civil rights plank, and one of the southerners objected strenuously to creeping civil rights advocacy. As a national party loyalist who had fought the Dixiecrats, and as "a very liberal Democrat," Mrs. Lennard Thomas of Alabama said that she "could not afford" to support such a resolution. Her explanation must not be written off as entirely disingenuous, any more than the northerners' urge to fight for civil rights should be written off as entirely idealistic: for both, black votes were involved. Thomas explained, "The Negro race is not a minority in the South and we don't consider them as such." In the black belt of the Deep South, enfranchisement would create black majorities in many counties: if they voted Republican, that would mean the end of Democratic rule in the South, and probably in Congress. The northern liberals were pushing too hard too fast, she argued, with little understanding of the South and the likely consequences of their actions there or in Congress. People like her could not yet think about expanding civil rights; they were too busy, in Thomas's words, "trying to preserve the Civil Rights we already have." Still, her Deep South colleague, Camille Gravel of Louisiana, stated that as a southerner he supported the civil rights resolution, provided that it did not go beyond the platform of 1956, and Mrs. Bryan Everett of North Carolina voted for it for the same reason.[5] The resolution carried.

Having passed its first explicit statement in favor of civil rights, the DAC immediately softened it. The members agreed to bury the potentially controversial announcement of it underneath other resolutions that would get equal coverage in the national press, so that it wouldn't "look like [they had come] to California to talk about civil rights and nothing else." The tactic had been suggested by a southerner, National Committeeman Hugh Clayton of Mississippi.[6]

In fighting for civil rights within the Democratic party, most Democrats were not free from their institutionalized deference to the white South. Some black voters, inspired by the movement, sought to undermine that deference by making the two parties compete with each other. But no more than a few northern liberals were willing to defy the South to get those black votes. Northern liberals depended on the Democratic party, which had built into its structures at every level a southern veto. Even a new, northern-dominated institution like the DAC felt the power of white southerners impinge on its advocacy of black rights.

A Southern-dominated Congress's Response to Party Disunity

The Democrats had another shadow government operating in the late 1950s, the Democratic Policy Committee of the Senate; it too was preoccupied with party unity.[7] While the DAC tried to live down a reputation for anticongressionalism with conciliatory statements, the DPC, from the advantageous position of elected office, felt no compulsion to go easy on the "presidential" wing. The DPC just ignored the DAC. Unlike the DAC, the DPC did not need to appeal to the media or the public. It already had all the authority it needed and therefore tended to operate so quietly that most newspaper readers were not aware of its existence. But it set the agenda for legislation, disregarding DAC efforts to make Congress conform to the platform. The DPC walked more softly and carried a bigger stick.

A principal motive behind the DAC's formation was opposition to Johnson's largely successful effort to appear as *the* national spokesman for the party. The DAC preferred Stevenson, or at least someone who agreed with Stevenson. There were reasons why the Stevensonians failed to rid themselves of the nuisance. Lyndon Johnson was a southerner who enjoyed the respect of southern voters and the friendship of many segregationist heroes, including Senator Richard Russell of Georgia, a pioneer in massive resistance and leader of the segregationist forces in the Senate. Yet Johnson had refused to sign the Southern Manifesto, one of only three southern senators who did. Unlike the other two (Kefauver and Gore), Johnson had a plausible excuse: an extreme show of sectionalism would weaken him as a national leader, the *South's* national leader.[8] As Senate majority leader he could be more useful to the South than he could be as a 100 percent correct southerner. Russell and others recognized this and defended Johnson's stance. In this way Johnson, though northern liberals envied and feared him, became the closest thing to a southerner they could work with, a southerner with a national face.

Johnson's motives for refusing to sign the manifesto and other signs of deviance from southern orthodoxy were similar to those that led the DAC to make gestures of conciliation to the South: a desire for party unity. But there was a difference: if Johnson unified the party sufficiently to carry a Democrat into the White House in 1960, the Democrat would likely be he.

This was the context in which the congressional Democrats began unmistakably, if glacially, to move toward support of civil rights legislation.

The Majority Leader Becomes the Standard-Bearer for Constitutional Rights

In a DPC meeting in June 1956, Senator Thomas Hennings of Missouri revealed the dilemma Johnson faced. Hennings stated that his position on civil rights was "a little more complicated [than that of] other Senators because of the large Negro vote in Missouri." At his latest count, that vote was 125 thousand-odd in the St. Louis area, plus 50 thousand in Kansas City. According to the meeting minutes, Johnson "said that this presented a problem for all Democrats because 'the Republicans would like to see us at each others' throats.'"[9]

In April 1956, Johnson's aide James Rowe noted that the press and political leaders were eyeing the southern Democrats expectantly, waiting for their legislative response to the judicial mandate for desegregation and the impending presidential message on civil rights. The Court and the White House seemed to be pointing the way. Would the South follow? What would it demand in return? "Unless something is done," Rowe urged, ". . . the attitude or actions of the South will be irrelevant." Southern Democrats and the Senate leadership could not prevent Congress from taking civil rights action because circumstances were "forcing the Northern wing of the Party to take the initiative." Northern Democrats had to prove their liberalism to black voters.[10]

Before this time, southerners had grown accustomed to cooperation from their northern brethren in Congress, who, after all, tended to need southerners — whose one-party states and demagogic talents gave them a corner on the seniority market and thus on chairmanships — more than southerners needed them. Since southern Democrats had disfranchised the poor voters of their states (including the vast majority of blacks in the country) at the end of the nineteenth century, there was never a serious threat of civil rights legislation during Progressive and New Deal eras.

But in the mid-1950s, with a Republican chief justice drawing black voters back to the party of Lincoln, Rowe noted that the northern liberal attitude had "hardened," not because liberals themselves had become more militant but because nonliberals now had new political reasons to favor civil rights. The Democrats' urban machines faced increasingly militant black voters, who would just as soon vote for liberal Republicans. In 1952, Dem-

ocratic bosses had supported the South to guarantee a Democratic majority. "In 1956 the 'bosses' will be leading the struggle to drive the South out,
while the 'Liberals' who at the past two conventions initiated the struggle
will go along somewhat reluctantly." Pennsylvania's large urban black electorate had gone 80 percent Democratic in 1952, but by the spring of 1956
this figure was already down to 55 percent.

To illustrate the hardening of the northern wing on civil rights, Rowe
told LBJ the story of a New Jersey boss who told Adlai Stevenson to abandon his "gradualism" on civil rights, which would cost him New Jersey.
The boss said that his area in New Jersey had fourteen thousand Negroes
who had voted solidly with him in the last several elections but had recently
become "so touchy" that neither he nor his leaders could talk with them.
The South was a "millstone around his neck," and his power depended on
the Democrats' delivering some kind of school integration law soon.

Another LBJ aide told his boss that the South was "rapidly losing its
ability to prevent the Congressional passage of civil rights legislation." The
pro–civil rights groups were growing bolder, and the vast group of northerners who were "really indifferent to civil rights" had been attracted by
the argument that the Senate had been frustrated by an "'irresponsible'
group of southerners."[11] The GOP was moving into the big cities to make
up for Eisenhower's losses in the Farm Belt. Some Democratic bosses, to
compete for black votes, wanted to drive the South out of the party even if
it meant turning over congressional chairmanships to the Republicans:
"They argue they would be no worse off than they are now."[12]

After Eisenhower's first term of inaction on civil rights, the GOP was
now capitalizing on the adventitious *Brown* decision. The president sent a
civil rights bill to Congress in 1956, and though he did not do much to support it, he did not have to do much to appear better than the party of Jim
Eastland, as some black voters came to call the Democrats. Eisenhower's
cautious steps paid off in black votes in the 1956 election: though he won
only 21 percent of the total black vote in 1952, he won 39 percent in 1956.
More important, he won a majority of the black vote in ten northern and
twelve southern cities in 1956 and the votes of such luminaries as Adam
Clayton Powell, Clarence Mitchell, and Martin Luther King, Sr.[13]

When Eisenhower sent his 1956 bill to Congress again in 1957, DPC
staff member Harry McPherson, a Texan, recalled that the southern Democrats "faced an unprecedented situation. Their traditional friends on the
Republican side were under great pressure to support the bill. Most of
them quickly succumbed. Thus in the showdown, it was the South against

the country." Republicans wanted civil rights now because they could make inroads in northern cities and in doing so "spli[t] the Democrats asunder." To McPherson, "there were many possible outcomes" for the Democrats, "most of them bad." If the administration's bill died in a Democratic Congress, the continuing shift of black votes would produce a spirit of vengefulness among northern liberals, which the southern bloc in Congress might survive but which would be fatal to any member of it who had national ambitions. On the other hand, if the bill passed after the South put up a long fight, the northern victory would humiliate the South and elevate Eisenhower as "a second Lincoln."[14]

Circumstances therefore presented southern Democrats with two choices: either accept a mild civil rights bill now or resist any bill "and have a drastic measure crammed down their throats later."[15] To Johnson's staff the first was obviously preferable, but if southerners voted for a mild civil rights bill, DPC staff director George Reedy doubted whether southern people — so many of whom were "genuinely bewildered by the 'hate the South' campaign of recent years — would understand that their representatives were acting in their best interests." It would be especially difficult for them to understand if a majority of their representatives did *not* act in their best interests, for the second road, a bombastic and futile campaign against *any* civil rights bill, was probably the path of least resistance that most southern members of Congress would take.[16]

Avoiding the Issue in the Search for Order and Unity

The Democratic coalition that formed behind civil rights legislation, as Reedy sketched it in December of 1956, consisted of four groups. "Liberals" had a "passionate addiction" to civil rights, the only remaining issue that still stirred "deep emotions." Organized labor needed to overcome its internal difficulties and saw civil rights as an opportunity to gain power in the party. (Most of this impulse came from the most politically minded faction within labor, the "Reuther group," which not incidentally consisted of the unions with the highest black memberships.) Newly animated urban bosses, whose power had been shrinking, saw Negroes as the last cohesive voting bloc to be won. "Negro groups," whose attraction to civil rights needed no explanation, were the only bloc whose power was increasing.[17]

Though Johnson's men could see nothing constructive coming out of this lineup, they could not wish it away. The most dangerous temptation the party faced in this situation was to try to recover lost votes, especially those of Negroes.[18] Liberals, who urged that course, might have regained the Negro vote, but then they would lose "almost every other vote." The ensuing North-South battle would take the limelight, allowing the Republicans to get away with murder in the dark. Republicans would quietly become the majority party, by picking up the white-collar voters repelled by Democratic infighting. The white-collar vote was the dominant political force, in the Johnson staff's analysis, and it sought social peace and stability, not radical revisions of the Constitution and the social order.[19]

For a time, this alarm-driven analysis of the crisis was pillowed by a comforting assumption: that the unnatural furor over civil rights would soon die down. Everything from events in Eastern Europe and the Middle East to the approach of Christmas at the end of 1956 gave LBJ's staff reason to believe that some of the storm over civil rights was "bound to blow itself out."[20]

But this assumption kept breaking down. On Christmas Day itself, Reedy came to the realization that his hopes had been premature, so premature that he could not even take the day off. After opening their presents, Reedy and Horace Busby tore away from their families to write urgently to the majority leader that "some action" was necessary on civil rights. The administration's bill, which Eisenhower had made clear he was going to push in the New Year, might in some diluted form be acceptable and provide a chance to wash their hands of the whole divisive issue.

Though the public's attention had returned to civil rights after Suez, Hungary, and even Christmas, Reedy and Busby reached for ways to restore their assumption that the issue would die down. They looked for ways to quiet the public's alarm. Congress needed to act to "reassure" the people that Congress was capable of acting, that its leaders were not ignoring or shrinking away from a real issue. Southern opposition had kept Eisenhower's bill from getting off the ground in 1956, but a bill crafted to avoid antagonizing the southerners might be more successful. Reedy suggested legislation to repeal the poll tax through constitutional amendment and to establish a civil rights commission with no subpoena powers and carefully controlled membership to ensure that it would be staffed by "reasonable men."[21] If, Reedy wrote, the public could be shown that "Congress can act in this field—even in a minor way—the interest in the question will abate rapidly."[22]

To make it go away: that was the goal toward which Reedy and others in the DPC continued to press, in the same ominous, plaintive tones. Their work, and their assumption, became more difficult when, on the eve of the next session of Congress, Eisenhower, having reaped the fruits of Republican appeals to black voters in his reelection of 1956, told the nation that he would reintroduce his civil rights bill and support it far more vigorously than he had before.[23] Democrats had some catching up to do. According to *Time* magazine, black defections in 1956 had convinced northern Democrats that their party had to "pay more than lip service to civil rights."[24]

A Bill to Match Johnson's Ambition and a National Leader to Protect the South

Though southerners in the House and Senate tied up the bill in committee for three months, the new interparty competition for black favor limited the collaboration of southerners and Republicans and thus permitted the House to pass a bill on June 18, after voting down amendments to weaken it.[25] As the bill fell on the Senate, Reedy summed up the situation: The South needed to assess "coldbloodedly" the debate and the political realities that lay behind it, he said, for it risked "punitive, vengeful, and possibly even disastrous legislation." Southerners could not fall back on old habits. "In the past, it was possible to kill off *all* legislation simply because Republicans were willing to cooperate. That is no longer true." The fears he had voiced in his memos for the last year had come true. "The Republicans have made a calculated decision to build their party by appealing to the minority vote. The South is now completely without allies." The South had to swallow a little civil rights or die.[26]

Using this logic, LBJ urged his southern colleagues to make some conciliatory gestures. He got his friend Richard Russell to pledge not to lead a filibuster when the bill came to the Senate floor for a vote.[27] In public, Johnson chided the "extremists" on both sides, while information about the deals he had made leaked into the press. His role as a conciliator became the subject of much editorial praise, from North and South. Reading the editorials in mid-July, just before the big Senate votes on the bill, Reedy concluded that Johnson was going to "come out looking mighty good."[28]

The important development here was not simply that LBJ had found a way to advance his career as a leader the nation needed in time of sectional disunity. It was also that the white South had found a leader who offered a way to withstand the civil rights movement's attack on its institutions without surrendering its control over events.

Johnson's greatest challenge was getting the northern liberals to go along, and the way he met it showed his great skill and luck in riding the waves of party discord. He got help from the heart of his rival shadow cabinet. One of the Democratic Advisory Council's most influential spokesmen was Dean Acheson, the head of its foreign policy committee. A member of the old New Deal *apparat* and former secretary of state, Acheson languished through the hottest years of the Cold War at the sideline offices of Covington and Burling. Easily flattered, and feeling lonelier and lonelier with his hard-line views on foreign policy, Acheson was eager to play the role of tough realist for someone who had real power. Johnson's power, kinetic and potential, was enormous, and his attention flattered Acheson enormously.[29] Johnson needed Acheson for his connections to northern liberals.

Johnson first called Acheson in to help knock Title III out of the bill; that title would have empowered the attorney general to seek injunctions against individuals and agencies that violated civil rights. Acheson told Johnson's staff how happy he was to join the effort "to convince those damn fool northern liberals not to nail their flag to the mast." Civil rights proponents such as Paul Douglas of Illinois, Acheson complained, were "saying that Russell eats Negro babies and all that kind of nonsense." Instead of Douglas's divisive language, Acheson said, "we need some understanding" in the Senate. He suggested getting Senators Clinton Anderson and Hubert Humphrey or "others with brains" to work on paring down the bill to an inoffensive provision or two.[30]

Acheson's advice symbolizes the kind of agreements northern Democrats were willing to make with southerners in the name of party unity. Johnson ended up getting sufficient northern Democratic support for weakening the bill: only thirteen Democrats voted to save Title III; it fell out of the bill on July 24 by a vote of fifty-two to thirty-eight. Johnson had unified the South with most of the North on the first big stage of a civil rights bill.[31]

Johnson soon used Acheson again at the next stage of the 1957 fight and found him even more helpful. The Title III fight depleted Johnson's limited capital with the liberals, which he needed to stake on a second weakening effort: a jury trial amendment. In the original bill, civil rights suits would be matters of civil law; in civil law, unlike criminal law, contempt citations do not carry a right to jury trial. A judge's order had to be followed. All one had to do to purge oneself of the civil contempt charge was to stop disobeying the order; no trial for contempt would be necessary, which made sense, since no penalty would normally be attached to the contempt citation. Only direct disobedience of an order would lead to a penalty. Eisenhower (who opposed the jury trial amendment) quoted Justice Taft as saying that putting a jury trial between the issuing and enforcement of court orders would lead to anarchy.[32] This is exactly what Johnson's amendment proposed to do. Johnson and other southerners stood on the principle that the Constitution guaranteed a right to trial by jury, however inconvenient it might be for those in power to observe that right scrupulously.

Northern liberals joined Eisenhower in fighting against the jury trial amendment on the grounds of realism. Experience with southern juries, which would rarely convict white defendants of civil rights violations, suggested that there were limits to the idealistic constitutional guarantee of a right to trial by jury.[33] Northern moderates looking for a way out needed strong arguments to pull them away from the liberals. To that task, Acheson lent his reputation as a lawyer. With fellow New Dealers Abe Fortas of Memphis and Ben Cohen of Indiana, Acheson helped write the text of the amendment itself, and he came up with lawyerly justifications for it.[34] They carried the day for Johnson.

In their analysis of the 1957 bill's passage, Rowland Evans and Robert Novak stress that Johnson's central task was to get northern liberals' support for both of his efforts to water down the bill. Acheson acted as Johnson's agent in securing the cooperation of the three most important liberals, Theodore Green and John Pastore of Rhode Island and John Kennedy of Massachusetts.[35] Kennedy came through in the final debate on the amendment, turning strongly in favor of the jury trial amendment and securing the last-minute endorsements of two famous professors and a former dean of Harvard Law to counter the Ivy League law school opposition to the amendment that liberals had previously mustered.[36] The Senate passed the new jury trial amendment by a vote of fifty-one (thirty-nine Democrats plus twelve Republicans) to forty-two (nine Democrats plus thirty-three Republicans) on August 1.[37]

So it was that LBJ succeeded in watering down—or as one witty historian says, drowning—the bill. The liberals won some things in return.[38] But on the whole the bill (which Eisenhower signed on September 9) was a victory for the South. The best that the bill's original supporters could say for it was, in the words of Roy Wilkins, "If you are digging a ditch with a teaspoon and a man comes along and offers you a spade, there is something wrong with your head if you don't take it because he didn't offer you a bulldozer."[39]

As Reedy predicted, LBJ had indeed come out looking good, miraculously good, in both the North and the South. The *Houston Post* praised him for his skill in avoiding "a deeper schism in the Democratic party," and the *Montgomery Advertiser*'s Ray Tucker lauded him as a "modern Henry Clay" who "saved his party . . . from splitting on the rock of civil rights." Washington columnist Roscoe Drummond was more to the point: "The senior senator from Texas is at one stroke removing from his path the single barrier which . . . has made it impracticable for the Democratic Party to select a Southerner for its presidential nominee—the barrier of opposition to civil rights legislation."[40] Yet Johnson had the support of southerners in all his efforts. Even on the final version of the amended bill, which the Deep South voted against, Senators Gore and Kefauver of Tennessee, Yarbrough of Texas, and Smathers of Florida joined him in defecting to the majority. Johnson was looking good as a national leader but also as a type of southerner.

The Civil Rights Issue Refuses to Die

But the issue did not, as LBJ's advisers planned, abate. Three days after the final vote on the civil rights bill, the Little Rock crisis began. While Congress took no action, Johnson's staff contrived new strategies of crisis management and damage control, preparing ways to put out another fire should the civil rights clamor ignite Congress again.[41] Now they had some success to build on.

The 1957 bill became a model of how to deal with civil rights trouble. Johnson and the DPC had warded off divisive legislation; they had discovered that voting rights, as distinct from civil rights, were acceptable (if undesirable) to southern Senators—if they were offered as a substitute for other (even more undesirable) rights. Early in 1958, Reedy wrote LBJ that they had embarked on "new directions" in civil rights thinking. Before 1957, all civil rights bills had been designed to punish the South, he said. Thus they were bound to fail and frustrate the northerners who introduced them. But in 1957 a mere voting rights act had passed rather smoothly.[42]

Reedy converted this lesson into a principle on which all future legislation would be based: racial minorities had to be convinced that they could not achieve the goals they really wanted "without a degree of acceptance— or at least acquiescence—from the 'white community.'" Reedy was discovering what the movement had already discovered independently. The minorities, that is, already were convinced. But he put their discovery to different use. While the movement offered to end disturbances for a measure of justice, the congressional leadership's role was, according to Reedy, "to smooth the transition"—given the inevitability of civil rights victories — to white acquiescence.

Reedy proposed two innovations in policy to give life to this new principle. The first was a "Federal Conciliation Commission," which could provide mediation or arbitration in local disputes, and the second was a new division in the Department of Labor to help minorities gain access to job opportunities. Reedy hoped that these new bureaucracies would divert protest energies into useful, small steps.[43] Here there was another transformation of the hope that drove the effort to pass the 1957 bill: no longer did Reedy assume the issue would simply *abate*. He now believed that the issue could be *removed from politics*, by creating a nonelective governmental authority for civil rights. Reedy argued for a permanent apparatus (which would supplement the Civil Rights Commission and the Justice Department's Civil Rights Division, both created in the 1957 act) to take the pressure off Congress and allow the heated debate to dissipate. In this belief that some legislative sleight of hand could remove conflict from the political arena, where it endangered careers, lay the seeds of the civil rights bureaucracy.

Master Plans for the Future Take Shape

The DPC had one more plan. McPherson proposed an off-the-record conference of prominent white southern leaders (such as *Atlanta Constitution* editor Ralph McGill, Senator Gore, Congressman Hale Boggs of Louisiana, and Governors Collins of Florida, Hodges of North Carolina, and Coleman of Mississippi). Such "moderates and conservatives" commanded "the respect of Southerners" and might therefore be the ones to "find a way out" of a predicament that threatened to destroy the South. Black leaders would not be part of these private policymaking sessions but would surely appreciate them. In return for white leaders' figuring out ways to implement desegregation, McPherson and other advisers felt they could ask for and expect "Negro self-restraint on litigation" and general "forbearance" from the NAACP. With proper leadership, such white efforts would "strengthen the forces of moderation in the South and the country at large and help prevent the split on civil rights in the Democratic Party and the Country that [was] growing every day." Johnson, it was almost unnecessary to add, was "in a unique position to break the log-jam."[44]

The white leadership conference originated in the minds of two white southerners who were then working for the new Civil Rights Commission, Harris Wofford and Robert S. Rankin,[45] who from this point forward played central roles in making Democratic strategy on civil rights. Their careers deserve some attention.

Harris Wofford was working as legal counsel to the Civil Rights Commission and had a well-established interest in civil rights. As a student for a few years in India after World War II, he had found inspiration in Gandhism. He and his wife Clare wrote a book, *India Afire*, published in 1950. As a law student in 1951, he helped organize a group of pickets to desegregate the lunch counter at Hecht's department store in Washington, D.C. He became a friend of Martin Luther King's, writing to him in 1956 as his "armchair strategist" to urge him to bolder use of Gandhian tactics of civil disobedience.[46] Wofford helped to edit and rewrite King's book about the Montgomery struggle, *Stride toward Freedom*, and helped King plan his trip to India. In addition to experience with Gandhism, Wofford had establishment connections that helped him in his effort to serve the movement. A Yale-trained lawyer, he worked for Acheson's powerful Washington firm, Covington and Burling. He was intimate with Clare Boothe Luce and Chester Bowles as well as the executives of well-endowed liberal foundations. These connections might have carried him much further into service to the movement. It became known that Dr. King needed a right-hand man, in the form of a top white establishment lawyer-adviser, and there is some speculation in the literature that Wofford was a top contender for that role, having been only narrowly beaten out by Stanley Levison, who became, in Taylor Branch's words, "King's closest white friend and the most reliable colleague of his life."[47]

In addition to all this, Wofford was the great grandson of a Confederate colonel (also one of the biggest slaveholders in Mississippi). Wofford began his life in Johnson City, Tennessee, and though he moved from there at the age of six to upstate New York, he felt at home in the South in many trips and when stationed in Alabama as an airman in World War II. After graduating from Yale College, he scandalized his very southern grandmother by choosing a black law school to further his education. Howard University was the best place to go to learn about civil rights law, to which Wofford's interest turned after his return from India. His mentor at Howard, George Johnson, persuaded Wofford to finish law school at Yale, so that he would "know both worlds." Wofford ended up getting degrees from both places and thus was the first white person to graduate from

Howard Law since the suffragists who, having been denied entry everywhere else, attended a half-century before.[48] By the late 1950s, frustrated in his efforts to play an active role in the direct-action movement, Wofford left his job at Covington and Burling to take a job with the Civil Rights Commission.

Less is known about Robert Rankin, then chairman of the political science department at Duke. Rankin was southern born and bred and had a long record of service in the Southern Regional Council, a breeding ground of the kind of middle-road white southerners who intervened without publicity in desegregation crises and tried to bring opponents to compromise. Much of the council's work had been the distribution of studies and factual reports among editors and academics to legitimize desegregation among southern intellectuals: to show, above all, that desegregation need not lead to violence. Rankin did some work for the Civil Rights Commission staff shortly after it was set up and would later be appointed as one of the six commissioners.[49]

The first proposal these men submitted to the Democratic Policy Committee, strongly supported by Johnson's Texan aide, Harry McPherson, is a window into the thinking of the southern moderate forces then angling for influence in the Democratic party. As southerners, these men felt that they alone had the credibility and experience to lead the South away from social upheaval and a dangerous party realignment. Many northerners ended up agreeing with these proposals (beginning with the head of the Civil Rights Commission, Notre Dame president Theodore Hesburgh, who endorsed Wofford and Rankin's proposal), which suggests partly that the proposals had the desired effect of convincing northerners that it was best to let the South deal with its own extremists and partly that northerners just did not have sufficient knowledge of the issue to come up with practical alternatives of their own.

The Rankin-Wofford proposal sought a compromise solution through off-the-record meetings of southern white men. On the agenda of those proposed meetings, Wofford and Rankin wanted to emphasize — either out of genuine interest or as a rhetorical carrot and stick — the benefits of compromise for the investment climate in the South and the effect of disorders on America's reputation abroad. As a more immediate danger, they stressed party disunity. Holding all these concerns together was the call for effective leadership, which implicitly meant Lyndon Johnson.

The concerns about America's reputation abroad and party disunity, and the faith in salvation through good leadership, created common ground between the DPC and the Democratic Advisory Council. On that common ground, the chairman of the DAC's foreign policy committee kept up his affair with the Senate majority leader.

The duty to correct the entire course of the U.S. party system and Congress was one that Dean Acheson would not shrink from. When Acheson realized that his former colleague from Covington and Burling had a way of getting the majority leader's ear, he was eager to improve the relationship by making himself the intermediary. A few months after McPherson introduced the Wofford-Rankin proposal to LBJ, Acheson wrote the majority leader with a new proposal that he was sure could break the crisis in the party by diverting the nation's expectations from Congress. This proposal consisted of two papers, "done in consultation" with Acheson, by Wofford and Rankin. Acheson's enthusiastic endorsement was useful: it suggested in prototypical form the plan's appeal to northern Democrats. The plan's attractiveness to a top member of the DAC must have increased its attractiveness to LBJ; certainly Acheson hoped it would.

Acheson informed the Texan who had benefited so much from his counsel in 1957 that this promising new "method of extricating [southern leaders] from the impasse in which they [found] themselves on the school and voting questions" came along just in the nick of time: "The thought that the present course of events may continue . . . really terrifies me," he confessed. Echoing the secret cold warrior manifesto of 1950, NSC 68 (drafted by Acheson's protégé at State, Paul Nitze), Acheson said that NATO lacked not only the weapons to measure up to the Warsaw Pact but also the social and ideological "determination." The Soviet threat made this the worst of times to try to work out racial difficulties at home. "The present trend of the North-South division will tear our country and our party apart." And according to Acheson, it would hand the Republicans the White House in 1960. Though he allowed for shortcomings in the Democratic party, the fact remained that the country could not "survive six more years of Republican government." A GOP victory in 1960 would last almost to the end of the current Soviet Seven-Year Plan, "way beyond any time within which [the United States could] survive Russian nuclear missile superiority." Acheson concluded, without the irony we instinctively read into all such statements today, "It is sheer treason to throw away this next election. A default to the extremists on civil rights will surely do this."

Acheson softened this rhetoric somewhat by philosophizing, as he often did, about the democratic process. At a loss for guiding principles and perhaps sensing the need to calm himself, Acheson drew on his Anglophiliac education: R.H.S. Crossman, he reminded Johnson, had once said with solemn British authority that "democracy means the civilizing of the struggle for power and the softening of rugged conflicts of principle by injections of sweet expediency." Lest this penetrating insight fall wide of the gritty Texan's learning (Johnson had probably never heard of R.H.S. Crossman), Acheson aimed at a larger target, his ego: "I turn to the one man in the Democratic Party whose rare gifts of leadership and equally rare courage make possible the solution of this seemingly insoluble problem."[50] Acheson fueled these flights of philosophy and flattery with earthlier substance: the enclosed memos from Rankin and Wofford showed that the two had been busy, since their last foray into the DPC's councils, putting flesh on the bones they had strung together for McPherson. Rankin had contacted some southern governors (Luther Hodges of North Carolina, LeRoy Collins of Florida, and Lindsay Almond of Virginia), who expressed some willingness to participate in a conference to solve desegregation "by southerners [in a way] that would be reasonably palatable to the South."

More important were Rankin's contacts with "various businessmen in the South," allied civic leaders, and local officials. "An overwhelming number approved the mediational approach to this matter."[51] As any southerner by this time knew, southern businessmen and civic leaders were numerous, diffuse, and disorganized enough to yield to a variety of pressures and temptations and to accept a variety of options for dealing with local civil rights activity. In that respect they stood in stark contrast to southern politicians, who kept a party discipline that would have impressed Lenin. If the businessmen or other local leaders worked without national attention, they could evade the politicians' deadly baiting—not because the politicians would fail to notice, but because low publicity would allow them to look the other way. However strong their commitment to segregation, the southern politicians' first duty was to save their public reputations by avoiding a battle that many of them sensed they stood to lose.

Wofford and Rankin wanted Johnson to take decisions about civil rights out of the hands of politicians, a mediagenic group, and put them into the hands of business and civic leaders, an invisible one. Removing the issue from public view would remove much of the temptation to make drastic gestures of resistance to change. If they could break a single Manichean fight up into a panoply of small, practical, and confusing "problems," then the issue, at last, would be out of the public eye and thus Congress's hair.

Depoliticization: LBJ's Ticket to Political Power

This urge to depoliticize had shaped the 1957 act, which created the Civil Rights Division at the Justice Department and the Civil Rights Commission—bureaucratic structures that, unlike an elected politician, offered no focal point for public anger and had no accountability to voters. Now the DPC was finding a new outlet for responsibility in what is today called the "private sector." Though that sector so often appears antagonistic to the "federal bureaucracy," its function was the same in this case: to relieve politicians of the terrors of politics.

By late 1958, the party's stewards of legislative policy had formed their strategy for responding to the shocks of mass direct action, which began at Montgomery in December 1955. After hoping it would go away, DPC staffers landed upon a way to depoliticize the spreading crisis by turning it over to southern moderates, preferably unelected ones who could work without publicity.

This plan was at odds with the movement's plan to force the same southern white leaders to grant complete desegregation, step by step. Pursuit of party unity pushed black demands for justice far into the background of legislative strategy. Rankin and Wofford gave first priority to meeting the southern white leaders, soothing their egos, appealing to their interests, gaining their confidence. Meeting black leaders came up only as a secondary concern. Once the carefully chosen white leaders were operating smoothly, Rankin wrote, "a group of Negro leaders might be invited to attend a conference to be held with such men later." Might be. And later rather than soon, so that "a plan of action could be prepared" before "disagreement and division" destroyed all hope of getting a plan.[52]

Wofford, despite his commitment to racial justice, had a countervailing commitment to Democratic unity. He and the DPC staff aimed to "modify the political and public attitude of absolute resistance throughout much of the South"; he saw no way to do that quickly. On the contrary, forcing the issue was the biggest danger. The increasing representation "in Congress and in the councils of both parties of militant northern and western champions of federal civil rights legislation" was already pushing the party to the brink of disaster. Johnson had to convince southerners to start compromising on their own, for continued southern resistance would provoke destructive "federal intervention in the field of public education on a massive scale."[53] Wofford was careful to make his alternative sound as palatable as possible: "the South must take the initiative"; "local resolution . . . by local communities" would result in "very gradual, voluntary plans of desegregation." He defined the party's goal narrowly as compliance with the Supreme Court's new constitutional interpretations, "with only token integration in most districts at this stage."

Even token integration was too much for the Deep South. These initiatives were to take place in the peripheral southern states — Florida, North Carolina, Tennessee, Texas, and (by this time) Virginia — where even on a "limited, gradual" scale, they would break up "the monolithic approach" that was "entangling everything" at the time, "even if some deep southern states did not immediately follow suit." Rather than apply civil rights to all parts of the South, which would unify the South and thus divide the Democratic party, Wofford thought it better to divide the South.[54] The trouble was, the Deep South was where the movement wanted to focus, for exactly the same reasons that Wofford wanted to avoid the region: focusing there politicized the issue. The issue, for all the Democratic Policy Committee's efforts, did not go away.

Lyndon Johnson Takes Center Stage – and Then an Intermission

T he plan to control the civil rights crisis through southern white moderate leaders did not remain confined within the Senate majority leader's offices. The Democratic Policy Committee staff was groping for a way to build a record of success in civil rights settlements, in other words, a way to keep northern liberals from taking the initiative on the issue and thus to keep the party's sectional wings at peace. More and more, this meant finding white business and civic leaders (and an occasional governor) in the South who could grant concessions to civil rights groups and supplant racist demagogues by presenting the public with a road to peace without radical change. Johnson needed large numbers of such leaders and he needed to organize them. They were the basis of his plan to make himself the party unifier. He was one of them and knew how to use them better than anybody. But the principles of his strategy, and one of his strategists, proved adaptable, and he soon had trouble keeping other candidates from reaping the rewards of their success.

A Provisional Unity: The Second Civil Rights Bill

The day after the new session of Congress opened, in January 1959, Johnson submitted Senate Bill 499 as an alternative to strong civil rights bills that were gaining liberal support.[1] He sought, as Reedy described it, a moderate bill around which "reasonable men" could rally.[2] The heart of Johnson's bill was a provision for a federal Conciliation Service, patterned after the Wofford and Rankin proposals. This new federal agency would set up meetings of local white leaders all over the South and help them frame successful negotiations with black leaders. The bill contained no provision to mandate desegregation or enfranchisement. Its purpose was to "restore communications between groups in the Southern states." The service could repair "washed out bridges." In the words of one of Johnson's assistants, "Like the U.N., if people can be kept talking they may be stopped from fighting."[3] Since the liberals were weaker now than in 1957, S.499 gave the South an opportunity to ward off intrusive legislation: "If a reasonable bill can be passed during this session," Reedy wrote, "it will probably be the last for many years."[4]

Congress took no action on civil rights in 1959, torn as it was between Illinois senator Paul Douglas's strong bill and Johnson's weak S.499. For the time being, the Conciliation Service died (it was later reborn in the act of 1964), but Johnson found other ways to serve the larger aims that the service was designed to meet. Through dilatory skirmishes, he held off the party schism long enough to keep his own leadership in the spotlight. More important, he put those who wanted a civil rights bill before the 1960 election on notice that they had better craft a bill closer to Johnson's bill than to Douglas's bill if they wanted to get any bill to come to the floor, let alone past a filibuster. LBJ had gotten a bill through in 1957. No one had been able to do it since. He was pointing the way Congress had to go.

Johnson's power provoked the presidential wing. The Democratic Advisory Council, under Paul Butler's leadership, had become the main weapon of pro–civil rights Democrats outside Congress, and in July 1959, Butler struck out at LBJ directly. He publicly accused him of breaking party discipline by working against the pledges made in the 1956 civil rights plank. The attack completely backfired, as Johnson rallied nearly every Democratic senator, and a good many members of the other house, to make public statements of disagreement with Butler.[5] Party unity, to congressional Democrats, now meant squelching the DAC. From then on, Butler's complaints about congressional obstruction of civil rights legislation seemed to be based on the desperate assumption that he had nothing more to lose. Far from bringing congressional leaders to heel, his complaints only succeeded in dividing the DAC itself. In mid-March 1960, the most prominent southern member of the DAC, Florida governor LeRoy Collins, joined the other five southern members, including significantly Senator Kefauver, who had taken his stand against southern racists in the past, in a public dissent from the DAC's call for stronger civil rights laws. This dissent portended not a split in the presidential wing but the death of the DAC's influence. As the convention of 1960 drew near, congressional

Democrats — Kennedy, Johnson, Symington, and Humphrey — dominated the field of contenders for the presidential nomination, and the prospects of the DAC's preferred candidate, Stevenson, faded. With the "presidential" wing sputtering sour grapes and Johnson riding high in Congress, the party seemed in better shape than ever to withstand a civil rights debate.

In the 1960 session of Congress, the impending presidential election created overwhelming pressure to pass some form of civil rights bill. The legislative battle over what became the 1960 Civil Rights Act followed the pattern of the 1957 battle. After Eisenhower announced in early January that he would push for passage of his previous year's civil rights bill, leading northern Democrats and liberal Republicans announced that they would make passage their top priority. Johnson, however, made it clear he would fight to restrict any bill to a narrow coverage of voting rights. Proposals for desegregation he wrote off as "extreme" and unlikely to survive a filibuster. "What is needed," he wrote, "is an effective bill that will satisfy the consciences of 67 senators." That could best be done "without punishing one section of the country for the alleged sins of its grandfathers."[6]

The bill evolved, under LBJ's stewardship, to avert such punishment. The Senate eliminated from Eisenhower's bill any explicit focus on the southern states and on specifically segregationist crimes. It passed a bill that created new criminal penalties for obstruction of federal court orders "by threats or force" and for interstate flight to avoid prosecution for use of explosives. It required preservation of federal election records for inspection by the attorney general and provided schools for military dependents in areas where public schools had been closed. Finally, it instructed federal judges to appoint special referees to register black voters in areas where the attorney general, after winning a voting rights case, had gone on to prove a general pattern of discrimination. To arrive at these provisions took nearly 400 hours of Senate debate, carried on over eight weeks, including one record-breaking filibuster of 125 uninterrupted hours.

The end product, as in 1957, was less of a bill and more of a majority leader. When the final bill passed both houses in April 1960, LBJ dominated the headlines, taking most of the credit when the papers, after weeks of critical reporting, quit the fray and in their relief accentuated the positive.[7] But civil rights proponents were disappointed. Senator Douglas said Congress, after weeks of bitter controversy, looked like "the mountain that labored and brought forth a mouse." What his colleagues had passed could "only by courtesy be called a civil rights bill." Senator Joseph Clark of

Pennsylvania said the act of 1960 left standing "only a pale ghost" of the law he had planned to create and was thus "a crushing defeat"; Senator Jacob Javits of New York called it "a victory for the old South." Outside Congress there was less restraint. The 1960 act, said Thurgood Marshall, was not worth the paper it was printed on.[8]

Though many of the southern segregationists made a last stand of opposition by voting against the watered-down bill,[9] their real feelings were summed up by Senator Robert Byrd of Virginia, who agreed with the liberal Javits that the bill's passage was "a victory for the South." Senator John McClellan of Arkansas (who during the debate proclaimed that he would have to be "arrested" before he would answer a filibuster-breaking quorum call) avowed that southerners, by "fighting with their backs to the wall," had succeeded in killing "the far more odious and obnoxious proposals" for civil rights.[10]

More to the point, in an election year, they had remained in the Democratic party, their destructive power spent on civil rights provisions rather than on party unity. Just a few months before final passage, Governor Collins joined his fellow moderate Governor Luther Hodges of North Carolina and a prominent segregationist, Governor John Patterson of Alabama, in a call for party unity. In Hodges' words, the Southerners would be "foolish beyond comprehension to run out of the party with the control we have in Congress."[11] Southerners were confidently saying they would fight northern liberal attempts to drive them out of the party rather than (as in 1948 and 1952) threatening to bolt. An intraparty peace had been achieved.

Slouching toward the White House

What was good for the party was good for Johnson. Johnson went into the convention with large numbers of southern delegates and a strong reputation as a party unifier: the northern Democrats might not like him, but they needed him. But although LBJ had held the party together enough to pass the civil rights acts of 1957 and 1960, and to gain the allegiance of such influential northern Democrats as Acheson, he just had not done enough to consummate his presidential ambitions by the end of Eisenhower's term. When the votes were counted in Los Angeles in the 1960 Democratic Convention, all that was left open to LBJ was a back door to the White House.

If LBJ's interest in the civil rights issue was limited to a majority leader's concern for party unity and a southerner's need to signify a repudiation of sectionalism, that much could not be said for Senator John F. Kennedy, the man who held that back door half open, somewhat grudgingly. The conflict of views on how Kennedy ended up with Johnson on his ticket obscures the basic fact that there was good sense, as well as ample precedent, behind his choice of a southerner—and more sense, if less precedent, in his choice of a southerner who was cagey enough about civil rights to hold wavering southern voters without driving away too many black voters. The choice did help solidify southern support, and though it was initially seen as a setback for Kennedy's chances with black voters, the new team immediately set up private meetings with black delegates to take the edge off an angry liberal threat of a floor fight over the choice of running mate. To these black delegates LBJ said that, although he had come as a candidate for first fiddle, he was not a "cry-baby" and he did not want to "pout." He promised to discourage southern efforts to gut the platform: "I want to campaign from one coast to the other on the platform." Kennedy needed someone who could unify the party: "I had no choice except to do my duty and I'm going to do it and I don't believe you folks will be sorry, I think you will be glad."[12]

It was remarkable that Johnson's image as a civil rights liability was something Kennedy had to overcome. For Kennedy's own record on civil rights never involved taking a stand on anything controversial. His driving fear was alienating his southern supporters, whom his father and every other political adviser urged him to woo. Back in the 1950s, Kennedy courted segregationist support and reaped promising rewards for doing so. In 1956, Mississippi governor J. P. Coleman and Georgia governor Marvin Griffin (the one who traveled to Little Rock to goad Governor Faubus into a last stand for white purity) led the southern movement supporting Kennedy's bid for the vice-presidential nomination. During the debate on the 1957 bill, though Kennedy reluctantly cast some votes against the southerners, he helped weaken the bill by campaigning for the jury trial amendment. As he warmed up for the presidential campaign of 1960, Kennedy secured promises of support from segregationist leaders including Mississippi senator John Stennis and Georgia senator Herman Talmadge. When Adam Clayton Powell and much of the black press attacked Kennedy's position on civil rights, Kennedy sent copies of their critical statements to southern leaders to remind them that he was their enemies' enemy.[13]

Kennedy's southern support was not solid, however, and he became vulnerable for indecisiveness on the issue. During the congressional debate on the 1960 bill Johnson taunted Kennedy for being absent from roll calls on crucial civil rights votes.[14] In a 1959 biography, James McGregor Burns suggested that JFK's record on civil rights was "a profile in cowardice."[15]

Kennedy wanted to keep his own stance (or rather lack of a stance) as quiet as possible. He tried hard to halt the NAACP's criticism, with some success—Roy Wilkins, after criticizing JFK in 1956 and 1957, ended up endorsing him in his 1958 Senate race, for example—but where Johnson sought to take command of Congress in order to neutralize civil rights as a national issue, Kennedy simply sought to neutralize the issue's effect on his own career. It was a northern leader's luxury that its effect on his career was separate from its effect on the national party alignments. By the 1960 campaign, JFK had few endorsements from either black leaders (who preferred Humphrey) or southerners (who preferred Johnson). But though he was preferred by neither, as historian Carl Brauer concludes, he had succeeded in becoming acceptable to both.

Kennedy's ambitions for the presidency, to the extent that they contained ideals at all, centered on a desire to remake foreign policy with strong executive "leadership." He did not crave reform of social life at home, let alone look forward to upsetting Congress with the legislation reform would require. "The Negro" was as far from the center of his concerns as an issue could be. Though he followed Congress in learning to tiptoe around civil rights, his chief confidant and apologist Theodore Sorensen noted that he just was not very interested in the issue.[16]

But the issue, to paraphrase Trotsky, was interested in him. Though he had beaten out all the candidates who competed for the presidential nomination, he had not beaten out black protesters who competed for the limelight of national imagination. As Congress wore itself out watering down the civil rights bill, sit-ins sprang up in Greensboro, North Carolina, and spread to Nashville and the rest of the South: the desegregation movement moved into its more youthful, more diffuse second phase. From then on, it was no respecter of politicians. Without any central leadership or organizational structure, the sit-ins took the politics of local confrontation, which the first phase of the movement had used to isolate, in sequence, Baton Rouge, Montgomery, Tallahassee, and Little Rock, into nearly every major city in the South at once. In doing so, they cleared a new avenue for southern black hopes and an equally wide one for Democratic leaders' fears, just at the time when it seemed that the Civil Rights Act of 1960 was warding off the advance of both.

A man who depended on his image as a decisive and clear-headed leader could not afford to appear to ignore a disruptive social conflict — as Eisenhower had done until it was too late in 1957. Pollsters predicted a very close election, which meant that black voters in northern cities might decide the outcome.[17] When the issue thus became irresistible to Kennedy, he had no experience to fall back on. He sought the services of someone who *was* very interested in the issue and thus could take his mind off it.

While Harris Wofford was helping Lyndon Johnson's Democratic Policy Committee deal with civil rights, his work for the Civil Rights Commission (Wofford was its legal counsel) caught the attention of Joseph Kennedy's son-in-law, Sargent Shriver. Shriver was facing his own civil rights crisis as head of the Chicago school board. He got some suggestions from Wofford, but before he had a chance to put them to use, Shriver resigned from the school board to devote himself to his brother-in-law's presidential campaign. Wofford followed him, with some hesitation. Wofford was not at all attracted to John Kennedy's positions on civil rights, but he had heard in Kennedy's foreign policy speeches a way to jump out of the frying pan of Dulles's Cold War nationalism without landing in the fire of Acheson's hard-line realism. Wofford believed Kennedy could create a "new" foreign policy, which would abandon both narrow-minded nationalism and Eurocentric power politics and respond instead to the needs of new nations fighting for independence (as he had seen India so movingly do). Wofford's fan letters to Kennedy focused on foreign policy as his earlier letters to King had focused on Gandhian tactics. John Kennedy, whose advocacy of Algerian independence had provoked Dean Acheson to attack the young senator's ignorance and inexperience, was particularly gratified to hear encouragement and praise from his influential critic's law partner. Wofford began writing foreign policy speeches for Senator Kennedy.

After the Kennedys won the Democratic nomination in 1960, they asked Wofford to join the campaign full-time. Since the candidate knew he was in trouble with black voters,[18] he assigned Wofford to head a new "civil rights section" in the campaign staff, which would report to Sargent Shriver. Wofford's careful work, though motivated by deep conviction, allowed JFK to maintain his equivocating stance. Wofford had the ear of prominent black leaders, including Martin Luther King and Roy Wilkins, as well as such northern liberal lights as Chester Bowles, Wofford's former employer.[19] He also had the ear of a wide range of white southerners. As staff counsel to the Civil Rights Commission, he had worked for the three prominent white southerners Eisenhower had appointed to that body. His work with Robert Rankin, coauthor of the proposals sent to the Democratic Policy Committee, had given him an in with LBJ's trusted Texan aide Harry McPherson. Wofford, as the one who developed the idea for local advisory committees to the CRC, plugged himself into a growing network of moderate white southerners, a network that rivaled the independent structure set up by the Southern Regional Council. These discreet ties to both of the crucial blocs of voters made Wofford the ideal navigator to chart the perilous course past the Scylla of antisouthernism and the Charybdis of indifference to the Negro.

Looking for a Way Out of Civil Rights and into the White House

Shortly after hiring Wofford, Kennedy told him bluntly to "tick off the ten things a president ought to do to clean up this goddamn civil rights mess." He gave Wofford five minutes. Wofford began to lay out a strategy of emphasizing executive, as opposed to legislative, initiatives, including the famous "stroke of a pen" order to end discrimination in government-financed housing. The idea of executive action appealed to Kennedy because it would allow a new president to circumvent the party division that seemed to require Congress to make such a "mess" out of the issue. The mess was getting deeper. The Democratic Platform Committee had passed, without the Kennedys' knowledge, a radical civil rights platform, on which Kennedy was bound to run. Republicans in Congress smelled blood and began to circle. By introducing bits of the Democrats' own plank as bills, they taunted Senator Kennedy with a chance to make himself an honest man: he could fight today in the Senate for what he promises to fight for tomorrow in the White House, could he not?[20] But of course he would not, needing as he did the help of southern Democrats to get to the White House. The potential for embarrassment here made a Harris Wofford necessary. More than what he would be able to do as president, JFK needed Wofford to figure out what he had to do to become president. To that task Kennedy now directed Wofford to devote himself, and allowed him considerably more than five minutes.

Wofford's first assignment was to combat the plausible Republican argument that Democratic majorities in both houses failed to make good on their own civil rights planks for the simple reason that their presidential nominee could not lead his own Senate. A statement that Wofford wrote for Kennedy countered that the GOP only introduced the bills to tie up Congress and thus prevent passage of minimum wage, health care, school construction, and housing bills. Congress had had its civil rights fight that year already. Kennedy promised he would put the power of the White House into the push for a better civil rights bill early in the next session and even asked Senator Joseph Clark and Representative Emanuel Celler (sponsors of strong bills in the past) to start drafting the bill. He produced the signatures of twenty-three senators who had consistently voted for strong civil rights provisions who now supported him on this pledge.[21]

The pledge had a strong appeal to the civil rights movement, which needed to hope and which, it must be said, was accustomed to trusting charismatic leaders. The juxtaposition of Eisenhower's bland countenance with a deadlocked Congress fed optimism about JFK's becoming the new chief executive: he might break the deadlock with his air of irrepressible determination. The first televised debates pitted a freshly suntanned Kennedy against Richard Nixon, who had lurked in the shadows of Eisenhower's indolence for eight years and was now pale and listless from campaign exhaustion. Despite a record that was at least as good as Kennedy's on civil rights, the Republican candidate was too much of a sourpuss, if he was not yet a consummate schnook, to engender high hopes for innovation in a controversial field.[22]

With little of substance to bank on from either candidate, black voters were at least getting campaign promises from Kennedy's civil rights section. The most thorough and sympathetic student of Kennedy's civil rights policies, Carl Brauer, notes that the candidate's early commitments were largely symbolic.[23] The question whether symbolic action "worked" during the campaign — and thus whether it would set a pattern for future presidential action — was whether it placated enough civil rights leaders to win their support, in light of the available alternative, without sacrificing southern white support.

The Politics of Symbolism

One of the campaign's symbolic moves suggests how much political energy it took to engineer a symbol. The sit-in movement, in addition to forcing JFK's organization to start devoting serious, if mostly indirect, attention to the demands of black voters, goaded Martin Luther King's SCLC to keep up with the suddenly ubiquitous young limelight stealers in SNCC. The black student leaders in Atlanta, Lonnie King (no relation) and Julian Bond, aided incidentally by such white southerners as Jane Stembridge and Bob Zellner, directly challenged King to make good on his Gandhian rhetoric about "filling the jails." King reluctantly joined the students in a sit-in at Rich's department store. "I had to practice what I preached," King told a reporter. He ended up for the first time in his life spending a night in jail.[24] The Kennedy campaign's opportunity for a symbolic gesture was also an opportunity to prove the value of covert assistance from southern white moderates.

Wofford enlisted one of his white southern contacts, Morris Abram, an Atlanta lawyer and Kennedy supporter who was close to the mayor, in the effort. Abram ended up getting Mayor William Hartsfield and the owner of Rich's department store to agree; both were middle-road white southerners already striving, as counterparts had done in Montgomery, Tallahassee, and Little Rock, for compromises that would restore order. Hartsfield, seeking accomplices in a risky move, appeared on television and announced that he was releasing King in response to Kennedy's direct personal intervention. There was a hitch, however: in joining the sit-in, King had unknowingly violated the terms of his probation for a previous traffic violation. Therefore the judge, turning down a hasty plea for release on bail until the traffic conviction came up for appeal, sent King up to the state penitentiary for four months for parole violation. Hartsfield could do nothing about that. All of the other demonstrators were released.

A rural southern prison was one of the most terrifying places a black man could imagine himself in. Coretta King was convinced that inmates and guards in the penitentiary, with or without the warden's direct encouragement, would get the white South's revenge on her husband. "They are going to kill him," she told Harris Wofford. Wofford and Louis Martin, the top black adviser in the civil rights section, tried to get Kennedy to intervene again, first by issuing a statement expressing his concern to the press. A promise from Georgia's Democratic governor, Ernest Vandiver, to resolve the matter without involving the candidate put the release of that statement on hold. Then Wofford and Martin asked Kennedy to apply the human touch by consoling the distraught Mrs. King over the telephone. After some wrangling, they got Kennedy to agree. From a Chicago hotel room, he took a moment to express his sympathy to her and said, without going into specifics, that he would do what he could for her.[25]

One day later, King's attorney, Donald Hollowell, presented his case for King's release pending appeal of the original traffic violation. The judge reversed his earlier rejection of a less thorough version of this case and let King out of jail.[26] The outcome might have been affected by the intervention of Robert Kennedy, who, apparently without the candidate's knowledge, called the judge and somewhat heatedly told him this kind of thing would be frowned upon if his big brother won. The judge gave no indication that he had been influenced by the Kennedys' interest in the case, of which he must have known (from Hartsfield's television broadcast) before sending King up in the first place. Whether he was influenced or not is impossible to say and entirely irrelevant to the political trends of the day: the temporal proximity of the famous Kennedy phone call to King's release made it easy to imagine a logical sequence in the chronological one.

Black voters were encouraged to believe that intervention from a merciful and benevolent candidate saved King from a four-month hell in rural Georgia. While it is every bit as possible that the candidate's intervention encouraged local keepers of the peace to put King away in the first place, just to show they would not let meddlesome Yankees push them around, many civil rights advocates found the Kennedy appeal irresistible. Martin Luther King, Sr., who until that day was not only Republican but anti-Catholic, told the press, "Because this man was willing to wipe the tears from my daughter's eyes, I've got a suitcase full of votes and I'm going to take them to Mr. Kennedy and dump them in his lap."[27] The civil rights section quickly printed a pamphlet contrasting the boldness of the "Candidate with a Heart" with the callousness of "No Comment Nixon," whose staff had failed to pick up the phone. The highly enfranchised black ghettoes of northern cities were flooded with these pamphlets. Southern eyes were protected from them.[28]

The exact effect of the call to Mrs. King is hard to measure. The shift of black voters to the Democratic party in the 1960 election (only 7 percent over Stevenson's 1956 showing) was not so overwhelming as to suggest that they thought Kennedy's symbolic politics were the answer to their prayers. To Kennedy's staff, however, it was sufficient to suggest that Wofford and his contacts had come up with a winning formula for getting out of the "civil rights mess." In crucial northern districts, where civil rights may have been secondary to the economic and social policies of the local machines, the Democratic totals of the black vote were often 80 percent.[29] LeRoy Collins, who was elected chairman of the Democratic National Convention of 1960, said Kennedy believed that massive distribution of the "No Comment Nixon" pamphlet in Chicago's black belt might have accounted for the narrow victory in Illinois. The pamphlet influenced black voters throughout the North, Collins said, "and, so far as [Kennedy] could determine, it had no damaging effect in the South."[30] If self-congratulation oversimplified the election data, at least bitterness confirmed the oversimplification: Eisenhower lamented that his side lost the election "because of a couple of phone calls."[31]

Election Strategy Becomes National Policy

The call to the King family during a crisis made it clear that the Kennedy way of tentative and private approaches could at least get prominent black leaders to soften their complaints about the Democrats' historic opposition to civil rights. Martin Luther King, Jr., though moved by Kennedy's call, did not go so far as to endorse the Democratic candidate, but he did announce he was indebted to Kennedy and stated privately that he increasingly saw Nixon, whom he had known much longer, as a moral coward who would not even make a minimal personal effort. The best thing of all was that this kind of jockeying, set up as it was by Wofford through white southern moderates like Abram and Hartsfield, suggested that the personal, piecemeal, symbolic touch could work without alienating southern Democrats. As Wofford assessed things in March 1961, Kennedy won because both black voters and "a large part of the white South" had voted Democratic. They did so because of a unique combination symbolized by Lyndon Johnson on the ticket and a strong civil rights plank in the platform. The Democratic ticket embodied "the combination of faith in a new South and determination to end racial discrimination everywhere." The campaign was "a combination of a strong appeal to the South and a strong civil rights campaign."[32]

But this was a paradox. Wofford's very position in the campaign was based on the axiom that these two things could not both be strong. The definition of each required any increase in the one to come at the expense of the other. What the civil rights section's work allowed the Kennedy campaign to do, then, was redefine the Democratic meaning of "civil rights." Wofford helped the Kennedy campaign finish squaring the political circle by redefining the issue as a symbolic one, expandable before black audiences, retractable before southern white ones. There was no guarantee, however, that Wofford would be able to translate the symbolic reconciliation into a real one — even if he were able to win the full devotion of Kennedy's staff to the issue.

The Kennedy administration's policies never departed from the pattern of making piecemeal, mostly symbolic moves in civil rights and checking each move out ahead of time with southern white leaders. The task of pushing those leaders into a position in which more and more of them had to make concessions was the work of the civil rights movement. However, since that movement increasingly used the federal administration as part of its strategy to force the changes it sought, it yielded more and more of the initiative, and ultimately the basic direction of the fight for civil rights, to the federal government. The government, in turn, took its direction increasingly from the white moderates of the South.

The effort to find a way through "this civil rights mess" continued after the election. The threat of party disunity continued to loom; though it no longer threatened Kennedy's election, it threatened his legislative program. As Kennedy told Sorensen, "If we drive [Alabama senators John] Sparkman and [Lister] Hill and other moderate southerners to the wall with a lot of civil rights demands that can't pass anyway, then what happens to the Negro on minimum wages, housing and the rest?"[33]

Wofford became chairman of JFK's Subcabinet Group on Civil Rights and his chief White House aide on civil rights. As the head of the subcabinet group, Wofford met with deputies, assistants, and undersecretaries of cabinet officers to plan the integration of black employees into the government bureaucracy and other quiet initiatives. The subcabinet group coordinated such actions as Defense Secretary McNamara's decision never to use federal troops to enforce segregation again and Health, Education, and Welfare secretary Ribicoff's requirement that beneficiaries of National Defense Education Act grants conduct their programs without discrimination.[34] Many in the civil rights movement viewed the long delays in other subcabinet initiatives, such as integration of the National Guard, as failures, but because the efforts were scattered and ever pending, they gave the administration the opportunity to inform black leaders that much progress was being made. Above all, the subcabinet group worked well in the overall scheme of White House policy because it was quiet and thus could not endanger southern cooperation with other programs in Congress.[35]

The Kennedy Policy Shows Signs of Strain

Wofford's work as the chief White House aide on civil rights consisted largely of responding to complaints from civil rights advocates, who achieved a rare unanimity in their belief that the Kennedy administration had abandoned them. Wofford's main line of defense was always that the administration had taken a number of steps "to secure full constitutional rights for all Americans." Wofford found his own responses as exasperating as his friends in the movement found them, but he had had reason to expect exasperation from the beginning.[36] He knew that his candidate saw civil rights as at best a nuisance and at worst a danger; the issue had never been on the list of those on which Kennedy wanted to exert his much-vaunted leadership. Kennedy's best and brightest shone in other fields. Since policy was shaped by Wofford's own ability to devise ways to get the problem out of their way, his largest hopes rested on the problem becoming bigger in the nation. The conflict within him was that his job was to make the problem smaller.

Kennedy gave his staff orders to restrict civil rights policy to things that did not involve Congress, lest he upset his entire congressional program.[37] From the start, Wofford supported Kennedy's decision to avoid legislation. Although he knew (as he told Kennedy) that it was "heresy in the civil rights camp" to favor "a minimum of civil rights legislation and a maximum of executive action," Wofford was on a first-name basis with the major civil rights leaders and spoke with confident authority of their ultimate willingness to go along. Civil rights organizations had not yet "adjusted to the idea of the primacy of executive action." Initially they would have greeted a decision to forgo legislation as a "sell-out," but, Wofford told Kennedy, once they tasted "the fruits of executive action," they would know "the barrenness of their legislative lobbying, and see that the logic of such executive action [would] lead to complementary legislation — and lead there sooner than a party-splitting legislative battle at the beginning of [Kennedy's] administration."[38] In the summer of 1961, Wofford's superior, Frederick Dutton, defined the purpose and limits of Wofford's executive action. "The dynamics both here and abroad compelling desegregation in this country are accelerating. How to provide leadership for those forces and moderate southern difficulties without destroying the Congressional coalition at mid-term is the nub of the problem."[39]

Civil rights leaders seemed willing to try dropping the legislative effort, provided that the administration delivered on its promises for executive action; so a report by the Southern Regional Council and an article by Martin Luther King suggested in early 1961, both spelling out executive actions the administration could take.[40] The civil rights leaders had no desire to antagonize southern Democrats per se; they had just found doing so unavoidable when pushing meaningful legislation in the past. Wofford was encouraged that there was a way to keep the confidence of civil rights leaders within the administration's constraints.

But as time wore on, executive action failed to quench the thirst for presidential leadership. The reason was that proposals for action that would actually satisfy the civil rights leaders were never as valuable to the Kennedy administration as proposals that would keep the issue quiet.[41] Wofford fervently believed in civil rights, and he believed that gradual progress in executive action would pave a path *to* a winnable legislative battle. He also believed that the Kennedys would follow that path. But to get the Kennedys' ear, he had to stress ways to defuse the issue more than ways to provide substantive aid to southern black people. For example, Wofford told Kennedy that the way to avoid "summit meetings with large delegations and great expectations was to hold occasional informal meetings."[42] He then persuaded Kennedy to meet with Roy Wilkins in order to "calm some of the Negroes' fears" that Kennedy was "dodging any formal meetings with Negro leaders."[43] Informal meetings would allow Kennedy close personal contact but, more important, would keep the coverage in the white press down to quiet speculation. Still, the basis of Wilkins' and other leaders' agreement to meet was their hope that Kennedy's promise of bold executive action in lieu of legislation was about to bear fruit. That hope became steadily less tenable.

The biggest specific campaign promise for bold executive action proved too much for Kennedy to live down. For two years after his election, Kennedy declined to issue the "stroke of a pen" housing order he had let Wofford persuade him to promise. In protest, civil rights advocates began sending the White House pens by the thousands; JFK said, "Send them to Wofford." Wofford had drafted and submitted the proposed executive order early after the election, but Kennedy kept yielding to Senator Sparkman's requests for delay and Senator Russell's insistence on watering it down. Wofford claims that he saw for the first time in these delays "the degree to which [Kennedy] was terribly responsive to the southern leaders in Congress." Wofford realized that in proposing the course of executive action to Kennedy in the first place he had failed to realize that the same forces who opposed legislative action would oppose executive action, too.[44]

The housing order, when Kennedy finally agreed to sign it, on November 20, 1962, was an anticlimax. It applied only to new federal housing, leaving out the vast majority of housing already built, and of course left all private housing undisturbed. To issue this order, Kennedy waited, as Sorensen said, till "the lowest key time possible," just after the midterm elections, and sandwiched announcement of the order in between dramatic headline material: an announcement on Soviet bombers leaving Cuba, and another one on Sino–Indian border clashes.[45]

Harris Wofford and Lyndon Johnson:
Central to the Policy, Dispensable to the Administration

Wofford became irritated with his role as "a buffer" for the administration, as he described it. "All the Negro leaders would see me and think they were getting something through to the president." The heat from his civil rights friends intensified as it became clear that the administration was not going to deliver the promised program of "bold" executive action. In the summer of 1962, he left the White House, returning to the dreams that had once attracted him to the Kennedys: the promise of an idealistic new foreign policy. He went to Africa to supervise Peace Corps operations there and began reporting again to his most sympathetic audience within the Kennedy family, Sargent Shriver.[46] When Wofford left, his position as a civil rights adviser was not filled. His duties were transferred to a regular White House staff adviser, Lee White. For a time, civil rights leaders lacked a confidant, and the administration a lightning rod, within the White House.

For Lyndon Johnson, walking the civil rights beat in the Kennedy administration was as frustrating as it was for Wofford, though for different reasons. Where Wofford had a passionate belief in civil rights, LBJ had a passionate belief in his own leadership. The administration's assigning Johnson to the low-priority field of civil rights may have been a way of keeping him away from the center stage of policy. But whereas Wofford had nothing to hope for by sticking it out, Johnson had everything to hope for.

As Wofford's subcabinet group followed the habits of the campaign, so did LBJ's domain, the President's Committee on Equal Employment Opportunity. Like the subcabinet group's action, the PCEEO's action was voluntary, gradualist, and piecemeal. It too met with very low publicity and aimed to show black leaders changes while keeping things quiet and voluntary enough to avoid antagonizing southern members of Congress. While the subcabinet group concentrated on government employment, the PCEEO concentrated on the private sector: its main activity was securing voluntary agreements from government contractors to improve minority representation in the high-paying jobs.[47]

The principal achievement of Johnson's PCEEO was the Plans for Progress program. Here the administration's strategy of doing things quietly and voluntarily met with its most encouraging success and found its most energetic exponent, Bobby Troutman, a white southern lawyer.

Plans for Progress began as a response to civil rights leaders who wanted the PCEEO to grow some teeth. They thought that employers would take it more seriously if they could make an example out of a company that resisted desegregation. They wanted one big government contract canceled, and Lockheed's plant at Marietta, Georgia, was a prime candidate.[48] The PCEEO, which had been investigating a complaint from a Lockheed employee, did not get very far before Troutman, an old schoolmate of the president's from Choate, intervened. Troutman, who had extensive political and social connections in Georgia, had been active in JFK's campaign, during which he had discouraged advocacy of civil rights in general and contact with King in particular. Troutman now put together a voluntary "Plan for Progress" for Lockheed and gained the enthusiastic backing of both Kennedy and Johnson in letting the plan go forward as an alternative to cancellation of Lockheed's contract.[49]

Soon Troutman, whose aggressiveness, ability to make the president laugh, and consequent ease of access to the Oval Office became something of a legend, persuaded the administration to set up similar Plans for Progress with other contractors across the nation and began reporting substantial progress in his plans. The PCEEO also set up an advisory council on Plans for Progress, composed of leading industrial managers, to encourage more voluntary efforts from southern white businessmen, even in companies that were not federal contractors. Voluntary programs always carry an implicit threat that if no one volunteers, a mandatory — and harsh — policy will follow. The reports of the participating businesses did provide a source of information for possible future policy initiatives, and the act of reporting itself often served as a goad to change. Wofford testified that the PCEEO "acted vigorously" on the six-hundred-odd complaints it received.[50] A handful of minority group members that each contractor hired in the top job category, "Officials and Supervisors," spread out over 112 firms, added up to a total of 506 new minority group members hired in those positions nationwide.[51] If the pressure of complaints could have been maintained, this change could have grown from a change of appearance into one of direction. But with the administration so keen on keeping its work quiet, and so disinclined to use coercion on a civil rights issue, the 123 major companies that volunteered for Plans for Progress could consider their mildest effort a virtual guarantee against government enforcement.[52] The diffusion and complexity of the gains — always in response to scattered, individual complaints — made further pressure extremely hard to focus. Moreover, as a voluntary program, the gains were tenuous: what the employer giveth, the employer taketh away.

The Plans for Progress program was frustrating to civil rights leaders, but frustration that expressed itself by asking for more of what was being done gave a certain advantage to the administration. This action, however scattered, was far more extensive than anything under Eisenhower.

President Kennedy's reliance on personal friends working behind the scenes could deflect movement pressure in more direct ways. In Albany, Georgia, as we have seen, Martin Luther King came in to give a flagging protest a jolt of inspiration at the end of 1961 and in doing so put Albany's white community into the same position as the Kennedy administration: wanting to quiet down King's effort. James Gray, publisher of the *Albany Herald,* the only paper in town, came to personify that common position. Gray had become a companion of Joseph Kennedy, Jr., on the Ivy League basketball circuit, and when Joseph died, he became a friend of Joseph's younger brother Jack. Gray's corner on the media market in southwest Georgia helped Kennedy during the 1960 campaign, as did Gray's chairmanship of the Georgia state Democratic Committee. Gray was an extreme segregationist.[53]

In the first half of 1962, Burke Marshall of the Justice Department, who had been looking into what the protesters at Albany said were false charges and other violations of black rights, got in touch with the mayor of Albany and urged him to compromise.[54] Others in the administration got in touch with Gray, who opposed any hint of compromise. Gray joined other respectable local citizens in a private investigation of the charges Marshall was considering and thereby lessened the administration's incentive to intervene. Gray's investigation led to the indictment and sentencing of more black protesters, rather than those accused of violating the protesters' civil rights.[55] Elsewhere in the South, cosmopolitan intellectuals with lots of money like Gray (who was a native New Englander) often lent legitimacy to desegregation compromises by speaking in favor of them or by participating in them, but Gray lent legitimacy to the opponents of compromise. Gray condemned and threatened local white leaders who hinted at compromise, and lobbied his friends in the administration to leave things up to the local authorities.[56] The administration became, by omission if not commission, complicit in Gray's efforts.

The administration was not consistent on Albany. The Justice Department filed an amicus brief supporting the Albany Movement's side in court, and the president stated in a press conference that the city of Albany's refusal to desegregate public facilities "as required by the Constitution" was preventing a settlement. In private, the administration continued, in the words of a presidential staff assistant, "to use all possible powers of persuasion" to settle out of court. The administration's contact with James Gray was a principal avenue of this private effort. It is not clear exactly what Gray asked and what the administration agreed to give him.[57] But far more important than the amicus brief and the press statement was Albany's contribution to the growing record of administration refusals to step in unambivalently and defend the rights of the protesters.

After King left the city, things in Albany got worse, and Gray was active in the worsening. The city of Albany closed its recreational facilities rather than yield to pressure to integrate them. Gray bought the municipal swimming pool from the city and immediately turned it into a "private" pool that could stay all white. The administration would do no more.[58] Perhaps its intervention would not have saved the movement from defeat there. But Gray's well-known friendship with Kennedy, and the administration's failure after repeated requests to defend the rights of the protesters, left Albany's black community suspicious and resentful of the administration.[59] Suspicion and resentment, as always, exaggerated the degree of active complicity; but the Kennedys had lived by the sword of political symbolism in campaigning for black votes in 1960 and could not have been too surprised to find it was double-edged. Indeed, they needed it to be double-edged, for they were always campaigning for votes of southern whites as well as those of blacks.

Despite the administration's alienating Georgia's black leaders through its quiet diplomacy in Albany in 1962, however, it soon lost its hold on Georgia's white leaders. In response to the Civil Rights Act of 1964, Gray would become the Georgia chairman of Democrats for Goldwater.[60] Georgia went Republican for the first time in its history in 1964.[61]

Old Habits Die Hard

If the contacts with Gray reveal the limitations of the administration's behind-the-scenes approach to white southerners, Harris Wofford told a revealing story that suggests why the administration nonetheless found the tactic so promising. After entering the White House, Wofford kept up his contact with the Civil Rights Commission, to which fell the responsibility to investigate violations of voting rights. The commission wanted to publicize violations in order to increase public pressure for redress. Though the Justice Department and the FBI resisted the commission's effort, a well-placed moderate white southern Democrat offered covert aid to the commission. "You're here to help niggers vote," Louisiana governor Earl Long told CRC staff director Berl Bernhard. "And I'm for you because they're my niggers and I want their votes." Long said that his rival Leander Perez, the political boss of Plaquemines Parish, was preventing pro-Long Negroes from voting. "Now we're never gonna talk about my helping you," Long said, "but I'm gonna get my state registrar to give you the records you need, and after you talk to him, you remember, you never saw me."[62]

This story, though probably true, could serve as an allegory. It reveals in one moment the main outlines of the predicament the administration was in. The bed of southern politics was as procrustean (and as colorful) as ever. The administration, always trying to keep the issue quiet, could not control the many forces who needed to publicize it. The white southern moderate was comfortable in the knowledge that everybody needed him more than he needed them. Just as local white business and civic leaders could play the civil rights movement against the local government to increase the demand for their own good offices as mediators, they could now play one part of the federal government against another. If only out of canny opportunism, the white southern moderate would make common cause with civil rights activism if such activism could hurt his enemies, which it very often could. That was enough to give the movement infusions of hope in government action. But the hope, for obvious reasons, paid off only irregularly, and government action remained vulnerable to manipulation in the other direction by the southern white moderates.

Policy in High Gear

From the Justice Department
to the Acts of 1964 and 1965

T he revolutionary innovations that came out of the Kennedy-Johnson administration's clash with the movement, the civil rights acts of 1964 and 1965, began to take shape midway through Kennedy's last year. Considered by their provisions, these two acts constituted a radical break from the first two years of Kennedy's policy (and from the earlier Democratic Policy Committee's policy, with which the Kennedy policy merged). Considered by the aims behind them, however, the two acts are of a piece with the previous policy. The acts of 1964 and 1965 grew directly out of the administration's efforts to keep civil rights quiet. Those efforts, which relied on assistance from white southern moderates, increased the power those moderates had and gave them the means and incentive to use their new power.

The difference between the early policy and the 1964 and 1965 acts was twofold. On the one hand, it was a vast quantitative increase in the number of white southern moderates brought into the administration's network of influence. On the other hand, it was a qualitative change in white southern moderation, which, under direct pressure of the movement in the late 1950s and early 1960s, came to mean taking concrete (if small) steps toward systematic desegregation. Prior to the movement years, it meant assurances of good will and occasional tokenism: moderates followed the lead of segregationists as long as segregationists had unchallenged power and rounded off some of the rough edges of their rule. In the late 1950s and 1960s, as the movement gained strength, moderation increasingly marched to the tune of desegregation. The moderates gained greater and greater authority through their ability to restore peace by outflanking intransigent segregationists and compromising with black leaders. They gained still greater authority from the private advice and occasional promises of support they got from Washington. In the center of the administration's civil rights policy, the Justice Department, the roots of these two changes, and their continuity with the administration's previous evasive action, appear most clearly.

The Heart of Administration Policy

While the White House remained timid and ineffectual, the Justice Department took center stage in civil rights policy early in the administration and, particularly in the personality of Robert Kennedy, developed a growing commitment to black rights as the years passed.[1] Quite unlike the White House, the Justice Department had a covering duty to carry out the law, strictly, rather than a naked responsibility to initiate policies, creatively. It should be immediately apparent that assigning the main burden of civil rights policy to the Justice Department was another way of divesting the issue of its potential to divide the Democratic party. Not presidential leadership but obscure legal arguments initiated civil rights policy—and left the final decisions to unelected, life-term judges, many of whom were Republican appointees.

The consignment of most civil rights policy to the Justice Department was consistent with Kennedy's only excuse for supporting Title III back in 1957 and with Johnson's partial deference to civil rights demands as Senate majority leader: the sanctity of the Constitution and law. Those who feared alienating southern Democrats could hide behind that. Obedience to law was the hardest thing for white southerners to disagree with; even Senator Russell conceded that the law had to be obeyed.

Since the judges who were making the laws were mostly white southerners,[2] deference to the law meant, in practice, deference to respected men with southern accents who could take the heat off the Yankee administration in Washington. Human intentions, which historians can rarely detect with any certainty, are not under scrutiny here: there may have been no conscious decision to move federal authority over civil rights southward. The point is that the Kennedy administration experimented and ended up devoting itself most to what "worked." As in the campaign, what "worked" was what placated enough civil rights advocates enough of the time to ward off the danger of defections of black voters, while at the same time reassuring white southerners that their party was not abandoning them. The reliance on the Department of Justice "worked" in this sense because the court cases were quiet and rarely made good copy for more than a day or two. They tended to diffuse, and thus defuse, the issue that civil rights activists tried to focus on a single city, a single restaurant, a single policy, one at a time.[3] Court cases produced lengthy, complicated, and often inconclusive proceedings. There were few dramatic climaxes. That took the sting out of the civil rights movement's strategy.

Moreover, while the Justice Department became the focus of civil rights activity in the new administration, civil rights activity did not become the focus of the Justice Department. The attorney general had no civil rights policy, in the sense that he had an organized crime policy.[4] Robert Kennedy would have no truck with moralizing crusaders, and that was how he viewed civil rights leaders. The culture of the Kennedy administration was marked by great displays of disdain for "preachy" men and causes. A charge of impractical zeal could chill any proposal, however sound. Yet the president's brother did not lack a crusader's drive. He was a missionary against the mob, just as McGeorge Bundy and Walt Rostow were missionaries against the Reds in Southeast Asia. The truth behind the displays of disdain was that the administration would not tolerate preachiness in politically divisive matters. The field was open against easy targets.

Civil rights was the most divisive matter of all: preachy men would offend the South, and from the start, the Justice Department strove, like the rest of the administration, to avoid that. Harris Wofford, Robert Kennedy said, would have been the logical choice to head his Civil Rights Division, but Wofford came off as too much of a crusader.[5] Wofford was one of the few white lawyers in the country who had studied civil rights law, certainly the only one the Kennedys knew. Burke Marshall, on the other hand, had never devoted himself to civil rights law and had no record of association with the movement. Byron White supported Marshall for the position because Marshall was simply a very competent lawyer who would ensure "that southerners would not think of [civil rights policy] as a vendetta, but as an even-handed application of the law."[6] Wofford himself approved the choice for similar reasons.

Marshall's staff at the Civil Rights Division followed the same strategy of conferring with local white southerners that Wofford had set up in the White House. Having a full staff and being lawyers, however, they were more methodical about it. The first step the DOJ took was to get clear information. The department's main apparatus for information gathering, the FBI, obstructed more than it facilitated investigations of civil rights violations in the South. Therefore the Justice Department had to have a duplicate investigating structure, which it began to construct out of a private network that already existed in the South and gathered precisely the kind of information the department needed: the Southern Regional Council.

The SRC had been gathering information for years and stood ready to provide the Civil Rights Division what the FBI could not or would not provide. Burke Marshall began receiving detailed reports of civil rights activity from the SRC's indefatigable agent, Benjamin Muse. The SRC sponsored Muse's research trips as part of an extensive program, whose main purpose was communicating with the white South.[7] It had become an interracial organization, and it often served the movement—with which Muse did not identify himself—directly. But it did so mainly by advocating desegregation as the sober white South's antidote to racist demagoguery. It quietly repeated that desegregation was inevitable; the only issue for realistic southerners was whether the change would be gradual and peaceful or needlessly destructive. If the administration had to make the South change, yet keep its white voters loyal, the SRC was an ideal source of know-how and know-who.

The SRC focused on moderate white southerners in an operational as well as a doctrinal sense. Though Muse always met with prominent black leaders, the task to which he devoted most of his intelligence and energy was locating possible avenues of negotiation and compromise with local white leaders. Muse, and following him the Civil Rights Division, saw in these avenues the way to keep the smoldering crisis from erupting.

To the Kennedys (and to many civil rights leaders) Muse's focus on the white South made perfect sense. The white South was, after all, the body that needed to change. But the administration's fear of offending the white South kept it from seizing the opportunities Muse created. John Kennedy, as historian Carl Brauer describes him, was driven by an image of history in which Reconstruction figured as the grand wrong turn to be avoided. He did not read Du Bois or the later revisionist historians but held to the D. W. Griffith–Claude Bowers view that northern impositions on the South were uniformly vengeful, unnecessarily destructive, and ultimately counterproductive. In the same way that the memory of Munich harrowed critical thinking out of foreign policy circles, the memory of *Birth of a Nation* harrowed it out of domestic policy circles. The Kennedy administration had what could be called a carpetbagger complex. It was always searching for, and more often finding, ways to avoid imposing itself on the South.

Muse continued to stake out a difficult path for Kennedy to take toward racial change, a path that would not remind the South of Sherman's March. The purpose of Muse's investigations is conveyed by his first report, sent from a trip to northern Alabama in June 1961. This report centered on Muse's effort to "appraise the amount of liberal or moderate sentiment on the race question," an effort handicapped by "an almost universal care on the part of white liberals to conceal their liberalism." ("The instinct for survival has led to the development of almost incredible skill and ingenuity in this.") Still, under the surface, Muse discerned quietly germinating seeds of change. Though every white leader appeared superficially to be an "uncompromising segregationist," close observers could "go over a list one by one" and name a substantial number who were "gravely concerned" over the situation and were "prepared to accept desegregation."

Like the movement leaders before him, the more involved Muse became with civil rights, the more he felt drawn to middle-road white southerners who had enough credibility with the segregationist masses to maintain authority yet never had to prove loyalty to crowds of white voters or face electoral opposition. Muse spent most of his time in Birmingham with three politically active white lawyers, Charles Morgan, David Vann, and Charlie Nice. Vann and Morgan were "about as liberal as Roy Wilkins" and yet managed to keep top positions in the state and county Democratic organizations. With the help of these extreme liberals, Muse painstakingly identified who was who in the "Birmingham power structure," ferreting out those who were "moderate leaning" and those who were lost causes. Some who called themselves segregationists nonetheless accepted the need "for adjustment to the law of the land" and saw the need to keep racial issues from damaging "the state's economy and America's position."[8] In his meetings with black leaders, too, openings to white leaders were a major topic of discussion. More and more he saw the potential in unobtrusive, unelected white leaders.

In speaking with top figures in the "economic power structure," a group distinct from white liberals, Muse located potential sources of pressure to bring out the best in other white southerners. These leaders told Muse that racial disturbances "did more damage to Alabama's economy" than many realized. An executive of one big corporation feared long-term damage to executive recruitment after six top specialists scheduled to come to work for him in Alabama cited racial disturbances as the reason for changing their minds at the last minute. "If the national administration

wanted to help," a white lawyer well connected to the business establishment told Muse, it could have convinced "half a dozen people outside of
Alabama" to apply pressure for change. "New York bankers had a great
deal of influence with Birmingham bankers and industrialists, and they
might be the handiest to approach." If the Kennedy administration could
get U.S. Steel president Roger Blough and a few bankers to "point out
emphatically to their Birmingham associates" that this "anti-Negro business" threatened "the economic stability and progress of Alabama, things
would change."

The message of this and more than a dozen other detailed reports that
Muse sent to the Justice Department over the next few years was that white
leaders were waiting to find a way to compromise. Powerful white southerners would not only welcome changes but bring them about, *if* they
could get relief from local demagogues. The logic was geared to appeal to
the Kennedy brothers: only proper national leadership could provide such
relief. Muse did not neglect to mention that, on the other side, the segregationist extremists regarded the government of the United States as "the
enemy!" and that they often "ridicule[d] Attorney General Kennedy."[9]

Through the use of the SRC's extensive contacts, and others set up less
formally, Justice officials tried to set up, at least in their imaginations, negotiating committees to resolve expected crises.[10] Anticipating the trouble
that was to erupt in Birmingham in 1963, Burke Marshall began receiving
detailed reports directly from one of Muse's white contacts in Birmingham, Norman Jimerson, in May 1962. Jimerson was an official of the local
SRC affiliate, the Alabama Council on Human Relations.[11] Jimerson's
reports supplemented Muse's and would help the Civil Rights Division
develop its policy of behind-the-scenes negotiation to the fullest extent
ever. Then, in the fall of 1962, Marshall's office made direct contact with
the Alabama Council on Human Relations and another group of local moderates, the Alabama Advisory Committee to the Civil Rights Commission.[12]
Both of these groups included black as well as white leaders who had an
interest in ending racial conflict but studiously avoided identification with
the direct-action movement.

These informal contacts allowed the administration to show black
leaders that it was active in encouraging change. But they also allowed it to
maintain what could be called plausible deniability of involvement with
these mostly private initiatives if southern politicians ever raised the issue.
This is not to say that those politicians were too stupid to notice the
thumbprints of John and especially Robert Kennedy on these initiatives.

Far from it. The elaborate evasion of obvious government involvement worked well because it allowed southern senators — who mostly recognized the irresistibility of the pressure on the administration to do something, especially as much of that pressure was coming from their own white constituents — to look the other way. It was not the stuff of headlines, and thus of little use to aspiring or incumbent demagogues.

Federal Intervention in Civil Rights Adds to yet Divides Pressure for Change in the South

It must be borne in mind that the Kennedy administration was not the only organization making contacts among southern white moderates. In the meantime, movement leaders continued to make the same kind of contacts that Muse was making, and of course much of the SRC's systematically collected information inevitably made the rounds in movement circles.[13] The difference was that now the Justice Department increasingly had the same or better information. Should a crisis boil over, the department would know where to apply its resources and its authority to turn down the heat. Movement leaders had triumphed over opponents in Montgomery, Tallahassee, Little Rock, and other places because they understood southern white society better than its putative defenders. But now the movement's tactic of studying the power structure was no longer a solo effort. The federal government was becoming a competitor for that kind of understanding, as much as an uneasy ally. The government's information gatherers, with greater authority and resources, were able to get what they needed to keep even with the movement's intelligence. But for the government this information gathering, as long as tensions did not flare up enough to ignite the headlines, was not its top priority. For the movement, it always was. That was only one of many differences of approach that made cooperation difficult between government and movement. The total pressure for change in southern race relations, while unquestionably stronger with the government's force added to the movement's, was no longer single-minded and indivisible. Now the middling white moderates of the South (the main sources of the government's information) had someone else to deal with. They could call the shots.

The federal government, for its part, consciously developed its contacts with white moderates in the South, without publicity, in order to have someone to negotiate with besides the black leaders and the extreme segregationists. The Justice Department led the way. Rather than develop an adversarial, public relationship with the white South, it sought cooperative, quiet relationships with disparate white southerners. This was true even in the field of litigation, usually an adversarial field; in the vast number of suits the Civil Rights Division initiated, the general tendency was to avoid confrontation, to avoid publicity. Victor Navasky quotes Burke Marshall as saying that "federal policy under Attorney General Kennedy was to try to make the federal system in the voting field work by itself through local action, without federal court compulsion." This meant negotiation first, even in seemingly hopeless areas. Sometimes negotiation worked, Marshall said, as in the southwest Georgia county where no black person had been registered for decades: "Repeated visits by a southern-born lawyer from the Department to the county board of registrars finally led to a policy decision by the board members that Negroes should be registered on the same basis as whites. More than three hundred Negro citizens were registered in the county in less than two weeks. State officials never became involved at all." Marshall said there were countless other examples. Behind-the-scenes negotiations with white southerners dominated the department's operations. Only if they failed would the department go to court.[14]

Outside the field of litigation, a curious pattern developed in the department's civil rights activity. The department's files show that, in addition to expansion of staff and caseloads in the Civil Rights Division, the Lands Division, the Tax Division, and the attorney general's special assistant, also devoted their time and expertise to the Civil Rights Division's work. For a department that saw civil rights investigations more as an unavoidable burden than a positive good, it was remarkable that it should go out of its way to divert additional resources to them. Part of the explanation for this extracurricular activity lies in the Kennedy administration's generally covert approach to civil rights. If someone from Tax or Lands came down, black voters would be aware that someone from the Justice Department had intervened in their neighbor's, their cousin's, or their preacher's case, while white southerners (including those who reviewed the department's budget in Congress) would not necessarily see increased activity in "civil rights." But a larger part of the explanation lies in the personal backgrounds of the special assistant, John Seigenthaler, the head of the Tax Division, Lou Oberdorfer, and the head of the Lands Division, Ramsey Clark: all three were white southerners.[15]

Seigenthaler, a Nashville newsman who crusaded against labor racketeers in the 1950s, got to know Robert Kennedy during the latter's tenure as counsel to the Senate Permanent Committee on Investigations. The two became very close when Seigenthaler moved in with Kennedy to help Kennedy write his book *The Enemy Within* (1960). Their collaboration continued in the 1960 campaign, in which Seigenthaler served, among other things, as a contact for southern leaders. When the new attorney general chose Seigenthaler as special assistant, one of the first tasks he assigned him was a racial survey of the department's lawyers. Seigenthaler found there were only 10 black lawyers among the department's 955, and that result spurred Kennedy to ask the top law schools to send him their top black graduates. Soon the department had more black lawyers quietly working for it than ever.[16]

Seigenthaler also served the department's civil rights effort in an informal capacity. He greased the wheels of the general approach, described by Burke Marshall, of setting up out-of-court negotiations with local southern officials—out of the range of publicity and therefore of politics. Robert Kennedy sent Seigenthaler around the South to investigate school desegregation plans and prepare the school officials for compliance. "I'd go in," Seigenthaler said, "my southern accent dripping sorghum and molasses, and warm them up. Burke would tell them what the law was: . . . a pretty effective team." That these negotiations worked became clear when the New Orleans, Atlanta, and Memphis schools desegregated in September 1961 without violence.[17] That those desegregations were of the gradual, token kind prescribed by Wofford and Rankin in their memos to Johnson's staff—and that this kind of desegregation exasperated the movement's ranks and whetted their sense that society owed them a great deal more than it was giving—suggests that Democratic policy grew quantitatively under Kennedy but did not change qualitatively.

Seigenthaler became famous during the Freedom Rides of the spring of 1961. He had gone in the name of the Kennedy brothers to escort wounded protesters out of Alabama, where mobs had beaten them and set fire to their bus. Seigenthaler wheedled promises of protection for the riders out of the Alabama governor, John Patterson, and the head of the state police, Floyd Mann. Mann's men escorted the bus along the state roads but would not intervene, after the riders entered Montgomery, without an express invitation from Montgomery police or clear signs that order had broken down. Montgomery police vacated the scene, and the mob beat the riders with impunity. The only protection they had was Seigenthaler and Marshall's assistant John Doar.[18] When Seigenthaler, with a touch of chivalry, went to the aid of a female rider trying to escape in a taxicab, the mob beat him into unconsciousness, as it beat other white southerners that day, including news reporters.

The patience of the administration snapped, and Robert Kennedy ordered in federal marshals, first to protect the riders and then to protect Martin Luther King, who came to Montgomery for a mass meeting the next day.[19] The southern white press, without approving of the riders, excoriated the mob that day for violence and the local police for dereliction of duty.[20] The administration's boiling point was approximately the same as that of "respectable" white opinion in the South: willing to tolerate segregationism as long as it refrained from brutality and disorder. It was never clear whether the administration was outraged at the segregationist mobs or the riders who provoked their anger. Either way, it responded to the movement's pressure to do something, in other words, to politicization of a moral issue. The administration did its best to unpoliticize it, through a southern-born emissary's negotiations with local authorities.

To concerned liberals outside the administration, Seigenthaler's failure to avert violence in Montgomery suggested that peace in the South required less negotiation and more force. For once, the Kennedys seemed to agree: in Seigenthaler's concussion, the Kennedys finally had a precedent, a bloody shirt, to justify use of coercive federal power. The impulse to use force did not develop into a consistent policy, however. The sending of marshals was a desperate last resort. The administration still hoped the issue would abate and that wholesale, federally mandated change could be avoided.

During his tenure at Justice, Seigenthaler had acted as a kind of emissary-at-large and confidant for the attorney general. (He left the department early in 1962 to become editor of his old paper, the *Nashville Tennessean*, a voice of the liberal South.) Lou Oberdorfer's official beat was a much duller affair of settling cases for the Internal Revenue Service. Oberdorfer had the plodding intelligence to fill a position that called as much for an accountant as for a prosecutor. He had a driving ethic of hard work and loyal service and never took credit for what he did. He made no waves, and no history, at the Tax Division. No one could accuse him of being a crusader.

If that did not make Oberdorfer perfect enough for making Kennedy-era civil rights policy, he was the one man in the administration who had grown up in Birmingham, Alabama. When Martin Luther King's SCLC joined forces with Fred Shuttlesworth's Alabama Christian Movement for Human Rights and chose that city as the battlefield for Project C (as in confrontation), the administration turned to him. The record suggests that Oberdorfer devoted as much of his energy to civil rights as to tax investigations in the summer and fall of 1963.

Burke Marshall had prepared Oberdorfer for this role by forwarding copies of Muse's reports on Alabama to him. In June 1963, Oberdorfer began making reports of his own. These became the main source of the Civil Rights Division's information on compliance with desegregation rulings. The making of these reports, through informers in business, the clergy, and the professions, took Oberdorfer's eyes and ears all over the South and thus supplemented his firsthand knowledge of Birmingham with a comprehensive understanding of the movement's tactics and achievements. They afford a penetrating view into the department's thinking.

Oberdorfer first started checking the progress of desegregation of private businesses through hundreds of individual reports and the records kept by trade associations (such as the National Restaurant Association). The main question his reports addressed was, did the (usually) voluntary action of white owners, individually or collectively, put an end to the demonstrations? If the answer was no, the fallback question was, what impediments are there to a satisfactory compromise that *would* end the demonstrations? The reports, not infected by any preachy attitude toward justice and equality, sought ways to restore social order.[21]

Oberdorfer's running tallies of progress arranged southern cities into three columns: those where desegregation had been accomplished, those where it was "imminent," and those that had activated the "civic machinery" to try to reach a settlement.[22] Nearly every day at 5:30 P.M., Oberdorfer reported new events as signs of change. Where failures and delays gave the protesters a sense of pessimism about the immediate future, which translated into a need for drastic federal action, Oberdorfer's vast compilation of local details strengthened the Justice Department's faith in the progress of local, voluntary compliance.

The reassurance that progress was being made without massive federal intervention was an indirect function of Oberdorfer's daily reports. They also had a direct function in the formation of policy: they pulled together not merely information but information sources — white southern men and women who would develop confidence in their government contacts and thus become sources of government initiative and control.[23]

The president met with these southern white leaders at the White House in June and July 1963. Kennedy wanted the meetings to give isolated individuals who were groping for a way to ease tensions in their communities the feeling that they were not alone. Their vast numbers, all there in one room, suggested that changes that seemed so difficult to each of them working in isolation were in fact possible.[24] Whether all of the individuals gained such confidence remains unclear; it was crucial at that moment for the *administration* to gain confidence.

The administration's efforts to stimulate voluntary changes, Oberdorfer wrote the attorney general on June 17, 1963, demonstrated that the South was not a "monolithic bastion of resistance to desegregation." On the contrary, "a great many people in the area" were ready to make changes. Oberdorfer merely added the isolated efforts together, however, and that was a major shortcoming of the administration's policy. He did not integrate them into a comprehensive program. The vicissitudes of voluntary compliance with desegregation were as frustrating to the civil rights movement as the vicissitudes of segregation and disfranchisement themselves — which, as we have seen, rarely functioned as a monolithic system. On the contrary, segregation and disfranchisement consisted of a piecemeal series of escape hatches from the Fourteenth and Fifteenth amendments. The movement discovered that the escape hatches could swing both ways — the black community could win concessions by hitting local pressure points in the white leaders' sense of decency or in their opportunism — but it could not nail them shut. Once the pressure was off, the escape hatches would swing open again. More and more the movement demanded a monolith, the closing of all escape hatches once and for all.

The isolated efforts of the president's volunteers, taken together, bolstered the administration's argument against a comprehensive, federally imposed policy with uniform contours for all. They did not give an assurance of minimal justice across the South. They did not free the black protesters (or the white moderates) from the need to work on race problems full-time. The shortcomings of this policy should have been obvious to the administration that proposed them as an alternative to comprehensive civil rights legislation. If a solution to the civil rights crisis was too much to ask of Congress, it might easily prove too much to ask of white moderates.

Strains in the Policy of Voluntarism

The Kennedy policy faced a severe test when the crisis in Birmingham came, in the summer of 1963. Informal negotiations there worked for a time. With the help of Oberdorfer's contacts, and those whom Muse and

Jimerson had sounded out, the Justice Department recruited virtually all of the cabinet members to call their business contacts in the city and urge them to work for a compromise. Oberdorfer was particularly active in this effort.[25] When the president sent Burke Marshall there as a negotiator on May 4, he came with as much information as the civil rights movement itself had, perhaps a great deal more. By having discussions with moderates in the white business community, Marshall gained their confidence. These included such men as David Vann, Sydney Smyer, and the new mayor-elect, Albert Boutwell, Bull Connor's rival and eventual successor. (Boutwell was a segregationist and had courted segregationist support but opposed Connor's style and tactics. "I am determined . . . to defend, I hope maintain, segregation," Boutwell vowed in the campaign against Connor, "but we are not going to be a city of unrestrained and unhampered mockery of the law.")[26] Those men outflanked the extremists and, through the good offices of Burke Marshall, secretly communicated with King, Shuttlesworth, Andrew Young, and other representatives of the movement.[27]

Marshall tried to dissuade King from conducting demonstrations until the moderate white leaders could get public safety commissioner Bull Connor and the rest of Mayor Hanes' administration out of power. (Connor and Hanes, by virtue of a legal dispute over the laws that changed the city's form of government, remained in power after their election defeat — Connor had run for mayor that year and lost to Boutwell but remained in office under Mayor Hanes as safety commissioner.) The merchants, through a wiretap on King's phone, learned of Marshall's efforts to keep King off the streets and realized Marshall was a man they could deal with. His mediation between the moderate merchants and the civil rights activists strengthened the hand of the moderates and allowed them to reach a settlement with the protesters on May 10. Enough pieces of this settlement were enacted by July 14 that King could announce he was pleased with implementation of the settlement. By July 30, black customers were served at five different lunch counters and, as historian Bob Corley concluded, "it was clear beyond any doubt that the city of Birmingham had now chosen to walk down a path from which it could never return, and that its community leaders had committed themselves as never before to racial harmony, and racial justice."[28] The businessmen had settled things at least in the private sector.

But however thorough Oberdorfer's work with the business community was, the policy left too much undone. The businessmen in Birmingham could not desegregate the public schools as readily as they could the lunch counters and theaters they owned. Racist terror returned with the opening of the schools, and Governor Wallace rewarded the terrorists by closing the schools. Though the Kennedys talked Wallace into reopening them a few days later, they could not stop vigilantes: bombings went off first in the home of Arthur Shores, a local black attorney, then most dramatically in the Sixteenth Street Baptist Church on September 15. The protests in Birmingham picked up after these events with renewed fervor.

From the start, Birmingham had inspired protests all over the South and, even more ominously, a few in the North. They broke out like "chicken pox," one administration official said. These strained the mental geography of the administration, which was simultaneously being forced to focus on Birmingham. Things were getting out of hand.

As the voluntary efforts continued, important voices in the administration lost faith in them. Assistant Attorney General for Lands Ramsey Clark — the third white southerner who moonlighted as a civil rights policy-maker for the Justice Department—called attention to the shortcomings of the administration's policy at the very moment when Oberdorfer's reports were lauding its greatest progress. Clark toured the South to report on the major trouble spots and ended by recommending an overhaul of the entire piecemeal approach. He concluded on August 28, 1963, that private prosecution of school desegregation was "ineffective, unfair, and capricious." Not only were the majority of southern school children at the mercy of a slow and piecemeal approach, but the federal government was in effect having its policy dictated by the NAACP Legal Defense Fund, a private organization, which chose and prosecuted the cases that were shaping federal law. "There is a great need for coordinated, long-range planning for effective integration in depth in all areas where segregation exists whether under color of law, or de facto, and an apparent present lack [of] any such approach."[29] Other southern supporters of the administration echoed this frustration and called on JFK for more decisive action.[30]

Oberdorfer, for all his optimism, also gave evidence of the limitations of the policy. He interpreted his reports as maps of "remarkable progress" toward a new South, but he was too careful, too concerned, and too honest not to notice that the progress had another pattern: it was confined pretty strictly to the cities in the peripheral southern and border states. Mississippi, Louisiana, and Alabama, by contrast, remained "hard core." "In Mississippi," Oberdorfer wrote, "whites who would advocate a moderate course are still subject to violent reprisals from extremists." Georgia, South

Carolina, and Arkansas, which he categorized as "softening," showed great progress in the urban areas, but in these states, "as in the 'hard core' states, the rural areas remain adamant." The remaining states, Virginia, Texas, North Carolina, Florida, Tennessee, Kentucky, Oklahoma, West Virginia, and Maryland, were "gaining momentum," but even there, "fierce opposition" existed "in isolated instances, e.g., the Delta region of Southwestern Tennessee, parts of Eastern Texas, and some small cities in inland Florida." All that would "complicate enforcement" of civil rights laws.[31] The civil rights leaders complicated it further: while the administration tried to draw attention to the quietly desegregating periphery, the movement drew attention to newsworthier "hard core" areas.

In June 1963, after years of agonizing over seemingly endless protests and, perhaps just as important, a dismal decline in congressional action on his legislative program, Kennedy's reluctance to force the issue began to melt away. On June 11, he sent federal marshals to Alabama a second time, this time to compel the state university to admit two black students. That night, he made what amounted to a victory speech over Governor George Wallace, who had stood in the university door to block the students' entry and was compelled to back down. In the speech, he stated civil rights was a moral and not merely pragmatic issue.[32] The extremists in the South, quite rightly, took the June 11 statement as a declaration of war. They shot Medgar Evers in the back that night. (Evers was scheduled to testify in favor of legislation.) On June 19 Kennedy confirmed the change of course. Reversing his earlier decision to avoid legislation, he introduced a civil rights bill.

Saving Voluntarism by Force of Legislation

Though the bill's introduction was a departure from the administration's antilegislative policy, it was a continuation of its emphasis on voluntary, which is to say white southern moderate, compliance with civil rights. Oberdorfer's carefully formed network, for all its inadequacy, formed a prototype for the administration's new structure of implementation of civil rights policy, the Community Relations Service, to be created by the Civil Rights Act of 1964.[33]

The administration wrote and lobbied for the civil rights bill with this voluntary network in mind, and it continued to develop the network with the bill in mind. For example, after the bombing of the Sixteenth Street Baptist Church on September 15, 1963, President Kennedy appointed a new team of mediators to go to Birmingham to try to calm the waters again. The Royall-Blaik mission, as this team was called, consisted of General Kenneth C. Royall, a New York lawyer and former secretary of the air force who was raised in the rural South, and Colonel Earl H. Blaik, a former West Point football coach and director of the AVCO corporation. The administration viewed the team as a prototype, "patterned on the Community Relations Service proposed in the Administration's civil rights bill" pending before Congress.[34]

The Royall-Blaik mission showed the Kennedy administration's desire to continue to handle the white South with kid gloves, even in the wake of an apparently total breakdown of law and order. Royall and Blaik reported that trouble had returned to Birmingham because "misunderstandings" persisted over just what had been agreed to in the May compromise and that black people needed "fair job opportunities." To keep the peace, however, they said black people would have to refrain from demonstrations, which would "only lead to further difficulty and danger." Their main conclusion was that the racial situation in Birmingham would eventually have to be "determined by residents of the Birmingham community."[35] Burke Marshall's assessment of Royall and Blaik's discoveries was the opposite: "Whites do not have the sense or courage to take sufficient steps to give the local negroes enough gains to enable them to oppose further demonstration." Accordingly, Marshall wrote, "The situation will get worse again."[36]

The U.S. government, having followed the lead of the civil rights movement in focusing on moderate white southern leaders, was now facing the same paradox of using coercion to achieve cooperation. Though Marshall and others in the administration such as Ramsey Clark looked forward with some despair to continuation of their policy of negotiated, voluntary agreements, they dared not abandon that policy.[37] Though the tactics Oberdorfer engineered in the quiet outer reaches of the administration did not end racial disturbances, they were habit-forming. They had worked enough to prevent experimentation with other tactics. That made it virtually inevitable that the legislation the administration offered would only expand, rather than change qualitatively, the policy already in place. Oberdorfer wrote to the attorney general on February 18, 1964, "[The] experience of the last six months has taught us many valuable lessons in how to deal with racial problems. We ignore these lessons at our peril. Change can be peaceful and orderly. If the legislation passes, lawsuits and enforcement problems can be held to a minimum." To the civil rights advocates, the legislation was a promise of massive federal intervention, but to

Oberdorfer it was something else, a new variation on encouragement of voluntary compliance with evolving rights. Even with a new law, social peace required southern white cooperation. "The decision is basically up to responsible leaders in local communities. The business community has a great stake in seeing that changes are made voluntarily and peaceably and can exercise significant influence toward that end." Southern business and civic leaders were to be the cornerstone of policy after the passage of a civil rights act as they were before.

Despite its basic continuity with previous policy, the administration's bill threatened to enlarge and organize the existing voluntary efforts to such a great extent that it immediately provoked opposition. The previously unlegislated, ad hoc patchwork of compromises had been very hard for southern Democrats to oppose (or not worth the bother). Logically enough, the administration's previous policy became a weapon to fight against its proposed new policy. Republican senator and presidential candidate Barry Goldwater, who opposed civil rights and was actively encouraging conservative southern defections from the Democratic party, for example, really had to laud President Kennedy's earlier, voluntary approach. Goldwater said that the president, "with his ability to persuade people," did a great thing "to point out the economic and moral stupidity of maintaining racial prejudice in the case of job acquisition." Once a businessman himself and always a defender of businessmen's honor in the Senate, Goldwater may have found JFK's willingness to let businessmen do their own reporting on desegregation more attractive than the actual desegregation; but the conscientious conservative expressed a genuine desire to overcome economic and moral stupidity. The president's very success in encouraging voluntary chipping away at segregation became the strongest argument against coercive legislation. To Goldwater, the impressive numbers of voluntary acts of desegregation reported by the National Retail Merchants Association made it clear that results may be achieved "without having to upset constitutional processes by resorting to enactment of law."[38] Opponents and proponents of the bill shared the premise that the previous policy had been worthwhile.

The administration, in preparing for the act's possible passage, made a heated effort to get white leaders in southern cities to commit themselves to working for compliance. The administration held a meeting with private leaders for this purpose in April 1964, resolving that their goal was "to have in as many cities as possible the responsible elements of the community ready to take at the appropriate time a concerted and definite stand for compliance with the law . . ."; Johnson's forces hoped to obtain such a public commitment from responsible citizens in those cities where it was feasible.[39] But as Goldwater's remarks suggest, that very public commitment could backfire by obviating the need to pass the legislation at all. Many of the businessmen involved surely hoped it would.

Part of the administration's unwillingness to repudiate its stress on voluntary action stemmed from its continuing fear that coercive legislation would not pass Congress. Oberdorfer, working for the department that was lobbying hard to pass the bill, urged businessmen of the South to continue what they had started in Plans for Progress and in the informal committees of businessmen, women's groups, clergymen, and lawyers which had been set up in meetings with President Kennedy in the summer of 1963. Oberdorfer recommended carrying on such voluntary action "if the legislation passe[d]—or if it fail[ed] of enactment." The importance of the new law itself paled next to voluntary action, which would have to continue with or without a new law: "If the Civil Rights legislation passes, such action will be necessary to insure peaceful acceptance of the law with a minimum of litigation and enforcement problems. If the legislation does not pass, the need for community action, without the help of the federal courts, will become even more critical."

Here the paradoxical relationship between voluntarism and coercion in civil rights policy became clearest. Oberdorfer reminded his readers, "While trouble spots have dominated the headlines, remarkable progress has been achieved in many cities without publicity in the last six months." Almost two-thirds of the desegregated facilities in the 566 southern and border-state cities he had surveyed had desegregated between May 1963 and February 1964. While Oberdorfer (and Goldwater and many southern opponents of legislation) took that impressive number as an indication of all that could happen voluntarily without legislation, the opposite interpretation seems more plausible, namely that coercion—the growing threat of the bill's passage, behind which lay the direct pressure of mass demonstrations of unprecedented size and duration—was the cause of increased "voluntary" progress.

In fact, Oberdorfer's own words, full of urgency, show the imprint of that coercion. In meetings with businessmen and other white southerners in early 1964, he warned his audiences that resistance to integration "could lead to severe disorders and economic dislocations." Every community with segregated facilities had to face up to the need for change. "Business leaders and other citizens can and should start now to see that the law [assuming it passes] is accepted and that local and state political officials are informed that the law will be complied with and that businessmen need and demand police protection." Businesses could take a number of steps on their own, before passage: elimination of "white only" signs would be easy. He appealed to common sense, emphasizing the absurdity of maintaining segregation: "A retailer said that until recently one of his stores in south Texas had twelve restrooms, with classifications for sex, for the general public or employees, and for whites, Negroes, and Mexicans. As he said, 'at times I wondered if I was running a store or a restroom concession.'" They could start using titles of respect in billing black customers. As in all the operations, control of information was crucial: "The difference between a smooth transition and a tumultuous and agonizing one is frequently the local newspaper. Try to persuade your local publisher and editor that it is in the best interest of the community to take a responsible position in editorials and to report the facts in a fair and rational manner. Even where the papers are hostile, the Letters to the Editor column provides a forum in which community leaders can challenge inaccurate or slanted news coverage or present the opposing arguments to editorial positions."

Oberdorfer was aware of the coercion lurking behind him: he was playing the good cop. The movement, now armed with a bill that might pass Congress, was playing the bad cop. But, as in his reports, he spent his energy finding ways to avert coercion. The last tactic he urged upon southern businessmen was to maintain contact with black students. "The most militant Negroes are the college age students. They are frequently not responsive to the counsel of older Negroes, even those older Negroes who lead in the civil rights movement." Oberdorfer tried to encourage efforts to bring "such students or student leaders . . . into contact with the leaders of the White community." Such contacts would allow exchange of ideas and opinions; thus "pent-up emotions" would not "spill over into street demonstrations." He urged business leaders to "take the students on tours of plants, show them urban renewal plans and progress; acquaint them with the facts, the difficulties, and the good faith of the white community. Contacts could be arranged through local Negro colleges, through older Negro civil rights leaders, or through civil rights groups, particularly the Student Nonviolent Coordinating Committee." Oberdorfer also stressed the necessity to provide legal counsel and job opportunities for black people.[40] That was the message thousands of southern businessmen were hearing from the Justice Department as their senators and representatives listened to Robert

Kennedy and Burke Marshall testify in favor of the law's passage on Capitol Hill.

The Culmination of the Administration's Policy and the Movement's Strategy

This background puts the passage of the Civil Rights Act of 1964 in a new light. The act declared discrimination in public accommodations and private employment illegal for the first time, and since those two forms of legal discrimination were cornerstones of the social structure of the South, the act was revolutionary. But the act did not guarantee that black customers would feel welcome in formerly segregated accommodations. Nor did it guarantee that employers and lawmen would refrain from devising brilliant stratagems to evade the law, as they had done with the Fourteenth and Fifteenth amendments for nearly a century.

The administration's hopes for making reality conform to law now rested on one provision of the act: the one that created the Community Relations Service, a new federal agency. President Kennedy made clear the motive for the creation of the Community Relations Service in his first proposal for a new civil rights act, saying that progress in race relations would come more "solidly and peacefully" when "buttressed by voluntary action." Robert Kennedy, testifying in favor of the bill, praised the Justice Department's "yeoman service" in setting up informal voluntary structures of mediation but defended the bill's provision for a new agency, separate from the prosecutorial arm of the executive branch: the "confidence of all," he said, would be greater than had been the case in Birmingham if there was an intermediary agency that was "separated from departmental functions of investigation or litigation."[41] Needless to say, this arrangement would get much of the civil rights problem out of his office.

The CRS was created to "implement" the new law primarily by setting up negotiations between civil rights groups and local white leaders. "Implementation" and "compliance" from this point forward became the key words in the administration's discussions of civil rights policy. Significantly, "enforcement," the constitutional definition of the executive branch's role, was never a key word. Implementation and compliance were more voluntary, less threatening, more properly bureaucratic things to do.

The Community Relations Service was to be a loose and voluntary network, like the business and professional networks set up through Oberdorfer's contacts, like the Plans for Progress, like the Civil Rights Commission's local advisory committees, and like the nongovernmental network of Human Relations Councils (organized and monitored by the Southern Regional Council), on which all governmental projects built. The CRS had virtually the same personnel as these. John Seigenthaler was called back into service as a private contact and adviser.[42] Harold Fleming, a former executive director of the Southern Regional Council, became the deputy director of CRS.

In putting a Community Relations Service into the heart of the bill, the administration showed it had been backed into the same position the black preachers had been backed into a decade earlier when they began massive and systematic direct action: they needed to apply conciliation at the same time as force. Conciliation without force yielded only stasis. Force without conciliation would only lead to evasion and counterattack, and the administration dared not try it. The bill, which was to make racial discrimination unequivocally illegal for the first time, would be the force—if it passed. The inclusion of a CRS in that bill reflected the belief that force would require more rather than less conciliation.

The Community Relations Service embodied all the voluntarism, all the scattershot diffusion, of the administration's first two years of evasive action. Likewise it embodied all of Majority Leader Lyndon Johnson's dreams of depoliticizing the issue: by an act of Congress, Johnson, now president, finally found a way to get civil rights out of Congress.[43] Efforts to get out of the civil rights "mess" had come together fitfully and tentatively, almost by accident, during the Kennedy-Johnson campaign. The groping, ill-defined aims had metastasized into a policy. They now had something they had not had before, a bureaucracy all their own: the Civil Rights Commission and the Justice Department's Civil Rights Division were, properly speaking, informational and prosecutorial bodies, respectively. The former could not "do" anything. The best the latter could do was prosecute, and during Kennedy's time, it took it as its duty to settle out of court by negotiation. To implement was a compromise, a way to make government force unthreatening.

With a vast network of white southern moderates institutionalized in the CRS, the Johnson administration continued to press for peaceful resolution of local conflicts. The CRS mediated in the last major struggle of the movement, at Selma, Alabama, in 1965. The CRS director, former Florida governor LeRoy Collins (whose name had been circulating among LBJ's staff since 1956 as a likely leader of any attempt to organize southern moderates), made a personal visit there. He took along with him Ramsey Clark, who presented the U.S. government's plea for order to the local white leaders. Collins reported that many of Selma's white leaders wanted to shut down businesses to prevent desegregation. Ramsey Clark explained the government's position to the white leaders: "We felt very strongly that this would be inadvisable, both because visitors would need services from many businesses and also because clerks, etc., should be kept busy to avoid other movements their idleness might encourage."[44] That logic appealed to the businessmen but was not enough to cool the local protest. Congress felt compelled to pass the Voting Rights Act of 1965 to ward off continuing disorder in Selma and elsewhere in the South. The movement had been especially lucky in Selma in finding Sheriff Jim Clark, the last of a dying breed of die-hard segregationist lawmen, who brutalized protesters in spite of growing moderate sentiment in town: the continuing southern brutality convinced Congress that it would require more force still to restore order in the South.

When the dramatic brutality of Sheriff Clark came to an end, and when Congress with the acts of 1964 and 1965 declared the two institutions of southern racism, segregation and disfranchisement, illegal, the movement could declare a moral victory. But the group of moderates the CRS represented, which had been legitimized and strengthened by federal policy under Kennedy and Johnson, were the political victors. They assumed the positions of power in southern society—and in time shared some of those positions with like-minded black leaders—while the Bull Connors and Sheriff Clarks died out or, as in George Wallace's case, were reborn as moderates who campaigned with remarkable success for black votes.

It would be a mistake to see the victory of the white moderates as detracting from the victory of the black civil rights leaders: the black leaders had not fought for governorships and other worldly offices but for an end to racial injustice. In defeating two great institutions of injustice, they achieved one of the most significant social changes in American history. But it would also be a mistake to think that the black leaders could have been satisfied with their victory: injustice continued without institutional sanction. In an understandable but ultimately disastrous step, southern black leaders turned their energies (and the attention of the nation) to where that uninstitutionalized injustice was most fully developed, the North. There desperate urban poverty could provide the dramatic evidence of racial injustice that southern sheriffs no longer would provide. But northern injustice, however ugly it was, did not create a crisis of party unity. Thus it could not impel the congressional leadership or the president to do something about it. Nor did there lurk behind northern injustice a class of white moderates who had something to gain from removing the injustice; since no class of white demagogues owed their careers to the defense of racial injustice in the North, let alone maintained that injustice at the expense of economic favor from big corporations and the federal government, there was little incentive for powerful white leaders to aid the destruction of injustice. Nor was there even a potential corps of unalienated dissenters, like Virginia Durr and Glenn Smiley, who could challenge basic institutions of injustice without feeling that they were attacking their own cultural traditions. White people who attacked racial injustice in the North were (or were trying to be) self-made outsiders. They did not stand on the Bible and Constitution, as southerners did. They could not resist the growing temptation toward nihilism in thought and self-destructiveness in deed which soon overwhelmed the North in that decade of protest, the 1960s. In contrast to the South, the North had no white insiders to whom the movement could appeal with confidence and hope or to whom the ever risk-averse federal authorities could defer. Without hope of victory, the competitive tendencies of movement leadership could no longer be held in check. The movement, with partial victories under its belt, fell to internal divisions; those divisions had always existed, but struggle over them could always be deferred as long as victories in the outside world were in sight.

Epilogue
Interpreting the Movement

The civil rights movement was an effort to transform an existing relationship between black and white southerners. Black leaders all over the South found that relationship oppressive, degrading, and offensive. Yet they also found it full of opportunity. Having an acute, empirical knowledge of white southerners, they knew their designated opponents in the struggle often lacked the will, the resources, or the inclination to fight effectively.

This observation does not imply that the civil rights movement had an easier job than we once thought. On the contrary, it directs our attention to the excruciating skill that allowed civil rights leaders to take advantage of subtle, shifting divisions among their white southern neighbors. More important, it directs our attention to the moral difficulty of fighting against a hateful system without condemning its beneficiaries *en bloc*. The civil rights movement was far more strenuous, morally and politically, than any black-versus-white, minority-versus-majority interpretation of it can capture. The principal result of letting ourselves think of the movement's opposition as overwhelming and monolithic is to make our task of remembering the movement (and living with its legacy) easy to bear.

Civil rights leaders had years of accumulated evidence that white southerners could learn to live without racial discrimination. The influential white newspaperman Virginius Dabney emphasized in 1932 that the South's progressive leaders, who had "hoped that the wholesale disfranchisement of the Negroes . . . would remove the blacks from the political picture," were disappointed by the continuation of racial demaguery into the 1930s.[1] This was a great portent of Jim Crow's vulnerability. It was people like Dabney—New South liberals—who conceived, institutionalized, and defended the segregation-disfranchisement system a generation before Dabney took up his pen (Henry Grady, Edgar Gardner Murphy, and Woodrow Wilson being some of the more prominent founders). And they did so for the very reason that Dabney (like John Spencer Bassett before him) identified: to remove the destructive Negro issue from politics.

One should not be too hasty, then, to attribute to a man like Dabney newly awakened sympathies for the downtrodden race around him, or a new interest in righting historical wrongs. Segregation was designed to establish social peace and allow government to concentrate on the economic development of the region (which meant, as always, the economic security and prosperity of the ruling elite). The conversion of Dabney to a softened position on disfranchisement in the 1930s therefore seems based on a pragmatic conclusion that the experiment of Grady was failing to do what it was designed to do. To redeem the spirit of Jim Crow laws, in other words, it might now be necessary to abandon Jim Crow laws in practice.

This logic, inchoate in Dabney's 1930s, became irresistible to southern liberals thirty years later, when a stick was added to the carrot Dabney saw materializing before his eyes—when the boycotts and marches drove home the idea that Jim Crow's maintenance led to *disorder*. But Dabney had revealed that the soul of southern liberalism was no longer in the institutions that southern liberalism had created to secure its rise to power around the turn of the century. The institutions had become a threat to southern liberalism and were becoming more useful to southern liberalism's enemies. By tapping into the idealism as well as the opportunism of Dabney and other white southerners, the civil rights leaders of the 1950s had to keep that delicate and confusing shift of forces in focus. That was the prize their eyes were on.

In Montgomery, behind the scenes of a showdown between black and white was a more complex and interesting struggle among human beings. The best accounts of Montgomery begin to capture this complexity but do not bring it fully to light. J. Mills Thornton, to choose just one of the very best, lays bare an intricate, high-tension game of local politics, which escalated into a decisive struggle in world history. With great subtlety and analytic flair, Thornton finds in the intransigence of Jack Crenshaw and other guardians of segregation, especially when lawyers, the root cause of Montgomery's projection onto the world stage. (Thornton also sees the uncompromising stance of the MIA as important, but he seems to put the weight on the side of the segregationists.) In other words, it would have remained a local battle had the bus company and the city commission compromised with the MIA.

This is an incomplete picture. It is certainly true that Montgomery's segregationist leaders were inflexible (as were those in Tallahassee, Albany, St. Augustine, Birmingham, and Selma) and that their inflexibility precluded negotiated change. But segregationist leaders elsewhere in the South were often the opposite of rigid. In Little Rock, notably, they were divided and remained so. Even in Montgomery, there were initial sources of flexibility, though these dried up and the segregationists' position (at least at high levels) hardened. But in other cities—notably Little Rock— the local white leaders remained flexible and a *mob* (often from outside, in Little Rock's case led by the governor) contributed the element of inflexibility. In still other cities, the flexible leaders prevailed.[2] True, in most of these cases their flexibility led only to tokenism—which reinforces Thornton's larger point that *only by provoking federal intervention* could the movement really root out segregation as a system.

But white southerners' growing flexibility explains that revolutionary change as much as their abiding rigidity explains it. More important, their flexibility explains the *timing* of the change (the 1950s and 1960s as opposed to the 1920s and 1930s). I do not deny the existence or the importance of the rigidity that Thornton emphasizes. But this rigid resistance is important precisely because it contrasted with the growth among moderates of a flexible acquiescence in desegregation. This does not mean, of course, that waiting for the moderate leaders to replace the intransigent ones would have led to victory. That would have produced only uneven tokenism, and perhaps backlash. But the emergence of the moderate leaders—or more precisely, the redefinition of moderate as meaning willing to abandon elements of Jim Crow—was significant. Precisely because their emergence was not enough, the moderates provoked militant black action in the streets and in the courts; they indicated a division in the system, that is to say a weakness, which made it vulnerable.

To put a finer point on it, if a black movement had struck only against rigidity (in the late 1890s, say, or 1920s), it would have had much less success than it actually had in the 1950s and 1960s. I maintain that the awareness of white moderation—and true awareness includes awareness of its ineffectuality—is a principal reason why the movement struck in the 1950s, and not before, and why it succeeded with means considerably short of civil war.

White moderation was a mixed blessing for the protesters, however.

The black leadership faced manifold temptations to settle for half-loaves. The victory at Montgomery was incomplete. White supremacy, and specifically segregation, remained intact everywhere but on the buses. Its destruction on the buses was significant, but perhaps we exaggerate it in hindsight because it launched the career of the man who became the symbol of the larger, longer struggle.

Some readers may wonder whether I am blinded by that symbol: whether my emphasis on black leaders' understanding of white southerners as human beings relies too much on Martin Luther King's Christian idealism. But my belief is that King was significant because he was a realist. His realism, far more than his idealism, accounts for the long-term devotion of his huge following in the southern black community. Idealists preach forgiveness every Sunday — or they preach an equally idealistic revenge. King (and others allied with him) showed a particular kind of forgiveness that brought results in the here and now. He delivered. The black masses of the South made King into the figure he was because they believed he expressed their own best ideas. I do not think in "King-centric" terms. His words are not simply his words but a distillation of the views of masses bound inextricably to their chosen moral leader. Accordingly, I reject the choice between "the great man theory of history" and "history of the inarticulate masses" as a false choice between two forms of romanticism. What happens when the allegedly inarticulate masses themselves have a great man theory, as an honest observer must admit they sometimes do? When I asked rank-and-file black women in Montgomery why their civil rights movement worked, they said things like "because God sent us that man." Historians may think it diminishes the masses to attribute greatness to the masses' leaders. There is no evidence that the masses share that opinion. I am not saying it is bad political history to rewrite the history of the movement as though King's ideas were not central to it. I am saying it is bad social history.

In any case, the Tallahassee and Little Rock cases show that even when King was not on the scene, similar patterns of conflict appear.[3] Little Rock was projected onto the stage of world history by two men with considerably less theatrical sense than King. Faubus and Eisenhower exposed to the world the hesitations and weaknesses of the so-called white community. The world has largely forgotten the hesitations and weaknesses, remembering the much more photogenic anger and brutality. Yet we ought to remind ourselves that Elizabeth Eckford shared with Roy Harris an uncertainty as to whether Faubus called out the troops *"for* us or *agin'* us." Faubus's armed resistance to federal law and Eisenhower's armed defense of it steal attention, as displays of force so often do, from the deep uncertainty of both men's positions. Daisy Bates, the leader as well as the outstanding chronicler of the Little Rock movement, emphasizes the complexity, the irony of the battle she understood well enough to win: she was much more definite in her view that Chief Smith's suicide was a central tragedy of the Little Rock story than Faubus and Eisenhower were about anything.

In Tallahassee, the dynamics of the black leaders' relationship with local white leaders are not obscured by the projection of the struggle onto the stage of world history, for it remains a relatively unknown one. Aldon Morris is surely right when he writes that Tallahassee is more typical of the southern movement than Montgomery, since the Tallahassee movement was a wholly local operation. What is interesting, though, is that the relationship of the movement to the white community there was largely the same fruitful, complex one found in Montgomery and Little Rock, as again the recollections of the local black leaders show.

The head of the Tallahassee boycott's transportation committee, Dan Speed, made clearer than anyone how irresistible a moderate southern segregationist could be. Speaking of a visit from police chief Frank Stoutamire, Speed said:

> He always called me Dan. . . . He talked to me like a kid. He came by one day and . . . said "Dan why don't you stop wasting time and go on about your business? You're too good a businessman and everybody in Tallahassee knows it." I said, "thank you sir, I enjoy that, I appreciate that and I can reflect upon the things that you have made reference to, but I'd also like to see a better reaction among the Blacks and Whites when they come to public places like the buses, the courthouse and other places. . . . I just want to be honest. I don't believe in no two fountains, one for Whites and one for Blacks. I don't believe in no two toilets."

Speed found Stoutamire's response remarkable: "You know what he said? . . . He said, 'I don't either but we're in the damn thing like that.'"

Speed's interviewer (Jackson Ice, a northerner) found it even more remarkable: "I always thought you were going to tell me that you couldn't get through to him because he was reared in a southern climate."

Speed replied, "As I say, people are peculiar." Stoutamire "really felt like that." Speed and Stoutamire "got along" (throughout the boycott, the two maintained a business relationship: Stoutamire's farm supplied eggs to Speed's store).[4]

Another boycott leader, K. S. DuPont, said Stoutamire, who went to great lengths to discipline his own men ("when they got too high, he'd beat them down"), protected civil rights workers when they insisted on camping out at the scene of a Klan rally. DuPont was not swayed by mere professions of good will: Stoutamire earned his trust, which other white leaders did not earn, by action. "If it hadn't been for Stoutamire—and I'm telling you the truth—we probably would have ended up in a race riot. . . . He done much more than they give him credit for."[5] The head of the Tallahassee boycott organization, C. K. Steele, said Stoutamire was "an uncannily wise person" and "one of the most unusual persons" he had ever met. "He was a dyed in the [wool] segregationist, but he knew that to overly persecute us would have made the movement mushroom. And the error they had made in Montgomery, he saw to it that they did not make it here."[6]

Though Stoutamire's attitude had all the condescension of paternalism, it was an aging paternalism, in which the father figure was suddenly capable of recognizing, with the usual bewilderment, that his "children" were capable of self-reliance and self-assertion. Perhaps he even recognized that, having lost the means to support them, he was too weak to control them much longer. Elsewhere in the South the father figures, like literal fathers, were often unwilling to face these truths or to relinquish control without a fight. The basis of their authority, originally absolute power, had imperceptibly been supplanted, in uneven, overlapping stages, by degrees of consent. This family metaphor makes sense, for there is often compassion, affection, and mutual interest, along with the violence and domination, in relations across the color line in the twentieth-century South. Those relations are more distant, which is to say less coercive, than those of the slave South, but that is true of family relations in general since the Civil War. The metaphor makes further sense because, as in a family, those born into it did not choose their position in it. Only those with an idealized notion of parent-child relations could interpret the label "paternalist" as a romantic one: literal fathers, all too often, abuse their children and shirk their responsibilities. Certain lower-class white men and women were often fed the illusion that they were equal to the recognized heads of the southern household, and were designated as favored siblings, but only provisionally so. The members of this family grew estranged. Perhaps the relationship had been dysfunctional (to use today's execrable neologism) from the start. But the civil rights movement was not a complete escape from the human relationship inherited from the past, or a repudiation of it, but a development of it.

It may be objected that Speed's, Steele's, and DuPont's descriptions of Stoutamire suggest that Tallahassee was not very different from Albany, whose nonviolent white leader, I argue, was unique. But the difference is that in Albany police chief Laurie Pritchett, a nonviolent segregationist, had the full faith of the city leaders and kept the ranks of segregationists united behind his leadership. In Tallahassee, Chief Stoutamire never achieved such unity.

There were *always* white leaders somewhere in the power structure who wanted to treat the protesters with respect and caution. But Albany was the only battle site where such a white leader fully succeeded. Despite the views of Tallahassee's black leaders that Tallahassee avoided "the error they made in Montgomery," Tallahassee had a visible Klan presence, unlike Albany, where Pritchett kept the Klan out. There was a higher level of violence in Tallahassee than in Albany, which was partly a cause and partly a result of Tallahassee's much more deeply divided white leadership.

One cannot write about Albany without stepping into a crossfire. It remains the most controversial of all the civil rights struggles, and the controversy extends to disagreements among the sources over the role of local white residents. The sources agree that there were no local white supporters of the movement there, but to Andrew Young, this made Albany an exception to the general rule of southern cities. To Charles Sherrod, however, this just proved that Albany was another typical southern racist town. Sherrod said that white people everywhere were too scared to show any sympathy for the movement.

Both may be remembering correctly. The difference probably comes from the histories of the two men's organizations, which led each man to observe two distinct areas of the South. Sherrod's SNCC was known for taking on the most difficult areas—the rural, black belt counties, especially in Mississippi—while Young's SCLC tended to work the major cities. Albany was the smallest and most rural of the targets the SCLC took on.

This may be the key, incidentally, to the SCLC's relative success and SNCC's relative failure. (As James Bevel said, "The trouble with SNCC is that it has never had any clear successes.")[7] It may also be a key to the limitations of the SCLC's strategy. The SCLC walked in the valley of the shadow of death, but it always brought along a spotlight; SNCC walked in the valley of death itself. The SCLC's victories (and those of its predecessors, the MIA and ICC) in the cities inevitably grew dissatisfying under the weight of persistently unreconstructed rural counties (partly because the protesters simply ran out of cities). Yet if the SCLC avoided the most intractable (not to be confused with the most visibly violent) districts, SNCC could be accused of impossibilism. The SCLC types, during their heyday, did at least deliver the victories that bolstered morale. In the long run, target selection may have been the most important strategic decision.

My argument about Albany bears restating here to make its differences clear from other accounts in the sources and secondary works. It rests on two contentions. First, I contend that Chief Pritchett was substantially correct in his claim to be nonviolent during the time that national attention was focused on his city. Pritchett said, "I even took up some of the training the SNCCs originated there — like sitting at the counter and being slapped, spit upon. I said [to policemen], 'If they do this, you will not use force. We're going to out-nonviolent them.'"[8] Though there were lapses into violence, Pritchett was careful to dissociate himself from them and in fact bore no direct responsibility for them. More important, politically speaking, the lapses did not presage a general resort to brutal repression — until the national spotlight was gone.

Coretta King corroborates the essence of Pritchett's claim: "One redeeming aspect of that period was that Police Chief Laurie Pritchett was not at all typical of southern policemen. He was not brutal, though some of his officers engaged in brutality. He tried to be decent, and as a person, he displayed kindness. . . . Our people were given fair warning. Often they would refuse to disperse and would drop to their knees and pray. Chief Pritchett would bow his head with them while they prayed. Then, of course, he would arrest them and the people would go to jail singing."[9] So too Marion Page, one of the founders of the Albany Movement: there were "never any overt cruelties" in Albany. Speaking in particular about the girls in the movement in Albany, Page said, "We have yet to see a policeman slam one with a billy." (In other cities, of course, police set upon women and men alike.) "That was the real strength of Pritchett's part in the whole thing, that he did not turn the entire country against the white people of Albany."[10] Wyatt Tee Walker, executive director of the SCLC, who was in Albany with King most of the time, criticized Pritchett — "in his role as Chief of Police he is as villainous as the system in which he is hopelessly caught" — but still granted that "he is a cut of man who sincerely abhors police brutality and will not allow it." He also noted that Pritchett became "the darling of the press because he . . . abstained from police brutality."[11] Walker later denied Pritchett was "nonviolent" but insisted on using the term "nonbrutal."[12] One of the SNCC members in Albany, John Lewis, said that Pritchett "did things very cool. He knew if there was violence or retaliation on the part of policemen . . . that this would tend to increase the participation of the Negro community and would give a greater sympathy to the movement in Albany, from people not only in Albany, not only from white people but from people throughout the country and throughout the State of Georgia. And Pritchett had this whole thing that he would meet non-violence with non-violence, . . . a very interesting point."[13]

Even those SNCC veterans who most fiercely denounce Pritchett's pose of nonviolence as a hypocritical sham concede the basic point that for the time his city was in the public eye he managed to maintain a credible nonviolent image. The fiercest is Charles Sherrod. In discrediting Pritchett's reputation for nonviolence, he cites an instance of two of Pritchett's own police manhandling movement leader Samuel Wells, dragging him "by his gonads."[14] This almost surely refers to an incident that took place in 1963, after the media lost interest in the city and (as SNCC observers on the scene stated at the time) Pritchett's tactics changed.[15]

Throughout my chapter on Albany, I concern myself with nonviolence during the time media attention was focused on Albany — until August 1962, when the SCLC withdrew from the city and the Albany Movement discontinued mass protests.[16] The unity and discipline of the movement in Albany, already showing signs of severe strain in the summer of 1962, completely broke down afterward, as cadres of SNCC workers, including a number of northern white students, attempted to carry on scattered actions and voter registration the following year. From then on, there was sporadic violence and much testimony as to police brutality, some involving Pritchett's own men. At that point, however, Pritchett's forces were out of the national press's limelight, and, a related point, they no longer faced a completely nonviolent opposition: their political need to behave nonviolently had fallen away, and they could resume more orthodox methods of police work. None of my emphasis on Pritchett's restraint is to deny the oppressive and violent nature of his role, which was, after all, enforcement of the inherently brutal system of segregation. The point is that Pritchett's tactics in the battle for public opinion — local and national — were shrewd and effective; he beat the movement at its own game of nonviolent strategy without any inner conversion to the nonviolent way of life.

My second contention is that the movement in Albany was a failure. This is the heart of the controversy over Albany. Among early King biographers, David Lewis and Lerone Bennett both argue that Albany was a failure.[17] King himself, cited in my chapter as admitting he had no victory at Albany, was inconsistent. In an article written shortly after Albany, he voiced concern that the movement had lost its momentum and called for a revival of the militant spirit. Then, in his *Playboy* interview in January 1965, he went into the mistakes that were made at Albany but disavowed the idea that it was a failure.[18]

Marion Page, secretary of the Albany Movement, and Wyatt Tee Walker, on the other hand, both assert that there was no failure at Albany.[19] The Albany Movement president, William Anderson, and Bernice Reagon, a local leader who was active in SNCC, along with Wyatt Walker and Charles Sherrod, collectively reveal the weakness of their claim of success in their interviews in Henry Hampton and Steve Fayer's collection, *Voices of Freedom*. They say that although there were no tangible or symbolic gains in Albany, the movement learned something there and developed a kind of spiritual strength and resolve, which they imply was not present before. In Reagon's case, Albany was a turning point because it demonstrated the spiritual power of singing; there developed at Albany "a real sense of platformness and clearly empowerment." David Garrow's otherwise insightful account takes a similar line: like the leaders he cites, Garrow seems to define "success" as learning from one's mistakes.[20]

This is far too indulgent a definition of success. John Lewis, without dismissing the importance of learning from Albany, puts the emphasis more credibly on the failure—and on Chief Pritchett: "I think the Albany movement . . . was successful in only one way. The fact that you got the Negro community aroused." His interviewer (Emily Stoper) asked whether there were any concrete results. "No victories," he replied, "or concrete gains. And a lot of people have said it was Dr. King's serious defeat. I don't know. If it was a defeat for SCLC, it was a defeat for SNCC also, for there were two organizations working there. But nothing really significant or meaningful in terms of change or victory came out of Albany. Chief Pritchett, the police official there, played it very cool."[21]

James Forman, perhaps the most extreme of the memoirists, is also the least consistent. Forman glorifies SNCC (especially his own role and that of Bernice Reagon), minifies the divisions in the local black community, as well as those in the local white community, and comes close to blaming the whole debacle on Martin Luther King's coming to town—except that he denies it was a debacle. He argues that Albany was not a failure yet feels compelled to blame it on someone anyway.[22]

The controversy over whether Albany was a failure usually shades into controversy over why it was a failure. In the secondary works, Aldon Morris is most compelling and thorough when he attributes the failure at

Albany to poor planning in the movement and to tensions within the black community—rivalry between SNCC and the SCLC, in particular SNCC leaders' resentment over King's encroachment on their turf (SNCC had gotten there first). The white power structure understood and exploited these tensions and rivalries. The drawback in this as an explanation of Albany's failures, though, is that similar tensions and rivalries existed in the black community everywhere and grew more intense under the pressure of movement action. (Those at Montgomery were arguably as intense as those at Albany; those at Birmingham and Selma certainly were.) Moreover, tensions and rivalries existed in the white community, too. There was no predetermined winner: where movement organizations worked brilliantly and tirelessly to maintain at least an outward show of solidarity, and where the white community fell to bickering, working at cross-purposes with itself, and shooting itself in the foot, the movement won. Where the positions were reversed—Albany—the movement lost.

David Garrow also emphasizes lack of black unity but (echoing Howard Zinn and Anne Braden's analyses, as well as the judgment of King himself) adds the absence of federal intervention that had been crucial at Little Rock and in the Freedom Rides the year before Albany. My analysis suggests, however, that federal intervention depended upon the relationship of the local black and white communities. Had the protesters found fissures and fifth columns within the Albany white community, that is, black unity would have been easier to maintain. The competing protest organizations would have seen the hope of victory, which would have strengthened their faith in the strategy being pursued—not a strategy for "platformness and clearly empowerment" but for tangible changes. What happened instead was that Pritchett's resistance strengthened their impulse to dissociate themselves from their failing strategy, point fingers of blame at one another, and put forth new, conflicting strategies. That meant that the federal government, always reluctant, found no incentive to intervene. Since the local power structure had the confidence of local white folks—indeed, insofar as Pritchett represented that power structure, it had the confidence of a substantial number of black protestors—it provided no justification for intervention. Elsewhere, the federal government found itself compelled to intervene (including St. Augustine, Birmingham, and Selma, after Albany) only because the white leadership, being divided against itself, could not maintain order.

Most other arguments about Albany focus on what "the black community" did—and immediately the controversy runs aground, since this is a misleading phrase. The black persons involved were first of all not all local residents, and even the local residents were divided by class, denomination, and organizational affiliation. Just as important as what the black people did was what the white people did. The white people were also divided, but in Albany more than in any other locale that was tested by direct action in the 1950s and 1960s, they held a remarkable unity and discipline behind Chief Pritchett. Elsewhere, only the black people maintained such unity. The relationship, the contrast, of solidarity levels between the local black and white groups is what matters.

Howard Zinn's firsthand account is one of the few that take the white people's role into consideration in explaining the movement's failure in Albany. Zinn maintains that Albany's white residents had only one source of facts and opinion on civil rights, the militantly segregationist *Albany Herald*, in contrast, for example, to white people in Atlanta, who had the more moderate *Constitution* of Ralph McGill and Eugene Patterson.[23] But the analysis should begin rather than end there. Why did the Albany newspaper maintain a hard line, when newspaper editors who once supported segregation elsewhere (for example, in Montgomery, Little Rock, and for that matter Atlanta) argued in varying degrees for moderation and compromise? My argument suggests that the newspaper editors, like the civic, professional, and business leaders with whom they associated, sought to steer their cities back to social peace. In Albany, there was no·division among white leaders as to which way that goal lay: the way Pritchett was pointing. It is a strange and illuminating coincidence that Pritchett could save a racist system only by rejecting racist assumptions about the protesters: he was smart enough to see that they were smart enough to win. Therefore he was able to organize a strong enough force to defeat them.

But the rest of the white South did not follow Pritchett. It resorted increasingly to armed resistance, most dramatically at Birmingham and Selma. That reaction directs our attention again to the strategy of coercion that is the key to the civil rights movement's success. For all the complexity they faced in the white community, the civil rights leaders thought of their struggle against discrimination as war. That means that they lived, not always willingly, by the severe obligations and restraints that war imposes on military leaders, and they felt those obligations and restraints not merely as Christians but as practical men and women who were gambling with the lives of their followers. That theirs was, in King's words, a nonviolent army made their moral task a special case in some details of tactics, but no different in its fundamentals from that of any other army in war. They were using force against enemies to achieve political ends. The general philosophical question and the general historical tradition they were involved in was that of the just war, and the principles of just war provide the best summary of the relationship they developed between ends and means.

Having taken the first step—breaching the moral injunction against the use of force—the civil rights leaders could not hope to inspire the confidence and discipline of their followers through exhausting and dangerous struggles, let alone consider themselves Christians, if they threw all further moral concerns to the winds. Their decision to take that first step was a grave one: it did not indicate that the morality of their cause superseded other moral rules—that once the threshold of using force was crossed, anything goes. Rather, that first step entailed special, more austere ethics than those of normal, peaceful times. The leaders of this army, regardless of its being a nonviolent one, could not be vindictive in their treatment of enemies. They had to use means that were proportionate to the wrongs they hoped to right.

To say that the decision to use force entails special moral restraints is perhaps to state the obvious. What is less obvious is that those special moral restraints, whose purpose is to limit tactical choices, are hopelessly utopian unless they take into account the relationship that runs the other way: that tactical choices also impose limits on the moral choices. That is why just war doctrine is so important and so interesting. It is one area of ethics that does not easily degenerate into abstractions, or ideal "problems." It is based on special real-life situations in which the practical demands of survival impinge so obtrusively on every choice that those demands cannot be relegated to the background. (It may, therefore, be a better starting point for everyday morality than those theories of ethics that begin and end with ideal, laboratory-type situations.) The basic premise of just war doctrine is that the need for victory does not obviate concerns about right and wrong. But equally crucial is the less often recognized premise that the need for ethical rightness does not obviate concerns about victory and defeat.

In warfare it is wrong, that is, to be so constrained by morality as to lose sight of winning—just as it would be wrong to be so impelled toward winning as to lose sight of being just. That just war theorists take this into account is in part a recognition that the commander in the field will ignore their injunctions if they require suicidal restraint. All morality is lost if our side loses in war. But that is not merely a concession that morality makes to practicality. It is itself a moral principle: a commander, no matter how just his cause for making war, ceases to be just if he leads his own troops to slaughter. If he does not have a reasonable hope of victory, then the justness of his cause becomes immaterial. His moral obligation in the face of certain or even near-certain slaughter is to call a retreat.

It follows from the observation that morality does not obviate concerns about victory that morality does not obviate concerns about strategy. The civil rights leaders' moral actions were strategic. We must evaluate them not merely on the basis of their moral righteousness but on their political efficacy. By looking at the matter through the lens of just war doctrine, we can see around the sterile distinction between suasion and force, between "working within the system" and claiming a stance outside it. We can see clearly that winning matters, and that winning is contingent on the often arbitrary opportunities of an imperfect, immoral world. We can also see clearly, without any contradiction, that winning is not the only thing that matters in a world where people still have principles. The civil rights protesters maintained the delicate balance just long enough to crystallize as an example that remains to this day both morally and politically inspiring.

Whether southern mayors and governors in the 1950s understood the civil rights movement this way or not, they could never fully endorse violence against such protesters if they hoped to maintain their legitimacy, locally as well as nationally. Even the greatest fire-eaters among southern politicians sensed this, as the difference between their incendiary public statements and their conciliation toward federal authorities often reveals. There was terrible disorder in the streets of southern cities, disorder that the local civic and business elite wanted to suppress even more than distant bureaucrats in Washington, and more than the so-called American public (meaning middle-class white northerners) who watched the whole thing on television and were allegedly driven by conscience to demand federal intervention. When local authorities proved many times over that they could not or would not suppress the disorder, they made intervention almost risk free for extremely risk-averse presidents—partly because the bureaucrats did want order and partly because the so-called American public did care, but *primarily* because the local authorities needed to shunt the responsibility of suppressing segregationists onto a distant authority.

The question why the authorities did not seek help in suppressing the desegregationists, rather than the segregationists, is not answered by vague references to the deep constitutionality of civil rights or to some "American creed" that ensured that Americans would become fed up with persistent inequality of opportunity. The principle of states' rights is embodied in the

Constitution as indisputably as racial equality is and certainly has a longer constitutional pedigree, despite its being morally offensive to most nationalists and liberals. Americans tolerate all sorts of inequality, and other contradictions, in their various creeds. The answer lies in the superior strategy of civil rights protesters, based upon their superior understanding of southern society. Such protesters were able to seize the initiative and show themselves, by their discipline and persistence, to be the stronger of the two belligerents. For that reason they gained the federal government as an active ally.

When the direction of the war became clear, the Second Reconstruction began to take shape in the councils of Lyndon Johnson's Democratic Policy Committee. This was not to be a northern Republican imposition like the first Reconstruction, however, but a southern Democratic one. The roots of the Second Reconstruction's limitations are easy to see in the policy discussions Johnson's men had, in which they sought above all to avoid taking responsibility for race relations in the South. Their discussion was partly a philosophical one about whether the executive or the legislative or the judicial branch was the most appropriate one to act in the civil rights field. It was partly a practical one about which branch could get away with real action. Above all it was a political one about how best to remove responsibility from the southern politicians who were intolerably accountable both to the Democratic party and to southern voters. Just who would assume the responsibility was a secondary question. There were three main possibilities: the first consisted of leaders of the enemy party like Eisenhower, who obliged by alienating the segregationists and other states' righters with federal troops in Little Rock. When that was not enough, the next choice, southern governors and local politicians, would be useful, since although they were Democrats, they were not accountable to the national party. The last and best choice was southern businessmen, who were accountable to neither, especially if they operated off the record. These were useful because they were unobtrusive, and they were unobtrusive because they did nothing until the issue was forced.

It was the southern black movement that forced the issue, and it did so by refusing to take the opinion of white southerners as the end of the story of racism. The movement faced a population whose majority told opinion pollers it favored segregation. This ought to call our attention to our persistent, enervating habit of thinking of racism as primarily a matter of opinion, even of subconscious opinion. Like all historical phenomena, it is partly a matter of opinion, but primarily of something else: of political power, wherefore the decisive question is not "Do you favor segregation (or whatever racist institution)?" but "What are you willing to sacrifice, today, to defend it?" That deeper question the movement posed to white southerners in the 1950s and 1960s, and it produced at once greater realism and less cynicism than questions about mere opinion.

The movement's moral and political strategy put pressure on an evolving southern paternalism, eliminated segregation and disfranchisement from the laws, and in doing so redefined the status of those with black skin. It did not eliminate racial considerations from the hearts and minds of all white southerners, which may be a way of saying it did not eradicate the tendency of all people in all times and places to draw distinctions between themselves and other groups. But it did something of enormous historic significance: it brought down those specific instruments of oppression that gave racism sanction and institutional reinforcement. It forced serious southern racists to become artists of nostalgia (among other deceptive emotions), and freelance artists at that. That made them quite like northern racists, who since the Great Migration began in 1915, were making it clear to the world, and belatedly to themselves, that race could no longer be written off as a southern question.

While the nonsouthern character of race will be acknowledged widely today, something else will not, which is that race—by which I mean specific historical institutions, practices, and ideologies, as distinct from the timeless tendency of groups of people to be exclusive of and nasty to other groups—is not primarily a question of opinion, revealed to us in slips of the tongue and other unorganized, politically invulnerable ways. It is a question of what people will give up to maintain specific racial practices (once other people have raised the question, by giving up enough to fight credibly against them). Those practices *are* hard to specify as political targets today, but we should remember that they were hard to specify in the 1950s and 1960s as well, and that the first step in making them vulnerable was noticing that their beneficiaries were divided and uneasy about them.

ABBREVIATIONS

ACHR   Alabama Council on Human Relations (in ch. 3)
        Arkansas Council on Human Relations (in ch. 5)
CRDP   Civil Rights Documentation Project, Founders' Library,
        Howard University, Washington, D.C.
DAC   Democratic Advisory Council
DNC   Democratic National Committee
DPC   Democratic Policy Committee
FCHR   Florida Council on Human Relations
H&M   *Hearts and Minds: The Anatomy of Racism from Roosevelt to
        Reagan,* by Harry Ashmore (McGraw-Hill, 1982)
JFKL   John F. Kennedy Library, Boston, Massachusetts
LBJA   Lyndon Baines Johnson Archives, LBJ Library, Austin, Texas
LBJL   Lyndon Baines Johnson Library, Austin, Texas
MBP   Montgomery Boycott Papers, Martin Luther King Center,
        Atlanta, Georgia
MLKA   Martin Luther King Papers, and other related collections,
        Martin Luther King Center, Atlanta, Georgia
MLKB   Martin Luther King Papers, Mugar Library, Boston University,
        Boston, Massachusetts
NYT   *New York Times*
OH   Oral History (interview transcript)
PPP   *Public Papers of the Presidents*
R&R   Jane Record and Wilson Record, *Little Rock, U.S.A.: Materials
        for Analysis* (San Francisco: Chandler, 1960)
SMS   *A Southern Moderate Speaks,* by Brooks Hays (Chapel Hill:
        University of North Carolina Press, 1959)

SNCC   Student Nonviolent Coordinating Committee
SOHP   Southern Oral History Project, Wilson Library, University of North Carolina, Chapel Hill
SRC   Southern Regional Council
WHCF   White House Central Files

NOTES

Introduction

1. I do not think the role of white northerners in the Freedom Rides of 1961, the Freedom Summer of 1964, or in movement support groups at other times is similar to the role of the white southerners upon whom the movement more regularly relied. The mere similarity of skin color is trivial compared to the psychological and cultural differences between northerners and southerners in the period. Two northerners expressed this difference. One white New Yorker involved in the student movement said he did not have any "problem" mixing with black people in the North: that was not "a challenge" to the person he thought he was, as mixing in the South was. "I could have my beliefs without cost in New York . . . whereas in the South, beliefs were more expensive, so expensive that the bill was sometimes too high to pay. That was why there were so many liberals in the North and so few in the South. Being a liberal in the South meant losing business or a job or being ostracized or even attacked. In New York, it usually meant attending meetings" (W. J. Weatherby, *Love in the Shadows* [New York: Stein and Day, 1966]), 13. A student in the Freedom Summer project wrote, "As a white northerner I can get involved whenever I feel like it and run home whenever I get bored or frustrated or scared. I hate the attitude and position of the Northern whites and despise myself when I think that way" (*Letters from Mississippi*, ed. Elizabeth Sutherland [New York: McGraw-Hill, 1965], 193).

2. I differ here with David Garrow, who, in *Protest at Selma* (New Haven: Yale University Press, 1978) and more moderately in *Bearing the Cross* (New York: Morrow, 1986), sees an evolution in Martin Luther King's strategy from a reliance on moral suasion in the 1950s to a coercive realism by the time of the Birmingham and Selma struggles. I argue that King emphasized the coercion as much as the suasion, right from the beginning of the Montgomery struggle in 1955–56, and indeed even earlier, from the time he read Reinhold Niebuhr in divinity school. See King's "Pilgrimage to Nonviolence," in *Stride toward Freedom* (New York: Harper, 1958), 97–99. The evolution was in the minds of white southerners: the years of direct action up to 1964 and 1965 made resistance to coercion appear to them increasingly futile, and therefore King and others found it prudent to attempt more radical, systematic changes in 1964 and 1965 than in 1955 and 1956. But the attempts were coercive from the start and involved suasion till the end.

3. Numan Bartley makes this point in his excellent *Rise of Massive Resistance: Race*

and *Politics in the South during the 1950s* (Baton Rouge: Louisiana State University Press, 1969).

Chapter 1: The "Silent South": The Founding Fathers of Southern White Dissent

1. Atticus Greene Haygood, *Our Brother in Black, His Freedom and His Future* (St. Louis: Advocate Publishing House, 1881), 129, 131–38, 141. See also *The New South: Thanksgiving Sermon, 1880, by Atticus Greene Haygood*, ed. Judson C. Ward, in *Emory University Publications Sources and Reprints*, 6th ser. (1950), no. 3, v–xi; Haygood, *Pleas for Progress* (Cincinnati: Cranston and Stowe, 1889).

2. This and next three paragraphs: Haygood, *Our Brother*, 138–42, 133, 142–43.

3. Ibid., 144.

4. John Cell, *The Highest Stage of White Supremacy: The Origins of Segregation in South Africa and the American South* (New York: Cambridge University Press, 1982).

5. Haygood, "The Negro Problem: God Takes Time—Man Must," typescript for *Methodist Review* (Sept.–Oct. 1895), Haygood Papers, quoted in Joel Williamson, *A Rage for Order* (New York: Oxford University Press, 1986), 76–77.

6. Haygood, *Our Brother*, 116; Morton Sosna, *In Search of the Silent South* (New York: Columbia University Press, 1977), 30–31.

7. Carl Degler, *The Other South: Southern Dissenters in the Nineteenth Century* (New York: Harper, 1974), 308–9, and see Joel Williamson: "Haygood was one of the first and probably the greatest of the southern churchmen to revolt against the abandonment of black Christians," *Rage for Order*, 73.

8. Lewis Harvie Blair, *The Prosperity of the South Dependent upon the Elevation of the Negro* (1889); reprinted as *A Southern Prophecy: The Prosperity of the South Dependent upon the Elevation of the Negro*, ed. C. Vann Woodward (Boston: Little, Brown, 1964; hereafter *Prosperity*), 184, 70.

9. This and previous paragraph: Blair, *Prosperity*, 48–49, 122–51.

10. C. Vann Woodward, "A Southern Brief for Racial Equality," in *American Counterpoint: Slavery and Racism in the North-South Dialogue* (Boston: Little, Brown, 1976), 196.

11. Blair, *Prosperity*, 68.

12. Woodward, "Southern Brief," 209–11.

13. See C. Vann Woodward, *The Strange Career of Jim Crow* (New York: Oxford University Press, 1955), and *Tom Watson: Agrarian Rebel* (New York: Macmillan, 1938).

14. This and previous paragraph: Blair, *Prosperity*, 118, 171 ff.

15. George Washington Cable, "The Silent South" (1888), in Cable, *The Negro Question*, ed. Arlin Turner (New York: Doubleday, 1958), 116, 114.

16. Blair, *Prosperity*, 73–74, 52, 81.

17. Cable, "The Freedmen's Case in Equity," in *The Negro Question*, 51.

18. Cable, "The Negro Question," in *The Negro Question*, 124, and "Silent South," 116–17. Haygood argued that the best growths are slow ones and that the North had no right to expect overnight miracles from a region trying to recover from war. Haygood, *Our Brother*, 101–3.

19. Haygood, *Our Brother*, 151, 156, 116, 155–56; 96–97.

20. Blair, *Prosperity*, 29.

21. Cable, "Silent South," 80–81, and "Freedmen's Case," 73–74.

22. See Cable's celebration of the statue of Lee at the beginning of "Silent South," 77–78, and Blair's rhapsodies on "mammy," *Prosperity*, 143–45, and on southern kindness, ibid., 86–87.

23. Haygood, *Our Brother*, 88–89, 96, 187–88, 232–33. Those who raised the specter of "social equality" whenever black rights were discussed suffered from "a sort of hysteria," but Haygood never questioned whether his own eagerness to dismiss *fears* of social equality stemmed from the same malady.

24. At any rate, Blair returned to his main point: "[If the issue is mixed schools or no schools,] it would be the height of folly to allow feeling or sentiment to rob us of the inestimable blessings of education." Blair, *Prosperity*, 142–46. This was an awfully big if.

25. Cable, "Silent South," 83–84, 89, 95–99.

26. Richard H. Edmonds, in 1900, quoted in Paul Gaston, *The New South Creed: A Study in Southern Mythmaking* (1970; reprint, New York: Vintage, 1973), 105.

27. Woodward, *Origins of the New South* (Baton Rouge: Louisiana State University Press, 1971), 632, 163–64.

28. "Memorial" to Louisiana Legislature from American Citizens' Equal Rights Association of Louisiana Against Class Legislation, in Official Journal of House of Representatives of Louisiana, 1890, pp. 187–88, in *The Thin Disguise: Turning Point in Negro History, Plessy v. Ferguson, A Documentary Presentation, 1864–1896*, ed. Otto H. Olsen (New York: Humanities Press, 1967), 47–50. C. Vann Woodward, "The National Decision against Equality," in *American Counterpoint*, 215–18.

29. Otto Olsen, *Carpetbagger's Crusade: The Life of Albion Winegar Tourgee* (Baltimore: Johns Hopkins Press, 1965), 326–28.

30. Brief for Homer A. Plessy by Phillips and F. D. McKenny, in Olsen, *Thin Disguise*, 106. Phillips here accepted the idea that there are "races" and that no "race" could be interested in "its own destruction."

31. Blair, *Prosperity*, 144, and see Woodward, "Southern Brief," 184. Cable, "Segregation," in *The Negro Question*, 30, and "Freedmen's Case," 64–65, 70–72. Separate schools were already sanctioned by Congress — the same Congress that created the Fourteenth Amendment — in District of Columbia legislation, as Justice Brown noted in his opinion, *Plessy v. Ferguson* 163 U.S. 550–51, and by Massachusetts chief justice Lemuel Shaw — whose authority made him a sort of "tenth Supreme Court Justice" — who had endorsed separate schools as early as 1849. Woodward, "National Decision," 228–29.

32. See above and Haygood, *Our Brother*, 143–44. Also, Henry Grady: "Whites and blacks must walk in separate paths. . . . As near as may be, these paths should be made equal — but separate they must be now and always. This means separate schools, separate churches, separate accommodation everywhere — but equal accommodation where the same money is charged, or where the state provides for the citizen." Grady, *The New South*, ed. Oliver Dyer (New York: Robert Bonner's Sons, 1890), 244–45.

33. *Plessy v. Ferguson*, 163 U.S. 544 (1896).

34. *Plessy*, 163 U.S. 561 (1896).

35. *Plessy*, 163 U.S. 562, 559–60 (1896).

36. Olsen, *Thin Disguise*, 21, 18.

37. Woodward, "National Decision," 231.

38. In some sense, Walling was no longer a southerner: he had been educated in Edinburgh and at the University of Chicago and (briefly) Harvard Law School, as well as in Louisville, and had moved to New York just after the turn of the century. For biographical information here and in the next paragraph I have drawn from *American Reformers*, ed. Alden Whitman (New York: H. W. Wilson, 1985), 839–41; Mary White Ovington, *Walls Come Tumbling Down* (1947; reprint, New York: Schocken, 1970), 101–3; and Richard Kluger, *Simple Justice* (New York: Knopf, 1975), 96.

39. William English Walling, "The Race War in the North," *Independent* 65 (Sept. 3, 1908), 529–34.

40. The core group that issued "the Call" on white liberals to join with the Niagara Movement in a biracial organization held its first meetings in Walling's New York apartment. It was Walling who took the initiative to engage Du Bois as an executive of the new organization and to attack Booker T. Washington's conciliatory policies head-on with repeated calls for social as well as political equality. Ovington, *Walls*, 100–110; Du Bois, *Autobiography* (New York: International, 1968), 254; Du Bois, *Dusk of Dawn* (1940; reprint, Franklin Center, Pa.: Franklin Library, 1980), 98–99, 235–37; Charles Flint Kellog, *NAACP: A History of the National Association for the Advancement of Colored People*, 1: 1909–20 (Baltimore: Johns Hopkins Press, 1967), 10–12, 15–16, 44, 28; Langston Hughes, *Fight for Freedom: The Story of the NAACP* (New York: Berkeley Medallion, 1962), 20–23.

Chapter 2: From Silence to Futility: Southern White Dissent Gets Organized

1. Southerners who wrote on the subject tended to remember the Negro "as a slave"; they considered "him and his rights from a position of proud and contemptuous superiority, and would deal with him on the antebellum basis of his servile state." Andrew Sledd, "The Negro: Another View," *Atlantic Monthly* 90 (July 1902), 65–73, reprinted in *Forgotten Voices: Dissenting Southerners in an Age of Conformity*, ed. Charles Wynes (Baton Rouge: Louisiana State University Press, 1967), 91–105.

2. Cable, in exile, wrote about these changes, too, but found them highly reprehensible. He had still not renounced his belief in Negro inferiority or his disdain for "social equality," however. See "The Southern Struggle for Pure Government" (1909), in *The Negro Question*, 213–44; "My Politics," in ibid., 1–25.

3. This had not always been so. Before 1885, more than half of lynching victims were white. After that turning point, the proportion of black lynching victims to the total number of victims steadily increased. Robert Zangrando, *The NAACP Crusade against Lynching* (Philadelphia: Temple University Press, 1980), 6–7; Sosna, *Search*, 35.

4. "If it were strictly the fact," as most southerners defensively tried to convince themselves, "that violent rape is the cause of most of our lynchings; if it were true, moreover, that the man were suddenly and violently slain by the husband, lover, father, brother, of the dishonored one, in quick tempest of wrath and agony unspeakable — while we must still condemn, we might, in sympathy and sorrow, condone the deed of hurried vengeance. *But neither of these things is true.*" The more common view, promoted

by Rebecca Latimer Felton, one of the early crusaders for increased restriction of black southerners, was that lynching was appropriate punishment and a necessary deterrent to black men who had already lost too much of their proper sense of "place." Felton to the *Atlanta Constitution*, Dec. 19, 1898, quoted in Williamson, *Rage for Order*, 94–95.

5. It should be noted that outside the white South, thanks to the investigations of Ida B. Wells, the rape justification was being discredited at the same time. See Zangrando, *NAACP Crusade*, 4.

6. See Bruce Clayton, *The Savage Ideal* (Baltimore: Johns Hopkins University Press, 1972).

7. Henry Y. Warnock, "Andrew Sledd, Southern Methodists, and the Negro: A Case History," *Journal of Southern History* 31 (Aug. 1965), 251–71.

8. John Spencer Bassett, "Stirring Up the Fires of Racial Antipathy," reprinted in Wynes, *Forgotten Voices*, 110.

9. Bruce Clayton, in his otherwise reliable and insightful study, seems to misread Sledd, claiming he was merely "paying lip service to the dogma of Negro 'inferiority.'" Clayton implies that Sledd dismissed "talk about 'social equality' as 'ill-advised cant.'" But what Sledd dismisses as "ill-advised cant" is not *talk* about social equality but rather the belief held by "misguided friends" of the Negro that Negroes *are* equal to white people. Sledd states that widespread acceptance of the fact of Negro inferiority should put to rest all "schemes" that attempt to *establish* "social equality." Far from "demolish[ing], one by one, the popular shibboleths about racial relations in the South," as Clayton writes, Sledd uses "social equality," "amalgamation," and "negro inferiority," to serve his own rhetorical ends. Clayton, *Savage Ideal*, 82–83, 102.

10. Virginius Dabney, *Liberalism in the South* (Chapel Hill: University of North Carolina Press, 1932), 339–41; Clayton, *Savage Ideal*, 90–91.

11. Clayton, *Savage Ideal*, 94–95.

12. James Kilgo, "An Inquiry regarding Lynching," *South Atlantic Quarterly* 1 (Jan. 1902), 4–13; Sosna, *Search*, 31.

13. Clayton, *Savage Ideal*, 94, 95–96.

14. Clayton sees the Bassett Affair as emblematic: after it, southern dissenters were much more timid than they had been before. *Savage Ideal*, 103, 182. An interesting footnote on the whole affair: William A. Dunning wrote Bassett in November 1902 that Columbia University would hire him if he was forced to leave Trinity — the same Columbia that provoked Charles Beard's resignation in 1917 by firing faculty with anti-war views.

15. For this and the next five paragraphs: John J. Culley, "Muted Trumpets: Four Efforts to Better Southern Race Relations, 1900-1919" (Ph.D. diss., University of Virginia, 1967), esp. 94–112; E. Charles Chatfield, "The Southern Sociological Congress: Organization of Uplift," *Tennessee Historical Quarterly* 19 (1960), 328–47, and "The Southern Sociological Congress: Rationale of Uplift," *Tennessee Historical Quarterly* 20 (1961), 51–64; and Sosna, *Search*, 17-18.

16. Culley, "Muted Trumpets," 114–68; Sosna, *Search*, 16–19.

17. Material in this and the next three paragraphs: Wilma Dykeman and James Stokely, *Seeds of Southern Change: The Life of Will Alexander* (1962; reprint, New York: Norton, 1976), 45–46, 62–65; Sosna, *Search*, 20–21.

18. Sosna, *Search*, 22. See also Ann Ellis, "The Commission on Interracial Coopera-

tion, 1919-1944: Its Activities and Results" (Ph.D. diss., Georgia State University, 1975), Edgar Burrows, "The Commission on Interracial Cooperation: A Case Study in the Interracial Movement in the South" (Ph.D. diss., University of Wisconsin, 1955), and R. W. Miles, "The Virginia Interracial Committee," *Journal of Social Forces* 1 (1923), 153.

19. *Cooperation in Southern Communities*, ed. T. J. Woofter and Isaac Fisher (Atlanta: Commission on Interracial Cooperation, 1921), 21, 24–25; Woofter, *The Basis for Racial Adjustment* (Boston: Atheneum, 1925), 11, 25–28, 30–37, 235–41; Sosna, *Search*, 25; Dykeman and Stokely, *Seeds*, 66.

20. Sosna, *Search*, 26.

21. Woofter, *Basis for Racial Adjustment*, 139–47.

22. Walter White, *Rope and Faggot: A Biography of Judge Lynch* (1929; reprint, New York: Arno, 1969), esp. 208–26. The literature on southern antilynching efforts often obscures the independent effort, led by the NAACP, which maintained its headquarters and most of its membership in the North and which, besides creating tremendous publicity and political pressure in its own right, was a constant goad to the quieter efforts of the southern antilynching organizers. A useful corrective is Zangrando, *NAACP Crusade*.

23. Sosna, *Search*, 30–36.

24. This and previous paragraph: Jacquelyn Dowd Hall, "The Mind That Burns in Each Body," *Southern Exposure* 12 (Nov.–Dec., 1984), 61–71; Hall, *Revolt against Chivalry: Jesse Daniel Ames and the Women's Campaign against Lynching* (New York: Columbia University Press, 1979); Dykeman and Stokely, *Seeds*, 143–52.

25. Dykeman and Stokely, *Seeds*, 146, 152.

26. Johnson quoted in Harvard Sitkoff, *A New Deal for Blacks* (New York: Oxford University Press, 1978), 296.

27. Zangrando, *NAACP Crusade*, 105, 116–17, 126–27, 143; Dykeman and Stokely, *Seeds*, 143–52; Sosna, *Search*, 20–41.

28. Sosna, *Search*, 29–36. Daniel J. Singal, *The War Within: From Victorian to Modernist Thought in the South, 1919-1945* (Chapel Hill: University of North Carolina Press, 1982), 330–34, offers an insightful explanation for the southern acceptance of Raper's book on lynching but points out, pp. 335–38, that Raper was otherwise seen as something of a renegade and exiled himself from the South in the mid-1940s.

29. Zangrando, *NAACP Crusade*, 143; Sosna, *Search*, 36.

30. Dykeman and Stokely, *Seeds*, 152; Sosna, *Search*, 34. One southern sociologist, whom Sosna cites, offers a thin reed of statistical support for the idea of a relatively swifter decline of lynching in those counties in which the ASWPL was most active: John Shelton Reed, "An Evaluation of an Anti-Lynching Organization," *Social Problems* 16 (Fall 1968), 172–82. Hall, "Mind That Burns," 343, notes other possible causes of the decline in lynching during the years of the southern white crusade. Cf. Raper's own explanation, cited in Singal, *War Within*, 333, and 413 n. 57, and the obvious secular decline in the figures.

31. See Bartley, *Rise of Massive Resistance*.

32. Sosna, *Search*, 36–37.

33. Sosna, *Search*, 36–37; Walling in Ovington, *Walls*, 157.

34. Dan Carter, *Scottsboro: A Tragedy of the American South* (Baton Rouge: Louisiana State University Press, 1969), 83–87, 116–21; Sosna, *Search*, 37–38.

35. Though racism declined in educated liberal circles—even in the South, as educated southerners grew less and less isolated in the twentieth century—red-baiting seems to have filled the vacuum. Irrational fears of association seemed irresistible to the conscientious, socially aware liberals who were nonetheless afraid to challenge their social order: such fears provided a reason not to take the risks necessary for social change, and an excuse not to aid those who were taking such risks. Racial difference, a fabrication that could not survive forever in a culture that was bound to respect the results of scientific discovery, was rather easily replaced by the new Communist menace in the minds of those very liberals who began, however haltingly, to take a stand for racial equality in the late 1940s and 1950s.

On the impact of red-baiting on southern dissent more generally, see Anthony Dunbar, *Against the Grain: Southern Radicals and Prophets, 1929–1959* (Charlottesville: University Press of Virginia, 1981), and Virginia Durr, *Outside the Magic Circle: The Autobiography of Virginia Foster Durr*, ed. Hollinger F. Barnard (1985; reprint, New York: Simon and Schuster, 1987).

36. See remarks on this in the Epilogue.

37. Dabney, *Liberalism in the South*, 238–39.

38. For contrasting views of the South and the influence of its liberals in the region, see Clarence Cason, *Ninety Degrees in the Shade* (1935; reprint, Tuscaloosa: University of Alabama Press, 1983), and W. J. Cash, *Mind of the South* (New York: Knopf, 1941).

39. Virginia Durr, *Outside the Magic Circle*, 110–14; John Salmond, "'Miss Lucy of the CIO': A Southern Life," in *The South Is Another Land: Essays on the Twentieth Century South*, ed. Bruce Clayton and John Salmond (Westport, Conn.: Greenwood, 1987), 107–21, and *Miss Lucy of the CIO* (Athens: University of Georgia Press, 1988); Dunbar, *Against the Grain*, 187, 192–93; Thomas Krueger, *And Promises to Keep: The Southern Conference for Human Welfare, 1938–1948* (Nashville: Vanderbilt University Press, 1967), 16–17.

40. The general outline of events in this and the preceding three paragraphs comes from Krueger, *And Promises to Keep*, 24, 37–38, 42, 124, 43, 17, 194–96, and George Tindall, *Emergence of the New South, 1913–1945* (Baton Rouge: Louisiana State University Press, 1967), 611, 624. The interpretations are mine.

41. See J. Saunders Redding, "Southern Defensive—I," and Lillian Smith, "Southern Defensive—II," both attacking the SRC, in *Common Ground* 4 (Spring 1944), 36–45, and Guy B. Johnson (SRC executive director), "Southern Offensive," defending the SRC, in *Common Ground* 4 (Summer 1944), 87–93.

42. See Irwin Kilbaner, "The Southern Conference Educational Fund: A History" (Ph.D. diss., University of Wisconsin, 1971).

43. See James R. Green, "The Brotherhood of Timber Workers, 1910–1913: A Radical Response to Industrial Capitalism in the Southern U.S.A.," *Past and Present* 60 (Aug. 1973), 161–200, and especially Dunbar, *Against the Grain*.

44. Dunbar emphasizes the effect of red-baiting, especially from within, in the decline and fall of neo-Populist organizations in the 1940s and 1950s. He ends his history of these organizations with the tantalizing suggestion that the civil rights movement that took over their integrationist agenda might have been much more revolutionary, and

much more effective, had red-baiting not forced it to ask for half a loaf from the start. "In effect, the Cold War and the pressures of agencies like [the House Un-American Activities Committee] forced the issues of economic equality and racial equality to become separate and pushed the civil rights struggle in a direction that posed no challenge to the vital elements of the American economic system." Though movement leaders remained sincerely concerned about black-white inequality within that system, they rarely challenged the more general inequality on which that system was premised. "Their struggle altered the fundamental characteristic of southern society, the second-class citizenship of blacks, but it set aside for consideration by future generations many of the historic demands of [neo-Populist] southern dissenters: 'land for the landless,' 'full and decent employment,' a halt to the invasion of carpetbag industry, the holding in common of 'all natural resources and all scientific processes,' and 'the liberation of all workers from the enslavement to the machine.'" *Against the Grain*, 258.

45. Sosna, *Search*, 82, 84–85, 95–96; Daniels quoted in Sosna, *Search*, 107.

Chapter 3: The Montgomery Bus Boycott, 1955–1956

1. For example, Jonathan Daniels ended *A Southerner Discovers the South* (New York: Macmillan, 1938) with a lament that the South's leaders had failed it. With bitterness in place of Daniels' sympathy, W. J. Cash ended his monumental *Mind of the South* on the same point. Harry Ashmore's treatment of the same theme mixes lament with hope, *Epitaph for Dixie* (New York: Norton, 1957), esp. 26–44. See also Richard King, *A Southern Renaissance: The Cultural Awakening of the American South, 1930–1955* (New York: Oxford University Press, 1980), and Morton Sosna, *In Search of the Silent South.*

2. Virginia Durr was head of the National Committee to Abolish the Poll Tax. Clifford and Virginia Durr OH, no. 1, LBJL, 29–33. On the Durrs being well known in the black community (Clifford was the only available lawyer for black clients for many years), Johnnie Carr, interview with author, Montgomery, July 14, 1989 (hereafter Carr interview).

3. *NYT*, Mar. 20, 21, 22, 23, 1954.

4. Clifford and Virginia Durr OH, no. 1, LBJL, 37–51. Virginia Durr, *Outside the Magic Circle*, 180, 207, 254–73, and passim. Mrs. A. W. West, Johnnie Carr, Virginia Durr, joint OH, King Library and Archives, MLKA, 6.

5. Virginia Durr in the West-Carr-Durr OH, MLKA, 6.

6. Lamont Yeakey, "The Montgomery, Alabama, Bus Boycott, 1955–1956" (Ph.D. diss., Columbia University, 1979), 151; Taylor Branch, *Parting the Waters* (New York: Simon and Schuster, 1988), 120–23. Virginia Durr in the West-Carr-Durr OH, MLKA, 6. Virginia Durr, interview with author, Vineyard Haven, Mass., Aug. 18, 1988 (hereafter V. Durr interview). Virginia Durr to Curtis McDougall, Apr. 11, 1955, MBP, MLKA, folder 67.

7. Durr in West-Carr-Durr OH, MLKA, 9–10, 6–7.

8. Durrs OH, no. 1, LBJL, 26–27. V. Durr interview; Charles Gomillion, interview with author, Washington, D.C., Mar. 21, 1989 (hereafter Gomillion interview).

9. See Aimee Horton, "The Highlander Folk School: Pioneer of Integration in the South," *Teacher's College Record* 68 (Dec. 1966), 242–44, and *The Highlander Folk School: A History of Its Major Programs, 1932–1961* (Brooklyn: Carlson, 1971); Frank

Adams, "Highlander Folk School: Getting Information, Going Back, and Teaching It," *Harvard Educational Review* 42 (Nov. 1972), 497–520; Frank Adams (with Myles Horton), *Unearthing Seeds of Fire: The Idea of Highlander* (Winston-Salem, N.C.: J. F. Blair, 1975); and Dunbar, *Against the Grain.*

10. Aldon Morris, *Origins of the Civil Rights Movement* (New York: Free Press, 1984), 144; Branch, *Parting,* 121.

11. On Rosa Parks at Highlander and Virginia Durr's role in arranging the visit: Septima Clark OH, MLKA, 48–49. Rosa Parks to Mrs. H. Shipherd, July 6, 1956, MBP folder 29. Virginia Durr to Hortons, Jan. 30, 1956, MBP, folder 32. V. Durr to Hortons, Feb. 24, 1956, MBP, folder 31. Rosa Parks to M. Horton, Feb. 25, 1956, MBP, folder 29. V. Durr to Hortons, Mar. 2, 1956, MBP, folder 7. V. Durr to M. Horton, Nov. 5, 1956, MBP, folder 35. On Mrs. Parks' relationship with Highlander, see also M. Horton to Septima Clark, Aug. 13, 1957, Septima Clark manuscripts, supplementing her file in SOHP, and the Septima Clark interview transcript, SOHP, 82–83.

12. Rosa Parks to Mrs. H. Shipherd, July 6, 1955, MBP, folder 29. According to Mrs. Durr, "When she came back she was so happy and felt so liberated and then as time went on she said the discrimination got worse and worse to bear AFTER having, for the first time in her life, been free of it at Highlander. I am sure that had a lot to do with her daring to risk arrest." Durr to Hortons, Jan. 30, 1956. Rosa Parks wanted to return to HFS, which was "the promised land to her. . . . It was the contrast with her life there that made Jim Crow completely unbearable and it was the first time she had ever lived in a free society." Durr to Hortons, Feb. 24, 1956, MBP, folder 31.

13. Irene West OH, MLKA, 17.

14. Yeakey, "Montgomery, Alabama, Bus Boycott," 151; Branch, *Parting,* 120–23. Fred Gray, interview with author, Tuskegee, Ala., July 12, 1989 (hereafter Gray interview). Gray became the main lawyer representing Rosa Parks in court. He continued to rely on Clifford Durr for strategic advice as well as mundane things like use of his library (Gray and his young, impoverished practice did not have a collection of law books, and being black he was not able to use public facilities). As Lamont Yeakey noted, "Although quite capable (in fact having the confidence of both Nixon and Mrs. Parks and being one of the more knowledgeable lawyers in town), perhaps better able to handle the case than Gray, Clifford Durr was most respectful of the wishes of all the parties concerned, and mindful of not upsetting what might be thought to be the prerogative Fred Gray had or should have in the case." Yeakey, "Montgomery, Alabama, Bus Boycott," 276. Gray discussed with Clifford Durr his decision to supersede Parks' case (which bogged down in state court) with a federal suit (filed Feb. 1, 1956), which directly challenged the constitutionality of segregation. Branch, *Parting,* 129–31, 158–59, 167.

15. See V. Durr to M. Horton, Feb. 18, 1956, and V. Durr to Hortons, Feb. 24, 1956, MBP, folders 34 and 31. Georgia Gilmore, interview with author, Montgomery, July 14, 1989 (hereafter Gilmore interview); Carr interview; Gray interview; Ralph D. Abernathy, interview with author, Atlanta, July 7 and July 11, 1989; Gomillion interview; and V. Durr interview.

16. Branch, *Parting,* 133–34. On Graetz, see Rosa Parks OH, CRDP, 17–18.

17. *Birmingham News,* Jan. 11, 1956, quoted in Thomas J. Gilliam, "The Montgomery Bus Boycott of 1955–1956" (M.A. thesis, Auburn University, 1968), reprinted in

The Walking City: The Montgomery Bus Boycott, 1955–1956, ed. David J. Garrow (Brooklyn: Carlson, 1989), 209–10.

18. Steven M. Millner, "The Montgomery Bus Boycott: A Case Study in the Emergence and Career of a Social Movement" (Ph.D. diss., University of California at Berkeley, 1981), reprinted in Garrow, *Walking City*, 498.

19. King, and King quoting Graetz, Martin Luther King, Jr., *Stride toward Freedom* (New York: Harper, 1958), 169. Rosa Parks, J. E. Pierce, and Robert Graetz, "The Montgomery Story," transcript of a television broadcast, Aug. 21, 1956, pp. 18–19, 26–27, MBP, folder 5. On Ray Wadley, see also King, *Stride*, 32–33, and V. Durr interview.

20. Coretta Scott King, *My Life with Martin Luther King, Jr.* (New York: Holt, Rinehart, and Winston, 1969), 128. King, *Stride*, 175. Millner, "Montgomery Bus Boycott," 497–98. Septima Clark OH, MLKA, 47. David L. Lewis says Graetz was the sole white person involved in MIA deliberations. Lewis, *King* (1970; 2d ed., Urbana: University of Illinois Press, 1978), 61. Gilliam says he was the only white member. Gilliam, "Montgomery Bus Boycott," 222.

21. Durrs OH, nos. 1 and 2, LBJL; V. Durr interview; Smiley OH, CRDP, 1–9; Smiley, tape recording, Glendale, Calif., Jan. 23, 1990 (in author's possession; hereafter Smiley tape); Smiley, Report [to the Fellowship of Reconciliation] from Montgomery, Aug. 15, 1956, MLKA, box 10, folder 15, pp. 1–2, 4.

22. Bayard Rustin, "Montgomery Diary," *Liberation* (Apr. 1956), reprinted in *Down the Line: The Collected Writings of Bayard Rustin* (Chicago: Quadrangle, 1971), 55–61. Smiley, CRDP, 35–37. Smiley to John and Al, Feb. 29, 1956; Smiley, Report from the South [to FOR], Feb. 29, 1956; and Smiley, Report from the South, Number Two [to F.O.R.], Aug. 15, 1956, all in MLKA, box 10, folder 15. Smiley to MLK, Feb. 28, 1956, MLKB, box 57, file 7.43B. On the background of CORE, see also James Farmer, *Lay Bare the Heart: An Autobiography of the Civil Rights Movement* (New York: Plume, 1985), and August Meier and Elliott Rudwick, *CORE: A Study in the Civil Rights Movement* (New York: Oxford University Press, 1973).

23. Smiley OH, CRDP, 35–37. On Smiley's efforts with "the white community," which fared as poorly as Graetz's (Smiley tape), see also Graetz to Hassler, May 15, 1957; Smiley to John and Al, Feb. 29, 1956; Smiley Report from the South [to FOR], Apr. 1956, pp. 2–4; and Smiley, Report from the South, Number Two, Aug. 15, 1956, pp. 1–2; all in MLKA, 10:15. Smiley did propose a meeting of a hundred or so black and white Alabama clergymen, to "meet in a rural setting so that they would not feel afraid, and without any publicity." He discussed this matter with the Reverend Andrew "Doc" Turnipseed, a white preacher from the Montgomery area who was sympathetic to the movement, and others: "and we did gather together on one occasion 23 men . . . [and] discussed the possibility of some sort of rapprochement among the ministers themselves. One minister, though not in Montgomery, wept when I talked with him about this matter because, he said, 'I am so ashamed of myself that as a Christian I cannot even return the love that my black brother has offered to me.'" This group planned to go "barnstorming on the subject of openness and listening to the cries of our brother," but the plans broke down when two of the most prominent ministers were transferred out of Alabama. Smiley tape.

24. Smiley, letter to author, Dec. 26, 1989. Smiley later stated he attended only one

Klan meeting. The Klan did not hold many public meetings, partly because "as the Montgomery bus protest matured, the people came to a point where they did not fear the Klan and many of them felt sorry for them." And on the one occasion they paraded when Smiley was present, the black people "greeted the parade with a sort of enthusiasm and there was much laughter"; Smiley said he felt sorry for "these poor, ridiculously dressed men who were attempting to create fear, being met with this type of cordiality instead of the expected hostility." Smiley tape.

25. Smiley, letter to author, Dec. 26, 1989; Smiley tape. Smiley also held a workshop attended by some seventy white residents of Montgomery, most of them women, the overwhelming majority of them upper-class, the night before the buses were finally desegregated in December 1956. Smiley says the workshop was conducted exactly as the ones in the black churches, with role plays — "psychodramas and sociodramas" — simulating the anticipated encounters on real-life buses. The idea was to prepare them for riding side by side with blacks in the face of hostility from segregationist holdouts and to deal nonviolently with incidents. Some of those at the workshop showed up the next day to demonstrate white acquiescence in desegregation of the buses right from the beginning. Smiley OH, CRDP, 37–38, and Smiley tape.

26. Smiley tape. King, *Stride*, 168. Other sources on Smiley's activity include Graetz to Hassler, May 15, 1957, MLKA, 10:15; MLK to Smiley, Nov. 19, 1962, and Smiley to MLK, Sept. 28, 1962, and Dec. 5, 1962, MLKA, 10:16; Muste to MLK, Feb. 4, 1963, and Smiley to "Friend," Feb. 19, 1963, MLKA, 10:17; Hassler and Smiley to MLK, June 15, 1963, MLKA, 10:19. Exchange of letters between MLK and Smiley, Sept. 13–Nov. 14, 1961, MLKB, box 57, file VII.43.B.

27. Branch, *Parting*, 196.

28. Branch, *Parting*, 138.

29. The task of the movement, King said, was not only to free the Negro but to free "his white brothers from the bondage of fears concerning integration." *Stride*, 206, 216. See also Martin Luther King, Jr., *Why We Can't Wait* (New York: New American Library, 1963), 38, and Rustin, "Montgomery Diary," 57.

30. ACHR, *Newsletter*, Oct. 1955, 4, MBP, folder 75. On the Birmingham-Nixon deal, see Yeakey, "Montgomery, Alabama, Bus Boycott," 168–70. The *Montgomery Advertiser* (quoted in Yeakey, 169) editorialized that the hiring was "wise" and "should have been done years ago." The paper admitted that white police had "needlessly bullied Negroes on occasion" and that black people consequently had a "natural resentment" of the "guardians of the law." Black police would thus lead black people to have "more respect for the law." White politicians, from Mayor Gayle down, told white audiences that the black officers were hired "on a trial basis" only and that they would patrol only in black neighborhoods and could arrest only "colored people." White people could be arrested by black police "only under the most extreme, emergency conditions," Mayor Gayle said. But black officer Arthur G. Worthy said that he and his fellow black officers received no such instructions and that in his first fifteen months of duty 95 percent of his arrests were of white people for drunk driving. The *Advertiser* reported on March 25, 1955, that elections in Montgomery were "notoriously close" and that black voters had "the balance of power." Yeakey, "Montgomery, Alabama, Bus Boycott," 168–70, 174. On Dave Birmingham, see also J. Mills Thornton, "Challenge and Response in the Montgomery Bus Boycott of 1955–1956," in Garrow, *Walking City*, 326–36.

31. ACHR, *Newsletter*, Oct. 1955, 4, in MBP, folder 75.

32. Yeakey, "Montgomery, Alabama, Bus Boycott," 168.

33. Morris says that Parks was ejected from a seat in the 1940s by the same driver who had her arrested in 1955. *Origins*, 51.

34. Rosa Parks OH, CRDP, 3–4.

35. Branch, *Parting*, 120.

36. Branch, *Parting*, 144.

37. This moderate approach led to trouble later on, however: Smiley reported that the failure of negotiations came about largely because "the MIA asked for too little in the beginning which [left] little room for negotiation." Smiley, Report from the South [to F.O.R.], Feb. 19, 1956, MLKA, 10:15, p. 3.

38. Numan Bartley and Hugh Graham, *Southern Politics and the Second Reconstruction* (Baltimore: Johns Hopkins University Press, 1975), 39–41.

39. Bert Collier, "Segregation and Politics," in *With All Deliberate Speed: Segregation-Desegregation in Southern Schools*, ed. Don Shoemaker (New York: Harper, 1957), 128, 123–24. McKeldin of Maryland, Wetherby of Kentucky, Clement of Tennessee, Cherry of Arkansas, and Marland of West Virginia were the other governors to vote against the segregation resolution at the Southern Governors' Conference of 1954.

40. Yeakey, "Montgomery, Alabama, Bus Boycott," 477–78. Rufus Lewis told Yeakey that Folsom fought against segregation, which he saw as an issue that divided black from white in order to maintain undemocratic rule in the black belt. Yeakey, "Montgomery, Alabama, Bus Boycott," 477. See also Gilliam, "Montgomery Bus Boycott," 250–52, 290–91.

41. *Atlanta Daily World*, Feb. 4, 1956, quoted in Yeakey, "Montgomery, Alabama, Bus Boycott," 478. The *Minneapolis Star and Tribune* called Folsom a man "with most of the attributes of a demagogue" but who had never baited the Negro. As a result, he had the solid Negro vote, which, however, was not "very big—probably 50,000 out of a half million." Quoted in Collier, "Segregation and Politics," 123.

By 1956, Folsom began to pay the price for racial moderation. He lost a bid for Democratic National Committeeman, by a three-to-one vote, against a vocal segregationist—the author of the "interposition" resolution, Charles W. McKay, Jr. Steven Lawson, *Black Ballots: Voting Rights in the South, 1944–1969* (New York: Columbia University Press, 1976), 383. By the end of his second term (1958), Folsom's actions suggest he felt he had nothing more to lose. In a land where symbol had at least as much force as reality, his invitation to Harlem's congressman Adam Clayton Powell to come and have a Scotch with him in Montgomery in 1958 had a deadly effect on the future of his brand of politics. Drinking, as one political scientist put it, went over badly enough in the rural, fundamentalist South, but to do it "with an uppity black who entered the governor's mansion through the front door . . . became too much for many whites to accept." Folsom, unable to succeed himself, may not have cared, but the state turned. According to Numan Bartley and Hugh Graham, "The vigorous if sometimes chaotic rural liberalism so prevalent in Alabama during the 1940s and early 1950s . . . fell victim to the race issue." All the contenders for the governor's seat in 1958, including Folsom's protégé George C. Wallace, disavowed "Folsomism," which in addition to class consciousness carried the taint of booze (and no doubt a lingering whiff of Folsom's famous paternity suit in 1951), but especially and most untouchably a soft attitude on race. Wallace, who emerged as a frontrunner in 1958 along with the sensational race-baiting attorney general John Patterson, lost the runoff. In defeat Wallace vowed, ominously, that he would never be "outniggered again." Bartley and Graham, *Southern Politics*, 38, 67. Wallace denies the exact wording of this, but no one seems to believe him. At any rate, he did not deny the substance: he claims he said he would never be "out-segged" again. Jack Bass and Walter DeVries, *The Transformation of Southern Politics: Social Change and Political Consequences since 1945* (New York: Basic, 1976), 57, and Earl Black, *Southern Governors and Civil Rights* (Cambridge: Harvard University Press, 1976), esp. 52, 189, 296.

42. Branch, *Parting*, 144; later, Hall also came out in opposition to the indictments of boycott leaders on the tactical grounds that indictments made martyrs of a flagging leadership. Branch, *Parting*, 183.

43. Smiley tried again a few months later, in June 1956, and asked Hall if he would meet King, to which Hall replied, "No, he's still a son of a bitch, but I will admit that he's the smartest son of a bitch I ever saw." Finally, toward the end of the boycott, Hall agreed to meet King, saying, "Dr. King is one of the great minds of the South." Smiley OH, CRDP, 37.

44. King, *Stride*, 176.

45. Hall's editorial, warning all Montgomerians to consider the "consequences of economic warfare as a matter of economic self-interest," may have been intended as an appeal to the black protesters to desist, but it could also be read as a warning to the white leaders that any compromises necessary to end the boycott would be far less painful than sentimental and stubborn adherence to strict segregation. Hall, in Yeakey, "Montgomery, Alabama, Bus Boycott," 444.

Inadvertently, the paper gave enormous aid to the boycott by publicizing it ahead of time—printing the WPC flyer verbatim on its front page. Movement leaders swore that this free publicity improved the rate of compliance (typically estimated at 99 percent) from the first day far more than their own frantic efforts to contact all the churches could have done.

Johnnie Carr and others told of Gould Beech, who worked for the *Advertiser* for many years but left Montgomery before the boycott. They say he strongly supported black efforts to achieve civil rights. Carr interview. See also Beech's papers at the MLKA.

46. Letters to the editor, *Montgomery Advertiser*, Dec. 9, 1955, quoted in Yeakey, "Montgomery, Alabama, Bus Boycott," 438–39, and in Jo Ann Gibson Robinson, *The Montgomery Bus Boycott and the Women Who Started It: The Memoir of Jo Ann Gibson Robinson*, ed. David J. Garrow (Knoxville: University of Tennessee Press, 1987), 101–2. On Mrs. Rutledge, see also E. D. Nixon OH, CRDP, 16–17.

47. Letter to the editor, *Montgomery Advertiser*, Dec. 25, 1955, quoted in Yeakey, "Montgomery, Alabama, Bus Boycott," 416A.

48. A count of the letters the *Advertiser* printed would be helpful, and a count of the letters it received even more helpful, but still the sample—which selects in favor of literates—would not be representative of all white opinion. No count of the *Advertiser*'s mail has yet been conducted.

49. ACHR, *Newsletter*, Dec. 1955, 4, in MBP, folder 76. On white carpool drivers, see also Rosa Parks OH, CRDP, 17–18.

50. The evening *Alabama Journal* noted on the first day of the boycott that "many"

white employers of cooks, maids, and nurses were seen "on the street in their automobiles fetching their employees along with the Negro motorists." At least "one white man," the story went on, "was carrying Negroes in his automobile and parked in the downtown area until he got a load." The morning *Advertiser*, however, tried to explain this away by saying the white drivers came out in response to a newspaper story the day before, which had quoted black domestic workers as saying that "they would not show up for work Monday unless the employer came for them in an automobile or agreed to pay their taxi fare." *Alabama Journal*, Dec. 5, 1955, and *Montgomery Advertiser*, Dec. 5, 1955, both quoted in Yeakey, "Montgomery, Alabama, Bus Boycott," 305–6.

51. King and other leaders of the MIA said that white carpool drivers showed up at mass meetings of the MIA: R. D. Nesbitt (finance committee of MIA) OH, MLKA, 37. King also reported that letters of support came in from white Montgomerians who told the MIA, "Carry on, we are with you a hundred per cent." Frequently, King said, these letters were signed simply "a white friend." *Stride*, 142. Cf. Moses Jones: there were whites at the meetings, he said, but he did not think they were "local"; "local people were afraid of reprisals. . . . There were one or two that were really out in the open, but not many." Moses Jones OH, MLKA, 16. Virginia Durr wrote that Mrs. McLeod, the Moreland Smiths, and Paul Woolsey were the only local white people who attended MIA meetings regularly. Durr to "Norman," ca. 1957, MBP, folder 70.

For other testimony that white sympathizers occasionally attended MIA meetings and marches, see Alfrieda Thomas OH, MLKA, 41–42. See also the list of meeting attendees, which included the Reverend Thomas Thrasher, R. Hughes, and other local white folk, MBP, folder 43. Irene West said, "Some white people asked me how I kept going like I did; they said 'the Lord really must be with you.'" Irene West OH, MLKA, 13. E. D. Nixon recalled how over the years a corps of between one and two dozen white women, with Mrs. Rutledge at their head, supported his cause just by coming to court and keeping a stern, watchful eye on the proceedings. Nixon swore that this had an effect on the judge and perhaps saved justice from miscarriage on several occasions. He could call on these white women when he needed them, and Mrs. Rutledge would usually be able to enlist a whole courtroom full of white women. "I had influence with a whole lot of white people here." Nixon OH, CRDP, 16–17. Mrs. Johnnie Carr, who was a member of the Women's Political Council and secretary of the MIA transportation committee, said that some of the white people who drove did so out of their own interest, but "some of them were sympathetic." Some of those who drove would not only take their own maids but other passengers. Carr also recalled that the Reverend Andrew "Doc" Turnipseed, a local white Methodist minister, attended MIA mass meetings, which Turnipseed corroborated. Carr interview. Turnipseed, interview with author, Ada, Ala., July 13, 1989.

52. Robinson, *Montgomery Bus Boycott and the Women*, 107–9, e.g., and see Branch, *Parting*, 164.

53. West-Carr-Durr OH, MLKA, 27 ff.; and West OH, MLKA, 10. The *Montgomery Advertiser* reported in January 1956 on rumors that white businessmen were financially aiding the boycott. The national press had already begun to pick up on the implications of the boycott tactics on the business climate, not just in Montgomery but potentially everywhere. *Business Week*, assessing the situation in March 1956, concluded that the boycott was "difficult to find a defense against." *Montgomery Advertiser*, Jan. 17,

1956. *Business Week,* Mar. 24, 1956. Both quoted in Yeakey, "Montgomery, Alabama, Bus Boycott," 472.

54. "One such maid stated that she loved her white employers as she did her own family and felt that they loved her, too. The wife would often 'slip a few extra dollars' in her hand for the boycott movement without telling her husband. At the same time the husband would leave a few extra dollars for the boycott under her purse in the kitchen where she kept it while she worked. Then, when neighbors visited this home to deplore the boycott activities of the audacious blacks, the man and wife joined in the conversation as if they felt the same way. When she, the maid, was called in to bring food or drinks to the guests, each of the two hosts would wink at her to assure her that they were merely being polite hosts.

"Similar reports came to the WPC from other workers in private family or public employment whose employers were sympathetic toward the cause and contributed to its maintenance and promotion." She added "many whites, too, were boycotting to sympathize with black boycotters' protests." Robinson, *Montgomery Bus Boycott and the Women,* 108, 109.

55. West-Carr-Durr OH, MLKA, 27 ff.

56. Rosa Parks OH, CRDP, 17–18.

57. Years later, she said Robert Kennedy and Martin Luther King negotiated there in secret. Gilmore's house at 405 Dericote Street (formerly Stewart Street) was a venue for secret MIA meetings, some of which were attended by local white folks. The white grocers and butchers who supplied her massive feeding operation, and knew what they were doing, had an interest in keeping the fact quiet, as did various white families who employed her from time to time taking in laundry, preparing meals, and the like. This provides a glimpse of how extensive was the conspiracy of silence in which many local white people, if they did not support the boycott in any other way, passively participated. Gilmore interview.

58. Gilmore interview. Jimmy Harper, interview with author, Atlanta, June 30, 1989. See also Millner, "Montgomery Bus Boycott," 490–91. Gilmore estimated that she collected money from "more than a hundred" white people, who together contributed "about a quarter" of all the funds she collected. These contributions came covertly: "They was liberal but didn't want to become known as liberal." She said that there was very little difference between the attitudes of black and white contributors: "Quite a few of the colored peoples, who had good jobs . . . were afraid to let their employers know, because they could get fired and then they had their families to support." Moreover, there were a substantial number of black people who were as vehement in their condemnations of the movement (for stirring up trouble, for undermining the progress already made) as the white racists were.

Gilmore had attended a school run by two white sisters who were run out of town in the early 1930s by the Klan for teaching black children. But she was used to integration most of her life because Montgomery had only two Catholic churches and black worshipers attended both of them along with white ones as far back as the 1930s.

59. Robinson, *Montgomery Bus Boycott and the Women,* 154.

60. On the peaceful desegregation of facilities in many southern cities, which historians have on the whole ignored, see the 1957 reports of the Southern Education Reporting Service, published as *With All Deliberate Speed: Segregation-Desegregation in*

Southern Schools, ed. Don Shoemaker; Benjamin Muse, *Ten Years of Prelude* (New York: Viking, 1964); Assistant Attorney General Don Oberdorfer's memoranda tallying desegregation events in Lee White Papers, box 22, "Justice Department" file, JFKL; and the Southern Regional Council Report, published as "Bus Integration Spreads," *New South* (Jan. 1957), 14ff., and the SRC's unpublished reports (including those by Anna Holden and Harold Fleming in 1954–55), in SRC Papers, Woodruff Library, Atlanta University, Atlanta, Georgia (on microfilm), ser. III, file 237 (reel 116).

61. Sellers, with 43 percent of the vote, defeated Birmingham (37 percent). Birmingham, as in 1953, got most of the black vote. Sellers tried to use Birmingham's appeal to the blacks against him. This was the first campaign on the race theme in Montgomery since the 1920s when the Ku Klux Klan had (unsuccessfully) put up candidates against the Montgomery establishment. In March 1955 Birmingham held not only the black vote but also the poorest white precincts; but he lost the lower-middle-class areas of east Montgomery, on which his majority in 1953 had depended, to Sellers. A runoff would normally have been necessary between the two top vote-getters, since no one won a majority, but Birmingham's doctor advised him to withdraw, and Birmingham took his advice. J. Mills Thornton, who reports and analyzes all this information thoroughly, suggests persuasively that Sellers' victory pushed Mayor Gayle into a militant segregationist stance, which he and his political forbears in Montgomery had not taken before. See Thornton, "Challenge and Response," esp. 335–37.

62. Gilliam, "Montgomery Bus Boycott," 239.

63. Branch, *Parting,* 146.

64. King, *Stride,* 111. On Crenshaw's intransigence, see also Gilliam, "Montgomery Bus Boycott," 240; Millner, "Montgomery Bus Boycott," 471; and especially Thornton, "Challenge and Response," 342, 362–63, 366–67.

65. Branch, *Parting,* 150.

66. Branch, *Parting,* 157. Thornton, "Challenge and Response," 333–34, 348, 355.

67. Branch, *Parting,* 154, 168.

68. Thornton, "Challenge and Response," 356, 376.

69. Crenshaw quoted in Thornton, "Challenge and Response," 348. The floodgates explanation is central to Yeakey's argument, less so to Thornton's.

70. *Montgomery Advertiser,* May 12, 1957; in Weldon James, "The South's Own Civil War," in Shoemaker, *With All Deliberate Speed,* 23.

71. See Yeakey, "Montgomery, Alabama, Bus Boycott," 422; Gilliam, "Montgomery Bus Boycott," 237–38, 243.

72. See Yeakey, "Montgomery, Alabama, Bus Boycott," 430–37, 445–46, 449, 454, 469, 473.

73. Durr to Hortons, Feb. 18, 1956, MBP, folder 34. On business being hurt by the boycott, see *NYT,* Feb. 28, 1956; *Business Week,* Mar. 24, 1956, 32. The *Amsterdam News* reported on Jan. 7, 1956, that by that time already the boycott had cost the city of Montgomery $1 million. See also L. D. Reddick, "The Bus Boycott in Montgomery," *Dissent* 3 (Spring 1956), 116; *Newsweek,* Mar. 26, 1956, 73; Opie Sheldon, "The Role of Business Leaders," *New South* 11 (May 1956), 2–3, 12; and William Gordon, "Boycotts Can Cut Two Ways," and Douglas Smith, "Industrial Progress at Stake," both in *New South* 11 (Apr. 1956), 1–4, 5–11. These are cited in Yeakey, "Montgomery, Alabama, Bus Boycott," 471–72.

74. Graetz in "Montgomery Story," transcript, Aug. 21, 1956, 14–15, MBP, folder 5.

75. King, *Stride,* 169–70, 121–22. Thornton, "Challenge and Response," 338–39, 357–62, 376–77.

76. King, *Stride,* 124–26; Branch, *Parting,* 155–57; Gilliam, "Montgomery Bus Boycott," 257–58.

77. Branch, *Parting,* 152.

78. Branch, *Parting,* 154.

79. "Montgomery Story," transcript, 18, MBP, folder 5. Thornton, "Challenge and Response," 359–62.

80. ACHR, *Newsletter,* Jan. 1956, 2, MBP, folder 77.

81. Durr, in West-Carr-Durr OH, MLKA, 19–20.

82. West-Carr-Durr OH, MLKA, 20–21.

83. ACHR, *Newsletter,* Jan. 1956, 2, MBP, folder 77.

84. King, *Stride,* 137.

85. Excerpt from leaflet, printed in Rustin, "Montgomery Diary," 59.

86. ACHR, *Newsletter,* Feb., Mar., Apr. 1956, 2, MBP, folder 78.

87. ACHR, *Newsletter,* Jan. 1956, 2, MBP, folder 77.

88. ACHR, *Newsletter,* Feb., Mar., Apr. 1956, 2, MBP, folder 78.

89. *Time,* Feb. 18, 1957, 17–20, quoted in Ralph D. Abernathy, "The Natural History of a Social Movement: The Montgomery Improvement Association" (M.A. thesis, Atlanta University, 1958), printed in Garrow, *Walking City,* 142.

90. Rustin, "Montgomery Diary," 57.

91. Graetz, in "Montgomery Story," transcript, 18; Rustin says the middle ground was wearing away by this time and forcing whites who had always thought of themselves as liberal to take a stand one way or another. "Montgomery Diary," 58–59.

92. Rustin argues that the one thing the middle insisted on was to "condemn overt violence." This fear immobilized them, often keeping them from support of desegregation but also keeping them from opposition. "Montgomery Diary," 59.

Chapter 4: Tallahassee, 1956–1957

1. Charles Smith and Lewis Killian, *Tallahassee Bus Protest* (New York: Anti-Defamation League of B'nai B'rith, 1958), reprinted in *We Shall Overcome,* vol. 3, ed. David Garrow (Brooklyn: Carlson, 1989), 6. Unless otherwise specified, I have relied on Smith and Killian's chronicle for the narrative outline of events in this chapter. Speaking about the late 1940s, George Conoly, a member of the NAACP and later the ICC, said that "the NAACP at that time in Tallahassee was one man." Conoly, interview by Jackson Lee Ice, Florida State University Archives (hereafter cited as Ice interviews), Aug. 1, 1978, 21. On the lack of activity by the Tallahassee chapter of the FCHR, the only desegregated organization in Tallahassee, see also Ice interview with Charles Smith, pp. 2–3, and Marshall Jenkins to George Mitchell, Sept. 16, 1954; Mitchell to Jenkins, Sept. 21, 1954; Fred Routh, "Report on Florida Trip, February 11–20, 1955"; Fred Routh to A. L. Kidd (associate dean of Florida A&M), June 17, 1955; Routh to Burke G. Vanderhill of FSU, June 17, 1955; all in SRC Papers, file 256. The SRC's "Report for September, FCHR," Sept. 30, 1955, in SRC Papers, file 262, and subsequent reports through 1957, show almost no activity in Tallahassee. The CHR's meetings were illegal, since a

city ordinance banned integrated gatherings. Jackson Ice, "An Oral History of the Civil Rights Movement in Tallahassee: A Report," a.

2. David Chalmers, *Hooded Americanism: The First Century of the Ku Klux Klan* (Garden City, N.Y.: Doubleday, 1965), 333, 335–41.

3. Smith and Killian, *Tallahassee*, 6–7.

4. Estimates vary somewhat. Figures in the text come from Numan Bartley and Hugh Graham, *Southern Elections: County and Precinct Data, 1950–1972* (Baton Rouge: Louisiana State University Press, 1978), 59, and U.S. Civil Rights Commission, *Report* (1959, 1960). The total population of Florida, according to the census figures, was 21.8 percent nonwhite in 1950 and 17.9 percent nonwhite in 1960. U.S. Bureau of the Census, *Historical Statistics of the United States*, ser. A 195–209.

5. Five urban Florida counties went Republican in the presidential election in 1948, giving Dewey one-third of the statewide vote; Eisenhower carried the state in 1952 and 1956 and Nixon in 1960, though Democrats continued to control the state level and congressional delegations. Bass and DeVries, *Transformation*, 131, 134, 120, and Donald Matthews and James Prothro, *Negroes and the New Southern Politics* (New York: Harcourt, 1966), 148–53.

6. Smith and Killian, *Tallahassee*, 5. See also George Conoly, Ice interview, Aug. 1, 1978, 23.

7. Smith and Killian, *Tallahassee*, 6.

8. The Reverend K. S. DuPont, who was vice president of the ICC, stated that the black section of the bus was crowded but "there was one long seat for the whites to sit down on the front. There was one white lady sitting there who was a very courteous white lady and two black girls standing over her and she said, 'Why [don't] y'all [unintelligible] sit down?' And they [took] the seat and the driver had 'em arrested." "The girls were invited to sit there by a white lady. . . . There were two empty seats. And she said, 'why don't y'all sit down?' And they went to sit down on the invitation of the lady, . . . a southern lady — runs a little store out there in the black community. Very nice southern lady. . . . The girls were not intending it. They would never have sat if the lady hadn't invited them. She had good meaning and she had business out there in the black community." DuPont, Ice interview I, 2, and interview II, 2–3.

9. Glenda Rabby, "Out of the Past: The Civil Rights Movement in Tallahassee, Florida" (Ph.D. diss., Florida State University, 1984), 10, 11, 13–15.

10. Morris, *Origins*, 64, 74–75.

11. Smiley said he helped craft appeals to local white folk and provided the movement ranks with a living example of a southern white man to "role-play" confrontations. Smiley, letter to author, Dec. 26, 1989; Smiley tape. Dan Speed quoted in Morris, *Origins*, 67. Dan Speed elaborated on Smiley's role and identified him as "the strongest expert" the ICC had. Speed, Ice interview, 32–35, 36, 44.

12. C. K. Steele, Ice interview, 27. Rabby, "Out of the Past," 5.

13. Speed, Ice interview, 15.

14. Quoted in Rabby, "Out of the Past," 79, 80, 161–62. Mrs. Lewis was also in the FCHR and worked with a religious group at FSU which organized interracial activity. Asked if there was any white person in the establishment who helped the cause, Charles U. Smith (a black sociology professor at A&M and president of the Tallahassee Council on Human Relations) said, "George Lewis was always right there. . . . George and

Clifton Lewis . . . [were] almost always on the right side . . . and they were stalwart."
Lewis lost accounts, including state government accounts, "but he stuck by it. And . . .
they put him out of the bank." Lewis later became regional director for the Civil Rights
Commission. Smith, Ice interview I, 25–26. K. S. DuPont said George Lewis and Jim
Shaw were "the best supports" the cause had. They put up bond money for jailed protesters, "walked that cell like they had their own daughters in jail." Asked if there were
other white people who helped, DuPont said, "No other two. Some did a few things like
on the side. Like [police chief Frank] Stoutamire." (See below.) DuPont, Ice interview I,
19–20, 22.

15. *Tallahassee Democrat*, May 29, 1956, quoted in Rabby, "Out of the Past," 16.

16. Gregory Padgett, "C. K. Steele and the Tallahassee Bus Protest" (M.A. thesis,
Florida State University, 1977), 40–41.

17. The FCHR commented that the bus company was "forced out of business by its
failure to recognize the trend of the times." FCHR, *Newsletter* 1 (July 1956), SRC
Papers, file 242 (reel 141).

18. Padgett, "C. K. Steele," 50; Smith and Killian, *Tallahassee*, 10; Rabby, "Out of
the Past," 44–46.

19. ICC Diary, July 13, 1956, as cited in Padgett, "C. K. Steele," 50.

20. The concession was a fulfillment of one of the ICC's stated demands but not officially acknowledged as such. Smith and Killian, *Tallahassee*, 9–10. Steele, Ice interview,
12. The FCHR interpreted the concession as a token gesture to co-opt the protesters.
FCHR monthly report for August 1956, SRC Papers, ser. IV, file 262 (reel 142).

21. Collins quoted in Rabby, "Out of the Past," 47. As happened in Montgomery,
segregationists also tried to locate a white "mastermind," on the assumption that blacks
did not have enough initiative or skills, or were not dissatisfied enough with their lot, to
protest on their own. In this case the target was Lewis Killian, the FSU sociology professor. Rabby, "Out of the Past," 149.

22. The paper's reporters were barred from a KKK rally, held six miles west of Tallahassee in early September 1956, because of the paper's "liberal" viewpoint on the boycott. *Tallahassee Democrat*, Sept. 2, 1956, in Padgett, "C. K. Steele," 54. Steele, Ice
interview, 18, 20–23. Rabby, "Out of the Past," 49.

23. Smith and Killian, *Tallahassee*, 12. The ICC formally abolished the carpool but
voted to continue the boycott. Steele said, "The war is not over; we are still walking."
The city canceled the franchise of the Economy Cab Company, one of whose two owners
was assistant transportation secretary of the ICC. Rabby, "Out of the Past," 60.

24. Smith and Killian, *Tallahassee*, 12–13. Rabby, "Out of the Past," 63.

25. Smith and Killian, *Tallahassee*, 13. Steele said that "the City and the bus company
were at loggerheads because the bus company was losing money." The company's "position ultimately prevailed because [the company president] threatened to go to court and
. . . the City knew that [it] could not win and was forced to give in at that point." Steele,
Ice interview, 13.

26. DeVane in *Florida Times-Union*, Dec. 17, 1957, in J. W. Peltason, *Fifty-eight
Lonely Men: Southern Federal Judges and School Desegregation*, 2d ed. (Urbana: University of Illinois Press, 1971), 147. DeVane's opinions in other cases give a very different
impression from his opinion here that segregation was dead as a doornail. On the
Meredith case, see Jack Bass, *Unlikely Heroes* (New York: Simon and Schuster, 1981),

177–79; James Meredith, *Three Years in Mississippi* (Bloomington: Indiana University Press, 1966); and Russell H. Barrett, *Integration at Ole Miss* (Chicago: Quadrangle, 1965).

27. Peltason, *Fifty-eight Lonely Men*, 146; the Florida Supreme Court on God and America for the red man is from *Florida ex rel Hawkins v. Board of Control*, 1 RRLR 89 at 95 (1955) in Peltason, 146. The U.S. Supreme Court declined to overrule the Florida Supreme Court's contention that it had a right to maintain order. In June 1958, DeVane ordered the opening of the University of Florida to all qualified Negroes. FCHR, Monthly Report for June 1958, SRC Papers, ser. IV, file 241 (reel 141).

28. Smith and Killian, *Tallahassee*, 13. Rabby adds: "Approximately 200 whites, many carrying poorly concealed hatchets, hammers, and other weapons," assembled at the scene where a mass black boarding of the buses was to take place at the end of 1956. Speed called off the test ride. Few black or white passengers rode the buses for the next few days. No incidents occurred in public. But many threats were received, and there was increased damage to black property before New Year's. "Out of the Past," 65–66.

29. Peltason, *Fifty-eight Lonely Men*, 147.

30. In his first election in 1954, against Charley Johns, race was not a big issue. The two candidates agreed on the *Brown* decision, which is to say they both avoided taking a stand on it. Collins did denounce Johns, however, for his 1951 vote against the Florida antimask law (an anti-Klan measure), which had passed easily. Even Johns had to tone down the race-baiting for Florida audiences. He admitted that his pro-Klan stance was a mistake and said that Collins' claims that he would try to restrict black voting rights were false. Black, *Southern Governors*, 93; Chalmers, *Hooded Americanism*, 340. Johns was the leader of the "pork chop gang" of rural politicians who had disproportionate power. Collins advocated reapportionment to strengthen urban areas. Collins, Ice interview II, 19.

31. Collins, as quoted in Black, *Southern Governors*, 93, 369. Collins admitted his segregationism, in his interview with Jackson (Ice II, 25). In a different interview, Collins claimed that while governor he refrained from coming out as an avowed integrationist; to have done so, he said, would have jeopardized his leadership. In that interview he also claimed that he had stood from the beginning for order under law and that he treated the Supreme Court's orders as law. Collins OH, LBJL, 8.

32. Later that year, Collins appointed a biracial commission to advise him on the segregation laws passed by the state legislature. FCHR, Reports for May and September, 1956, both in SRC Papers, file 262 (reel 142). There was a precedent for a southern governor bucking the legislature's interposition resolutions: Jim Folsom in Alabama. See Bass, *Unlikely Heroes*, 64.

33. Black, *Southern Governors*, 93–95; Bass and DeVries, *Transformation*, 108–9, 115. For further analysis of the politics of the 1956 segregation struggle, see Helen Jacobstein, *The Segregation Factor in the Florida Democratic Gubernatorial Primary of 1956* (Gainesville: University of Florida Press, 1972).

34. *Tallahassee Democrat*, July 3, 1956; ICC Diary, July 4, 1956, both quoted in Padgett, "C. K. Steele," 44–45; Smith and Killian, *Tallahassee,* 10.

35. Padgett, "C. K. Steele," 44–45.

36. *Tallahassee Democrat*, Jan. 1, 1957, quoted in Padgett, "C. K. Steele," 69, 48.

37. *Tallahassee Democrat*, July 1, 1956, quoted in Padgett, "C. K. Steele," 43. The

FCHR, which reported a widespread belief that the middle ground had been "disappearing in the South," saw itself as "a rallying point for the sensible," at a time when "small, emotional groups ha[d] drowned out the isolated voices of good people." Report of the executive director, FCHR, Nov. 1957, p. 5, SRC Papers, file 261 (reel 142).

38. In 1960 Collins said it was "morally wrong" for businessmen to refuse to serve black people in one area of their stores and welcome their business in other areas. See Collins' speech in *We Dissent*, ed. Hoke Norris (New York: St. Martin's, 1962), 103–14; Black, *Southern Governors*, 93.

39. The governor also called on "the Negro" to recognize "that he must merit and deserve whatever place he achieves in the community." Smith and Killian, *Tallahassee*, 14. Rabby, "Out of the Past," 76. See also Collins, Ice interview I, 2–3. Later that year, Collins harshly criticized and vetoed an interposition bill that the legislature passed — one of many state gestures of massive resistance that, in language reminiscent of Calhoun, sought to "interpose" the authority of the state between the federal courts and the people. The Florida Council on Human Relations concluded that Collins' veto "saved" Florida from "some of the South's most vicious legislation" that year. FCHR to SRC, Grant Request for October 1957 to September 1958, SRC Papers, file 257 (reel 142).

40. Smith and Killian, *Tallahassee*, 14.

41. Smith and Killian, *Tallahassee*, 14. The Tallahassee chapter of the FCHR seems to have grown from the boycott, too. Founded in December 1954, it still had only fifty-four members when the boycott began. Then thirteen joined in April 1956. FCHR Report for the Month of April, 1956, SRC Papers, ser. IV, file 262 (reel 142); and minutes of "Florida Meeting, December 20, 1954, Central YMCA, Jacksonville," SRC Papers ser. I, file 968 (reel 29).

42. There is some discrepancy in the reports here: Speed complained that at first the ICC could not find any black persons to take the test ride, but then "one of the boys from Florida State University [Joe Spagna]" said he thought he could "serve as one of the persons." After that, the test ride "really got moving." Speed, Ice interview, 16–17. Smith and Killian say that one of the white and two of the black riders were arrested and that the other three riders were taken in as "material witnesses." *Tallahassee*, 14. Rabby adds more detail to the account, including the press's discovery that other white students had been regularly attending ICC meetings. "Out of the Past," 80–83, 91. The FCHR states that all three white riders were arrested and received the maximum sentence of sixty days and fines. FCHR, Report for February 1957, Report for March 1957, and Report for April, 1957, SRC Papers, ser. IV, file 262 (reel 142). Steele claimed that Dan Speed's son and another black student, Johnny Herndon, spent some forty days in jail with Spagna (Ice interview, 28), but Speed says his son Leonard was arrested with "two white boys from Florida State University" (Ice interview, 7).

43. Smith and Killian, *Tallahassee*, 15. At least one other white person paid a price for supporting desegregation. John Boardman, a graduate student at Florida State, was expelled for his involvement in interracial activities, including attendance at ICC meetings. The official reason for expulsion was his bringing two black foreign students from A&M to the FSU International Club Christmas Party, but he told the press that the real reason was his public support of DuPont. Boardman claimed that he had not ever overtly violated the university's prohibition on participation in the protest and that the university's administrators told him he would be reinstated if he gave up his support for

integration, an allegation the university denied. He ended up moving to New Jersey. FCHR, Report for February 1957, SRC Papers, ser. IV, file 262 (reel 142). Padgett, "C. K. Steele," 74–75. Glenda Rabby adds: "At a meeting of Governor Collins' Advisory Commission on Bi-Racial Problems, [FSU president Doak] Campbell told the seven-member council that Boardman was part of 'a little group of ten [FSU students] who regarded themselves as the saviors of the world.' The president added that although Boardman was a 'very brilliant scholar as far as mathematics is concerned,' he was 'unstable otherwise.' When other members expressed the fear that Boardman might be turned into a martyr, Campbell assured them that the suspension had 'waked the students up to the fact that the University has broad authority, and that [the suspension] may scare some of the more rabid ones into quieting down.' When former FAMU president J.R.E. Lee told the five white commission members that black students considered Boardman something of a hero, they expressed the hope that the 'Negro students did not think that the solution to their problems lay with a man like that.' Campbell then added that he had been given profile reports on the students sympathetic to integration and that he believed that, like Boardman, they were somewhat 'erratic' or had something lacking in their backgrounds." "Out of the Past," 87.

44. This and other insights into southern political arithmetic are drawn largely from Bass and DeVries. Democratic strength was in the panhandle, above the "frost-proof line." Bass and DeVries, *Transformation*, 108–9.

45. Smith and Killian, *Tallahassee*, 23. (Smith and Killian went to press in February 1958.) Steele, Ice interview, 33.

46. Smith and Killian, *Tallahassee*, 23.

47. Padgett, "C. K. Steele," 79.

Chapter 5: Little Rock, 1957–1959

1. *Arkansas Gazette*, July 17, 1956, quoted in Black, *Southern Governors*, 100.

2. Bass and DeVries, *Transformation*, 90–91; Orval Faubus, interview transcript, SOHP, 23–24; Faubus, *Down from the Hills* (Little Rock: Democrat Printing and Lithograph, 1986), 187.

3. Irving Spitzberg, *Racial Politics in Little Rock, 1954–1964* (New York: Garland, 1987), 38; *SMS*, 89.

4. Faubus OH, SOHP, 20; Spitzberg, *Racial Politics*, 36; Bass and DeVries, *Transformation*, 90–91; Black, *Southern Governors*, 100. Faubus tried to keep segregation out of the campaign, declaring that it was not an issue because all three candidates agreed on it; his opponents accused him of "pussy-footing" on the issue. R&R, 16ff.

5. Faubus OH, SOHP, 24.

6. R&R, 16ff.

7. "Little Rock Board of Education Plan of School Integration—Little Rock School District," in R&R, 21–23, with elaborations in R&R, 29–30, and extracts from the U.S. district court opinion in *Aaron v. Cooper*, 143 Fed. Supp. 855 (Aug. 28, 1956), in R&R, 23–26; Wiley Branton, in *Voices of Freedom: An Oral History of the Civil Rights Movement from the 1950s through the 1980s*, ed. Henry Hampton and Steve Fayer (New York: Bantam, 1990), 40; *SMS*, 130–31; *H&M*, 251–52; Spitzberg, *Racial Politics*, 43–44; Virgil T. Blossom, *It HAS Happened Here* (New York: Harper, 1959), 16. According to a

local white advocate of integration, Blossom stated in two hundred–odd speeches to the white community that integration "was as distasteful to him and the school board as to anyone else" but that his gradual program would avert sudden, court-imposed integration. Colbert Cartwright, "Lesson from Little Rock," *Christian Century,* quoted in Spitzberg, *Racial Politics,* 46.

8. Rockefeller quoted in Fred Routh to Nat Griswold, Apr. 19, 1956, SRC Papers, ser. IV, file 220 (reel 141). Routh suggested that other big business leaders were making similar speeches around town.

9. According to Elizabeth Jacoway, Blossom "apparently sold his plan to many of the city's civic and social leaders by pointing out that their children would not have to attend integrated Central High School." Central was a lower-middle- and working-class school. Jacoway, "Taken by Surprise," in *Southern Businessmen and Desegregation,* ed. Jacoway and David Colburn (Baton Rouge: Louisiana State University Press, 1982), 20–21. Faubus referred to Hall High, which was not to be integrated in Blossom's plan, as "a refuge for the rich and well-to-do, some of whom 'preached' integration or 'the law of the land,' but didn't want any part of the practice themselves." *Down from the Hills,* 200, 246. It should be noted, however, that the students at Hall themselves voted overwhelmingly (70 percent) in favor of desegregating their own school in 1958. Fred Routh to Harold Fleming, Sept. 23, 1958, SRC Papers, ser. IV, file 220 (reel 141).

10. Spitzberg, *Racial Politics,* 49; Jacoway, "Taken," 22.

11. Though Faubus did have campaign contributions from the Arkansas-Louisiana Gas Company, Hot Springs gambling interests, and certain big liquor distributors, Little Rock's business community gave Faubus little support before 1962. Spitzberg, *Racial Politics,* 36. See also Black, *Southern Governors,* 33, 37–39.

12. *H&M,* 261.

13. R&R, 16–17.

14. R&R, 18.

15. Faubus OH, SOHP, 23–24. Tallies of desegregated school districts by state, in Shoemaker, *With All Deliberate Speed,* 226. One of the nine black students who desegregated Central in September 1957 recalled years later that "there hadn't been any trouble expected, given the fact that there had been other schools in Arkansas that had integrated—Fort Smith, Arkansas, and some others. The buses in Little Rock had been desegregated without any problem. The library was integrated, the medical school, and the law school at the University had admitted some blacks. So there was an expectation that there would be minimal problems, but nothing major that would put Little Rock on the map." Ernest Green interview, in Hampton and Fayer, *Voices of Freedom,* 38–39.

16. F. Routh to Nat Griswold, Aug. 7, 1957, and Griswold to H. Fleming, SRC Papers, ser. IV, file 220 (reel 141).

17. ACHR, Newsletter of Jan. 1957, in R&R, 16ff.

18. Jacoway, "Taken," 15–27.

19. R&R, 28; *SMS,* 131; Branton, letter to author, Oct. 26, 1988; George Haley, interview with author, Washington, D.C., Mar. 9, 1989.

20. *H&M,* 255.

21. Resolutions passed by referendum Nov. 6, 1956, general election, in R&R, 27.

22. Elizabeth Huckaby, *Crisis at Central High: Little Rock, 1957–1958* (Baton Rouge: Louisiana State University Press, 1980), 10–12; *H&M,* 256–57; R&R, 31.

23. It noted candidly, however, "All pupils will use restroom facilities regularly provided." R&R, 32.

24. For example, Robert Ewing Brown, president of the Capital Citizens' Council of Little Rock, accused Faubus of aiding the integrationists by his long silence after making his earlier statement that he would protect the people of the state against integrated schools. R&R, 31.

25. Harris quoted in *SMS*, 131–32. The story is also told in Fletcher Knebel, "The Real Little Rock Story," *Look*, Nov. 12, 1957, 31–33, in R&R, 245–47. Faubus painstakingly provides his version of the meetings, with extensive excerpts from the *Arkansas Gazette* and the *Arkansas Democrat*, in *Down from the Hills*, 191–95.

26. *H&M*, 255.

27. Faubus has stuck to that story to the present day. See *Down from the Hills*, 199–202, 206–7; and his interview in Hampton and Fayer, *Voices of Freedom*, 41–42.

28. R&R, 33–34; *H&M*, 256–57; *SMS*, 133.

29. R&R, 34.

30. Ashmore, "Untold Story," in R&R, 266. Potts, in R&R, 34. Faubus later claimed that Blossom was his source of the information about revolvers and knives and that Blossom privately asked him for protection. *Down from the Hills*, 199, 201–2.

31. R&R, 33–34; *H&M*,257; Judge Davies, justifying his opinion on September 7, said the mayor of Little Rock had stated that there had not been a single case of violence and there was not a single indication that there would be. R&R, 41–42.

32. *Arkansas Gazette*, Sept. 1, 1957, in R&R, 34–35.

33. *H&M*, 257, 259. Fletcher Knebel has Faubus telling substantially the same story to his attorney and friend, William J. Smith, in "Real Little Rock Story," 31–33, in R&R, 245–47. In his memoir, Faubus puts a different spin on this story: by saving his own candidacy he was protecting the state, and liberals like Rockefeller, from the likes of Johnson. *Down from the Hills*, 207.

34. *Arkansas Gazette*, Sept. 5, 1957, in R&R. Daisy Bates, *The Long Shadow of Little Rock: A Memoir* (New York: David McKay, 1962), 65–66, 70–75. There is some discrepancy in accounts of these events. Bates says the other eight students arrived after Eckford's escape and had a slight brush with the mob. The *Arkansas Democrat* has the other eight remaining in the background while Eckford, alone, tried to cross the line of soldiers. Then it has a second black student, Terrance Roberts, briefly attempting to cross the line also. *Arkansas Democrat*, Sept. 4, 1957.

35. *SMS*, 134.

36. R&R, 42, 48. *SMS*, 134, 136.

37. Peltason argues that this was part of the two-pronged strategy the segregationists followed after Clinton and Hoxie: they would encourage violence against blacks and then use the violence as a pretext for keeping the blacks out. *Fifty-eight Lonely Men*, 154.

38. Will Campbell, *Brother to a Dragonfly* (New York: Continuum, 1977), 108–30; Will Campbell, *Forty Acres and a Goat* (1986; reprint, New York: Harper, 1988); Will Campbell, "Vocation as Grace," in *Callings*, ed. Will Campbell and James Holloway (New York: Paulist Press, 1974), 272–73; Bates, *Long Shadow*, 67, 87; James Lawson OH, SOHP, 5, 11.

39. Bates, *Long Shadow*, 189–95.

40. *H&M*, 283.

41. *Southern School News*, Oct. 1957, in R&R, 37.

42. Ralph Brodie, in *Arkansas Gazette*, Sept. 10, 1957, in R&R, 43; Brodie had participated in a goodwill effort to help black students prepare for entrance to a new school. Huckaby, *Crisis at Central*, 12. Marcia Webb Lecky, a white girl who was secretary of the senior class that year, recalled thinking that the troops "were there because Faubus was causing problems," and most of the students "were glad when the resolution came with President Eisenhower taking charge." Lecky in Hampton and Fayer, *Voices of Freedom*, 50.

43. McMath, quoted in Bass and DeVries, *Transformation*, 92–93.

44. R&R, 41–42; Bass and DeVries, *Transformation*, 92.

45. McMath quoted in Bates, *Long Shadow*, 82, and in Faubus, *Down from the Hills*, 246.

46. *H&M*, 260–61. See Orval Faubus, *Down from the Hills, Two* (Little Rock: Democrat Printing and Lithograph, 1986), 273, and Faubus OH, SOHP, 1–3.

47. Jacoway, "Taken," 33–34.

48. Sherman Adams, *Firsthand Report: The Story of the Eisenhower Administration* (New York: Harper, 1961), 344. Eisenhower's adviser Emmett John Hughes quoted Ike as telling him that *Brown* had "set back progress in the South" and that it was "wrong to demand *perfection* in these moral questions." Hughes, *The Ordeal of Power: A Political Memoir of the Eisenhower Years* (New York: Dell, 1964), 201.

49. For this, Faubus criticized Eisenhower (and his more liberal attorney general, Herbert Brownell) as hypocritical and cowardly. Faubus justified his own armed resistance by saying the federal government's unwillingness to enforce its own Court's orders forced him into doing what he could to prevent violence. Faubus OH, SOHP, 34–36; Faubus, *Down from the Hills*, 207–8.

50. Graham, letter to Stewart Alsop, Oct. 6, 1957, quoted in Chalmers M. Roberts, *The Washington Post: The First Hundred Years* (Boston: Houghton Mifflin, 1977), 330–31; David Halberstam, *The Powers That Be* (New York: Knopf, 1979), 306–12; *H&M*, 261–62.

51. *SMS*, 135–40; Hays, "Inside Story of Little Rock," *U.S. News and World Report*, Mar. 23, 1958, 124–32, reprinted in R&R, 45–47; Adams, *Firsthand Report*, 346–53; Dwight Eisenhower, *The White House Years: Waging Peace, 1956–1961* (Garden City, N.Y.: Doubleday, 1965), 165. Graham's brother and others, including Halberstam, date the beginning of Graham's descent toward his suicide (June 1963) to the Little Rock crisis. Roberts, *Washington Post*, 331, and Halberstam, *Powers That Be*, 309–12.

52. *SMS*, 144–45; R&R, 44.

53. *Arkansas Gazette*, Sept. 21, 1957, in R&R, 56–57.

54. R&R, 56–57.

55. Smith quoted in *H&M*, 265. In October Smith's superior, police chief Marvin Potts, resigned, and three months later Smith, over the objections of the Mothers' League, was promoted to chief. Bates, *Long Shadow*, 182–83.

56. Melba Beals, in Hampton and Fayer, *Voices of Freedom*, 46.

57. *H&M*, 266. Herbert Brownell, in Hampton and Fayer, *Voices of Freedom*, 47. One of the nine black students recalled years later that "it was apparent that the mob was just overrunning the school. Policemen were throwing down their badges and the mob was getting past the wooden sawhorses because the police would no longer fight their

own in order to protect [the students]." Melba Beals, in Hampton and Fayer, *Voices of Freedom*, 45.

58. Daisy Bates OH, SOHP, 17–18.

59. Craig Rains, in Hampton and Fayer, *Voices of Freedom*, 43–44.

60. "A Random Report on [Emory Via's] Little Rock Trip, February 14–16, 1958," p. 3. SRC Papers, ser. IV, file 217 (reel 141).

61. Faubus, *Down from the Hills, Two*, 3, 8.

62. Daisy Bates OH, SOHP, 17–18; many black persons in Little Rock were hostile to her, saying she was an outsider, "stirring up trouble." She said that if one student had been killed, she would have had to leave town. Ibid., 53–54. On the *Gazette*'s loss of advertising revenues: Faubus OH, SOHP, 33.

63. One girl, Sylvia Jones, was allowed to sign out for the day with a one-word explanation: "Integration." Huckaby, *Crisis at Central*, 36.

64. Blossom, "Untold Story," in R&R, 63; *Sacramento Bee*, in R&R, 59–63.

65. Huckaby, *Crisis at Central*, 36.

66. Peltason, *Fifty-eight Lonely Men*, 47; Bass, *Unlikely Heroes*, 153–54.

67. Jacoway, "Taken," 31; *H&M*, 281.

68. Jacoway, "Taken," 33–34.

69. Jacoway, "Taken," 34–35. Henry M. Alexander, *The Little Rock Recall Election* Eagleton Institute Cases in Practical Politics no. 17. (New York: McGraw Hill, 1960).

70. Tucker quoted in Jacoway, "Taken," 37–38.

71. Bates, *Long Shadow*, 184–87.

72. Bates, *Long Shadow*, 195–210. Nat Griswold to H. Fleming, Mar. 4, 1959, SRC Papers, ser. IV, file 220 (reel 141).

73. Bates, *Long Shadow*, 180, 191–95; Faubus, *Down from the Hills*, 200, 69.

Chapter 6: Albany, Georgia, 1961–1962

1. There were white southerners outside Albany who aided the movement there. The Southern Regional Council in Atlanta, for example, helped Charles Sherrod find contacts in the Albany black community, especially C. B. King. Branch, *Parting*, 524. Near Albany was Koinonia farm, a well-known radical religious community run by white southerners but sympathetic to interracial action and openly supportive of the SNCC actions in Albany. Koinonia functioned as a retreat and meeting place for Albany movement activists, who credited the community with a crucial role in the protests. But Koinonia's support from outside never encouraged or touched off active white support beyond its own staff. See SNCC Papers, subgroup A: ser. XV, folder 32, MLKA (on microfilm, reel 37); Norma Collins to Dorothy Swisshelm, Oct. 22, 1962; Ruby Doris Smith to Conrad Browne, Nov. 5, 1962; Conrad Browne to "Friends," Nov. 12, 1962; all in SNCC Papers, subgroup A: ser. IV, folder 206 (reel 7); and Koinonia Newsletters nos. 21, 26, and 27, in Slater King Papers, MLKA, folder 1.

2. John A. Ricks, " 'De Lawd' Descends and Is Crucified: Martin Luther King, Jr., in Albany, Georgia," *Southwest Georgia Historical Quarterly* 2 (Fall 1984), reprinted in Garrow, *We Shall Overcome*, 3:8. Edith Snyder and Katherine Hawke, "Notes on Albany, Georgia: 1964," Charles Sherrod Papers, MLKA.

3. Howard Zinn, *Albany: A Study in National Responsibility* (Atlanta: Southern Regional Council, 1962), 18.

4. White southern SNCC operatives Casey Hayden, Bob Zellner, and Sally McCullom came to Albany at one time or another. Zinn, *Albany*, 1, 6–7. According to Clayborne Carson, "Sherrod's desire to free southern blacks from their fear of whites played a part in his decision to use interracial teams of civil rights workers. At first he attempted to recruit southern whites, but when no volunteers were found, he hired northern white students. Although aware of the need for local black support, he concluded that the use of white voter registration workers was necessary to 'strike at the very root of segregation, . . . the idea that the white is superior. That idea has eaten into the minds of the people, black and white. We have to break this image. We can only do this if they see white and black working together, side by side.'" Carson, *In Struggle: SNCC and the Black Awakening of the 1960s* (Cambridge: Harvard University Press, 1981), 75–76.

5. Sherrod, letter to author, Feb. 8, 1990; Andrew Young, interview with author, July 15, 1989 (hereafter Young interview). See remarks on this in the Epilogue.

6. Ricks, "'De Lawd,'" 12.

7. Vincent Harding and Staughton Lynd, "Albany, Georgia," *Crisis* 70 (Feb. 1963), 78; Zinn, *Albany*, 18; Bartley and Graham, *Southern Politics*, 68–71. A black movement lawyer, C. B. King, also ran for office and got five hundred white votes, which, along with Sanders' victory, prompted Anne Braden to write, "There may be more moderate sentiment [in Albany] than any one realized. . . . Many people, silent before, . . . spoke in the privacy of the voting booth." Draft article for *Southern Patriot*, in Braden to James Forman, Sept. 23, 1962, SNCC Papers, subgroup A: ser. IV, folder 339 (reel 9).

8. This and previous paragraph: Zinn, *Albany*, 14, 17.

9. Morris, in *Origins*, goes to great lengths to disprove once and for all the idea of the "spontaneity" of movement action. Equally important, however, is the question of the spontaneity of massive resistance, governmental and nongovernmental, legal and extralegal. Albany appears to be the only case where significant planning and organization took place on the segregationist side.

10. Albany Police Department, report to city manager for fiscal year 1961–62 (pp. 68–71 of city manager's report to city of Albany), in SNCC Papers, subgroup A: ser. VIII, folder 102 (reel 19); Pritchett OH, SOHP, 1, 3. Pritchett's last statement must be qualified: there were incidents of segregationist violence, some of it arguably involving the police (see below), during the 1961–62 period when the SCLC and the press were focused on Albany. Moreover, after the media spotlight was gone and the movement in Albany itself lost its nonviolent discipline and its hold over the black community of Albany, there was much evidence of police brutality. See remarks on this in the Epilogue.

11. Pritchett OH, SOHP, 1, 3–4.

12. Pritchett OH, SOHP, 19. Garrow, *Bearing the Cross: Martin Luther King, Jr., and the Southern Christian Leadership Conference* (1986; reprint, New York: Vintage, 1988), 665.

13. Pritchett OH, SOHP, 8–9; also in *My Soul Is Rested*, ed. Howell Raines (New York: Putnam, 1977), 364–65.

14. Pritchett OH, SOHP, 3–4. Pritchett is correct when he adds, "You never read anything in any of his books or his wife's where they said that I made mistakes or

mistreated anybody." He also said, "C. B. King never uttered a word of protest against me." SOHP, 14.

15. Pritchett OH, SOHP, 5, 12a.

16. Zinn, *Albany*, 21. Pritchett did not object to this interpretation, adding only, "Right: whites, blacks, anybody." SOHP, 14.

17. Pritchett OH, SOHP, 6. Total arrests between December 1961, when mass demonstrations began, and August 1962 numbered 1,100. Zinn, *Albany*, 13. Pritchett's annual report lists total arrests for fiscal year 1961–62 as 1,300; in SNCC Papers, subgroup A: ser. VIII, folder 102 (reel 19). Movement participants frequently testified to being arrested with "75 others," "54 others," and so on. Arrest reports, SNCC Papers, subgroup A: ser. XV, folder 30 (reel 37).

18. Pritchett OH, SOHP, 12a. On Shelton, see Chalmers, *Hooded Americanism*, 367–76. All references to the Klan in the SNCC Papers and other sources refer to their being assembled on the outskirts of Albany or in the other counties. In contrast to other major civil rights battles, most conspicuously St. Augustine, there were no direct clashes between masses of protesters and the Klan or other vigilante groups in Albany.

19. This and previous paragraph: Pritchett OH, SOHP, 12a, 16, 18–19.

20. Pritchett interview in Raines, *Soul Is Rested*, 365.

21. Pritchett OH, SOHP, 8.

22. Quoted in Pat Watters, *Down to Now: Reflections on the Southern Civil Rights Movement* (New York: Pantheon, 1971), 265.

23. Draft of article for the *Southern Patriot* (organ of the Southern Conference Educational Fund and virtual mouthpiece for SNCC in these years), apparently written by Anne Braden on the basis of dispatches from Dotty Miller and James Forman, pp. 6–7. Enclosure to Braden to Forman, Sept. 23, 1962, and see Braden to Forman, Sept. 9, 1962, SNCC Papers, subgroup A: ser. IV, folder 339 (reel 9).

24. Zinn, *Albany*, 15. Cf. the Reverend Joseph Jackson, president of the National Baptist Convention, an organization representing 5 million black Baptists: "It is hypocrisy for a delegation to leave Chicago and go to Albany to fight segregation." Quoted in Lewis, *King*, 158.

25. Lewis, *King*, 149.

26. Pritchett OH, SOHP, 7–8.

27. Garrow, *Bearing*, 210.

28. In Lewis, *King*, 155.

29. The whole scene of Pritchett's visit to Shiloh is from Watters, *Down to Now*, 204–8, and Branch, *Parting*, 604–5.

30. Statement by King and W. G. Anderson, July 25, 1962, SNCC Papers, subgroup A: ser. XV, folder 33 (reel 37).

31. James Forman, *The Making of Black Revolutionaries* (New York: Macmillan, 1972), 247–62; Watters, *Down to Now*, 213–16; Branch, *Parting*, 618–19. In fact, King and Anderson's call for penance did not fully blame the violence on the black community:

> While we are certain that neither the peaceful demonstrators nor persons active in the Albany Movement were involved in the violence that erupted last night, we abhor violence so much that when it occurs in the ranks of the Negro community, we assume part of the responsibility for it. . . . We must honestly say that

the City Commission's arrogant refusal to talk with the leaders of the Albany Movement, the continued suppression of the Negro's aspiration for freedom, and the tragic attempt on the part of the Albany police officials to maintain segregation at any cost, all serve to create the atmosphere for violence and bitterness. While we will preach and teach nonviolence to our people with every ounce of energy in our bodies, we fear that these admonitions will fall on some deaf ears if Albany does not engage in good faith negotiations. We sense a great deal of satisfaction and joy on the part of public officials when violence erupted in the ranks of the onlookers. This betrays the fact that the community has fallen to a new low in moral degeneracy.

Statement by King and W. G. Anderson, July 25, 1962, SNCC Papers, subgroup A: ser. XV, folder 33 (reel 37). A similar effort was Dr. Anderson's telegram on behalf of the Albany Movement to state trooper Claude Hill, who was injured in the rioting: "We sincerely regret the violence perpetrated by onlookers following our peaceful demonstration which resulted in injury to you. May your recovery be swift and sure in body and spirit." SNCC Papers, subgroup A: ser. XV, folder 33 (reel 37).

32. Watters, *Down to Now*, 217.

33. "A UPI newspaperman here recently told one of the SNCC people that if there's a peaceful picket in the city it isn't news but if there were violence to call him. The news people and every one else here have seen so many peaceful pickets in Albany and so few results." Albany office of SNCC, draft press release, July 17 [1963], SNCC Papers, subgroup A: ser. VIII, folder 102 (reel 19).

34. Bevel in *Newsweek*, Aug. 13, 1962, quoted in Garrow, *Bearing*, 216.

35. Watters, *Down to Now*, 165–67.

36. Zinn, *Albany*, 23–25; Watters, *Down to Now*, 165–66; Branch, *Parting*, 541–42. Sheriff Matthews admitted pushing Sherrod around and warning his prisoners, "I want it so quiet in this jail that you can hear a flea peeing in a wad of cotton." FBI agent Marion Cheek quoted in Branch, *Parting*, 971.

37. "Charlie was a kook or a commie," C. B. King believed at first. Watters, *Down to Now*, 144.

38. Biographical information on Slater King in SNCC Papers, subgroup A: ser. XV, folder 33 (reel 37); Branch, *Parting*, 543; Garrow, *Bearing*, 180.

39. See, for example, Bay Area Friends of SNCC, "Report on Federal Prosecution of Civil Rights Workers in Albany, Georgia" [n.d.], p. 6, in SNCC Papers, subgroup A: ser. VIII, folder 102 (reel 19), and "Albany, Georgia, City on the Edge of Racial Violence," SNCC press release [1963], SNCC Papers, subgroup A: ser. XV, folder 32 (reel 37).

40. Zinn, *Albany*, 21; Branch, *Parting*, 622–23; Garrow, *Bearing*, 211; Pritchett OH, SOHP, 15–16. The most gruesome incident that grew out of the Albany protests involved Marion King, Slater King's wife, who drove out to the Mitchell County Jail with several other Albany women to bring food to protesters in July 1962. The Mitchell County sheriff ordered the visitors away. Mrs. King, who was pregnant and was holding two small children in her arms, did not move fast enough to satisfy the sheriff, who slapped her, sending her children sprawling, then kicked her and knocked her to the ground, where he and a deputy kicked her several more times. Though not badly injured, she lost consciousness and feared the consequences of the jostling for her baby.

Slater King's brother, C. B. King, did not bring a lawsuit against the sheriff, who was already the object of a futile suit involving brutality against an earlier black prisoner, saying that Negro lawsuits against rural sheriffs were just a form of self-torture. Branch, *Parting*, 615–16. Pritchett's response to this incident has not been recorded.

41. Both quoted in Zinn, *Albany*, 20–21.

42. Marion Page OH, CRDP, 8, 42.

43. Quoted in Pritchett OH, SOHP, 14.

44. Pritchett, report to the city manager for fiscal year 1961–62, in SNCC Papers, subgroup A: ser. VIII, folder 102 (reel 19).

45. Zinn, *Albany*, 21.

46. Leslie Dunbar, then executive director of the SRC, in the introduction to Zinn, *Albany*, vi.

47. Young interview. Sherrod to author, Feb. 8, 1990. Sherrod does not believe that Pritchett's leadership explains the total silence of Albany whites, but he does not have an alternative explanation for the difference between Albany and elsewhere.

48. For Montgomery as a contrasting case in this regard, see E. D. Nixon transcript, CRDP, 16.

49. Garrow, *Bearing*, 208–10.

50. Mrs. Marion Page, E. D. Hamilton, Thomas Chatmon, and Laurie Pritchett, quoted in Ricks, "'De Lawd,'" 13.

51. Pritchett, in Raines, *Soul Is Rested*, 350, 362. Pritchett's words were: "a coalition . . . between some blacks and some whites that felt that if he was released from custody and left that the mass news media that was there would also leave and Albany would go back to their ways." He added that he "had sympathy for [King] because . . . this made him lose a lot of respect of the blacks." C. B. King claims that he discovered recently that it was not a black man who bailed King out. As Aldon Morris reported it: "A member of a prestigious local white law firm told [C. B. King that] he was present at a meeting in Washington with J. Edgar Hoover and Robert Kennedy at the time: 'Bobby Kennedy expressed a desire of greatest urgency that he wanted King out of Albany. And it was conceived in that meeting that [the Albany lawyer] would bond him out. . . . It was he who paid . . . about $200 to the city. . . . That was how Martin was released.'" Morris, *Origins*, 247.

52. Lewis quotes a city official actually using this phrase: *King*, 151.

53. *NYT*, July 30, 1962; *NYT*, Aug. 5, 1962, and Walker interview, all quoted in Ricks, "'De Lawd,'" 11.

54. *NYT*, Aug. 18, 1962; Lewis, *King*, 169; Stephen Oates, *Let the Trumpet Sound: The Life of Martin Luther King, Jr.* (New York: New American Library, 1983), 199; all in Ricks, "'De Lawd,'" 12.

55. Pritchett in Raines, *Soul Is Rested*, 366; Pritchett OH, SOHP, 21.

Chapter 7: The Late 1950s: Saving the Party from Civil Rights

1. Transcript of Executive Committee meeting, Nov. 26–27, 1956, p. 221, and form letter from Paul Butler, Dec. 7, 1956, DNC Papers, box 119, JFKL.

2. Kenneth S. Davis, *The Politics of Honor: A Biography of Adlai E. Stevenson* (New York: Putnam, 1957), 356.

3. That division, according to James McGregor Burns and others, defined the Democratic party during the 1950s. Burns, *Deadlock of Democracy: Four-Party Politics in America* (Englewood Cliffs, N.J.: Prentice-Hall, 1963).

4. Transcripts of DAC meeting, San Francisco, Feb. 15–16, 1957, pp. 44–57, DNC Papers, box 120; DNC Executive Committee meeting, Washington, D.C., Nov. 26–27, 1956, pp. 193–95, 198–99, 228–29, and especially 215–21, DNC Papers, box 119, JFKL. DNC, *Official Proceedings of the Democratic National Convention, 1956,* pp. 322–23, 329–32.

5. Both Gravel and Everett had been on the 1956 platform committee and had voted to approve the civil rights plank. Transcript of DAC meeting, San Francisco, Feb. 15–16, 1957, pp. 44–45, 51, DNC Papers, box 120, JFKL. According to Allen Ellender, Gravel was later ousted from the DNC for his advocacy of civil rights. Ellender OH, JFKL, 9, 11.

6. Transcript of DAC meeting, San Francisco, Feb. 15–16, 1957, p. 53, DNC Papers, box 120, JFKL.

7. Harry McPherson OH, LBJL, int. I, tape 2, p. 2, and int. I, tape 1, pp. 5, 10, 12; and McPherson, *A Political Education* (Boston: Houghton Mifflin, 1988).

8. Kefauver and Gore were both from Tennessee, like Texas a "peripheral" southern state, but unlike Texas and the rest of the South a state long besieged by a Republican presence and therefore a less drastic Democracy than prevailed in other states of the former Confederacy.

9. Minutes of DPC meeting no. 62, June 27, 1956, Papers of the Democratic Leader, "Senate Democratic Policy Committee Minutes," box 364, LBJL.

10. This and next three paragraphs: Rowe to LBJ, Apr. 4, 1956, Reedy Files, box 418, LBJL.

11. [Reedy?] memo, n.d. [ca. Feb.–May 1957], Reedy Files, box 418, LBJL.

12. Since mid-1956, Rowe noted, the "deliberate drift" of the GOP in a liberal direction on civil rights greatly disturbed the urban bosses. The GOP had obviously written off the South and was making a "deliberate play for the large minority blocs which ha[d] been Democratic since the New Deal." Nixon's statement about the "Republican Chief Justice" was an "ominous warning" of what was to come." Rowe to LBJ, Apr. 4, 1956, Reedy Files, box 418, LBJL. See also McPherson, *Political Education,* 142–43.

13. Carl Brauer, *John F. Kennedy and the Second Reconstruction* (New York: Columbia University Press, 1977), 58–59. Lawson, *Black Ballots,* 141, 162. "Summing Up Defeat," *Reporter* 15 (Nov. 13, 1956); Henry Lee Moon, "The Negro Vote," *New Republic* 135 (Dec. 3, 1956). *NYT,* Nov. 11, 1956, 60.

14. McPherson, *Political Education,* 142–43. Feeding the flames of this trend, George Reedy said, was the tendency of "isolated incidents" in the Democratic South, such as "shooting into buses, etc.," to get "magnified out of all proportions." [Reedy?] memo, n.d. [ca. Feb.–May 1957], Reedy Files, box 418, LBJL.

15. [Reedy?] memo, n.d. [ca. Feb.–May 1957], Reedy Files, box 418, LBJL.

16. Southern members would prefer to grandstand for white supremacist votes, even if doing so led to "legislation that [was] really vicious." [Reedy?] memo, n.d. [ca. Feb.–May 1957], Reedy Files, box 418, LBJL.

17. These four blocs had come together on the basis of cynicism on the part of labor

and the bosses and "extreme fanaticism" on the part of liberals and Negroes. Reedy to LBJ, Dec. 3, 1956; LBJ Papers, Senate Files, box 567, LBJL.

18. The Democrats deeply feared losing black votes. Working-class white voters in the North were less of a worry: Eisenhower's personality and coattails were all that pulled working-class districts out of the Democratic column. When Eisenhower retired in 1960, the GOP could not get that lucky again. An effort to lure lost voters back would "not produce civil rights legislation," but it could split the Democratic party and reduce it to minority status. Reedy to LBJ, Dec. 3, 1956, LBJ Papers, Senate Files, box 567, LBJL.

19. Any effort to "buy back" the Negro would be "so transparent" that it would "merely infuriate southerners" and convince Negroes that it was "good business to scare the Democrats by tossing Republicans a big bloc of votes." Reedy told Johnson to try "to produce legislation along the civil rights lines." That would not end the attack on congressional leadership, but "it would take some of the edge off the Negro groups" and allow the Democrats at last to "fall back upon economic issues," where, with Negro voters, the Democratic party had a "decided advantage." Reedy to LBJ, Dec. 3, 1956, LBJ Papers, Senate Files, box 567, LBJL.

20. Reedy to LBJ, December 3, 1956; LBJ Papers, Senate Files, box 567, LBJL.

21. If they allowed "a reasonable civil rights bill" to pass, then in the future "the rest of the nation [would] be far more sympathetic to the southern position against unreasonable legislation."

22. Reedy to LBJ, Dec. 25, 1956, Reedy Files, box 418, LBJL. They needed a "miracle," in McPherson's words, and they thought their leader might be able to deliver one. *Political Education,* 143; the chapter in Reedy's memoir devoted to this struggle, and that in what is probably the most informative and engaging journalistic record, by Rowland Evans and Robert Novak, are entitled "Legislative Miracle" and "The Miracle of '57," respectively: George Reedy, *Lyndon B. Johnson: A Memoir* (New York: Andrews and McMeel, 1982); Evans and Novak, *Lyndon B. Johnson: The Exercise of Power* (New York: New American Library, 1966; hereafter *Exercise*).

23. In his State of the Union message, Eisenhower explicitly endorsed Titles III and IV, which his attorney general had previously submitted to Congress against his orders and about which Eisenhower only spoke vaguely thereafter. He also explicitly requested that Congress enact the bill, which he had not done before. *PPP,* 1957, p. 23. Lawson, *Black Ballots,* 151–52, 155–56, 165–66.

24. *Time,* Dec. 24, 1956, quoted in Lawson, *Black Ballots,* 163.

25. Lawson, *Black Ballots,* 167, 171.

26. Reedy to LBJ, July 15, 1957, Reedy Files, box 418, LBJL, emphasis removed.

27. Lawson, *Black Ballots,* 184.

28. Reedy to LBJ, July 12, 1957, Reedy Files, box 418. LBJL. Evans and Novak, *Exercise,* 140, 143, 150–51.

29. Biographical information on Acheson after he left the State Department in 1952 (the endpoint of his autobiography) is hard to come by. An admirer of his recently recalled (from his correspondence and meetings with Acheson in late 1957 and 1958) that "Mr. Acheson's fortunes were at this time at a low ebb. The powerful secretary of state he had become under President Truman had vanished. Abused and traduced by the odious Senator McCarthy, he could expect no comfort or defense from President Eisenhower." He had so little comfort, apparently, and so little to do, that he found time to

travel across the ocean and spend two weeks as the guest of a perfect stranger for no other reason than to "see" what Cambridge — which his old friend Keynes had talked so much about — "was like."

The perfect stranger arranged an honorary degree for Acheson, which entailed a second visit the same year, and Acheson killed the time attending lawn parties and drinking tea with the students. Acheson was apparently aware of his weaknesses. The admiring stranger, in an unfailingly flattering eulogy, recalls Acheson fawning over the well-bred young aristocrats at Cambridge: " 'I find the excellence of their manners so very engaging.' 'Whoever tires of flattery?' he added. 'I may recognize it, but how I love it.' " Noel Annan, "Dean Acheson," *Yale Review* 77 (Oct. 1988), 467, 470. For Acheson's career before then, see Acheson, *Present at the Creation* (New York: Norton, 1969), and Gaddis Smith, *Dean Acheson* (New York: Cooper Square, 1972).

30. Reedy notes on phone conversation with Acheson, July 22, 1957, LBJA Famous Names, "Acheson, Dean," LBJL. Interestingly, Acheson did not refer to any damn fool southern conservatives or balance his criticism of Douglas with criticism of Russell, who it is true did not eat Negro babies, but did assert that Title III was "cunningly designed to vest in the Attorney General unprecedented power to bring to bear the whole might of the federal government, including the armed forces if necessary, to force a co-mingling of white and Negro children in the state-supported schools of the South." Douglas was impractical. Russell was a man you could work with. For other evidence of Acheson's role in the Title III fight, LBJ to Acheson, Aug. 8, 1957, LBJA Famous Names, LBJL; Acheson to LBJ, Aug. 13, 1957, LBJ Senate Papers, Solis Horwitz Files, box 408, LBJL.

31. Evans and Novak, *Exercise*, 143–44. Lawson, *Black Ballots*, 178, 182. "Notes on Johnson's Remarks to Clarence Mitchell and other Delegates," LBJ Senate Papers, Subj. Files, box 752, LBJL.

32. Lawson, *Black Ballots*, 172–73.

33. The liberals took comfort in the endorsement of this realism by the law school deans of Yale, Columbia, Fordham, and Penn. Lawson, *Black Ballots*, 171.

34. Reedy's notes on Acheson conversation, July 22, 1957, LBJA Famous Names, box 1, LBJL.

35. On Acheson's central role in winning northern liberal support for the two big amendments to the 1957 bill, see Evans and Novak, *Exercise*, 143–49, and Rowe to LBJ, Apr. 4, 1956, with attachments, esp. Acheson's typescript on the jury trial amendment. On LBJ's general tactic of persuading northerners to let a weak bill pass to pave the way for a stronger bill in the future, and persuading southerners to let a weak bill pass to avert the threat of a stronger one in the future, see McPherson OH, LBJL, 16.

36. *Congressional Record*, 85th Cong., 1st sess., pp. 13305–7.

37. Johnson thanked Acheson effusively for his efforts, and repeated his gestures of thanks publicly, by inserting Acheson's letter to the *Washington Post* into the *Record*, and privately, by kicking off the next meeting of the DPC by reading Acheson's letter to them.

Johnson and Acheson grew closer over the next few years, sharing the mission to unify the party, and their correspondence suggests a congruence of views and of scruples. LBJ told Acheson he would walk on water for him. Acheson wrote poetry to LBJ. See LBJA Famous Names, box 1, LBJL, esp. Acheson to LBJ, Feb 17, 1958, and LBJ to

Acheson, Feb. 24, 1958; Solis Horwitz Files, box 408, LBJL, esp. DA to LBJ, Aug. 13, 1957, and DPC Minutes, Meeting No. 68, Aug. 13, 1957, Papers of the Democratic Leader, box 364, LBJL.

38. For example, Frank Church further amended the jury trial provision with a clause that gave any U.S. citizen over twenty-one years old the right to serve on federal juries. Lawson, *Black Ballots*, 189. This was meant to be an inexplicit, back-door guarantee of integrated federal juries.

39. Wilkins quoted in Lawson, *Black Ballots*, 196. Even with Church's addition, the House cried foul and altered the Senate-amended bill a bit more, substituting one of Acheson's earlier drafts for the Senate-passed version. The final bill, which Eisenhower signed on September 9, required a jury trial for all contempt sentences over a three-hundred-dollar fine or forty-five days in jail. Evans and Novak, *Exercise,* 152. For more on the battle over the 1957 bill, the memoirs of two of the participants are particularly useful: Richard Bolling, *House out of Order* (New York: Dutton, 1965), and Paul Douglas, *In the Fullness of Time* (New York: Harcourt, 1972).

40. Lawson, *Black Ballots,* 199, 183.

41. Reedy to LBJ, n.d. [ca. late 1957 or early 1958], Reedy Files, box 418, LBJL. Acheson to LBJ, Sept. 20, 1957, LBJA Famous Names, box 1.

42. Reedy to LBJ, Jan. 4, 1958, LBJ Senate Papers, 1959 Subject Files, box 652, LBJL.

43. Reedy to LBJ, Jan. 4, 1958, LBJ Senate Papers, 1959 Subject Files, box 652, LBJL.

44. Harry [McPherson] to George [Reedy], Oct. 24, 1958, and attachment on the Wofford-Hesburgh proposal, LBJ Senate Papers, 1958 Subject Files, box 589, LBJL.

45. Rankin was not actually appointed to the CRC until July 5, 1960, but McPherson says both were working (Rankin perhaps voluntarily or as a consultant) with the CRC at the time of their memo of October 1958.

46. Wofford to MLK, Apr. 25, 1956, MLKB, box 8, folder 33.

47. Wofford, *Of Kennedys and Kings* (New York: Farrar, Straus, and Giroux, 1980), 29, 165–66; Branch, *Parting,* 207–8; Garrow, *Bearing,* 84–85, 111, 113.

48. Wofford, *Kennedys,* 108–9, 466. Speech, Mar. 23, 1961, Harris Wofford White House Files, box 14, Speech File, JFKL.

49. Wofford, *Kennedys,* 164; Acheson to LBJ, Dec. 18, 1958, Solis Horwitz Files, box 408, LBJL; John Macy File on Rankin, LBJL.

50. Acheson to LBJ, Dec. 18, 1958, in LBJ Senate Papers, Solis Horwitz Files, box 408, LBJL.

51. Rankin memorandum, attached to Acheson to LBJ, Dec. 18, 1958, in LBJ Senate Papers, Solis Horwitz Files, box 408, LBJL.

52. Rankin memorandum, attachment to Acheson to LBJ, Dec. 18, 1958, in LBJ Senate Papers, Solis Horwitz Files, box 408, LBJL.

53. "Northern and Western Democrats who would otherwise feel compelled to press for further Federal intervention would refrain . . . if they felt that . . . a process was in motion by which the South might . . . disentangle itself." Wofford memorandum, attached to Acheson to LBJ, Dec. 18, 1958, in LBJ Senate Papers, Solis Horwitz Files, box 408, LBJL.

54. Wofford suggested that LBJ tell southern audiences, "As southerners we . . .

believe that separate but equal schools for colored and white children would be better for both groups and regret that the Supreme Court reversed its long-standing previous rule. . . . But none of us should sacrifice our children on the altar of our stubbornness." Instead, they should seek "workable" ways to comply with the Court, "with the least possible damage to all concerned." LBJ was to emphasize that "mass mixing of the races in the schools [was] not required" to satisfy the Supreme Court. The important thing, constitutionally, was to provide choices to black students: "We believe that for the most part Negroes will prefer to be in their own schools and not be a minority in white schools." Wofford memorandum, attached to Acheson to LBJ, Dec. 18, 1958, in LBJ Senate Papers, Solis Horwitz Files, box 408, LBJL.

Chapter 8: Lyndon Johnson Takes Center Stage—and Then an Intermission

1. Reedy to LBJ, Feb. 5, 1959, and Reedy to LBJ, n.d. [ca. Feb. 1959], in Senate Papers, Office Files of Gerald Siegel, box 404, LBJL. *Congressional Record,* 86th Cong., 2d sess., 105, pp. 875–77, 871, 985. Also see analysis of the bill on Mar. 2, 1959, under comments by Senator Clark: *Congressional Record,* 86th Cong., 2d sess., 105, pp. 2805–7. The bill was referred to Judiciary. It was never reported out. Senate Judiciary Committee, *Hearings,* on HR 300, 351, 353 . . . [39 bills], 86th Cong., 1st sess., ser. no. 5, Mar. 4–May 1, 1959.

2. [Reedy to LBJ], date penciled in Jan. 23, 1959 [perhaps the date it was filed: this had to have been written before LBJ decided to submit S.499, which was January 1959], in LBJ Papers, Senate Files, box 652, LBJL (emphasis removed), and Wofford's attachment to Acheson to LBJ, Dec. 18, 1958, LBJ Senate Papers, Solis Horwitz Files, box 408, LBJL.

3. Fifth memo in stapled packet of five memos, mostly undated, in "1959 Subject Files Civil Rights," in LBJ Senate Files, box 652, LBJL. The same figures Wofford and Rankin proposed came up as possible participants in this group: "men like Luther Hodges . . . probably Governor LeRoy Collins . . . and mayors of such cities as Atlanta and Nashville," along with university leaders. "Confidential Memo on Better Understanding Between the North and South," unsigned, n.d., in file "1959 Subject Files Civil Rights," LBJ Senate Files, box 652, LBJL. See also, Harry [McPherson] to Solis [Horwitz], Feb. 26, 1959, "1959 Subject Files Legislation (LBJ) Civil Rights, S.499," LBJ Senate Files, box 652, LBJL.

4. Reedy to LBJ, n.d. [ca. Feb. 1959], in Senate Papers, Office Files of Gerald Siegel, box 404, LBJL.

5. Statements by various senators and representatives, June 8–July 12, 1959, in Senate, U.S. Leadership—Criticism of/Butler-Spivak (1959), LBJA Subject File, box 118, LBJL.

6. *NYT,* Jan. 7, 1960. "Notes on Sen. Johnson's Remarks to Clarence Mitchell and other delegates to January 13–14 (1960) Legislative Conference" [Johnson enjoined participants in this from making statements on the record about what they discussed]; and memorandum on "The problem in the civil rights debate . . . ," n.d. [ca. Jan.–Feb. 1960], in LBJ Senate Papers, Subject Files, box 752.

7. Throughout the debate on the civil rights bill of 1960, the press reported that his work did not damage his presidential prospects, as it constantly threatened to do if he went too far one way or another. The press hailed the final passage of the bill, by a seventy-one to eighteen majority in the Senate, as a victory for Johnson's leadership skill. *NYT,* Mar. 1, Mar. 6, Mar. 27, Apr. 9, 1960.

For this and other analyses of the 1960 bill, I have relied on Daniel Berman, *A Bill Becomes Law: Congress Enacts Civil Rights Legislation,* 2d ed. (New York: Macmillan, 1966); Lawson, *Black Ballots;* and the *New York Times.*

8. Brauer, *Kennedy,* 11. *NYT,* Mar. 10, Apr. 9, 1960. Berman, *A Bill,* 128.

9. Representative Colmer of Mississippi publicly averred that "even in the darkest days of reconstruction, the Congress never went as far as this nefarious referee, registrar, or overseer bill," which was "a vicious attack . . . upon the fundamental structure" of the country and discrimination "against white people in favor of Negroes." Similarly, Representative Overton Brooks of Louisiana denounced the bill: "[It was] as vicious an instrument as I have read since I have been in this Congress." Berman, *A Bill,* 100, 128.

10. Berman, *A Bill,* 125. *NYT,* Mar. 1, Apr. 9, 1960. Senator Russell of Georgia stated early in the debate that the provision for voting referees was "way down the line in the order of being obnoxious" to him and his colleagues and that the preservation of federal election records for inspection was "the least objectionable of all." *NYT,* Mar. 1, 1960; the next day he clarified this by saying he did not want anyone to get the idea that he was "wrapping the olive branch around a white flag" on voting rights. *NYT,* Mar. 2, 1960.

11. *NYT,* Oct. 12, 1959, Mar. 16, 1960. Collins and another DAC southerner had dissented from a similar DAC statement in December 1959. *NYT,* Dec. 7, 1959.

12. LBJ, in Brauer, *Kennedy,* 38. Wofford on LBJ appointment as setback, OH, JFKL, 71.

13. Brauer, *Kennedy,* 17–29. For more on southern support of JFK in the 1950s, see Herbert Parmet, *Jack: The Struggles of John F. Kennedy* (New York: Dial, 1980), 409–14; Evans and Novak, *Exercise,* 143–49; Luther Hodges OH, JFKL, 1–2; Hale Boggs OH, JFKL, 2–4; LeRoy Collins OH, JFKL, 2–7; Allen Ellender OH, JFKL, 8.

14. *NYT,* Mar. 10, July 13, July 7, 1960.

15. Burns, *John Kennedy: A Political Profile* (New York: Harcourt, 1960), 100–206; Brauer, *Kennedy,* 29.

16. Theodore Sorensen, *Kennedy* (New York: Harper, 1965), 17, 471.

17. In the judgment of two of JFK's closest advisers on the issue, Theodore Sorensen and Harris Wofford, both advocates of a strong stance in favor of civil rights, he treated the issue as a matter of political expediency: Sorensen in Parmet, *Jack,* 409; Wofford OH, JFKL, 7.

18. Wofford OH, JFKL, 7.

19. Wofford OH, JFKL, 1, 7–8.

20. Wofford OH, JFKL, 10, 46–47: when the GOP introduced "essentially the Democratic platform" as legislation after the convention in 1960, "it was exceedingly embarrassing. . . . There was never any question but that the Democrats were not going to go ahead with an attempt to get civil rights legislation that August." "It was during this month that most strongly the theme of executive action came out." Wofford, *Kennedys and Kings,* 58–61; *NYT,* July 13, 14, 15, 18, 20, 24, 25; Aug. 1, 2, 4, 5, 8, 9, 10, 11, 12, 13,

14, 15, 17, 18, 20; Sept. 14, 21, 1960. The campaign pledge for early legislative action is reported in *NYT*, Sept. 2, 1960.

21. He did not tell the press that he had toned this pledge down, at Senator Russell's behest, and then strengthened another portion of it to square with Senator Clark's conscience. *NYT*, Sept. 2, 1960; Wofford, *Kennedys and Kings*, 59.

22. Among civil rights proponents, even skeptics began to prefer Kennedy because Nixon appeared increasingly incapable of making even the right gestures. Two months before the election, the Republican nominee took on Eisenhower's only black adviser, E. Frederic Morrow, and promised him a significant role in the campaign. Morrow later complained that he never had any assistants, never even "a secretary or anyone to answer [his] considerable campaign mail; [he] never had a dime to spend for anything other than personal expenses." Black leaders who asked Morrow's assistance were turned down flat. Brauer, *Kennedy*, 41–42.

23. Brauer, *Kennedy*, 88.

24. Garrow, *Bearing*, 143–44.

25. This and previous paragraph, Garrow, *Bearing*, 144–49.

26. Garrow, *Bearing*, 145, 148.

27. T. H. White, *The Making of the President, 1960* (New York: Atheneum, 1961), 387. A similar message came from a different constituency: Atlanta's Mayor Hartsfield. Wofford OH, JFKL, 20–22.

28. "Candidate with a Heart," Campaign pamphlet, along with statements of praise for JFK from black leaders, in Wofford Papers, box 2, JFKL.

29. Brauer, *Kennedy*, 58–59.

30. Collins OH, JFKL, 51.

31. Eisenhower in Garrow, *Bearing*, 149.

32. Speech to National Civil Liberties Clearing House, Mar. 23, 1961, Wofford Papers, box 14, JFKL. William Taylor, then a staff member at the Civil Rights Commission, noted that the *northern* black vote was not all. "The Negro vote in the South was a significant factor in the election of a Democratic Administration." William Taylor, special assistant to staff director, CRC, and secretary of the Subcabinet Committee on Civil Rights, to Wofford, Jan. 5, 1960, Wofford Papers, box 10, JFKL.

33. Sorensen, *Kennedy*, 475–76. Theodore Hesburgh OH, LBJL, 5–6. As far as anyone knew, in the first half-year of the administration, Kennedy's legislative program included the civil rights bill he had promised during the campaign. On May 10, 1961, Pierre Salinger publicly repudiated the administration's commitment to such a bill. See Patrick Malin to Wofford, May 24, 1961, Wofford Papers, box 1, JFKL.

34. Though 6 southern colleges withdrew, some 150 northern and southern ones adopted the policy without complaint or controversy.

35. Wofford, *Kennedys and Kings*, 144–50; Arthur M. Schlesinger, *A Thousand Days* (Boston: Houghton Mifflin, 1965), 852; Wofford to Pierre Salinger, July 18, 1961, in Ex HU 2, WHCF, box 360, JFKL; "Kennedy Administration Accomplishments in Civil Rights," June 1963, in Lee White Papers, box 19, JFKL.

36. For evidence of his frustration, see Harris Wofford to Patrick Malin, May 27, 1961, box 1, and Wofford to Arthur Finn, Nov. 16, 1961, box 3, Wofford Papers, JFKL.

37. The president made his intention to break the campaign promise explicit in private: "It may be proper for [Celler and Clark] to hold hearings this year . . . and then

have the fight next year," he told his staff, "[but] I do not want statements made that we have withdrawn our support for this matter." Brauer, *Kennedy,* 62–63; cf. campaign statement in *NYT,* Sept. 2, 1960.

38. Wofford to JFK, Dec. 30, 1960, as quoted in Schlesinger, *Robert F. Kennedy and His Times* (Boston: Houghton Mifflin, 1978; hereafter *RFK*), 288, Brauer, *Kennedy,* 63, and partially reprinted in Wofford, *Kennedys and Kings,* 136–38.

39. Dutton to Wofford et al., July 8, 1961, WHCF, box 358, JFKL, as quoted in Brauer, *Kennedy,* 85.

40. Southern Regional Council, *The Federal Executive and Civil Rights* (Atlanta, 1961). King, "Equality Now: The President Has the Power," *Nation* 192 (Feb. 1961), 91–95. Brauer, *Kennedy,* 66–67.

41. Wofford noted that keeping executive action "quiet" was a top priority in July 1961: "The theme is the application of the maximum intelligence and the most effective and wherever possible quiet use of the federal power to solve civil rights problems that are within our power to solve." He followed the same course in "the informal weekly Ad Hoc Committee on civil rights problems," which met in his office. Under pressure from Robert Kennedy to let out some controlled publicity, he said he was "able until now to discourage interest" among newsmen in the actions of the two groups. Wofford to Salinger, July 18, 1961, Ex HU2, WHCF, box 360, JFKL.

42. Brauer, *Kennedy,* 72.

43. Wofford said that Wilkins' criticism of Kennedy's failure to push legislation "was a mild attack and necessary for him to do." Better yet, Wilkins' attack actually helped the president live down southern suspicions of covert sympathy with the civil rights movement: it helped "shield the President in Congressional relations." Wofford also encouraged JFK to meet Wilkins because a meeting would "help Wilkins greatly in his fight for leadership": the administration found Wilkins' emphasis on lobbying and litigation less threatening than the mass direct action of Wilkins' southern competitors. Wofford to O'Donnell, July 11, 1961, Wofford Papers, NAACP file, box 5, JFKL. Wofford said Wilkins stopped criticizing the administration after meeting JFK in January 1961. Wofford OH, JFKL, 32–33.

44. Wofford OH, JFKL, 48–50.

45. Sorensen, *Kennedy,* 485. Wofford, *Kennedys and Kings,* 170.

46. Wofford, *Kennedys and Kings,* 165–67. (He left in "mid-1962," fifteen months before the assassination.)

47. PCEEO Press Release No. 141 (Dec. 13, 1963), Lee White Papers, box 23, JFKL. See also material on PCEEO accomplishments in 1963 Subject Files, Accomplishments of the Equal Employment Opportunity Program, Papers of LBJ as Vice President, box 6, LBJL. The PCEEO was a new creation that assumed the role of the old Committee on Government Contracts, which had been headed by Nixon, and a Committee on Government Employment. Schlesinger, *Thousand Days,* 852. The PCEEO continued to concentrate on government contracts, but its overlap with the subcabinet group in the field of employment in government left it unclear whether changes in the government's hiring and promotion practice were due to the PCEEO or the subcabinet group, or both.

48. Wofford, *Kennedys and Kings,* 143–44.

49. Wofford, *Kennedys and Kings,* 143; Sorensen, *Kennedy,* 474; Lee White OH, JFKL, 16.

50. Wofford, *Kennedys and Kings,* 144.

51. Troutman's report to the president, Aug. 27, 1963, Lee White Papers, box 23, JFKL.

52. "Plan of Organization, Advisory Council on Plans for Progress" [ca. Oct. 1963], Burke Marshall Papers, Oberdorfer File on Southern Business, box 30, JFKL; PCEEO Press Release No. 141 (Dec. 13, 1963), Lee White Papers, box 23; Jerry Holleman to Ralph Dungan, Jan. 3, 1962, with thirty-page attachment from John Field and two-page attachment from Troutman, and Troutman's report to the president, Aug. 27, 1963, in Lee White Papers, box 23, JFKL; Lee White OH, LBJL, 16.

53. Branch, *Parting,* 554–55.

54. Garrow, *Bearing,* 182.

55. Charles Sherrod, proposal to set up a Student Interracial Ministry, Sherrod Papers, box 4, file 15, MLKA.

56. T. F. Reardon to John Dempsey, Aug. 17, 1963, Ex HU/ST 10, WHCF, box 366, JFKL.

57. Gray may have been involved with the secret bail arrangements, whereby King got "kicked out of jail" on July 12. Gray had been pushing this tactic with the city commissioners and may have informed the Kennedys of it. Branch, *Parting,* 554–55. T. F. Reardon to John Dempsey, Aug. 17, 1963, Ex HU/ST 10, WHCF, box 366, JFKL.

58. Burke Marshall to Lee White, Sept. 16, 1963, Ex HU2/ST 10, WHCF, box 366, JFKL. John Henrik Clarke manuscript and Clarke to Slater King, Mar. 16, 1965, Slater King Papers, Personal Correspondence, MLKA. J. Edgar Hoover to Lee White, June 27, 1963, Lee White Papers, box 21, JFKL.

59. Garrow, *Bearing,* 203, 207, 201.

60. Charles Sherrod, proposal to set up Student Interracial Ministry, Sherrod Papers, box 4, file 15, MLKA.

61. Bass and DeVries, *Transformation,* 29, 155.

62. Wofford, *Kennedys and Kings,* 162.

Chapter 9: Policy in High Gear:
From the Justice Department to the Acts of 1964 and 1965

1. Schlesinger, *Thousand Days,* 852–53; Brauer, *Kennedy,* 88, 94–95. Victor Navasky argues that Robert Kennedy's commitment to civil rights grew from the pressure of events rather than from philosophy, planning, or deliberation: *Kennedy Justice* (New York: Atheneum, 1979), 98–99.

2. During the battle over James Meredith's admission to Ole Miss, RFK reminded Governor Ross Barnett that the civil rights policy he was fighting had been created by southerners—the federal judges of the Fifth Circuit: "This is not a bunch of northerners telling you this." Transcript of phone conversation, Sept. 25, 1962, Burke Marshall Papers, box 20, JFKL; Brauer, *Kennedy,* 185; Branch, *Parting,* 649.

3. Ramsey Clark said the DOJ ended up finding that litigation was "much too feeble an instrument to effect any significant social change." The judicial process was slow and limited in scope, dealing with only one school district, one employer, one union, at a time. Ramsey Clark OH, IV, p. 3, LBJL. According to Nicholas Katzenbach, "[The

courts were] very, very slow [on voting rights]; people obviously qualified to vote . . .
were being turned down; then we had to bring a lawsuit; then we had to go through all
the appeals and another election would go by. By the time it had taken three years and
they were getting into the Court of Appeals, they would then say, 'Well the situation is all
changed now,' and the Court would send it back, remand it for a new look at the facts;
and then you'd find the facts were the same and you'd be going up again—it just took
forever." Such delay, coupled with the demonstrations, especially at Selma, made a legislative solution necessary. Katzenbach OH, p. 25, LBJL.

4. Navasky, *Kennedy Justice.*

5. Wofford, *Kennedys and Kings,* 93; Schlesinger, *RFK,* 288; Helen Fuller, *Year of
Trial* (New York: Harcourt, 1962), 117–19.

6. Quoted in Navasky, *Kennedy Justice,* 162.

7. Harold Fleming, interview with author, Washington, D.C., Apr. 4, 1988; Leslie
Dunbar, interview with author, Durham, N.C., Dec. 15, 1988.

8. One such white man was Tom King, the top rival of archsegregationist mayoral
candidate Art Hanes. King won a plurality in the first primary and then lost the runoff
to Hanes, who was the favorite of Bull Connor, the White Citizens' Council, and the
KKK.

9. Muse to SRC, Confidential Memo (16 pp.), "Visit to North Alabama, Birmingham
and Tuscaloosa, June 18–28, 1961," dated July 13, 1961, and forwarded to Marshall by
Muse. See Muse to Marshall, Sept. 26, 1961, and Marshall to Muse, Feb. 14, 1964. This
and fifteen other such reports are in Burke Marshall Papers, Special Correspondence,
Benjamin Muse, box 8, JFKL.

10. One example of less formal contacts: Secretary of Commerce Luther Hodges,
former governor of North Carolina, made a great impression on the reform-minded
moderate businessmen of Birmingham in an address to them in May 1962. James Head
(chairman of the Birmingham Committee of 100) to Hodges, May 8, 1962, in Burke
Marshall Papers, box 17, JFKL. Another: representatives of the reform-minded new
mayor of Birmingham, Albert Boutwell, visited the Commerce Department, and a
deputy assistant administrator of the Commerce Department visited with Vann, the
mayor's executive secretary, and the mayor. These latter men sought Commerce Department funding for development projects and formed a "blue ribbon committee," with 27
black members out of a total of 216 members, to carry on development plans that
included "group relations" and educational and health programs. Area Redevelopment
Administration to Burke Marshall, July 28, 1963, in Burke Marshall Papers, box 17,
JFKL.

11. See Bob Corley, "The Quest for Racial Harmony: Race Relations in Birmingham,
Alabama, 1947–1963" (Ph.D. diss., University of Virginia, 1967), 262. Jimerson is identified as a "Moderate White Leader" in Muse's report of Jan. 11, 1962, pp. 10–11, and in
several other reports from Birmingham, Burke Marshall Papers, box 8, JFKL.

12. See Norman Jimerson to Burke Marshall, Oct. 19, 1962; David Vann to Burke
Marshall, Jan. 19, 1963, Burke Marshall Papers, box 17, JFKL. See also memo of phone
conversation from the Reverend Powers McCloud [McLeod?], president of ACHR,
Sept. 18, 1962, and minutes of Alabama Advisory Committee to the Civil Rights Com-
mission's "Emergency Meeting," which David Vann and Virginia Durr attended, on
May 22, 1963, and the committee's memo to the Civil Rights Division, Sept. 1962.

Another informal contact between the DOJ and white moderates is the petition "A Plea for Common Sense," adopted by "a group of white business leaders . . . to be presented to the City Commission," Jan. 3, 1962, and Muse's report of Jan. 11, 1962. All these are in Burke Marshall Papers, box 8, JFKL. These documents show that the department was prepared (at least intellectually) for the crisis at Birmingham a year and a half before it happened. They also show local white leaders offering their services and asking the federal government to intervene.

Another example of the informal contacts was the Tweed-Segal Committee of prominent lawyers, including Atlanta's Morris Abram, which investigated complaints of brutality in the South, provided counsel for protesters arrested on spurious charges, and put pressure on local bar associations to stand against discrimination in trial procedures. This informal committee later became the Lawyers' Committee for Civil Rights under Law. See Oberdorfer's daily reports for July 18, Oct. 2, Dec. 26, and Dec. 27, 1963, in Burke Marshall Papers, Oberdorfer File on Southern Business, box 30, JFKL.

13. John Lewis stressed especially Charles Morgan's role in conveying SRC information to the movement. Lewis, interview with author, Washington, D.C., Mar. 20, 1989. Young interview.

14. Navasky, *Kennedy Justice,* 169, 170.

15. Arthur Schlesinger, Jr., wrote that Nicholas Katzenbach, Burke Marshall, and Marshall's assistant John Doar were the chief negotiators. But the attorney general "also used his two southern assistant attorneys general, Ramsey Clark of Texas, and Louis Oberdorfer of Atlanta, as well as his southern assistant John Seigenthaler of Tennessee. Preparing for the new wave of school desegregation in the fall of 1961, these men traveled about conferring with local educational officials." *RFK,* 294. Ramsey Clark says Oberdorfer was very active in civil rights, "in part because he was a southerner." Ramsey Clark OH, II, p. 4, LBJL. Lee White says Oberdorfer was involved in civil rights policymaking "simply because he happened to come from Birmingham." White quoted President Kennedy as saying he wanted Lyndon Johnson involved in all coordination of administration policy, first of all because Johnson was "pretty damned smart; and, second of all, [he was] a southerner and he [had] a better speaking voice for a lot of these people than [Kennedy did]." Lee White OH, I, p. 12, LBJL.

16. Schlesinger, *RFK,* 137–38, 189–90, 217, 290–91. Most of the material on Seigenthaler is based on interviews of Seigenthaler to which Schlesinger had special access. The transcripts are in the John F. Kennedy Library but have not been opened for general research.

17. Schlesinger, *RFK,* 294–97. A lesser white southerner who functioned in the same way as a negotiator on behalf of the DOJ was Jerry Heilbron. See John Griffin to Governor Collins, Oct. 2, 1964, Burke Marshall Papers, CRS file, box 31, JFKL; Brauer, *Kennedy,* 109; Branch, *Parting,* 408–9, 627–28; and Garrow (who does not mention that Heilbron was a southerner), *Bearing,* 279.

18. Floyd Mann, interview with author, Montgomery, July 13, 1989.

19. Wofford, *Kennedys and Kings,* 152–54.

20. Shuttlesworth's clipping files: *Anniston Star, Montgomery Advertiser,* and others, Shuttlesworth Papers, box 1, files 51 and 52, MLKA.

21. All of Oberdorfer's daily reports (toward the end they came less frequently than daily), June 1963 to July 1964, are in Burke Marshall Papers, Oberdorfer File on South-

ern Business, box 29 and box 30, JFKL. See especially the overview and update in the November 13 report; the year-end summary in the December 26 report; and the explanation of the relations among the various groups in the December 27 report.

22. The last of these two categories bore a crucial relationship to the previous two. In his narratives of each city, time and again Oberdorfer referred to the role of a local "biracial committee" or "community relations commission." Where desegregation could not be achieved, Oberdorfer found a notable sign of progress in the agreement of the mayor or city council to appoint such a committee. Sometimes "local business and civic leaders" formed such a committee "voluntarily."

23. Between May 22 and July 9, in response to the crisis at Birmingham, JFK personally met eleven times with religious, labor, business, legal, and women's groups to encourage voluntary desegregation; 1,558 leaders attended. RFK met with 143 business executives. Oberdorfer, report for Dec. 27, 1963. Some 7,715 letters to other southern leaders went out over the president's signature on July 12, 1963. Ex HU2, WHCF, June 22, 1963, box 361, JFKL.

On the meetings, see Lee White to JFK, June 4, 1963, Oberdorfer to RFK, June 4, 1963, and other documents in Lee White Papers, "Hotel Restaurant and Theater . . . ," box 21, and "Meetings with President . . . ," box 23, JFKL. See also Burke Marshall Papers, Alabama File, Correspondence, Apr.–Dec. 1962, and Alabama File, Presidential Briefing Papers — Birmingham Crisis, box 17, JFKL. Correspondence with attendees is in Ex HU2, WHCF, Dec. 26, 1962–June 20, 1963, box 360; Ex HU2, WHCF, June 22, 1963; and Ex HU2/ST 1 [Alabama], WHCF, box 366, JFKL.

24. The president's big meetings in Washington aimed to provide a sense of unity. But the artificiality of that unity was apparent in every meeting and report. The meetings pulled the southern white moderates together on a regional basis (ignoring rural-urban and peripheral–Deep South divisions) but divided them by profession. See the overview and update in the November 13 report, the year-end summary in the December 26 report, and the explanation of the relations among the different groups in Oberdorfer's December 27 report. "Record of Presidential Meetings with Leadership Groups" gives a breakdown of these, in "Meetings with President — Miscellaneous" file, Lee White Papers, box 23, JFKL.

25. See RFK to Frank Barton and twenty-five others, June 17, 1963, in Burke Marshall Papers, box 17, JFKL. On Oberdorfer: Ramsey Clark OH, II, 14, LBJL, and J. Vernon Patrick to Oberdorfer, Dec. 11, 1963, in Burke Marshall Papers, box 17, JFKL. Oberdorfer read and initialed much of the correspondence addressed to Marshall and others which pertained to Birmingham.

26. Quoted in Corley, "Quest," 247–48.

27. See Corley, "Quest," 262–63ff., and Fred Shuttlesworth, Ralph Abernathy, and Martin King to Smyer, Vann, Chalmers Hamilton, and Burke Marshall, May 17, 1963, in Burke Marshall Papers, Alabama File Memoranda, box 17, JFKL.

28. Corley, "Quest," 277–78.

29. He suggested as the first step pushing passage of an "Equal Education Opportunity Act," which he had proposed in a memorandum to RFK on May 15, 1963, or, if that failed in Congress, at least a "wholesale" program of intervention and filing of amicus briefs in civil rights lawsuits. Ramsey Clark to RFK, Aug. 28, 1963, in Navasky, *Kennedy Justice*, 184.

30. A Birmingham contact wrote in June 1963, "The new city council and mayor are delaying. . . . The council is deliberately dragging foot on such matters as golf course-park reopening. . . . and unless I misjudge my community, the atmosphere here is of no follow-through by the whites." Red Holland, ca. June 19, 1963, in Burke Marshall Papers, Alabama Files, Correspondence, June 1963, box 17, JFKL. Morris Abram wrote somewhat later that Birmingham was still "smoldering" and could damage the position of the Democrats and possibly the president. "I am sure that the last thing any of us would want prior to November 1964 is for the President to face the choice of whether or not to send troops into Birmingham. If, however, the conditions are not adjusted, this could well happen. The Birmingham situation cannot be solved without a change in attitude by the white power structure. I believe the problem can best be approached at a level requiring the direct intervention of the president." Abram to Moyers, Jan. 22, 1964, in Burke Marshall Papers, Alabama Files, Correspondence, box 17, JFKL. See also Wulf to Marshall, Sept. 25, 1963, in Burke Marshall Papers, Alabama Files, Correspondence, box 17, JFKL.

31. The areas that were "softening" also suffered from "an antagonistic attitude on the part of state officials." The conclusion of this summary was that the reports predicted "considerable difficulty in enforcing civil rights legislation in the 'hard core' states and rural areas." Oberdorfer report for Feb. 17, 1964, Burke Marshall Papers, box 30, JFKL.

32. "Radio and Television Report to the American People on Civil Rights," June 11, 1963, PPP, 1963, 468–71. Though this was not the first time he had made the point that civil rights was a moral issue, it was the first time he backed up his rhetoric with proposals for significant legislation. He first referred to civil rights as a moral issue three and a half months earlier: "It is not merely because of the Cold War, and not merely because of the economic waste of discrimination, that we are committed to achieving true equality of opportunity. The basic reason is because it is right." In that speech, he did urge legislation to extend the life of the Civil Rights Commission and hinted at legislated changes in voting rights—both uncontroversial issues. His praise for all that his administration had done on employment and public accommodations without legislation reads like a brief against legislation in those areas. "Special Message to the Congress on Civil Rights," Feb. 28, 1963, PPP, 1963, 222.

33. Johnson's remarks on signing the Civil Rights Act, his remarks on a survey of compliance with the Civil Rights Act on October 30, 1964, and his remarks on Collins' retirement from the CRS, on July 7, 1965, all emphasized the CRS's role, as did his Message to Congress setting forth his seven-point civil rights program on February 15, 1967. PPP, 1963–64, 2:842–43, 1528–29; PPP, 1965, 2: 723; and PPP, 1967, 1: 194. See also Johnson's remarks to the National Citizens' Committee for Community Relations, Aug. 18, 1964, PPP, 1964, II: 979–81.

34. Draft memo, Rosenthal–Department of Justice, Sept. 19, 1963, Ex HU2/ST 1, WHCF, box 366, JFKL.

35. Royall and Blaik to RFK, Mar. 12, 1964, Burke Marshall Papers, box 19, and draft press release from Rosenthal-DOJ, Sept. 19, 1963, in Ex HU2/ST 1, WHCF, box 366, JFKL.

36. Marshall to Salinger et al., Oct. 9, 1963, in Lee White Papers, box 19, Civil Rights—Alabama, JFKL.

37. Martin Luther King had detected this despair in Marshall earlier in the year, in May, at the height of the Birmingham demonstrations. Branch, *Parting*, 762.

38. *Congressional Record*, Senate, July 15, 1963, in Burke Marshall Papers, Oberdorfer File on Southern Business, box 29, JFKL.

39. Ad Hoc Committee Minutes, Apr. 22, 1964; Administrative History of CRS, LBJL.

40. Oberdorfer, attachment to memo to RFK, Feb. 18, 1964, in Burke Marshall Papers, Oberdorfer File on Southern Business, box 30, and Burke Marshall Papers, Compliance Meetings, Undated, box 29, JFKL.

41. "An Informal Legislative History of the Community Relations Service" and "Community Relations Service Departmental History," in Administrative History of the DOJ, vol. VII—Civil Rights, pt. XI, Community Relations Service, Narrative and Documentary Supplement, LBJL.

42. Minutes of Ad Hoc Committee, Apr. 22, 1964, in CRS Administrative History, LBJL.

43. In Aug. 1962, those preoccupied with the idea of a conciliation service still associated Johnson with the idea. In response to Albany, Lee White suggested "appointment of a joint federal-state-municipal commission to serve as an adviser to communities when civil rights problems [arose]." The commission would aim to "avoid the charge of federal intervention." Its recommendations "would not be binding." The commission could provide a face-saving device "for local officials who refuse[ed] to deal with negroes." Lee White to Andy Hatcher, [draft memo] Aug. 2, 1962, Lee White Papers, box 21, JFKL. William Taylor of the Civil Rights Commission staff then proposed that the president send LBJ to negotiate in Albany, "because of his knowledge of the South, his strong commitment to interracial progress, and his past interest in a federal conciliation service in the race relations field." Taylor said "dramatic" action that symbolized the "concern of the President" could "nullify the carping of the critics." The city and protesters would not compromise, but "a third force, in the person of a presidential representative," might bring them together. William Taylor to Lee White, "Draft Memorandum on Albany Georgia" (proposal worked out with Berl Bernhard and Harold Fleming [former director of the Southern Regional Council and later to be appointed as deputy director of CRS]), Aug. 15, 1962, Lee White Papers, box 21, JFKL.

44. Collins to LBJ, Mar. 24, 1965, Ex FG 155–18, WHCF, box 229, LBJL.

Epilogue: Interpreting the Movement

1. Dabney, *Liberalism in the South*, 238–39. For broader, and to my mind more persuasive, explanations of segregation's origins, see J. Morgan Kousser, *The Shaping of Southern Politics* (New Haven: Yale University Press, 1974), and Cell, *Highest Stage.*

2. Clinton, Tennessee, and Hoxie, Arkansas, were similar in showing local flexibility and then yielding to an outside mob. See the reports in Shoemaker, *With All Deliberate Speed;* Muse, *Ten Years;* and Jacoway and Colburn, *Southern Businessmen.*

3. As I note later in the Epilogue, the southern struggles led by the Student Nonviolent Coordinating Committee were, with the exception of Albany, inconclusive, and therefore I have not sought to explain their outcomes in detail in this book. But it bears noting that SNCC, like the SCLC before it, relied on white southerners in its operations

as well. The role of such important white southerners in SNCC as Anne Braden, Guy Carawan, Sandra Cason ("Casey" Hayden), Connie Curry, Mary King, Sam Shirah, Jane Stembridge, Sue Thrasher, Bob Zellner, and Sue Weber can be glimpsed from the SNCC papers, the many "oral histories," and the published literature on the student phase of the movement, though one will not always find these persons identified as white and southern. See especially Carson, *In Struggle,* and Len Holt, *The Summer That Didn't End* (London: Heinemann, 1966).

4. Speed, Ice interview, 22–24.

5. DuPont, Ice interview, 19, 22, 25. DuPont said he did not trust the city judge but did trust Stoutamire.

6. Steele, Ice interview, 8–9.

7. Bevel, interview with Emily Stoper, in Stoper, *SNCC* (Brooklyn: Carlson, 1989), 274.

8. Pritchett in Hampton and Fayer, *Voices of Freedom,* 106.

9. King, *My Life,* 210–11.

10. Marion Page OH, CRDP, 8.

11. Wyatt Tee Walker, "The Congo, U.S.A.: Albany, Georgia," *SCLC Newsletter* 1 (Sept. 1962), in SNCC Papers, subgroup A: ser. IV, folder 338 (reel 9).

12. Walker in Hampton and Fayer, *Voices of Freedom,* 106–7.

13. John Lewis, interview with Emily Stoper, in Stoper, *SNCC,* 209, 235. King himself, speaking of the restraint that Bull Connor's forces in Birmingham showed at the beginning of the protest there (restraint that soon broke down): "What observers probably did not realize was that [Bull Connor] was trying to take a leaf from the book of Police Chief Laurie Pritchett of Albany. Chief Pritchett felt that by directing his police to be nonviolent, he had discovered a new way to defeat the demonstrations." *Why We Can't Wait,* 69. David L. Lewis, in one of the earliest and still most important biographies of King, captured the importance of Albany by titling his chapter on it "Nonviolence in Black and White," and his next chapter, on Birmingham, "Nonviolence in Black, Violence in White." Lewis reported that "no clubs, hoses, or dogs" were ever used in Albany and that King "was curiously generous to his enemies and bewilderingly sanguine about the future of Albany race relations. He complimented the Albany police department on its courteous treatment of the demonstrators and stressed that the city's problems could best be dealt with on a local level." Lewis, *King,* 150–51.

14. Sherrod, in Hampton and Fayer, *Voices of Freedom,* 107.

15. See SNCC press release, "Albany, Georgia: City on the Edge of Racial Violence" [1963], SNCC Papers, subgroup A: ser. XV, folder 32 (reel 37), and Peter Titelman, "Report on Albany, Georgia" [1963], SNCC Papers, subgroup A: ser. XV, folder 30 (reel 37).

16. J. Forman to W. G. Anderson, Oct. 15, 1962, SNCC Papers, subgroup A: ser. XV, folder 33 [reel 37].

17. Lewis, *King,* 140–70. Lerone Bennett, *What Manner of Man* (Chicago: Johnson, 1968), 130.

18. King, "Bold Design for a New South," *Nation* 196 (Mar. 30, 1963), 259–62. The *Playboy* interview is in *Testament of Hope,* ed. James Washington (New York: Harper, 1986), 344.

19. Page, CRDP, 4. Walker, CRDP, 27.

20. Garrow, *Bearing,* 218. This marks a change of emphasis from Garrow's previous book, *Protest at Selma* (New Haven: Yale University Press, 1978), in which he emphasized the failure at Albany as a lesson. The movement heeded it well and therefore achieved success at Birmingham and especially at Selma.

21. Lewis, interview with Emily Stoper, in Stoper, *SNCC,* 209, 235.

22. Forman treats King as a self-serving *diabolus ex machina* who stole attention from Forman's (highly romanticized) "people's" movement, and whose disastrous effects on the movement Forman alone was prophetic enough to foresee. *Making of Black Revolutionaries,* 247–62, esp. 255–56, 260, 248.

23. Zinn, *Albany,* 16–17.

BIBLIOGRAPHICAL ESSAY

What follows is not intended as a list of accomplices in my interpretations but a reader's guide to the genealogy of the ideas explored in this book and to their further pursuit. This guide is broken down into the three parts of the book, though there is some overlap between them. For a fuller version of the notes and bibliography of parts two and three, see my dissertation, "White Southerners in the Civil Rights Movement" (Ph.D. diss., University of Rochester, 1992), available from University Microfilms.

Part One

Readers of chapter 1 will immediately detect the influence of C. Vann Woodward, whose works, *Tom Watson: Agrarian Rebel* (New York: Macmillan, 1938), *Origins of the New South* (Baton Rouge: Louisiana State University Press, 1971), *The Strange Career of Jim Crow* (New York: Oxford University Press, 1955), and numerous shorter pieces, have more than any others shaped my views of the post–Civil War South. Paul Gaston's *New South Creed: A Study in Southern Mythmaking* (New York: Knopf, 1970) weaves together the various strands of post–Civil War southern culture into a brilliant synthesis that manages to be comprehensive yet comprehensible. It also makes points that are original, and inimitably Gaston's, though it confirms many views that Woodward happened to express first. In spite of my love for these books, I have still been deeply influenced by the one they go very far to refute, W. J. Cash's *Mind of the South* (New York: Knopf, 1941). In this connection I have found Bruce Clayton's history of southern culture, whose core is an extended synthesis of Cash and Woodward, indispensable and inspiring: *The Savage Ideal* (Baltimore: Johns Hopkins University Press, 1972). My understanding of the ideological and institutional innovations of the New South has been shaped by John

278 ══ **Bibliographical Essay**

Cell's *Highest Stage of White Supremacy: The Origins of Segregation in South Africa and the American South* (New York: Cambridge University Press, 1982), which expands (brilliantly) on the Woodward view of modern southern history by synthesizing its essential elements in ways that Woodward himself never did (a task of synthesis that is roughly equal in difficulty to that taken up by Clayton). Other books mentioned in the notes have had a direct influence, too, but Woodward's and the four others named in this paragraph have pride of place.

Carl Degler's *Other South: Southern Dissenters in the Nineteenth Century* (New York: Harper, 1974) is a very useful history of white southerners who opposed slavery and succeeding racial institutions up to the turn of the twentieth century. Though Degler upholds one Woodward thesis, that the South is full of diversity and conflict, he more directly takes issue with another, that there is a sharp break between the Old South and the New. My argument suggests that the real issue is not the existence of diversity of opinion (for that may exist without undermining political institutions) but the usefulness of that diversity to those who are trying to destroy the system. My view is that diversity of white southern opinion did have some limited usefulness to opponents of slavery — the Confederacy lost some of its solidarity, and toward the end may have lost some of its will to fight, because its commitment to slavery had rifts in it. But by historical standards, that is about as insignificant as diversity ever gets: it took years of all-out war to make it politically consequential. During slavery, it was the slaveholders' success in keeping diversity of opinion to a manageable minimum that determined the outbreak, intensity, and duration of the war. Because of this, my view differs from Degler's implication that diversity in the age of slavery is terribly significant.

I disagree with Degler's view of the South after slavery and Reconstruction, and with his larger argument for continuity between the Old and New Souths, for different reasons. The diversity of white southern opinion in the age of segregation was superficially similar to antebellum diversity in that it did not become very useful to opponents of segregation until they fought the system head-on — that is, in the civil rights movement of the 1950s and 1960s. But at that very point, the discontinuity between the age of slavery and the age of segregation becomes clearest: in the conflict that ended segregation, diversity of southern white opinion proved far more useful than in the conflict that ended slavery. The violence the protesters of the 1950s and 1960s met, however terrible, did not become a civil war because the segregationists, unlike proslavery ideologues, did not have the hegemonic influence (and partly because of that, the determination) to lead the South into all-out war. White southern diversity of opinion was *never* as significant, that is, as Degler (and perhaps even Woodward, at times) would have us believe. But history provides us as sharp a contrast as it ever provides between the civil rights–era diversity and the Civil War–era diversity.

On southern white dissent in the age of segregation itself, my debt is strongest to two thoughtful works that brought me to the threshold of the story told in this book: Morton Sosna's *In Search of the Silent South* (New York: Columbia University Press, 1977) and Anthony Dunbar's *Against the Grain: Southern Radicals and Prophets, 1929–1959* (Charlottesville: University Press of Virginia, 1981). Sosna and Dunbar, whose narratives both end before the movement of the 1950s emerges (though Sosna adds an epilogue about his liberals to show that "they, too, had a dream"), each focus on very different and in many ways conflicting traditions: Sosna on upper-class liberalism, Dunbar on lower-class populism and Christian radicalism. The only thing the two traditions have in common may be their failure, which my account emphasizes much more than theirs.

The social and cultural climate in which these people struggled I came to understand best through Pete Daniel, *Breaking the Land* (Urbana: University of Illinois Press, 1986); Jack Kirby, *Rural Worlds Lost* (Baton Rouge: Louisiana State University Press, 1987); Richard King, *A Southern Renaissance: The Cultural Awakening of the American South, 1930–1955* (New York: Oxford University Press, 1980); Daniel J. Singal, *The War Within: From Victorian to Modernist Thought in the South, 1919–1945* (Chapel Hill: University of North Carolina Press, 1982); and John T. Kneebone, *Southern Liberal Journalists and the Issue of Race, 1920–1944* (Chapel Hill: University of North Carolina Press, 1985).

Several works on white southerners in general deepened my view of their subject. Especially important have been Lewis Killian, *White Southerners* (New York: Random House, 1970); George Tindall, *The Ethnic Southerners* (Baton Rouge: Louisiana State University Press, 1976), and three books by John Shelton Reed, *One South: An Ethnic Approach to Regional Culture* (Baton Rouge: Louisiana State University Press, 1982), *Southerners: The Social Psychology of Sectionalism* (Chapel Hill: University of North Carolina Press, 1983), and *Southern Folk, Plain and Fancy: Native White Social Types* (Athens: University of Georgia Press, 1986). Though these books omit any historical analysis of the effects of the civil rights movement on white southern identity and solidarity, let alone of the roots of the movement's strength among southern white dissenters, Marshall

Frady's *Southerners: A Journalist's Odyssey* (New York: New American Library, 1980) is an exception in that it does contain many instructive insights along both lines, though still not any comprehensive analysis.

On subcategories of white southerners I have been influenced by J. Wayne Flynt, *Dixie's Forgotten People: The South's Poor Whites* (Bloomington: Indiana University Press, 1980); Ann Firor Scott, *The Southern Lady: From Pedestal to Politics, 1830–1930* (Chicago: University of Chicago Press, 1970); Shirley Abbott, *Womenfolks: Growing Up down South* (New Haven: Ticknor and Fields, 1983); and Florence King, *Confessions of a Failed Southern Lady* (New York: St. Martin's, 1985). Along this line an important new work suggests the great extent to which some kinds of white women defined what it meant to be white in the twentieth-century South in terms of their relationship to black women: Susan Tucker, *Telling Memories among Southern Women: Domestic Workers and Their Employers* (Baton Rouge: Louisiana State University Press, 1989).

It will be obvious that the first two chapters of this book, written to provide background for the other seven, rely much more on secondary works than the others. My interpretations differ from the authors named below, but that does not diminish my debt to them. On the figures discussed in chapter 1, I relied especially on Woodward's foreword to his edition of Lewis Blair's *The Prosperity of the South Dependent upon the Elevation of the Negro* (Woodward's edition is entitled *A Southern Prophecy: The Prosperity of the South Dependent upon the Elevation of the Negro;* Boston: Little, Brown, 1964), reprinted as "A Southern Brief for Racial Equality," in Woodward's *American Counterpoint: Slavery and Racism in the North-South Dialogue* (Boston: Little, Brown, 1976), 184–211, and on the previously named works by Gaston, Degler, and Sosna. On Haygood, I also relied on Harold W. Mann, *Atticus Greene Haygood, Methodist Bishop, Editor, and Educator* (Athens: University of Georgia Press, 1965); Joel Williamson, *A Rage for Order* (New York: Oxford University Press, 1986), 73–79; and Stuart Towns, "Atticus G. Haygood: A Neglected Advocate of Reconciliation and a New South," *Southern Studies* 26 (Spring 1987), 28–40. On Blair, I also relied on Charles Wynes, "Lewis H. Blair, Virginia Reformer," *Virginia Magazine of History and Biography* 72 (1964), 3–18; and George Fredrickson, *The Black Image in the White Mind* (Middletown, Conn.: Wesleyan University Press, 1971). On Cable, I relied on Arlin Turner's introduction to his collection of Cable's writings, *The Negro Question* (New York: Doubleday, 1958); Paul Gaston, *New South Creed*, 127, 135–37, 140–41; and Woodward, *Origins of the New South*, 163–64, 429. On

Phillips, I relied on Otto H. Olsen's handy collection on the Plessy decision, *The Thin Disguise: Turning Point in Negro History, Plessy v. Ferguson, A Documentary Presentation, 1864–1896* (New York: Humanities Press, 1967), which contains an excerpt from Phillips' brief for the plaintiff and several other important documents. The full text of the opinion and Harlan's dissent is in 163 U.S. 537–64 (1896). On Harlan, the best work is Linda Carol Adams-Prybyszewski, "The Republic According to John Marshall Harlan: Race, Republicanism, and Citizenship" (Ph.D. diss., Stanford University, 1989), though Louis Filler's biographical piece in the second volume of *The Justices of the Supreme Court, 1789–1969*, 2 vols., ed. Leon Friedman and Fred Israel (New York: Chelsea House, 1969), 2:1281–95, and Alan F. Westin, "John Marshall Harlan and the Constitutional Rights of Negroes: The Transformation of a Southerner," *Yale Law Journal* 66 (1957), 637–710, were both enormously useful.

For the figures in chapter 2, Sosna was the single most important work. On Andrew Sledd and John Spencer Bassett, I also relied on Charles F. Smith, "Professor Sledd and Emory College," *Nation* 125 (1902), 245–46, Henry Y. Warnock, "Andrew Sledd, Southern Methodists, and the Negro: A Case History," *Journal of Southern History* 31 (Aug. 1965), 251–71; Virginius Dabney, *Liberalism in the South* (Chapel Hill: University of North Carolina Press, 1932), 338–41; Charles Wynes, ed., *Forgotten Voices: Dissenting Southerners in an Age of Conformity* (Baton Rouge: Louisiana State University Press, 1967), 89–90; and Bruce Clayton, *Savage Ideal*, 77–84. On the attempts to organize southern white dissent early in the twentieth century, in addition to Sosna I relied especially on John J. Culley, "Muted Trumpets: Four Efforts to Better Southern Race Relations, 1900–1919" (Ph.D. diss., University of Virginia, 1967); three works by Edgar Gardner Murphy, *The White Man and the Negro at the South* (n.p., 1900), "The Montgomery Race Conference," *Century* 40 (1900), 630–32, and *The Basis of Ascendancy: A Discussion of Certain Principles of Public Policy Involved in the Development of the Southern States* (New York: Longman's, 1910); and Hugh C. Bailey's biography, *Edgar Gardner Murphy: Gentle Progressive* (Coral Gables, Fla.: University of Miami Press, 1968). Also important were Sheldon Hackney, *From Populism to Progressivism in Alabama* (Princeton, N.J.: Princeton University Press, 1969); Jack Kirby, *Darkness at the Dawning: Race and Reform in the Progressive South* (Philadelphia: Lippincott, 1972), and Dewey Grantham, "The Contours of Southern Progressivism," *American Historical Review* 86 (Dec. 1981), 1035–59.

On the SCHW, its journal, *Southern Patriot,* is the best single source. Wilma Dykeman and James Stokely provide important background on the organization in *Seeds of Southern Change: The Life of Will Alexander* (1962; reprint, New York: Norton, 1976), and Thomas Krueger gives a complete history in *And Promises to Keep: The Southern Conference for Human Welfare, 1938–1948* (Nashville: Vanderbilt University Press, 1967). On the SCEF, Irwin Kilbaner, "The Southern Conference Educational Fund: A History" (Ph.D. diss., University of Wisconsin, 1971), is an important work, as is Linda Reed, *Simple Decency and Common Sense: The Southern Conference Movement, 1938–1963* (Bloomington: Indiana University Press, 1991), which also covers the SCEF's parent organization. On the SRC, its papers, in the Woodruff Library at Atlanta University and on microfilm in many libraries, and its journal, *New South* (which supersedes the CIC's *Southern Frontier*) are the best sources, but also indispensable are J. Saunders Redding, "Southern Defensive—I," and Lillian Smith, "Southern Defensive—II," both attacking the SRC, in *Common Ground* 4 (Spring 1944), 36–45, and Guy B. Johnson (SRC executive director), "Southern Offensive," defending the SRC, in *Common Ground* 4 (Summer 1944), 87–93. Secondary works on the organization are (again in addition to Sosna) William C. Allred, Jr., "The Southern Regional Council, 1943–1961" (M.A. thesis, Emory University, 1966), and Anthony Newberry, "Without Urgency or Ardor: The South's Middle Road Liberals and Civil Rights, 1945–1960" (Ph.D. diss., Ohio University, 1982).

Memoirs, autobiographies, and firsthand accounts by white southerners who participated in or supported the movement include the following. Some of the works listed—such as those by Ashmore, Dunbar, and Watters—are contemporary meditations on politics and society rather than memoirs in the strict sense, but since they contain much in the way of first-person remembrances, they are included here: Frank Adams with Myles Horton, *Unearthing Seeds of Fire: The Idea of Highlander* (Winston-Salem, N.C.: J. F. Blair, 1975); Harry S. Ashmore, *Hearts and Minds: The Anatomy of Racism from Roosevelt to Reagan* (New York: McGraw-Hill, 1982); Russell H. Barrett, *Integration at Ole Miss* (Chicago: Quadrangle, 1965); Wendell Berry, *The Hidden Wound* (Boston: Houghton Mifflin, 1970); Virgil T. Blossom, *It HAS Happened Here* (New York: Harper, 1959); Sarah Patton Boyle, *The Desegregated Heart* (New York: Morrow, 1962); Anne Braden, *The Wall Between* (New York: Monthly Review, 1958); Will Campbell, *Brother to a Dragonfly* (New York: Continuum, 1977); Will Campbell, *Forty Acres and a Goat* (1986; reprint, New York: Harper, 1988); James McBride

Dabbs, *The Road Home* (Philadelphia: Christian Education Press, 1960); James McBride Dabbs, *The Southern Heritage* (New York: Knopf, 1958); Leslie Dunbar, *A Republic of Equals* (Ann Arbor: University of Michigan Press, 1966); Virginia Durr, *Outside the Magic Circle: The Autobiography of Virginia Foster Durr,* ed. Hollinger F. Barnard (1985; reprint, New York: Simon and Schuster, 1987); P. D. East, *The Magnolia Jungle* (New York: Simon and Schuster, 1960); John Howard Griffin, *Black like Me* (New York: Houghton Mifflin, 1960); Brooks Hays, *A Southern Moderate Speaks* (Chapel Hill: University of North Carolina Press, 1959); Brooks Hays, *Politics Is My Parish* (Baton Rouge: Louisiana State University Press, 1981); Clarence Jordan, *Cotton Patch Evidence* (Koinonia, Ga.: Koinonia Farm, n.d.); Mary King, *Freedom Song: A Personal Story of the 1960s Civil Rights Movement* (New York: Morrow, 1987); Katherine DuPre Lumpkin, *The Making of a Southerner* (1946; reprint, Athens: University of Georgia Press, 1984); Florence Mars, *Witness in Philadelphia* (Baton Rouge: Louisiana State University Press, 1977); Ralph McGill, *The South and the Southerner* (Boston: Little, Brown, 1963); Melton McLaurin, *Separate Pasts: Growing Up White in the Segregated South* (Athens: University of Georgia Press, 1987); Thomas Merton, *Seeds of Destruction* (New York: Farrar, Straus, and Giroux, 1964); Charles Morgan, *A Time to Speak* (New York: Harper, 1966); Claude Pepper with Hays Gorey, *Pepper: Eyewitness to a Century* (New York: Harcourt Brace, 1987); Junius Scales, *Cause at Heart: A Former Communist Remembers* (Athens: University of Georgia Press, 1987); Frank Smith, *Congressman from Mississippi* (New York: Pantheon, 1964); Robert Penn Warren, *Segregation* (New York: Random House, 1956); Pat Watters, *Down to Now: Reflections on the Southern Civil Rights Movement* (New York: Pantheon, 1971).

There is an equally large number of firsthand accounts, memoirs, and autobiographies by black veterans of the movement which contain reflections on the significance of the white southerners. These include Maya Angelou, *The Heart of a Woman* (New York: Random House, 1981); Maya Angelou, *All God's Children Need Traveling Shoes* (New York: Random House, 1986); Daisy Bates, *The Long Shadow of Little Rock: A Memoir* (New York: David McKay, 1962); Julian Bond, *A Time to Speak, a Time to Act: The Movement in Politics* (New York: Simon and Schuster, 1972); Amelia Platts Boynton, *Bridge across Jordan* (New York: Carlton, 1979); Stokely Carmichael and Charles V. Hamilton, *Black Power: The Politics of Liberation in America* (New York: Vintage, 1967); Septima Clark, with Le Gette Blythe, *Echo in My Soul* (New York: Dutton, 1962); Septima

Clark, *Ready from Within: Septima Clark and the Civil Rights Movement*, ed. Cynthia S. Brown (Navarro, Calif.: Wild Tree Press, 1986); Mrs. Medgar [Myrlie] Evers, with William Peters, *For Us, the Living* (Garden City, N.Y.: Doubleday, 1967); James Farmer, *Lay Bare the Heart: An Autobiography of the Civil Rights Movement* (New York: Plume, 1985); James Forman, *The Making of Black Revolutionaries* (Washington, D.C.: Open Hand, 1985); Dick Gregory, with Robert Lipsyte, *Nigger: An Autobiography* (New York: Dutton, 1964); Fannie Lou Hamer et al., *To Praise Our Bridges: An Autobiography* (Jackson, Miss.: KIPCO, 1967); Len Holt, *The Summer That Didn't End* (London: Heinemann, 1966); Julius Lester, *All Is Well* (New York: Morrow, 1976); Coretta Scott King, *My Life with Martin Luther King, Jr.* (New York: Holt, Rinehart, and Winston, 1969); Martin Luther King, Jr., *Stride toward Freedom* (New York: Harper, 1958); Martin Luther King, Jr., *Why We Can't Wait* (New York: New American Library, 1963); Martin Luther King, Jr., *Where Do We Go from Here: Chaos or Community?* (Boston: Beacon, 1967); Martin Luther King, Sr., *Daddy King: An Autobiography* (New York: Morrow, 1980); Benjamin Mays, *Born to Rebel* (New York: Scribner's, 1971); James Meredith, *Three Years in Mississippi* (Bloomington: Indiana University Press, 1966); Anne Moody, *Coming of Age in Mississippi* (New York: Dell, 1968); Jo Ann Gibson Robinson, *The Montgomery Bus Boycott and the Women Who Started It: The Memoir of Jo Ann Gibson Robinson*, ed. David J. Garrow (Knoxville: University of Tennessee Press, 1987); Cleveland Sellers, with Robert Terrell, *The River of No Return: The Autobiography of a Black Militant and the Life and Death of SNCC* (New York: Morrow, 1973); Sheyann Webb and Rachel West Nelson, with Frank Sikora, *Selma, Lord, Selma: Girlhood Memories of the Civil-Rights Days* (University, Ala.: University of Alabama Press, 1980); Roger Wilkins, *A Man's Life* (New York: Simon and Schuster, 1982); Roy Wilkins, *Standing Fast: The Autobiography of Roy Wilkins* (New York: Viking, 1982); Malcolm X, *The Autobiography of Malcolm X* (New York: Ballantine, 1964).

A number of excellent biographies were useful to fill in the background on the white southerners who in one way or another challenged the South's racial system. The works of John Salmond have been especially important in this regard. See Salmond, *A Southern Rebel: Life and Times of Aubrey Willis Williams* (Chapel Hill: University of North Carolina Press, 1983), *Miss Lucy of the CIO* (Athens: University of Georgia Press, 1988), and *Conscience of a Lawyer: Clifford Durr and American Civil Liberties* (Tuscaloosa: University of Alabama Press, 1990).

Jurists form a special category in the history of southern white dissent. Jack Bass, J. W. Peltason, and others have shown that there were a goodly number of southern judges willing to rule in favor of black plaintiffs and suffer the consequences. See Bass, *Unlikely Heroes* (New York: Simon and Schuster, 1981); Peltason, *Fifty-eight Lonely Men: Southern Federal Judges and School Desegregation*, 2d ed. (Urbana: University of Illinois Press, 1971); Virginia V. Hamilton, *Hugo Black: The Alabama Years* (Baton Rouge: Louisiana State University Press, 1972); Robert Kennedy, Jr., *Judge Frank Johnson: A Biography* (New York: Putnam, 1976); Arthur S. Miller, *A "Capacity for Outrage": The Judicial Odyssey of J. Skelly Wright* (Westport, Conn.: Greenwood, 1984); and Tinsley Yarbrough, *Judge Frank Johnson and Human Rights in Alabama* (University, Ala.: University of Alabama Press, 1981), *A Passion for Justice: J. Waites Waring and Civil Rights* (New York: Oxford University Press, 1987), and *Mr. Justice Black and His Critics* (Durham, N.C.: Duke University Press, 1988).

Part Two

On the Alabama politics that form the background for the Montgomery struggle, see Sheldon Hackney, *From Populism to Progressivism in Alabama;* William D. Barnard, *Dixiecrats and Democrats: Alabama Politics, 1942–1950* (University, Ala.: University of Alabama Press, 1974); and Virginia V. Hamilton, *Lister Hill: Statesman from the South* (Chapel Hill: University of North Carolina Press, 1987). On Governor Folsom, see W. Bradley Twitty, *Y'all Come* (Nashville: Hermitage, 1962); Thomas Gilliam, "The Second Folsom Administration: The Destruction of Alabama Liberalism" (Ph.D. diss., Auburn University, 1975); Carl Grafton and Anne Permaloff, *Big Mules and Branchheads: James E. Folsom and Political Power in Alabama* (Athens: University of Georgia Press, 1985); and Earl Black, *Southern Governors and Civil Rights* (Cambridge: Harvard University Press, 1976); esp. 52, 189, 296.

The literature on Montgomery is vast. David Garrow's tireless work as an author and editor has eased and improved the work of all students of the civil rights movement, and especially of the Montgomery struggle. His biography of King, *Bearing the Cross* (New York: Morrow, 1986), is so thorough in its narrative of Montgomery and in its bibliography as to make further citation here redundant. *The Walking City: The Montgomery Bus Boycott, 1955–1956* (Brooklyn: Carlson, 1989), Garrow's unselfish collection of other important works, many of them difficult to track down or even learn about before he rescued them from out-of-print lists or brought them to light for the first time, is rich in evidence and perspective. The King papers in Atlanta and Boston, and parts of related collections at the King Center in Atlanta, now being published under Clayborne Carson's skilled and patient editorship by the University of California Press, will soon provide the best single collection of sources on the movement. Until then, students will have to travel to Atlanta to examine the papers firsthand.

On Tallahassee, Aldon Morris's analytic account, in *Origins of the Civil Rights Movement: Black Communities Organizing for Change* (New York: Free Press, 1984), is the most thorough and incisive one in published form. Gregory Padgett and Glenda Rabby have covered the local newspaper sources so thoroughly as to make their works the best place to start, and perhaps finish, more extensive research: Padgett, "C. K. Steele and the Tallahassee Bus Protest" (M.A. thesis, Florida State University, 1977), and Rabby, "Out of the Past: The Civil Rights Movement in Tallahassee, Florida" (Ph.D. diss., Florida State University, 1984). Jackson Ice's interviews with many of the participants in the boycott, local officials, and other eyewitnesses constitute the best single source available on the Tallahassee movement. The papers of the Florida Council on Human Relations (in the Southern Regional Council Papers, available on microfilm or at the Woodruff Library, Atlanta University) are very thin on Tallahassee but in some instances indispensable.

For background on Tallahassee, see the new biography by Tom Wagy, *Governor LeRoy Collins: Spokesman of the New South* (University, Ala.: University of Alabama Press, 1985), and Julia Sullivan Chapman's excellent thesis, "A Southern Moderate Advocates Compliance: LeRoy Collins and the Community Relations Service" (M.A. thesis, University of South Florida, Tampa, 1974).

Sources on Little Rock include an unusually large number of published memoirs: by the head of the local NAACP and principal organizer of the desegregation effort, Daisy Bates, *The Long Shadow of Little Rock;* by the superintendent of schools who was author of the desegregation plan implemented at Central High in 1957, Virgil Blossom, *It HAS Happened Here;* by the vice principal for girls of Central High, Elizabeth Huckaby, *Crisis at Central High: Little Rock, 1957–1958* (Baton Rouge: Louisiana State University Press, 1980); by a local white clergyman, Robert R. Brown, *Bigger than Little Rock* (Greenwich, Conn.: Seabury, 1958); and by a former white student at Central, who supplemented his recollections with such a considerable amount of scholarly research that his book almost ceases to qualify as an eyewitness account, Irvin Spitzberg, *Racial Politics in Little Rock, 1954–1964* (New York: Garland, 1987). The congressman from Arkansas's Fifth District (which includes Little Rock) at the time of the crisis has also provided, within the course of two memoirs that span years before and beyond the crisis at Central, his version of several important events that shaped the outcome there: Brooks Hays, *A Southern Moderate Speaks* and *Politics Is My Parish.* The editor of the *Arkansas Gazette* has also left behind a memoir that stretches to include events outside Little Rock and beyond the time of the crisis, most of which did not involve the author himself, but he also provides inside information and insight into events to which he was one of the most thoughtful witnesses: Harry Ashmore, *Hearts and Minds.* All of the above are written, with varying degrees of subjectivity, in favor of desegregation, though Hays nonetheless has some sympathy for Faubus.

On the other side of the Little Rock struggle, a leading segregationist crusader (who defeated Brooks Hays for Congress in a write-in campaign in 1958) has left his memoir, too: Dale Alford, *The Case of the Sleeping People* (Little Rock: n.p., 1959). Last but not least, the famous governor himself has contributed a sprawling, two-volume account, which contains not only his justifications for his course of action in 1957–59 but also an extremely large sampling of contemporary newspaper accounts, political cartoons, and other fragments not of his own creation, which by no means always show him in a favorable light, along with his corrective commentary: Orval Faubus, *Down from the Hills* and *Down from the Hills, Two* (Little Rock: Democrat Printing and Lithograph, 1986). The forthcoming biography of Faubus, by the incisive and insightful correspondent Roy Reed of the *Arkansas Gazette* and then the *New York Times,* promises to be illuminating on this enigmatic character.

Finally, some insight into the crucial role of the federal government at Little Rock can be glimpsed from the memoirs of the president and his closest adviser on Little Rock, each of which devote a chapter to the crisis: Dwight Eisenhower, *The White House Years: Waging Peace, 1956–1961* (Garden City, N.Y.: Doubleday, 1965), and Sherman Adams, *Firsthand Report: The Story of the Eisenhower Administration* (New York: Harper, 1961). Stephen Ambrose's exhaustive and balanced biography, *Eisenhower: The President* (New York: Simon and Schuster, 1985), seemed to make a trip to the Eisenhower Library (at Abilene, Kansas) unnecessary for purposes of this book, but his notes make clear there is much of interest there on Little Rock, and they would form a useful guide to it.

Faubus and Daisy Bates have both left very useful interviews on file at the Southern Oral History Project at the University of North Carolina at Chapel Hill, and Faubus has left additional ones at the Columbia University Oral History Project and the John F. Kennedy Library, though the latter of these has not yet been opened. Ashmore's favorite editorials on the crisis have been collected together under the title *Crisis in the South* (Little Rock: n.p., 1959). The papers of Bates, Faubus, and other participants (not used for this study) are in the University of Arkansas library, at Fayetteville.

A magnificent collection of documentary materials is also available and constitutes the best introduction to the subject: Jane Record and Wilson Record, *Little Rock, U.S.A.: Materials for Analysis* (San Francisco: Chandler, 1960). This may be supplemented with the interview transcripts contained in *Voices of Freedom: An Oral History of the Civil Rights Movement from the 1950s through the 1980s*, ed. Henry Hampton and Steve Fayer (New York: Bantam, 1990), and the papers of the Arkansas Council on Human Relations, in the SRC Papers in Atlanta.

Sources on the movement in Albany include Howard Zinn's pamphlet *Albany: A Study in National Responsibility* (Atlanta: Southern Regional Council, 1962); Martin Luther King, Jr., "The Case against Tokenism," *New York Times Magazine*, Aug. 5, 1962, reprinted in *Portrait of a Decade*, ed. Anthony Lewis (New York: Random House, 1964); and Vincent Harding and Staughton Lynd, "Albany, Georgia," *Crisis* 70 (Feb. 1963), 69–78. Pat Watters, who covered the Albany movement for the *Atlanta Journal*, has collected his reminiscences on Albany and much else of great value and insight in *Down to Now: Reflections on the Southern Civil Rights Movement*. An excellent secondary work that takes in a comprehensive series of interviews is John Ricks, " 'De Lawd' Descends and Is Crucified: Martin Luther King, Jr., in Albany, Georgia," *Southwest Georgia Historical Quarterly* 2 (Fall 1984), 4–14, reprinted in *We Shall Overcome*, vol. 3, ed. David Garrow (Brooklyn: Carlson, 1989).

These should be supplemented with the interview transcripts of Laurie Pritchett, Ed Gardner, and Andrew Young in *My Soul Is Rested*, ed. Howell Raines (New York: Putnam, 1977). The far more extensive "oral histories" of Pritchett and Charles Jones at the Southern Oral History Project at the University of North Carolina at Chapel Hill, and of C. B. King, Marion Page, and Vincent Harding at the Civil Rights Documentation Project at Howard University, are indispensable. The papers of two principals of the movement in Albany, Slater King and Charles Sherrod, are housed at the Martin Luther King Center in Atlanta, but the State Historical Society of Wisconsin at Madison also has collections of Slater King and Charles Sherrod papers. Other important records are in the Student Nonviolent Coordinating Committee Papers (available on microfilm), the Albany City Records division in Albany, and the Howard Zinn Papers at Boston University.

Part Three

On the division of the Democratic party, so central to the framework of part three: James McGregor Burns, *Deadlock of Democracy: Four-Party Politics in America* (Englewood Cliffs, N.J.: Prentice-Hall, 1963); Joseph Clark, *Congress: The Sapless Branch* (New York: Harper, 1964); Herbert Parmet, *The Democrats: The Years after FDR* (New York: Macmillan, 1976); David B. Truman, *The Congressional Party: A Case Study* (New York: Wiley, 1959); and Barbara Sinclair, "From Party Voting to Regional Fragmentation," *American Politics Quarterly* 6 (1978), 125–46.

No adequate treatment of the Democratic Advisory Council exists. My interpretation was based on the Democratic National Committee Annual Report for 1957 by Paul Butler, Washington, D.C., Feb. 21, 1958, p. 21; Transcript of DNC Executive Committee meeting, Washington, D.C., Nov. 26–27, 1956, pp. 186–239; and other documents cited above in boxes 119–22 of the DNC Papers for 1953–60, in the JFKL; the "Oral History" of Camille Gravel, Democratic Committeeman from Louisiana and active participant in the DAC, JFKL; Allen Drury, "Two Different Voices Speak for Democrats," *New York Times*, Feb. 8, 1958; Kenneth S. Davis, *The Politics of Honor: A Biography of Adlai E. Stevenson* (New York: Putnam, 1957), 356–57, 364–70, 377, 382–87, 423; Arthur M. Schlesinger, Jr., *A Thousand Days* (Boston: Houghton Mifflin, 1965), 18, 280; and George C. Roberts, *Paul M. Butler: Hoosier Politician and National Political Leader* (Lanham, Md.: University Press of America, 1987), esp. 106ff. The papers of Paul Butler, chairman of both the DNC and DAC, on which Roberts' book is based, have not been consulted for the present study. They are in the Notre Dame University Library. The papers of Charles Tyroler II, who served as executive director of the DAC staff, are in the JFKL but have not yet been opened.

On the equally important Democratic Policy Committee, I relied first of all on Harry McPherson, close friend of LBJ's and staff member of the DPC from 1956 to 1963, who described the DPC as preoccupied with party unity. See especially McPherson OH, LBJL, interview I, tape 2, p. 2, and interview I, tape 1, pp. 5, 10, 12, and McPherson, *A Political Education* (Boston: Houghton Mifflin, 1988). Other sources on the role of the DPC are LBJ to Mrs. A. A. Luckenbach, Jan. 20, 1958; Jim Wilson to LBJ, Jan. 8, 1960; Reedy to LBJ, n.d. [ca. Feb. 1960]; Reedy to LBJ, Jan. 11, 1960; and Staff Memorandum, Senate Democratic Policy Committee, "Legislative History and Composition of the Democratic Policy Committee," Jan. 8, 1960, all in "Senate, U.S., Committees, Policy and Democratic Conference," LBJA Subject Files, box 116, LBJL.

On LBJ, I found Robert Dallek's thorough, temperate, and consistent *Lone Star Rising* (New York: Oxford University Press, 1991) to be the single most useful biography, though on Johnson's congressional wheeling and dealing, Rowland Evans and Robert Novak's observations in *Lyndon B. Johnson: The Exercise of Power* (New York: New American Library, 1966) are almost as revealing as LBJ's own papers are.

On the politics of civil rights, especially in Congress, Steven Lawson, *Black Ballots: Voting Rights in the South, 1944–1969* (New York: Columbia University Press, 1976), was indispensable.

One of the pleasures of research for this book was discovering the great body of literature on southern politics, most of it by political scientists and journalists, which is essential to understanding the history of the civil rights movement. Pride of place goes to V. O. Key's magisterial *Southern Politics in State and Nation* (New York: Knopf, 1949), but my views were just as strongly influenced by one book that predates Key's, Paul Lewinson, *Race, Class, and Party: A History of Negro Suffrage and White Politics in the South* (New York: Oxford University Press, 1932), and by three later ones that provide historical background: Michael Perman, *The Road to Redemption: Southern Politics, 1869–1879* (Chapel Hill: University of North Carolina Press, 1984); J. Morgan Kousser, *The Shaping of Southern Politics: Suffrage Restriction and the Establishment of the One-Party South, 1880–1910* (New Haven: Yale University Press, 1974); and Nancy Weiss, *Farewell to the Party of Lincoln: Black Politics in the Age of F.D.R.* (Princeton, N.J.: Princeton University Press, 1983).

Jack Bass and Walter DeVries updated Key's work in what was the single most important work on the politics of the period covered in this book, *The Transformation of Southern Politics: Social Change and Political Consequences since 1945* (New York: Basic, 1976). Also indispensable were Henry Lee Moon, *The Balance of Power: The Negro Vote* (Garden City, N.Y.: Doubleday, 1948); Alexander Heard, *A Two-Party South?* (Chapel Hill: University of North Carolina Press, 1952); Numan Bartley and Hugh Graham, *Southern Politics and the Second Reconstruction* (Baltimore: Johns Hopkins University Press, 1975); and Earl Black, *Southern Governors and Civil Rights* (Cambridge: Harvard University Press, 1976).

Important to my interpretations of the Kennedy administration were two books: Carl Brauer, *John F. Kennedy and the Second Reconstruction* (New York: Columbia University Press, 1977), generally charitable (though not uncritical) in his view of Kennedy, and Victor Navasky, *Kennedy Justice* (New York: Atheneum, 1979), generally critical (though not uncharitable).

Epilogue

The ruminations on aging paternalism expressed in the Epilogue are my own, though obviously influenced by Eugene D. Genovese's work on slavery. Genovese contends that paternalist social relations could not be sustained in the capitalist society that supplanted slave society, a view I accept as axiomatic. Still, it makes sense that paternalism should take a full century to give up the ghost, especially when capitalism had as long and unhealthy a gestation period as it did in the American South. Genovese's masterpiece (so far), *Roll, Jordan, Roll* (New York: Random House, 1976), directed me to Earle Thorpe's *Eros and Freedom in Southern Life and Thought* (Durham, N.C.: Harrington, 1967), which contains the germ of the idea that the South's paternalism could grow into a more mature, balanced relationship. Ernest Gaines' allegorical novel, *A Gathering of Old Men* (New York: Knopf, 1983), suggests the same transformation, with full attention to the estrangement and embarrassment it had to entail.

My thoughts on just war doctrine were informed by Francisco Suarez, *On the Three Theological Virtues: On Charity* (1612), ed. James B. Scott (Oxford: Clarendon, 1944); Hugo Grotius, *The Law of War and Peace* (1625), trans. Francis Kelsey (Indianapolis: Bobbs-Merrill, 1925); Robert W. Tucker et al., *Just War and Vatican Council II: A Critique* (New York: Council on Religion and International Affairs, 1966); James Turner Johnson, *Just War Tradition and the Restraint of War: A Moral and Historical Inquiry* (Princeton, N.J.: Princeton University Press, 1981); Paul Ramsey, *The Just War: Force and Political Responsibility* (Lanham, Md.: University Press of America, 1983); Robert L. Holmes, *On War and Morality* (Princeton, N.J.: Princeton University Press, 1989); and especially Michael Walzer's lucid and penetrating *Just and Unjust Wars: A Moral Argument with Historical Illustrations* (New York: Basic, 1977). The relationship of the just war tradition to the tradition of nonviolent resistance, both of which grow

— uneasily — out of medieval Christian conceptions of natural law, came to light by comparing Suarez and Grotius to one of the founding fathers of nonviolent resistance: Étienne de la Boètie, *Discours de la servitude volontaire* (1548), translated in 1942 as *Anti-Dictator*, in *The Quiet Battle: Writings on the Theory and Practice of Non-violent Resistance*, ed. Mulford Q. Sibley (Boston: Beacon, 1969). Equally important was the relationship of twentieth-century Christian "realism" to both just war doctrine and nonviolent resistance. In the works of the so-called realists, I found strong affinities with (one might say concessions to) just war doctrine, especially in Hans Morgenthau's *Politics among Nations* (New York: Knopf, 1949) and *In Defense of the National Interest* (New York: Knopf, 1951). As I read it, the theory of nonviolent resistance that Gandhi and King developed has more in common with the "realist" school than with the Wilsonian "idealist" school that the realists (and implicitly, Gandhi and King) reject as naive and sentimental. The roots of this relationship are explicit in Reinhold Niebuhr, *Moral Man and Immoral Society* (New York: Scribner's, 1932), which both King and the realists cite as a formative influence.

There are too many important books on the civil rights movement in general to mention here. The ones that have left the most lasting impression on my own interpretation break down as follows. Frances Fox Piven and Richard Cloward, in *Poor People's Movements: How They Succeed, Why they Fail* (New York: Random House, 1978), attempt an explanation of the civil rights movement and its success, one that influenced especially part three of my book. They argue that economic and demographic changes led to party instability, which created the opportunity for the civil rights protesters to advance their cause. Aldon Morris, in *Origins of the Civil Rights Movement* (New York: Free Press, 1984), rightly takes Piven and Cloward to task for not putting at the center of their analysis the southern black communities from which the movement sprang, though I think he exaggerates Piven and Cloward's belief in the "spontaneity" of the movement, on which their conclusions do not entirely depend. Morris has had the greatest influence on part two of my study, and in many ways my book is an amendment to his: the black communities of the South are (as he shows) the central part of the story, but the white communities of the South are central to *their* consciousness, aspirations, and strategy. Still they are not the whole story, and therefore Piven and Cloward's approach is necessary to explain, if not the origins of the movement, its success and the timing of its success in national politics. Doug McAdam attempts a synthesis of the Morris view with the Piven and Cloward view in his *Political Process and the Development of Black Insurgency, 1930–1970* (Chicago: University of Chicago Press, 1985), and I try to follow his example by stressing that both the local and (especially after 1963, when Morris's narrative ends) the national trends are crucial components of the movement's history.

For historical background on the movement, many scattered studies and biographies suggest many interpretations. Richard Kluger's *Simple Justice* (New York: Knopf, 1975) provided a coherent thread of legal developments, as well as a gripping narrative through decades of detail. This made all the other scattered trends easier to organize — perhaps deceptively so, but there is always that danger.

David Garrow's already mentioned biography of King is the one book on the civil rights movement to be stuck with on a desert island. Since King's life touched every aspect of the civil rights movement, and since the reach of Garrow's research is as broad as King's life, I have found it useful at every stage, not least for its incomparable bibliography. It should be supplemented with Morris's book, which calls attention to important episodes of the movement in which King was not involved, and for similar reasons with Clayborne Carson, *In Struggle: SNCC and the Black Awakening of the 1960s* (Cambridge: Harvard University Press, 1981), a complete and coherent history of an organization whose records are neither. Carson's work as editor of the King Papers (which will be a documentary record of the whole movement, far beyond King's own papers), will ensure that they become the best single source on the movement. So far, only the first volume is out, from the University of California Press.

Taylor Branch's first volume of *America in the King Years (Parting the Waters)* is a comprehensive history that takes King as the central figure of the age, something very different from Garrow's biography. If the second volume, to cover the more difficult (from a historian's point of view) years after 1963, is as good as the first, we will finally have a history of the civil rights movement to rank with the great histories of the Civil War. It is already an impressive literary as well as scholarly achievement, and it may outlive other works mentioned for that reason.

INDEX

The reader is directed to the Notes and Bibliographical Essay for references to many names that do not appear in the index.

Marshall, Burke, 191–92, 196, 197, 199, 201, 207, 273–74n. 37; on need to use force, 204
Marshall, Thurgood, 172
Martin, Louis, 178
Martinet, Louis A., 19
Mason, Lucy Randolph, xii, 43
Matthews, Sheriff Zeke, 134–35
Maverick, Senator Maury, 44
McAdam, Doug, 293
McClellan, Senator John, 98, 172
McCullom, Sally, 257n. 4
McLeod, Mrs. Frances P., 65–66, 244n. 51
McMath, Governor Sid, 97, 99, 110
McPherson, Harry, LBJ aide, 155–56, 164, 176, 290
means. See ends and means
media. See press
Men of Montgomery, 74–75, 78, 81
Miller, Judge John E., 102
Mills, Congressman Wilbur, 149
Minor, Bill, xii
Mitchell, Clarence, 155
Mitchell, H. L., xii
moderation, changing definition of, 189, 214
Montgomery Advertiser, 65–66, 75, 76–77, 161, 243nn. 43 and 45
Montgomery Conference, 32–34
Montgomery Improvement Association (MIA), 56, 58, 67–68, 75–77, 218
moral suasion. See force and suasion
morality and politics, relationship between, xvii, xx–xxi, xxii–xxiii, 48, 49, 212–13, 220, 224–25, 227. See also force and suasion
Morgan, Charles, xii, 193, 271n. 13
Morris, Aldon D., 58, 216, 221–22, 257n. 9, 286, 292–93
Mothers' League of Central High, 103, 104
Murphy, Edgar Gardner, 33, 213
Muse, Benjamin, 192–94, 199, 200
Muste, A. J., 58, 59

NAACP Legal Defense Fund, 202
National Association for the Advancement of Colored People (NAACP), 23, 96, 234n. 40; campaign against lynching, 37, 40–41, 234n. 22; in Montgomery, 54, 56; national leaders of, on Montgomery, 64;

in Tallahassee, 84; in Little Rock, 106; and JFK, 268n. 43
National Emergency Council, "Number One Economic Problem" report, 44
national state. See federal government, role of
Navasky, Victor, 196, 269n. 1, 291
Nazi party, American, 127
neo-Populist disenters, 47–48
Nice, Charlie, 193
Niebuhr, Reinhold, 47, 55, 231n. 2, 292
Nitze, Paul, 150
Nixon, E. D., 54, 57, 62; house bombed, 79
Nixon, Richard M., xxiii, 177
northerners, white. See white northerners
Novak, Robert, 262n. 22, 290

Oberdorfer, Lou, 196, 198–203, 204–5, 206–7, 271n. 15, 272n.25
Odum, Howard, 49
Ogden, David, 108, 119–20
Ogden, Dunbar, 108, 119–20
Ovington, Mary White, 23

Padgett, Gregory, 286
Page, Marion, 138, 141, 219, 221, 288–89
Parks, Frank, 70
Parks, Rosa, 54–56, 62–63, 68, 69
party division. See Democratic unity, efforts to restore
paternalism, 11, 33, 34, 48, 217, 227, 291
Patrick, Congressman Luther, 44
Patterson, Governor John, 172, 197
Pauley, Mrs. Frances, 122
Peltason, J. W., 254n. 37, 285
Pepper, Senator Claude, 44, 45, 86
Percy, Walker, xii
peripheral South. See Deep South–peripheral South division
Perman, Michael, 290
Phillips, Samuel Field, 19–20
Pierce, J. E., 57
Piven, Frances Fox, 292–93
"Plans for Progress," 184–85, 208
Plessy, Homer Adolph, 19
Plessy v. Ferguson (1896), 18–22, 25
politics, repudiation of. See civil rights issue, depoliticization of; repudiation of politics

poll tax, 157; campaign to repeal, 44–45, 53
Potts, Police Chief Marvin, 105
Powell, Congressman Adam Clayton, 155, 173
President's Committee on Equal Employment Opportunity (PCEEO). *See* "Plans
for Progress"
press, local, 114, 198, 207. *See also Albany
Herald; Arkansas Democrat; Arkansas
Gazette; Montgomery Advertiser; Tallahassee Democrat and under other locations*
press, national: segregationists' relations
with, 80–81, 114; in Albany, 128, 129–34,
136, 138–39, 141, 219–20, 259n. 33; and
LBJ, 161; and JFK, 183
Pritchett, Police Chief Laurie, 124–43,
218–23, 257nn. 10 and 14
progress, idea of, 3, 11, 18, 23, 36, 48; and
repudiation of politics, 25, 28; in interpretations of civil rights movement, 131, 225;
in Kennedy administration's strategy,
199, 202

Rabby, Glenda, 87, 88, 286
racism, xviii, xxi, 3, 17, 42, 76, 107, 142,
210–11, 223, 226, 227, 233n. 30, 237n. 35
Raines, Howell, xii
Rains, Craig, 114–15
Raleigh News and Observer, 30
Ramsey, Brooks, 123
Randolph, A. Philip, 59
Rankin, Robert, 163, 164–68, 169, 176, 197
Raper, Arthur, 39–40, 236nn. 28 and 30
Rayburn, Congressman Sam, 150
Reagon, Bernice, quoted, 221, 222
Reagon, Cordell, 122
realism and idealism, xxiii, 215, 227, 292
red-baiting, 41, 54, 237nn. 35 and 44
Reed, John Shelton, 236n. 30, 279
Reed, Judge Murray O., 105
Reed, Roy, xii, 287
Reedy, George, DPC staff director and LBJ
aide, 156–58; discovers need for white
southern acceptance of civil rights,
161–62; efforts to end civil rights con-
flicts, 169–70, 262n. 22
removal of civil rights from elective politics.
See civil rights issue, depoliticization of

repudiation of politics, in New South ideol-
ogy, 25. *See also* civil rights issue, depoli-
ticization of
Ricks, John A., 257n. 6, 288; quoted, 123
Robinson, Jo Ann Gibson, 54, 68
Rockefeller, Winthrop, 99, 106
Roosevelt, Eleanor, 43
Roosevelt, Franklin D., 43–45
Rowan, Carl, 76
Rowe, James, LBJ adviser, 154
Royall, Kenneth C., 204
Russell, Senator Richard, 153, 158, 159, 183,
266n. 10
Rustin, Bayard, 59
Rutledge, Mrs. I. B., 66, 244n. 51

Salmond, John, 284–85
Sanders, Carl, 123
Scales, Junius, xii
Schlesinger, Arthur M., Jr., 271nn. 15 and
16, 289
Scott, Ann Firor, 280
"Scottsboro Boys," 40–41
segregation, reasons for establishment of,
18, 212–13, 233n. 31, 274n. 1, 278. *See
also* class differences
Seigenthaler, John, 196–98, 209, 271n. 15
Sellers, Clyde, 69–71, 79; compared with
Pritchett, 129
Selma, Alabama, 209–10
"separate but equal" formula, 18
Shanks, Cheryl, xiv, xv
Shelton, Robert, 127
Sherrod, Charles, 122, 218, 220, 221,
256n. 1, 257n. 4, 259n. 37, 260n. 47, 289;
assaulted by Sheriff, 134–35
Shirah, Sam, xiii, 275n. 3
Shores, Arthur, 202
Shridharani, Krishnalal, 59
Shriver, Sargent, 175, 184
Shuttlesworth, Fred, 198, 201
silent South, 4, 25, 48
Simmons, Furnifold M., 31
Singal, Daniel J., 236n. 28, 279
sit-in movement, 174, 177. *See also* Student
Nonviolent Coordinating Committee
Slater Fund, 5

Library of Congress Cataloging-in-Publication Data
Chappell, David L.
    Inside agitators : white southerners in the Civil Rights Movement / David L. Chappell.
        p.   cm.
    Includes bibliographical references and index.
    ISBN 0-8018-4685-4 (hc : acid-free paper)
    1. Civil rights workers—Southern States—History—20th century. 2. Civil rights
movements—Southern States—History—20th century. 3. Afro-Americans—Civil rights.
4. Southern States—Race relations. I. Title.
E185.61.C543   1994
323.1'196073—dc20   93-43128